**9** · Ask questions—When did the problem start? Does the user know how to make the problem happen, or how to make it go away? What were they doing when the problem occurred? Did anything change recently?

**10** · Document your network. Record the configurations of servers, workstations, bridges—any piece of equipment that you can't reconfigure from memory in less than a minute.

**11** · Keep a log of problems you've fixed—it'll give you an idea of where to start when something similar occurs, and makes it easy to tell your boss what you've been doing with your time.

**12** · Prepare for problems in advance. Create a disaster preparedness plan that details your strategy for recovering from theft, fire, flood, earthquake, or terrorist attack. Almost all businesses struck by disaster that don't have a plan are gone within two years. Most that do have a plan survive.

**13** · Read the documentation for your equipment. If you don't want to read the whole thing, look for exceptions to the normal behavior and troubleshooting tips. Also look at the README files on software distribution diskettes—this information may not be in the manuals.

**14** · Be prepared to use any available sources of information. Join the local NetWare User group, and the CNE Professional Association. Stay tuned to the CompuServe forums or the Internet news groups on NetWare.

# NOVELL'S PROBLEM-SOLVING GUIDE FOR

# NetWare Systems

# NOVELL'S PROBLEM-SOLVING GUIDE FOR
# NetWare® Systems

LOGAN G. HARBAUGH

Novell Press, San Jose

PUBLISHER: *Peter Jerram*
EDITOR-IN-CHIEF: *Rudolph S. Langer*
SERIES EDITOR: *David Kolodney*
ACQUISITIONS EDITOR: *Dianne King*
PROGRAM MANAGER: *Rosalie Kearsley*
DEVELOPMENTAL EDITOR: *David Kolodney*
EDITOR: *James A. Compton*
TECHNICAL EDITOR: *Michael S. Bryant*
EDITORIAL ADVISOR: *Kelley J. P. Lindberg*
BOOK DESIGNER: *Helen Bruno*
PRODUCTION AND LAYOUT ARTIST: *Claudia Smelser*
TECHNICAL ARTIST: *Cuong Le*
DESKTOP PUBLISHING: *Stephanie Hollier*
PRODUCTION ASSISTANT: *Lisa Haden*
INDEXER: *Ted Laux*
COVER DESIGNER: *Archer Design*
NOVELL PRESS LOGO DESIGN: *Jennifer Gill*
COVER PHOTOGRAPHER: *David Hiser*

Library of Congress Card Number: 93-84816

ISBN: 0-7821-1124-6

Manufactured in the United States of America

10 9 8 7 6 5 4 3

# Acknowledgments

If you're reading this, it's probably because you think your name is in here. I hope it is, but if I missed acknowledging your contribution to this book, I do apologize.

I would like to thank the people who made this book possible: David Kolodney, Rose Kearsley and Peter Jerram, of Novell Press, for their help, encouragement and support; Michael Bryant, for the timely job of technical editing that helped make sure that all the information in this book was accurate and that I was presenting it well; and most of all, Jim Compton, the editor of this book, who made it better than it would otherwise have been, and guided me through all the stages of completing the book.

I'd also like to thank the people who have helped me learn the techniques I passed on in this book, especially Russ Mitchell, Michael Bryant, and Laura Chappell, of Novell Education, and Brent Loschen, of NeXT, for their excellent training and support. Thanks to Jane Nulty and Pam Eaken, who let me go to all those classes, and to all the tech pubs department members who made it necessary for me to learn the techniques in the first place.

My parents are responsible for my love of learning and of reading, which helped get me where I am today. (I'll read anything—even manuals.)

Finally, this book is dedicated to the memory of my grandmother, Frances W. Flickinger.

# CONTENTS AT A Glance

· · · · · · · · · · · · · · · · · · · · · · · · · · · · · · · · · · ·

*Overview: Principles of NetWare Problem-Solving*    *xvii*

**PART I**    **BASIC ELEMENTS OF TROUBLESHOOTING    1**

1    **Servers**                                              3
2    **Workstations**                                        45
3    **The Physical Network**                                91
4    **Printing**                                           137

**PART II**    **DISASTERS    171**

5    **A Pound of Prevention**                              173
6    **Coping with Disaster**                               205

**PART III**    **LARGE NETWORKS    229**

7    **Troubleshooting WANs**                               231
8    **Connecting to Other Systems**                        267

**PART IV**    **ADVANCED TOPICS    285**

9    **Troubleshooting Network Applications**               287
10    **Upgrades to NetWare, Hardware, and Software**       303
11    **Tips and Techniques**                               323

**APPENDICES**

A    **Resources**                                          341
B    **Forms**                                              369
C    **Glossary**                                           381

*Index*                                                     *435*

# TABLE OF Contents

*Overview: Principles of NetWare Problem-Solving*                     xvii

## PART I   *Basic Elements of Troubleshooting*          *1*

### 1 · Servers  3

| | |
|---|---|
| Concepts | 10 |
| Fault Points | 11 |
| NetWare Version Specific Information | 13 |
| New Servers | 17 |
| Existing Servers | 26 |
| The Binderies | 30 |
| Upgrading NetWare | 30 |
| NLMS | 31 |
| System Fault Tolerance | 32 |
| Real-Life Stories | 34 |

### 2 · Workstations  45

| | |
|---|---|
| Concepts | 52 |
| Fault Points | 52 |
| The Basics | 56 |
| PC-Compatibles | 58 |
| Windows and NetWare | 66 |
| OS/2 | 68 |
| PS/2 (Micro Channel) | 68 |
| Macintoshes | 69 |
| UNIX Workstations | 75 |
| Real-Life Stories | 76 |

**3 · The Physical Network 91**

| | |
|---|---|
| Concepts | 98 |
| Fault Points | 99 |
| Topology | 100 |
| Data Communications Protocols | 105 |
| Hardware Standards | 108 |
| Cabling: Lengths, Termination, Grounds, Connectors, Connection Order | 115 |
| Patch Panels, Repeaters, and Concentrators | 116 |
| Routers, Bridges, and Gateways | 117 |
| Documenting the Cabling Plant | 117 |
| Real-Life Stories | 118 |

**4 · Printing 137**

| | |
|---|---|
| Concepts | 144 |
| Fault Points | 144 |
| The Printing Process | 147 |
| PostScript Printers | 154 |
| NetWare for Macintosh | 154 |
| NFS Printing | 155 |
| Real-Life Stories | 157 |

**PART II** *Disasters* *171*

**5 · A Pound of Prevention 173**

| | |
|---|---|
| Introduction | 174 |
| Backups | 175 |
| Capacity | 176 |
| Speed | 176 |
| Software | 177 |
| Cost of Media | 177 |
| Cost of the Unit | 177 |
| Reliability | 178 |

| | |
|---|---|
| Support | 178 |
| Strategy | 178 |
| Workstation Backups | 179 |
| Power | 180 |
| Quality Equipment | 182 |
| Preventive Maintenance and Related Precautions | 183 |
| Dust and Other Contaminants | 183 |
| Connections | 184 |
| Anti-Static Precautions | 184 |
| Maintaining a Return Path | 185 |
| Fault Tolerance | 185 |
| Network Plans and Logs | 188 |
| Baselining | 190 |
| Monitoring the Server | 190 |
| Utilities | 195 |
| Training the User | 196 |
| Viruses | 197 |
| Security | 198 |
| Physical Security | 198 |
| Passwords | 199 |
| Rights | 199 |
| Logins | 200 |
| Dial-In Access | 200 |
| Other Access | 201 |
| Recovering from Disaster—in Advance | 202 |
| Recovery Services | 202 |
| The Recovery Plan | 202 |
| Data Recovery in Advance | 203 |

## 6 · Coping with Disaster   205

| | |
|---|---|
| Attitude: Keeping Your Head | 207 |
| Recovering from Mechanical Failure or Destruction | 208 |
| Your Emergency Kit | 209 |
| What to Try First | 209 |
| Physical Recovery | 210 |

| | |
|---|---|
| Data Recovery Software | 211 |
| Restoring from Backups | 212 |
| Recovery Services—How Much Is All Your Work Worth? | 216 |
| Recovering from Software Problems and User Errors | 217 |
| LAN Failures | 218 |
| Reconstruction—When All Else Fails | 219 |
| Viruses | 220 |
| Prevention | 221 |
| UPSes and Surge Protectors | 221 |
| Quality Equipment | 222 |
| Preventive Maintenance | 222 |
| Precautions | 222 |
| Fault Tolerance | 222 |
| Baselining | 223 |
| Training | 223 |
| Security | 223 |
| Disaster Preparedness | 224 |
| Disaster Planning | 224 |
| Data Recovery in Advance | 226 |
| Documenting Your Disaster Plan and Your Network | 226 |

**PART III** *Large Networks*    *229*

**7 · Troubleshooting WANs  231**

| | |
|---|---|
| How LANs Are Connected to Form WANs | 232 |
| Multiple LANS at One Site | 233 |
| Connecting LANS between Buildings | 235 |
| Connecting LANS across Long Distances | 236 |
| Connecting LANS around the World | 239 |
| Additional Fault Points of WANs | 240 |
| Hardware | 240 |
| Telephone Company Services | 244 |
| Software | 245 |

Network Management Tools                                       248
   What's Available                              249
   Cost Analysis                                 251
Diagnostic Tools                                               251
   Hardware-Based Products                       252
   Software-Only Products                        254
Managing without Diagnostic Equipment                          256
Services across WANS                                           257
   Printing on WANS                              257
   Managing Multiple Logins                      258
NetWare Directory Services                                     259
   The New Structure of NetWare 4.0              259
   The New Management Tool                       262
   Troubleshooting NDS                           262
Glossary                                                       264

**8 · Connecting to Other Systems   267**

Other Systems                                                  270
Other Operating Systems on PC Workstations                     272
   OS/2                                          272
   Windows                                       273
   NeXTStep                                      273
   UNIXware                                      274
AppleTalk and Macintoshes                                      274
   NetWare for Macintosh                         275
   Adding Appletalk Support to PC Workstations   277
   IPX for Macintoshes                           277
   AppleTalk Gateways                            278
   Accessing Other Environments from AppleTalk   278
TCP/IP and UNIX Connectivity                                   278
   NetWare NFS                                   280
   NetWare on UNIX Systems                       283

P A R T   I V   *Advanced Topics*                    285

**9 · Troubleshooting Network Applications   287**

Applications Accessing NetWare Services                288
    File Services                                      289
    Printing from Applications                         290
    Accessing NetWare Services from Windows            292
Applications Running from the Server                   294
    Running LAN WorkGroup                              296
    Running Windows from the Server                    296
Electronic Mail Applications                           298
Networked Modems                                       299
    Networked Data Modems                              300
    Networked Fax Modems                               300

**10 · Upgrades to NetWare, Hardware, and Software   303**

Planning an Upgrade                                    304
Upgrading NetWare                                      305
    Upgrading without Disrupting Work Flow             305
    Planning the Upgrade                               306
    Methods                                            310
    Example: 2.15 to 3.11                              312
    Example: 3.11 to 4.x                               315
Upgrading Hardware                                     319
Software                                               321
    Networking Software and Operating Systems          321
    Applications                                       322

**11 · Tips and Techniques   323**

PCs (DOS Computers)                                    324
    Boot Errors                                        324
    AUTOEXEC.BAT and CONFIG.SYS                        325
    IRQs                                               326
Windows 3.1                                            327

Windows Versions before 3.1                   328
Macintoshes                                   330
UNIX Workstations                             333
NetWare                                       334
    BINDFIX                                   334
    PRINTCON                                  335
    After Abends or Power Failures            335
    Login Scripts                             335
NetWare 2.*x*                                 336
NetWare 3.*x*                                 336
NetWare 4.*x*                                 337
Printing                                      339

▶ · · · · · · · · · · · · · · · · · · · · · · · · · · ◀

**A P P E N D I C E S**

**A ·  Resources  341**

**B ·  Forms  369**

**C ·  Glossary  381**

*Index*                                       435

# Overview

Most businesses have been using PCs for years, usually in the same way that typewriters were used previously—as individual tools to enhance productivity. Now, many companies are discovering that computers can be networked in Local Area Networks (LANs) and Wide Area Networks (WANs) to increase productivity dramatically. But the resulting networks are being built piecemeal; first one department networks its computers, then another, and eventually the whole company, but not necessarily according to any overall plan.

Such networks consist of several different kinds of workstations—PCs running any of several operating systems, Macintoshes, UNIX workstations—all tied together through servers of one sort or another, and perhaps also tied to the old mainframe or mini computer as well. One of the best tools for this purpose is NetWare. Its ability to allow many different environments to work together also makes it possible to create networks of incredible complexity.

Because the use of networks is growing so rapidly, and because training programs turn out far fewer graduates than are needed, network administrators are in very short supply. Often this means that users who know only a little more than their colleagues about computers or networks find themselves pressed into service as administrators, and administrators who have begun by administering a small departmental network may find themselves responsible for a half-dozen servers and hundreds of workstations. These people may be able to set up basic configurations of their workstations or LANs, but often have little or no formal training or background in troubleshooting. This book is intended to help the knowledgeable user to understand the principles of troubleshooting, and to apply those principles to fix problems with workstations and networks.

There are many books on troubleshooting that are full of information on what to do in specific situations—if X happens, do Y. There are others that try

**This book will show you how to isolate the cause of a problem, find the information to fix it, and apply that knowledge.**

to present the material contained in the software documentation in a more accessible way. These are both useful resources, but the one thing almost never touched on is the approach to troubleshooting. This book is not about how to get a particular network driver to work with a particular adapter. Instead, it will show you how to isolate the cause of your problem, find the information necessary to fix the problem, and apply that knowledge.

## Who Should Read This Book?

To use this book effectively you should have a basic understanding of the equipment you are working with—you should be able to move around the file system, understand the basics of configuring a system, and so forth. If the manuals that came with your hardware and software are not satisfactory, there are many alternatives available in your local bookstore. Appendix A will cover resources for learning more about your system. You don't need to be an expert. Following the principles in this book will help even a relatively inexperienced user to isolate and correct most problems.

## An Approach to Troubleshooting

Many people involved with computers and networks of computers regard setting them up and fixing them when they stop working as an arcane art. To the average user watching an expert troubleshoot and fix their system, the process might seem like magic. However, whether the expert consciously follows them or not, there are certain basic principles common to all troubleshooting.

The basic process of troubleshooting is simple to state: determine that there is a problem, isolate the problem, determine the cause of the problem, and fix the problem. The biggest difficulty in applying this relatively simple process to a Local Area Network (LAN) or Wide Area Network (WAN), or even to a single workstation or server, is caused by the enormous number of possible combinations of hardware, software and configurations involved.

The simplest approach to this complexity is to break it down—isolate the WAN into LANs, each LAN into server, workstations and cabling, each server or workstation into hardware, DOS and networking software, and the physical cabling into segments. Each of these subsystems can be further divided as necessary, until each element can be determined to be the cause of the problem or not.

Often an experienced troubleshooter will have a seemingly intuitive "feel" for what might be wrong. But what appears to be intuition is usually a rapid process of elimination based on long and often painful previous experience. This experience is useful in rapidly finding and fixing a problem, but it is not essential. Most users, by following a logical and methodical approach, will be able to solve the same problem, although probably not as quickly.

The optimum approach to becoming a good troubleshooter is to try things out. As long as basic precautions are followed to avoid irreparable changes, experimentation is fine. In fact, this is often the way that even a highly experienced troubleshooter will approach a problem; to simply try a few different things until the system is fixed. He or she will simply have a better feel for which things to try first—which "fault points" are the most likely to be broken.

> **To become a good trouble-shooter, try things out. Try the simple things first.**

There are a couple of basic ways to determine what things to try first, and how to continue from there. Try the simple things first. It's much easier to verify that a PC is plugged in than to disassemble it and check the hard disk to be sure it's receiving power. It's also much more likely that the PC has been accidentally unplugged than that the power connection for the hard disk has failed or worked loose. Also, don't change more than one thing at once; for instance, replacing all the cards in a PC might well fix the problem, but it won't tell you which of the cards has failed. Unless you need to get that PC back on line immediately, it's better to switch cards one at a time, replacing the old one if there's no change, until the problem is isolated.

Each chapter in this book will help you to determine the most likely failure areas for your particular setup. These vary from system to system, but as you become familiar with the trouble spots for your system, you will be able to rapidly check a few items and often solve your problem within a few minutes. Not only does this save time when irate users are waiting to get back on-line, it makes you seem like a wizard to your boss.

Two of your best tools to determine likely areas of failure are a well-kept log and a baseline of the system; that is, a collection of statistics which represent the normal operation of your equipment. These are discussed further on in this Overview, and in Chapter 5, A Pound of Prevention.

Almost all systems that need troubleshooting fall into one of two categories: systems that were working and have failed, or new systems that don't work as expected (this includes existing systems that stopped working when something new was added). Each requires a certain basic approach, but the essential underlying principle of all troubleshooting is to eliminate possible causes of the problem, until the actual cause is isolated.

**Eliminate possible causes of the problem, until the actual cause is isolated.**

## NEW SYSTEMS AND ADDITIONS TO EXISTING SYSTEMS

With a system that is new, or to which something has been added, the basic approach is to achieve a minimum configuration that works, or to return to the configuration that worked before things were changed, and build from there. For instance, a networked workstation will often have a number of cards in it; network adapter, video display, floppy/hard disk controller, mouse, and possibly others, such as a serial/parallel adapter, expanded or extended memory board, coprocessor or accelerator card, internal modem, host adapter, or SCSI controller. Each of these can potentially interfere with the others.

To begin with, it's best to fall back to a basic minimum, perhaps only the floppy/hard disk controller and video adapter. If the PC will boot with just these cards, then add others until you discover what isn't working, or what is conflicting with the basic system.

With new additions that cause problems it is unlikely that the new part is defective, so the solution is usually to isolate the conflict between the new item and something in the system. Unless you have specific suspicions about where the conflict may be, the most certain procedure is to remove any extraneous parts from the system. If the new addition works with a basic system, begin adding the remaining components back in until the problem recurs.

It is important to keep track of each card in a PC, and what interrupts and memory segments it uses. Actually checking each card's manual and writing down what its configuration is may be the only way you will discover that it is attempting to use the same memory segment as another card. You may discover that the default configurations of all the cards in the PC will not work together. In this case, you must determine which cards have alternate configurations, and how to set them, and then possibly reset the appropriate software. There are also programs that will help you determine what interrupts and memory each card in a system uses—see Appendix A for further details.

Some network cards, like the NE2000, have over a dozen possible configurations, but only two or three that are normally used. Unfortunately, the advisable configurations on some cards can be difficult to discover, depending on the quality of the documentation. This is also true in general of all the cards you might find in a PC. Even expensive cards may have terrible documentation—it is one of the few instances where paying more will not necessarily gain you anything.

If you cannot find the information you need in the manual for the card, or cannot make sense of what is there, your best bet is to find someone else who has already been through the problem and pick their brains. Possible sources of information include the manufacturer's tech support line, the dealer you bought the equipment from, your local MIS organization, the Support Alliance, various forums on CompuServe or the Internet, and the local CNE user group. A detailed discussion of various groups you may wish to contact appears in Appendix A.

### EXISTING SYSTEMS

With an existing system that was working and has failed, the basic approach is to determine what has changed. This may require a methodical approach involving swapping cards or checking connections, or it may be as simple as discovering that the user has added a new piece of software that is incompatible with other software on the system.

Talk to the user—does she know of a way to make the problem go away? Is there a certain time of day or particular piece of software, or a certain server associated with the problem? Has he changed the configuration of his PC recently? What was the user doing when the problem occured?

> **Keep a record of the system configuration for each workstation on your network.**

Getting the information from a user can be difficult. Users may not remember the critical change, or may be reluctant to admit having done something that may be causing a problem. There are a couple of things you can do to make the necessary information easier to find. The first is to keep a record of system configurations on each workstation on your network. This information can be tedious to acquire, although inventory programs can produce most of the information you will want automatically. Another useful approach is to standardize the workstations on your network as much as possible. Make sure that they are all using the same version of DOS, the same network shell and adapter, and so on.

Sometimes, the change to a system is not intentional. It may be a connection that has worked loose, a corrupted file, or a broken cable. You will still have clues to investigate, but you may have to dig for them. It is still basically a process of elimination which is determined by the break points of the system. These will be covered in the appropriate chapters in detail.

# Attitude: The Single Most Important Thing You Can Get from This Book!

When I meet with other troubleshooters, system engineers, or networking experts, the conversation often turns to troubleshooting, and what makes a good troubleshooter. The consensus is that the single most important ingredient to make a good troubleshooter is not knowledge, or experience, or intelligence. It is *attitude*. A determination to keep trying until you figure the problem out is essential. Any system that worked once can be made to work again. The critical thing is to keep trying until the problem is solved.

> The single most important attribute of a good troubleshooter is attitude. Keep trying until you figure the problem out.

The biggest stumbling blocks for most troubleshooters are the mistaken impression that they have "tried everything," and the feeling that the problem is too complex—that they'll never be able to understand the problem. The first idea is usually caused by looking at the system too quickly, but it may also result from failing to consider the possible effects of elements apparently outside the problem. The second feeling can be avoided by breaking the problem down into more basic components— break a WAN into LANs, a LAN into server, workstations, and cabling plant, and so on.

You can be successful at troubleshooting as long as you are willing to keep trying. You may not be as fast at first as someone with a lot of experience or knowledge of the system, but you can get results. The more familiar with your system you are, of course, the more capable of fixing it you will be. This is one of the functions of performing the baselining and collecting the log sheets for every workstation and server on your network. See Record Keeping, below.

# Record Keeping

It is utterly impossible to overdo documentation of your network. Time spent collecting information on your network might seem like a waste at the time, particularly to your supervisor, but it could make many, many hours of difference in the time required to get the network running again if there is trouble. It's cheap insurance.

One of the most useful aids in troubleshooting is good record keeping. It's difficult to isolate what might be causing a problem if you don't know what's in the system. Likewise, if you need to reconfigure a system back to its last working state, it's easier if you don't have to rediscover the settings that got it to work in the first place. Finally, your records for a similar system and how you got it to work may give you a lead on fixing your current problem.

You should have a record of each system that includes the date it was installed and the original configuration, and the dates and details of each update or addition to hardware or software, and perhaps a printout of the AUTOEXEC.BAT and CONFIG.SYS files. Such a record can greatly simplify the problem of isolating the latest change to a system. It will be easier to keep such records if you establish a database or use a standard worksheet when you set up or modify a workstation. Some suggested worksheets are presented in Appendix B.

In addition, an archive of the standard software used on your workstations can make your life much easier. It's far easier and faster to simply copy COMMAND.COM, AUTOEXEC.BAT, CONFIG.SYS, IPX.COM or NETx. COM from your standard set of floppies than to copy them from the original floppies, recreate them, or regenerate them, as required.

A daily log is another useful tool for the network administrator. It can provide a history of a particular problem, making it easier to isolate things which may occur at long or irregular intervals. A good log can make it much easier to justify new purchases or upgrades, if you can show that the same part has failed four times in the last 10 months, and will also show your supervisor just what you've been doing with your time.

## Resources

Because of the enormous number of possibilities inherent in LANs, no single book can address all the possible combinations, or provide all the information necessary to understand your LAN. Among the additional resources available to you, and which I hope you will use are:

- ▶ The NetWare manuals.

- ▶ The hardware manufacturer's manuals.

- ▶ Third-party books on NetWare (including other Novell Press books), networking, applications you may be using, etc.

- ▶ Trade publications—between the weekly and monthly magazines, there are thousands of pages published every month on hundreds of topics related to networking.

- ▶ Computer bulletin boards and services. CompuServe has a large section on NetWare—any question you might have has probably been discussed on one of the forums.

- ▶ Your local NetWare Users Group.

- ▶ The local chapter of the Certified NetWare Engineer Professional Association. Even if you're not a member you can probably get either free advice or professional help through the Association.

- ▶ Your Authorized Reseller. The dealer you bought NetWare from should have technical support personnel who can help you with your problem.

- ▶ 1 800 NETWARE—Novell's technical support hotline.

## Tools for Troubleshooting

This book provides a number of tools designed to help you implement the approach to problem-solving just outlined.

## SNAPSHOTS

The Snapshot section of each chapter in Part I is a quick-reference chart that will lead you through the basic process of isolating the cause of your current problem. It will ask you whether the problem is with a new system or an existing one, and then take you through a series of steps designed to help you find the source of the problem. It will then direct you to the section of the chapter that discusses that part of the system, which will discuss the principles involved and how to fix the problem. The process you should follow to isolate a problem with your LAN is in the same order as the chapters—check the server first, the workstations second, and the physical network third.

Your first indication that there is a problem will often be a complaint from a user. If a cursory examination shows that the workstation itself seems to be in order, then check to make sure that the server is operational. If it is, then check to see whether other workstations are also exhibiting problems. If they are, then you should check the physical network before a thorough investigation of the server. If not, the problem is probably with the workstation.

The best course is usually to quickly eliminate the most obvious possible causes before doing an in-depth analysis. Your first check of the server should simply be to see that it is on and responding to the keyboard. If it is, there could still be problems, but it's best to then find out how many workstations are experiencing problems, and then to do some simple tests to determine whether the physical connections could be causing the problem, before doing a really thorough examination of the server.

> **Within any system there are a limited number of points where something can go wrong.**

## FAULT POINTS

Rather than a typical flowchart, which cannot cover anything close to all the possibilities inherent in a network, I have developed a system that looks at the places where things can go wrong. This approach does require a certain degree of understanding of your system, but is also adaptable to any system. The idea is that there are, within any combination of different types of workstations, Network Interface Cards (NICs), LAN topologies, servers, cabling, software, and so on, a limited number of points where something can go wrong.

For instance, the connection between the NIC and the physical wiring is a fault point. Depending on your system, the connector may be any one of a dozen types, each with its own unique way of going bad. Rather than attempt to teach you what all of these are and how to tell if they are the problem, I'll attempt to show you how to isolate your problem to that particular fault point, and leave the rest to you.

The fault points are all the essential links in a network chain. For instance, the workstation hardware and operating system, the software and hardware that allow the workstation to talk over the cabling, the cabling system, and the server itself are all parts of the network chain that connects the user to the server. Other chains may include the chain from the user to the printer or to a modem, from the server to a remote LAN, from the LAN to another LAN, and so on. Each item in the fault point chain can affect the chain in three ways—it can fail, or its links to the previous or next item can fail. For instance, a power cord could be broken, or it could have a faulty connection to the wall socket or the power supply of the equipment it's attached to.

In every case, the key to finding the fault points and checking them for failure is an understanding of the principles involved in that chain. This does not mean that you must know and understand the seven levels of the OSI model, for example, but you should understand that the network adapter and network driver in a workstation combine to send a message through the wire to the network adapter and network driver in the server. You should also know that, depending on the type of network and whether the packet goes straight to the server or is passed along from one workstation to the next, a missing "t-connector" at the unused workstation in the next cube might be the problem.

For quick reference, the fault-point chain for each chapter in Part I is represented as an illustration like that shown in Figure O.1.

**FIGURE 0.1**

*The Fault Point chain.*

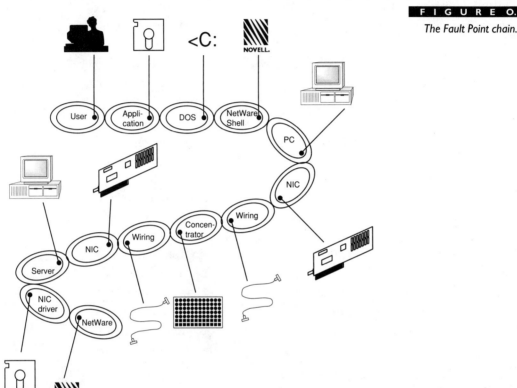

## REAL-LIFE STORIES

Each chapter in Part I will also have a narrative section describing typical problems and how a troubleshooter would go through the process of isolating the fault and fixing it. Two fictional companies and their administrators will be used as examples. They combine the equipment and experience of a number of actual businesses.

Itsy-Bitsy, Inc. is a small company with one building housing several departments and about 200 users. They have one system administrator, John, who is responsible for several NetWare servers, the networking hardware, and for supporting the workstations, most of which are PCs, with a few Macintoshes. The NetWare servers include both NetWare 2.*x* and 3.*x*.

Fran, the system administrator for Great Big, Inc., is responsible for a three-building campus, one of several sites scattered across the country. She has two assistants: Jethro, who is experienced with Macs, but not particularly with NetWare, and Marilyn, whose primary area of expertise is with UNIX, although she is learning NetWare. Marilyn was formerly the administrator for the engineering department, which runs UNIX workstations on a UNIX server.

Between them, these three are responsible for 14 servers, including two UNIX servers, networking hardware that includes links to company sites in other cities and abroad, and about a thousand workstations, including PCs, Macintoshes, and UNIX workstations. The internetwork is typical, having grown up from a number of departmental networks—there are several different types of wiring and network protocols, different types of workstations in different departments, and no real program for integrating the whole mess into a coordinated whole. The evolution of this internetwork will provide examples of what to do and what not to do in planning and evolving a network.

## Organization of This Book

This book is organized as follows.

Each chapter in **Part I: Basic Elements of Troubleshooting** shows how to troubleshoot a major component of the network: servers, workstations, the cabling, and print services.

> ▶ **Chapter 1: Servers** discusses the configuration of new server hardware, where it differs from the configuration of PCs in general. It also discusses the configuration of NetWare, versions 2.x, 3.x and 4.x, and the troubleshooting of existing hardware

and software. Includes a Snapshot section to help you quickly troubleshoot specific problems.

▸ **Chapter 2: Workstations** covers the setup and troubleshooting of new hardware and system software, and troubleshooting of existing hardware and system software, for PCs running DOS, Windows or OS/2, Macintoshes, and UNIX workstations. Includes a Snapshot section to help you quickly troubleshoot specific problems.

▸ **Chapter 3: The Physical Network** covers the theory and practice of network cabling—the types of topologies, the installation and maintenance of cabling and associated equipment such as patch panels, repeaters and concentrators, bridges, routers and gateways, and troubleshooting techniques. Includes a Snapshot section to help you quickly troubleshoot specific problems.

▸ **Chapter 4: Printing** covers the various ways of networking printers and fax modems, the theory of the printing process, typical problem areas, and solutions. Includes a Snapshot section to help you quickly troubleshoot specific problems.

**Part II: Disasters** covers steps you can take to prevent or minimize disasters, and what to do if they strike anyway (or before you have a chance to implement the suggested measures).

▸ **Chapter 5: A Pound of Prevention** discusses the things you can do in advance to make your life easier when problems occur. Both preventive measures and things that will help you recover after problems are included. You'll also see how to teach users to handle some common problems by themselves.

▸ **Chapter 6: Coping with Disaster** shows what to do after disaster strikes. Suggestions will also include graphic comparisons of the difference following the procedures outlined in the previous chapter can make, but will not rely on them.

**Part III: Large Networks** covers the issues involved with multiple LANs connected to form WANs, and heterogeneous LANs and WANs comprised of different types of operating systems and protocols.

▶ **Chapter 7: Troubleshooting WANs** covers multiple LANs and WANs, and how to isolate problems within the complexity of larger internetworks.

▶ **Chapter 8: Connecting to Other Systems** discusses the many additional services that NetWare will allow beyond linking PCs to a server. This chapter covers other protocols such as AppleTalk and TCP/IP, telecommunications, connections to several sorts of mainframe and mini computers, and connections to physically distant locations.

**Part IV: Advanced Topics** covers additional issues beyond the scope of a basic LAN, including troubleshooting application programs running in a network environment, upgrades to your network, and some tips, tricks, and techniques that may help you get through stubborn problems.

▶ **Chapter 9: Troubleshooting Network Applications** covers troubleshooting applications on a network. The functionality of a networked application program depends not only on NetWare, but also on how well the programmers understood NetWare in the first place. This chapter discusses the problem areas and how to isolate and fix them. Applications intended to run from the server, and the special considerations involved with them, will also be discussed.

▶ **Chapter 10: Upgrades to NetWare, Hardware, and Software** covers upgrades to applications and utilities, to workstation system software, to NetWare, and to hardware. This chapter discusses planning an upgrade, upgrading without disrupting work flow, and the precautions to take.

► **Chapter 11: Tips and Techniques** suggests things to try for particular problems, especially solutions that may not be logical or covered in the documentation.

► **Appendix A: Resources** covers using tech support, training available, on-line resources, the NSE, 900 numbers, and how to pick consultants.

► **Appendix B: Forms** contains forms that you can copy to use in inventorying your network, and to record the configurations of your workstations, servers, and network devices.

► **Appendix C: Glossary** covers terminology and acronyms you are likely to encounter not only in this book but in the NetWare manuals and other discussions of networking.

# PART I

# Basic Elements
# of Troubleshooting

The four chapters in this part each show how to troubleshoot one major component of a NetWare network: file servers in Chapter 1, workstations in Chapter 2, the physical network in Chapter 3, and print services in Chapter 4. The chapters share a common structure, designed to help you both troubleshoot current problems as you go and develop a firm understanding of where and why problems can occur.

Each chapter begins with a Snapshot chart, a series of questions and information that will lead you through the basic diagnostic sequence for that part of the network. At each step you'll be guided to the appropriate part of the Concepts section of the chapter, which explains the basic parts of, say, a server or a workstation and what is likely to go wrong with them. Here you'll find a Fault Point Chain diagram, as introduced in the Overview. The chapters conclude with a Real-Life Stories section that leads you through actual problems encountered with new and existing systems, using the fictitious companies also introduced in the Overview.

# CHAPTER 1

# Servers

# *SnapShot*

**N**etWare began to take over the PC-networking marketplace when it was changed to run on IBM-PC compatibles rather than the original proprietary servers. The first servers were 286-based IBM AT-compatibles, and as new chips and capabilities have become available, NetWare has grown to accommodate and make use of the new resources. As PC-based networks have grown, the demand for more capabilities has also grown, to the point that there are now *superservers* available that incorporate many of the features of the mainframes they are replacing, such as the ability to replace defective cards or even hard drives without needing to turn the server off, multiple processors, and Error Correction Code (ECC) memory, that can self-correct hardware memory errors. Memory and disk storage sizes have expanded by several orders of magnitude, from 640 KB of RAM, to 64 MB, 128 MB or more, and from 10 or 20 MB hard disks to 2 GB (2000 MB) and larger.

As the speed and capabilities of servers has grown, NetWare has also grown in the services it provides. From a relatively simple file- and print-sharing service, NetWare has grown to provide access to other types of computers and computer networks, including Macintoshes, UNIX, and IBM minis and mainframes. NetWare now supports many network protocols, dozens of network adapters, and can run on hundreds of PC-compatibles. As its capabilities have grown—*because* they have grown—NetWare has become much more complex and more difficult to troubleshoot. This chapter will lead you through the troubleshooting process for servers.

## IS THIS A NEW SYSTEM?

### *Does It Boot DOS?*

If not, go to Chapter 2, and see the section on new workstations. The Concepts section on hardware, on page 17, contains procedures and information on the specialized hardware found in servers, such as multiple network adapters and hard disk adapters. For NetWare 2.x, it is not strictly necessary that the server boot DOS, but it's a good test—if it won't boot DOS, then NetWare is unlikely to load either. You may need to boot from a floppy, especially with a 2.*x* server.

### It Boots DOS, but Then Fails to Load NetWare.

Look at the error messages that appear while NetWare attempts to load. These are your best clues to the problem. See the Concepts section on the NetWare loading process, starting on page 22. If you are running NetWare 2.*x* and using a Novell DCB, you should also check to see if the PROM on the DCB that allows the PC to boot from a SCSI drive has been installed. If the chip has not been installed, or has been installed incorrectly, the PC will not recognize the SCSI drive as a bootable disk. Look for bent pins, and make sure that the chip is facing in the correct direction. BE SURE TO OBSERVE STATIC PRECAUTIONS WHEN HANDLING CHIPS AND BOARDS! If you aren't familiar with proper static precautions, see Chapter 5, A Pound of Prevention, for more details.

### NetWare Loads, but Some Devices (Such as Network Cards or Disk Drives) Are Inaccessible.

This is likely to be a hardware problem. Either a piece of hardware is not functioning correctly, or the driver program for that hardware is not functioning correctly. See the Concepts section on new server hardware on page 17 below.

## IS THIS AN EXISTING SYSTEM?

### Is the Server Up?

If the server is working (the screen is lit, the prompt responds to keyboard input, you can switch to different NLM monitor screens), then the problem is likely to be in either the workstation or the physical network (the cabling, repeater, MUX, and so on). You can quickly check with MONITOR or FCONSOLE to make sure that all LAN adapters are sending and receiving packets. If they are, then you should next determine how many workstations are experiencing problems. If one, then go to Chapter 3, Workstations. If several or all have similar problems, then go to Chapter 4, The Physical Network. Finally, if the physical network checks out, then you'll need to begin a deeper analysis of the server. This is covered in the Concepts section on MONITOR, on page 26 below.

### Reboot the Server.

If the server does not appear to be working—if, for instance, the cursor is frozen or the screen is dark, or doesn't respond to keyboard input, reboot the server. If the server reboots correctly then the problem may have been a system error of some sort. Check the Error Message Log using SYSCON to see if there are any unusual error messages. You should also make note of any new NLMs or new applications that may have been running on the server—if the problem recurs, they are a good place to start.

### Will the Server Boot DOS?

If the server reboots without error messages, but NetWare doesn't load, try just booting DOS. With a NetWare 2.x server, you will need to boot from a floppy. If the server will not boot DOS, then it is likely that the problem is a hardware failure, although it's possible that COMMAND.COM has been corrupted. See Chapter 2 for information on isolating hardware failures.

### Will NetWare Load?

If NetWare fails to load, on a server that was working before, one of two things is likely to have happened. Either there is a hardware failure, or the NetWare system files may have become corrupted. There are other possibilities, such as a network "storm" causing so much interference that NetWare cannot function, but the first two possibilities are the most likely.

With NetWare 3.x or 4.x, watch the messages that come up as SERVER.EXE attempts to execute. They will normally give you the necessary clues to determine what has failed. If you have a copy of SERVER.EXE you may wish to try replacing the one on the boot drive.

With NetWare 2.x the problem may also be with the DCB or the3 PROM on it that allows NetWare to boot from a SCSI drive. If you are using this feature, you should see a message from the BIOS on the DCB that tells you it is making the SCSI drive available as a boot drive. You should also keep a backup copy of NET$OS.EXE—it is also subject to becoming corrupted.

### NetWare Loads, but Some or All Server Functions Cannot Be Accessed.

If the server appears to be functioning, but workstations cannot access it, and the physical network appears to be functional, then

MONITOR or FCONSOLE is your first step to isolating the problem. The two most likely areas of failure are the LAN adapters and the disk drive systems. See the Concepts section on software problems with existing servers, beginning on page 27.

### Intermittent Problems.

There are many possible causes of intermittent failure of a server, and this can be one of the most frustrating types of troubleshooting to attempt. The causes could be anything from a power surge caused by nearby heavy equipment (or even the power draws from another facility on the same power grid) to faulty equipment, to the applications running on the server or even on a workstation.

The important thing to look for to isolate intermittent problems is the thing that changes just before the crash. This seems obvious, but can be difficult to actually discover. Some starting points:

- ▸ What time does the crash occur?
- ▸ Do the crashes happen at regular intervals?
- ▸ Was there any particular software that was always in use when the crashes occured?
- ▸ Which workstations were attached every time the server crashed?
- ▸ Are there any unusual error messages in the System Error Log?
- ▸ Do any of the workstations get a message other than "The connection to the file server myserver is no longer valid?"
- ▸ Are there stages to the problem? If you can isolate events that lead up to the crash, they will give you a clue to the root cause.

Investigating some of these items will take research: talking to the users, discovering what new software has been installed on the server or workstations, who was logged in, and so on. You can simplify this job considerably with the use of network inventory systems, network monitoring equipment, and other software that will help keep track of the various parts of your network and its configuration. You can manually keep track of all installed software and hardware on your server and all the networked workstations, but it's much easier to run a network inventory program regularly to get the information. There's less chance that a user will forget to mention that new program they installed, too.

Of course, some problems may be impossible to isolate without some sort of network sniffer, and anyone with an installation that is larger than a couple of servers or runs more than one or two protocols should consider getting some type of monitoring software and/or hardware. These can range in price from a few hundred to tens of thousands of dollars in price. The best resources for determining which system is right for you are the trade magazines, your local NetWare Users Group, and your Authorized Reseller.

# Concepts

Fault Points

NetWare Version-Specific Information

    Netware 2.*x*

    Netware 3.*x*

    Netware 4.*x*

New Servers

    Hardware

    Software

Existing Servers

    Hardware

    Software

    Other Diagnostic Tools

The Binderies

Upgrading NetWare

NLMs

System Fault Tolerance

    Mirroring and Duplexing

    SFT Level III

In general, the principles of troubleshooting workstations are equally applicable to servers. In fact, servers are usually more straightforward in basic configuration than workstations—they aren't usually personalized with add-on software. The differences that can make servers a problem to troubleshoot include the high performance enhancements common to most servers, such as large amounts of RAM, large hard disks, specialized, faster interfaces, and NetWare itself. These differences are covered in this chapter; the basics of getting a workstation to work are covered in Chapter 2.

> **The basic principles of troubleshooting servers are the same as those for workstations.**

The biggest difference between the 2.*x* series of NetWare and 3.*x* and 4.*x* is that the configuration of 2.*x* cannot be changed once the operating system is installed. Versions 3.*x* and 4.*x* can be configured "on the fly," and the configuration can be changed without even bringing the server down, let alone re-doing the installation. Version 4.*x* adds additional functionality for large networks, principally the NetWare directory services, which allow access to server functions from anywhere on a large internetwork.

## FAULT POINTS

The Overview introduced the concept of a chain of Fault Points as a guide to troubleshooting networks and network components. Within any combination of different types of workstations, Network Interface Cards (NICs), LAN topologies, servers, cabling, software, and so on, there are a limited number of points where problems can occur.

Because a conventional flowchart cannot cover anything close to all the possibilities inherent in a network, it makes more sense to look only at those places where things can go wrong.

Figure 1.1 shows the fault chain for troubleshooting NetWare servers. Each item in the chain depends on the previous items for proper operation. For instance, the server will not operate at all without power to the wall socket. A complete fault chain would also include the connection between

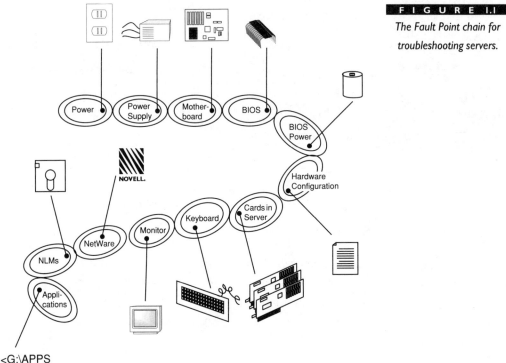

F I G U R E I.I

*The Fault Point chain for*
*troubleshooting servers.*

the wall socket and the power cord, the power cord and the connection to power supply. Similarly, the power supply link in the fault chain also includes the connections from the power supply to the motherboard and disk drives. The BIOS controls the motherboard and the beginning of the boot process, and can cause failures if it isn't recent enough, or if its battery power fails. The hardware configuration includes the values stored in the BIOS that tell the PC what type of floppy and hard disk drives it has, as well as the settings on the various cards installed in the server.

The cards themselves can also fail because of their connection to the motherboard, their connection to whatever device they're attached to, or because of a failure of some component on the card itself. Be aware that many cards now have BIOS of their own that operates in addition to the

BIOS on the motherboard, to add further functionality to the server.

A failure in the keyboard or monitor or in their cables or connections may result in a crash, a server that won't boot, or a server that seems dead when it isn't. NetWare, even though it is software, has the same three failure points. It can fail in its connection to previous links—a driver that accesses the LAN adapter, for instance or in the connection to the next item—which might be an NLM written for a different version of NetWare, or it can fail internally (crash). NLMs (or VAPs) add functionality to NetWare, and can fail, usually causing the loss of that functionality, but sometimes causing the whole server to crash. Finally, applications running on the server have been known to cause servers to crash, if they attempt to access NetWare services with an illegal function call.

## NETWARE VERSION SPECIFIC INFORMATION

NetWare, as a PC-based Network Operating System (NOS), has evolved through three major versions. The first PC-based versions of NetWare had to be generated with all operating system configurations set up in advance. These versions include NetWare 2.0, 2.0a, 2.10, 2.11, 2.12, 2.15 and 2.2, known collectively as 2.x. The next evolutionary step for NetWare was 3.0. NetWare 3.0 was the first version of NetWare written for the 80386 processor. It took full advantage of the additional capabilities of the 386 over the 80286, and also allowed reconfiguration of nearly every aspect of the operating system while the server was running. More recently, NetWare 3.10 and 3.11 have been released, and all are collectively known as 3.x. The third evolutionary step for NetWare is NetWare 4.0. This version adds features specifically designed for large corporate networks.

### NetWare 2.x

From a floppy, the loading process is this: DOS is loaded from the floppy, then NET$OS.EXE is executed, either manually, or from the AUTOEXEC.BAT file. NetWare takes over completely from DOS. When the server boots from a hard disk, it boots from the NetWare cold boot loader, which is written to track 0 of the disk when the hard disk is formatted. The cold boot loader is executed when the server is turned on, and in turn executes NET$OS.EXE, which is the only operating system present—DOS is never loaded. If the server boot drive is a SCSI drive, the PROM on the DCB, or the BIOS on later model SCSI adapters, is what allows the server to boot from a drive that is not supported by the PC's BIOS.

Commands in SERVER.CFG and AUTOEXEC.SYS allow you to automatically run Value Added Processes (VAPs), set up printers, and execute other commands which add functionality to NetWare in the same manner as an AUTOEXEC.BAT file on a workstation.

Communication buffers are used to hold data packets arriving from workstations. They don't use much memory, so set the number twice as high as you think you'll need; too low a number will degrade network performance, as the server will ignore packets it doesn't have room for in the buffers, forcing the workstations to resend the packets. Changing the number requires regenerating the operating system with INSTALL.

### NetWare 3.x

The biggest difference between NetWare 2.x and NetWare 3.x is that 3.x can dynamically allocate and deallocate memory as resources or NLMs are loaded or unloaded. See Figure 1.2 below.

Some resources are normally loaded permanently, such as disk drivers or protocols bound to LAN adapters, and some may be loaded and unloaded as needed. All remaining free memory is used for file cache buffers, which hold the files last requested, so disk access isn't required if the file is accessed again. NLMs are of four types:

▸ Disk drivers to allow the use of different types of disk drives (*.DSK).

▸ LAN drivers for running different protocols on various LAN adapters (*.LAN).

▸ Name space modules to allow operating systems other than DOS to access and store files on the server. These include the Macintosh, NFS (UNIX) and OS/2 (*.NAM).

```
                          Disk Driver      Name
                              ▼            Spaces
                                            ◄
   Core Printing          Network     ◄         ►      Disk Driver
   Services               Interface                        ▼
            Disk Driver       ▼
      NetWare                          NetWare
       Core                ▲            Core       ◄       Network
                                                           Interface
   Network                                   ►
   Interface              ◄                 ▲
               ►                                       MONITOR.NLM,
                  ◄                   ►                 INSTALL.NLM,
              Value Added        PSERVER.NLM           Other utilities
              Processes
     NetWare 2.x                  NetWare 3.x
                                  and 4.x
```

> ▸ Management Utilities and Server Applications. These include
> MONITOR, INSTALL, UPS, and others. They allow you to con-
> figure and manage the server, or add functionality (*.NLM).

The loading process is the same from a floppy or a hard disk. You boot
the server with DOS, then run SERVER.EXE. SERVER takes its configuration parameters from STARTUP.NCF and AUTOEXEC.NCF. If you will be
booting from a DOS partition on the hard disk, it doesn't need to be more
than about two MB, but I recommend at least four. This will give you
enough room for a directory where you can place backup copies of SERV-
ER.EXE, and STARTUP.NCF, in case those files are corrupted or accidentally
changed or removed. It will also give you room to grow if future versions
of NetWare require more space for SERVER.EXE or the equivalent.

### NetWare 4.x

The most complex addition to NetWare 4.x is NetWare Directory Services
(NDS), which uses a distributed NetWare Directory database, to manage all
services over a large internet. A large internet is organized logically, by Country,
State, Organization, Organizational Group, Organizational Role, and so on
down the line, rather than according to what hardware is plugged in where.

This means that users on a server in one building can access volumes, printers, or other services on servers in other buildings, or even other states or countries, without having to know the other server's name, or having to go through complex procedures to set things up first.

"Objects" are the basis of NDS—they contain information on various parts of the network, such as drives or printers. Each object contains information on who is allowed to access it, including users and groups, domains or workgroups, titles , and sites. Additional information has been added to many objects' properties—for example, you can record the telephone numbers and address of each user, or the locations of printers.

User accounts and groups are also set up globally, which means that users can log in to their account from any server, and get the same services they would have on their "home" server.

The entire network structure, including servers and their volumes, can be viewed as a tree, and browsed by the user. This makes it easier for users in large networks to locate resources without knowing in advance the exact name of the server or device.

Files, directory structures, and volumes can be replicated and updated automatically on multiple servers, or at different sites, providing additional fault tolerance and faster access to data (local vs. remote).

Other new features include:

▸ File migration—the ability to automatically move files that aren't being used to other media, such as optical disk, conserving hard disk space.

▸ Automatic compression and decompression of files.

▸ Suballocation of blocks on a hard disk, which means that on a disk with 4 KB blocks, a 512-byte file will no longer use up 4 KB.

▸ The beginnings of protected mode operation, which in the future will prevent badly written applications from being able to crash the server.

▸ Additional network management tools to make running the network easier and to allow the remote management of servers and their devices.

▸ SFT Level III—the mirroring of not just disks, but entire servers.

The first part of each section below will cover setting up the hardware and the second part will cover setting up the software.

## NEW SERVERS

The problems that afflict new servers are conceptually different from those affecting existing servers. You can generally assume that the hardware is all functional, at least until you have eliminated the other possibilities. The most common problems will be configuration errors, possibly including conflicts between hardware or software settings.

> **The most common problems with new servers will be configuration errors.**

### Hardware

With NetWare 3.x, the server must be able to boot DOS before you start NetWare. With NetWare 2.x, it is not strictly necessary—NetWare boots from the cold boot loader on track 0 of the hard disk. However, if the server will not boot DOS, either from the DOS partition on the hard disk or from a floppy, it probably won't be able to load NetWare either. You can try to boot from a floppy if there is not a bootable hard disk in the server. If you are having problems getting the server to boot DOS, see the Workstations chapter first. The problems addressed here will be the specialized ones relating to server hardware and getting NetWare running.

The usual differences between a NetWare server and a PC workstation are these: a large hard disk or disks, often with more than one hard disk adapter; lots of RAM; multiple Network Interface Cards (NICs); a faster processor; a faster bus; and of course, the NetWare operating system.

A NetWare server could be anything from a 386 PC with one floppy and a hard drive, one LAN adapter, and a monochrome video adapter to a high speed

**NOTE**
See Chapter 2 for information about hardware problems that affect both workstations and servers.

486 EISA bus PC with 32 MB of RAM, an IDE disk drive adapter with 3.5" and 5.25" floppies and a hard disk to boot from, two SCSI hard disk adapters with two or more 1 gigabyte hard drives on each adapter, two LAN adapters, and a VGA monitor and adapter. As your configuration approaches the latter, it can be very difficult to set up. Below are the most common problem areas.

**RAM (Over 16 MB)**   There are two problems that may occur with large amounts of RAM. The first happens when an additional RAM board is used to add the RAM, and the other is simply a function of the way some devices and NetWare itself react when there is more than 16 MB of RAM in the system. Many PCs will allow up to 64 MB of RAM on the motherboard. However, older machines which may only allow 4 MB on the motherboard will require additional boards. These boards can be difficult to configure—be sure to set the interrupts correctly, and to keep the segments of RAM contiguous.

Additionally, you may need an updated driver for your SCSI adapter or NIC, or may need to load the driver with a parameter that tells it that your server has over 16 MB of RAM. You may also need to use the REGISTER MEMORY command to tell NetWare that the server has over 16 MB with ISA bus PCs. With EISA bus PCs, you may need to add the following SET command to the AUTOEXEC.NCF file.:

### SET AUTO REGISTER MEMORY ABOVE 16 MB = ON

The default setting is ON, but some PCs may not register the memory unless you include the command in AUTOEXEC.NCF.

**SCSI Adapters**   It is common to have two SCSI adapters in the same server, to provide for mirrored drives. It is often the case that SCSI host adapters from different manufacturers will not work in the same PC. For that reason, it is best to use the same manufacturer's cards, and even the same model of card, when more than one adapter is required.

SCSI adapters do not interface with the PC in the same way as IDE and MFM/RLL adapters. If you wish to use a SCSI drive as a boot drive, you may need an additional BIOS, typically added to a network adapter to allow this, or a special SCSI adapter. In addition, you should take care that the interrupt used by the SCSI adapter is not used by other floppy or hard disk adapters, particularly if you have a motherboard with a built-in adapter.

Remember to check the termination and IDs of SCSI drives—instead of an outright failure, you may get an intermittent problem that will drive you crazy. Only the last drive in the SCSI chain should be terminated and all devices on any one chain must have different SCSI IDs, from zero to six (seven is used by the adapter). If there are both internal and external drives attached to a SCSI adapter, the last drive in both the daisy chains should be terminated and the terminator should be removed from the SCSI host adapter.

> **Check the termination and IDs of SCSI drives—instead of outright failure, you may get an intermittent problem that will drive you crazy.**

**Formatting and Partitioning the Drives**   Disk drives to be used with NetWare will not normally need to be formatted, just repartitioned. You may wish to use COMPSURF, ZTEST, or INSTALL to test the drive. Be careful—these utilities may destroy any data on the drive. COMPSURF does a comprehensive test of a drive under NetWare 2.x. ZTEST reformats track 0, which is used for the cold boot loader. Both of these will destroy any data on the drive. The INSTALL NLM in NetWare 3.x and 4.x will perform non-destructive tests as well as formatting the drive.

Mirrored partitions should be the same size—any additional space in the second partition will be unused. There can be multiple partitions on a disk, or a single partition that spans multiple disks. Be careful about creating partitions above 2.0 GB. Some file systems cannot handle more than 2 GB in a single partition.

If a large number of bad blocks show up, try formatting the drives. If there are still large numbers of bad blocks, the drive may be damaged. I would highly recommend replacing it at this point. Once the drives have been tested, or formatted if necessary, then a NetWare partition can be created.

**Multiple LAN Adapters**    LAN adapters typically use both an interrupt and a memory segment. If you have more than one adapter, they must not use the same interrupt and memory segment. Further, different manufacturers' cards will have different sequences of interrupts and memory segments that they expect to use; thus, it is not always sufficient to set the first adapter to its first configuration and the second adapter to its second configuration. Be sure to check the manufacturer's documentation for the usable interrupts and memory segments and make them different.

**Network Addresses**    In a Wide Area Network (WAN), especially a large one, a common problem is duplicate network addresses. The hex number used to identify the server must be unique. Fortunately, this is an easy problem to diagnose. A repeating error message will occur at the console on all servers on the LAN, with the text "Router Configuration Error: Servername is claiming my same internet address," or something similar. This is another case where having your network well documented comes in handy. All you get on the screen is the server's network number—a long hex number. If you have those numbers in a list with their corresponding servers, it'll be much easier for you to track down the other server.

**VGA Adapters**    VGA adapters use both an interrupt and a memory segment. This can cause conflicts with network adapters, SCSI adapters, or any other cards in the server that use interrupts or memory segments. Be sure to check the interrupt and memory segment used to ensure that it doesn't conflict with other cards.

**Automatic Loading of BIOS into Upper RAM**    Shadow BIOS, or loading the BIOS into the RAM between 640 KB and 1 MB, is intended to allow the faster execution of BIOS instructions, by execution from the inherently faster 16- or 32-bit RAM, instead of the BIOS. Problems can occur when other hardware (such as a VGA adapter or LAN adapter), or NetWare attempts to access this same area of memory.

**Interrupts/EISA Configuration**   Any PC with an ISA bus (or an EISA-bus PC using interrupts), has a limited number of possible interrupts. The problem is that typically, there are several cards which want to use interrupts in a particular range. For instance, NICs, mouse adapters, and some display adapters, among others, all want an interrupt between 2 and 5.

Things may be complicated further by cards that limit your choice to one or two of the four possible interrupts. In these cases, careful planning may be required to avoid conflicts. Of course, you should record the interrupts in use for each PC as you configure the cards in it, both to facilitate troubleshooting if it won't boot, and to make the addition of other cards at a later date easier.

EISA bus PCs in bus mastering mode no longer have a problem with interrupts. However, in exchange for the old problem, you are now faced with a much more complicated installation procedure. You will need to know the manufacturer of each card, and often the version of the card as well, and what memory, if any, it uses. Then you must run the EISA configuration utility that came with your server to tell it what cards are installed.

**Security**   NetWare provides several levels of security within the operating system. However, none of them can prevent someone from accidentally unplugging a server or turning it off. I recommend that your server be placed in a lockable room, and that the door be kept locked unless someone is present.

## Software

Only the most basic DOS configuration is needed to set a server up. When NetWare boots, it takes over as the operating system—DOS is not used and may be removed from memory. Thus, if the server will boot with DOS, nothing further needs to be done before installing NetWare. Again, the purpose here is not to instruct you in the process of installing NetWare, but rather to help you debug that process when it fails.

**Installing NetWare**   The basic process of installing NetWare is a relatively simple one of copying files onto the hard disk of the server. If you have problems, they are likely to be either with the configuration of NetWare after it's installed, or with hardware. SERVER.EXE and NET$OS.EXE are essentially programs like any other. If there are errors in loading them, they will typically be due to memory errors or hardware configuration. With NetWare 2.x, you will get an error when starting if the LAN adapter or cold boot PROM is defective.

**Formatting Drives**   NetWare does not use a standard DOS partition for disk drives. There will be a small DOS partition on the server's boot disk with NetWare 3.x or 4.x, but the rest of that disk and any others on the system must be partitioned with NetWare partitions. You do this with INSTALL. You can also choose to do a low-level format and test of the drive with INSTALL under 3.x and 4.x and ZTEST or COMPSURF under 2.x. Unless you buy the drive preformatted and certified for NetWare, I heartily recommend this with new systems. It can't hurt in any case (it will destroy any existing data, of course), although it may take some time.

Once the drive is formatted and partitioned, a "hot fix" redirection area is set up. This is used if bad blocks are encountered on the disk. If you use MONITOR, you can see the total number of blocks on the drive, and the number of Redirection Blocks. This is normally two percent of the total number of blocks. You will also see the number of Redirected Blocks. This number starts out at zero and, ideally, will never grow.

If you notice a large number of redirected blocks, or if the number of redirected blocks is growing regularly, it is a good indication that the disk is deteriorating physically. It's a very good idea to replace such a disk at once. You may wish to try a low-level format, followed by a thorough test of the disk, but since the cost of a disk is usually much less than the value of the information on it, and the cost of down time if the disk quits in the middle of a busy day (you are doing regular backups, aren't you?), it pays to just replace the disk.

NetWare allows you to create volumes that span multiple partitions and multiple disks. This can allow you to create volumes with very large effective sizes. This can be a problem with some operating systems that may have trouble with partitions over 2 or 2.5 GB. If you set up a volume over 2 GB, and you either cannot see the volume or it shows as a different size from a workstation, the problem is not with NetWare, but rather is an inherent limitation of the operating system of the workstation. The only solution is to decrease the size of the volume.

**Configuration Files**    The names of the server configuration files change in different versions, but they perform the same functions. In 2.*x*, the files are SERVER.CFG, and AUTOEXEC.SYS; in 3.*x* and 4.*x*, they are AUTO-EXEC.NCF and STARTUP.NCF.

Keep a hard copy of these files. It is easy to change a configuration in trying to troubleshoot a problem, and lose track of how it was configured in the first place. If you intend to remove a line for troubleshooting purposes, it may save you headaches to comment it out first, using # (the pound sign). This way, if the problem turns out to be something else, putting it back is a matter of erasing one character, instead of typing in a long string.

It seems ridiculous, but the most common problem with the configuration files is misspelling. Be very sure that commands and parameters are spelled correctly and that the values given are within the proper ranges. Case is usually not an issue, but some parameters, especially ones relating to Macintosh or UNIX support may be case sensitive.

> It is easy to change a configuration in the .NCF files and lose track of how it was originally configured. To remove a line for troubleshooting purposes, comment it out rather than deleting it.

**Device Drivers**    Each device in a server uses a driver. For example, the driver for a Novell NE2000 is named NE2000.LAN. Particular care must be used to make sure that the driver is the proper one for the hardware installed, and that it is the version recommended for the version of NetWare you are using. You should be able to get the proper driver from NetWire if you don't have it. Watch the messages as NetWare loads. If the server freezes after a driver is loaded, it may be the wrong driver, or an incorrect version of the right driver.

**NOTE**
See Appendix A for information about NetWire and other resources.

**Protocols**    NetWare 3.11 allows you to run multiple protocols as if they were native. Protocols supported include IPX, SPX, TCP/IP, Apple-Talk, NetBIOS, OSI, and SMB. It is possible to have a number of these protocols running on the same NIC. Each protocol must be loaded and bound to the board. The LOAD and BIND commands for each board include certain parameters. If the parameters are not set correctly (if the wrong numbers are used, or the spelling is incorrect) the statements may not work for that protocol.

Or the LOAD and BIND commands may work, but conflict with other devices on your internet. This problem occurs more often in a WAN environment than with single LANs. In a single LAN, not connected to anything else, the AppleTalk zone names and zone numbers, the TCP/IP numbers, subnets, and so on, that you specify are not critical. In a WAN environment, or a LAN which may someday be expanded into a WAN, these settings become crucial—they must be coordinated throughout the WAN. It is extremely important to carefully document and structure the Apple-Talk zone setup you use, and the TCP/IP setup you use.

If the server boots, and DOS workstations can log in, but UNIX workstations or Macs cannot see the server, the first place to look is in the INSTALL configurations. Double check the settings and remember that some items (for instance the Mac zone names) are case sensitive. For more information, see Chapter 8: Connecting to Other Systems.

**NOTE**
See Chapter 8 for more information about inter-networking and multiple protocols.

▶ • • • • • • • • • • • ◀

**The most common problem with the configuration files is misspelling.**

There is a saying among system administrators that 90 percent or more of the day-to-day problems that users encounter on a network involve permissions. Between permissions for users, and groups, and ensuring that all the proper people are in the proper groups, it's no wonder the issues are complex. They are potentially further complicated by different permissions at different levels of a directory hierarchy and on the files themselves.

One of the best investments a system administrator can make early on is to study NetWare's permissions structure until thoroughly familiar with it. Particularly, make sure that you understand completely the difference between the inherited rights mask and trustee rights and how they combine.

Bear in mind that the way permissions flow down through the directory structure and are granted changes greatly from NetWare 2.*x* to NetWare 3.*x*. If you use both, or are upgrading from 2.x to 3.*x*, make especially sure that you understand the differences in how permissions are implemented.

**Login Scripts**    There are three login scripts that may execute when a user logs in: the default, the user, and the system. The default login script will execute if no system or user login script exists. This script should normally not be used. The system login script executes first, and should contain commands that are necessary to set up all users. The user's login script executes next, and contains the commands that configure the user's environment.

NetWare 4.*x* adds another login script for groups, which takes the place of the IF MEMBER OF construction in the system login script under previous versions. This is necessary because groups are global in a network and can be accessed by members from any server. In addition, the system login script is executed for members of an organization, rather than on a server-by-server basis, because users are no longer tied to a particular server.

**ABEND**    With a new installation, an error message beginning with ABEND means that something in your software or hardware configuration is wrong. The first thing to try is rebooting the server.

If the problem recurs, it could be resulting from an NLM that is incorrectly configured, corrupted, or simply badly written, from an incorrectly entered SET command, or from a printer set up incorrectly. Try unloading all the NLMs and reloading them one at a time, checking the SET commands in the AUTOEXEC.NCF and STARTUP.NCF for correct spelling and values within the range allowed (check the *System Administration* manual for details), and check the setup of all printers configured.

It could also be a hardware problem. Make sure that the server memory is sufficient for the configuration you are running, and check the server as a workstation for hardware problems using the procedures listed in the next chapter.

## EXISTING SERVERS

With existing servers, you are unlikely to run across configuration errors or interrupt conflicts, unless you have just changed something. The principal problem with existing equipment is failures, either of hardware or software. The one exception to this is that some interrupt conflicts may cause intermittent, long-term problems that will only disrupt things occasionally.

> The principal problem with existing equipment is failures, either of hardware or software.

### Hardware

Other than changes, which you should troubleshoot using the steps outlined above, the most likely hardware problems are not unique to servers, but are equivalent to workstation problems. See the next chapter for details. Many hardware problems will produce error messages, either in the system error log, or when DOS or NetWare loads, that will make them easy to spot.

NetWare has the following tools which allow you to diagnose and sometime correct hardware problems.

**MONITOR and FCONSOLE**    MONITOR (3.x and 4.x) and FCONSOLE (2.x) are invaluable tools for deciphering network problems. They will tell you a lot about the normal operation of the server and can help you pinpoint problems that are otherwise very hard to isolate. For instance, if several workstations are having problems connecting with a 3.x server, and the server is running, and you can't find any problems with the physical network, go to the LAN Information selection. You will be able to see whether the server is sending and receiving packets, whether there are many bad packets, collisions, and similar information. Likewise, if network performance slows down radically when there are lots of users on a 2.x server, and FCONSOLE shows that the Peak Used number of communication buffers is close to or equal to the number of buffers set, you should increase the total number of communication buffers. (This will require regenerating the operating system.)

You should also be aware of the usual state of your server, as shown in MONITOR or FCONSOLE. There are a number of particular things to look for (and record in your log for that server).

**NOTE**
See Chapter 5 for more information about recording your system's normal state.

**VREPAIR**    VREPAIR is a very useful tool to fix software problems with hard drives. It won't diagnose a problem with the electronics of a drive, or tell you about a SCSI conflict or termination problem, but it does a good job of getting the directory entries back in sync with the files they represent.

The most important thing to know about VREPAIR is that it will only handle one set of problems at a time. Each time it scans a disk it finds problems, and, if you tell it to, it fixes them. However, the process of fixing one set of problems may uncover further problems, which will require another scan. You should continue running VREPAIR until no errors are reported.

**System Error Log**    The System Error Log is accessible through SYSCON from a workstation, and from some of the add-on modules in INSTALL.NLM on the server. You should become familiar with typical messages that occur in the log. Then, when problems occur, you will have a better chance of picking out the relevant error message.

Of course, the messages are in chronological order in the log and if you know when the problem began, this will give you clues as to which messages you should pay special attention to. Chapter 5 has more information on baselining—accumulating the statistics that your network produces normally, and how to use those baseline figures to determine what is wrong.

## Software

**Corrupted SERVER.EXE or NET$OS.EXE**    It is possible (though unlikely) for SERVER.EXE or NET$OS.EXE to become corrupted, so it is a good idea to back this file up onto a floppy. Then, if you suspect that the file has been corrupted, you can copy it from the floppy onto the server's hard disk, overwriting the existing file. If it won't fit on one floppy, another method is to create a directory on the DOS partition of the server's boot disk, and place a copy of the NetWare executable file (NET$OS.EXE or SERVER.EXE) in it.

Other than the slight possibility of a corrupted SERVER.EXE, the software on an existing server is only likely to cause problems if it is changed, or if some other part of your network is changed in a way that conflicts with the configuration of your server. These problems should be treated as changes—see the section above on new installations.

**ABEND**   You will occasionally see an error message on the server's screen that begins with ABEND. This means that the server software has crashed. (This message appears only on the server's screen.) In an existing system, this is usually a fluke, possibly caused by an application running on the server that is misbehaving, by an NLM that is not functioning correctly, or by a hardware memory error. The text following the ABEND part of the message will tell you something about the problem. The *System Messages* manual may be useful in decoding the error message. If the problem recurs, try to find out what applications were running on workstations when the server crashed. If any of them are new applications, or new versions, they may be causing problems with the server.

It could also be a hardware problem. Make sure that the memory in the server is sufficient for the configuration you are running. If you have recently added new NLMs, additional disk drives, or new name spaces on existing drives, or additional protocol drivers, the server may need more RAM to function correctly. Check the server as a workstation for hardware problems.

**NOTE**
See Chapter 2 for hardware problems that affect both workstations and servers.

**BINDFIX**   BINDFIX is a utility program in NetWare 2.*x* and an NLM in 3.*x* and 4.*x*. It will repair many problems that occur with the binderies: a user cannot log in, you can't modify or delete a user account, a password cannot be changed, trustee rights can't be changed, or you get error messages on the console that mention the binderies, for example.

Be sure to have a backup of the bindery files before running BINDFIX. If you do keep separate copies of the bindery files, you may be better off replacing them, rather than using BINDFIX. The names of the files you will need to back up are listed under "The Binderies," below.

### Other Diagnostic Tools

There are many levels of diagnostic tools available to the system administrator. They range from $195 software-only products that will allow you a little more capability than MONITOR, to $50,000+ WAN analyzers that will produce a map of an extended WAN, monitor traffic, inform you if anything unusual happens, and suggest solutions.

Other available software can inventory the software on each workstation on your network, upgrade all workstations on the net with the newest versions of software as they come out, or tell you what hardware is installed in the workstations. There are others that enhance the NetWare utilities, producing more detailed reports than MONITOR can, with tracking over time, and with nice formatting of the printed reports.

While many of these products can save you time, or be invaluable in a complex WAN environment, you can often produce the same results yourself with a little advance preparation, the tools available to you in NetWare, and a little deductive reasoning.

For example, a protocol analyzer might be able to monitor network traffic, detect bad packets coming from a server and notify you of the problem, which server is producing it, and where it is located. However, by assigning network numbers to servers that will allow you to identify them (office number, followed by extension, or something similar), you can get the same information by inspecting the system error logs of your servers regularly.

Of course, this is more work, and if you can get the money in your budget for a network analyzer, I highly recommend it. Similarly, the network hardware or software inventory programs are very useful, especially for large networks, but you can gather the same information manually, using the forms provided in Appendix B.

## THE BINDERIES

The binderies are hidden files that contain all the information you have set up on your users, their passwords, trustee rights, ownership of files, default printers, and so on. SBACKUP, NBACKUP, and backup programs designed to work with NetWare give you the option to back up the binderies. Be careful—if you restore from an older tape, and restore the binderies, any changes you or the users have made to passwords and the like will revert to what they were as of that backup. If you wish to back the binderies up manually, they consist of two hidden files, NET$BIND.SYS and NET$BVAL.SYS, in 2.x, and three files, NET$OBJ.SYS, NET$PROP.SYS, and NET$VAL.SYS, in 3.x. These files are located in SYS:SYSTEM.

In NetWare 4.x, the bindery is replaced with the NetWare Directory, under NetWare Directory Services. This is a new and much more capable way of making the services on the server available to clients, and it requires a more extensive database, with many additional properties. NetWare 4.x can be configured to emulate the old style of binderies to maintain compatibility with older servers and workstation shells. The NDS database is in a hidden directory, SYS:_NETWARE, in five files: VALUE.NDS, BLOCK.NDS, PARTITIO.NDS, ENTRY.NDS and 00006f00.000. This database can and should be replicated on other servers on your network.

If a user cannot log in, if you can't modify or delete a user account, if a password cannot be changed, if trustee rights can't be changed, or if you get error messages on the console that mention the binderies, try running BINDFIX.

## UPGRADING NETWARE

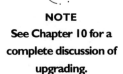

**NOTE**
See Chapter 10 for a complete discussion of upgrading.

Upgrading NetWare using the UPGRADE utility is usually a relatively pain-free operation. It is well documented, and this book will not go into the details of a normal upgrade. However, even in a straightforward upgrade, there are a number of things that can go wrong. NEVER upgrade without doing a complete backup of your file system first.

The most complicated part of upgrades is the changes in names and structures. In NetWare 2.x SERVER.CFG and AUTOEXEC.SYS are used to run parts of NetWare; in 3.*x*, the files are called AUTOEXEC.NCF and STARTUP.NCF. Permission structures—how permissions flow in the directory structure, and how users inherit permissions—change considerably from NetWare 2.15 and below, to 2.2 and above, to 3.*x*. NetWare 4.*x* has a still different system. Make sure that you understand the differences before you do an upgrade.

Another aspect of upgrades is the hardware requirements of the new system, as discussed in Chapter 10.

### NLMs

The installation process for NLMs under NetWare 3.x and 4.x is fortunately very simple. Just run the INSTALL NLM and the appropriate files will be put in the proper places on your server. Configuring the NLMs for your particular requirements is another matter.

Each NLM comes with appropriate documentation—this book is not intended to replace the user documentation, or even to supplement it. However, the troubleshooting process may certainly be applied to NLM installations that you believe are installed correctly, but refuse to function for one reason or another.

There are four types of NLMs:

▶ Disk drivers to allow the use of different types of disk drives (*.DSK).

▶ LAN drivers for running different protocols on various LAN adapters (*.LAN).

▶ Name space modules to allow operating systems other than DOS to access and store files on the server. These include the Macintosh, NFS (UNIX) and OS/2 (*.NAM).

▶ Management utilities and server applications. These include MONITOR, INSTALL, UPS, and others. They allow you to configure and manage the server, or add functionality (*.NLM).

**NOTE**
See Appendix A for
details about NetWire
and other soures of
software and information

If you are having regular ABENDs or problems with server performance, make sure that you have the latest version of all the NLMs you are using. (Updated NLMs and patches are often available on NetWire.) If necessary, reduce the number of NLMs loaded to the minimum necessary for basic server functions, and add the rest back in one at a time until you can determine which is causing a problem, or conflicting with other NLMs.

## SYSTEM FAULT TOLERANCE

System Fault Tolerance (SFT) is Novell's method of ensuring system reliability in the event of hardware failures. SFT II protects the data on a server. SFT III allows for entire servers to be protected.

### Mirroring and Duplexing

Both mirroring and duplexing are intended to allow the server to continue to provide file services even if a disk fails. All the data on a disk is duplicated on the mirrored disk, and if one disk fails, the other provides continued access to the data. These systems also provide the additional advantage of reducing the disk access time by half—NetWare will read or write to whichever disk is available, and then update the other in the background. Data can also be read from both disks at once, alternating blocks, which doubles throughput.

The only drawback to mirroring or duplexing is the added cost—for each volume required, two disks must be purchased; with duplexing, two controllers and two disk enclosures with power supplies are also required. However, given the relatively low cost of disk storage, this is cheap insurance against the lost time a crashed disk will cause on even a small network—obtaining a new drive and restoring from backup will take a minimum of hours, and perhaps days and of course, anything on the server that has been changed since the last backup will be lost as well.

> Mirroring or duplexing costs more—up to twice as much. However, this is still cheap insurance against the lost time a crashed disk will cause on even a small network.

The difference between mirroring and duplexing is the level of duplication of components. Mirroring uses two disks attached to the same controller, and usually the same power supply. Duplexing uses separate controllers, disks and power supplies, providing continuing functionality even if the power supply or controller fails. See Figure 1.3 below.

▶ . . . . . . . . . . . . . . . . . . . . . . . . . . . . . . ◀

*Mirroring and Duplexing.*

**Mirroring -**
**1 Controller**
**1 Power Supply**
**2 Hard Disks**

**Duplexing -**
**2 Controllers**
**2 Power Supplies**
**2 Hard Disks**

### SFT Level III

SFT level III allows you to mirror an entire server, rather than simply the disk drives. This provides a level of fault tolerance previously only available on mainframes and minis. All data written to one server is also written to the second server, which may be in a remote location. If any part of one server fails, the other server takes over. This is particularly important in mission-critical applications where any loss of connectivity might cause extensive business losses, such as in banking or airline applications. See Figure 1.4 below.

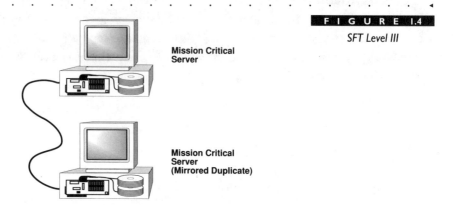

F I G U R E   I.4

*SFT Level III*

**Mission Critical Server**

**Mission Critical Server (Mirrored Duplicate)**

The two servers don't have to be identical, but the lowest configuration will apply to both servers—for instance, if one has 16 MB of RAM, and the other 32 MB, they will both effectively have 16 MB.

## Real-Life Stories

This section describes typical problems and how a troubleshooter would go through the process of isolating the fault and fixing it. The two fictional companies introduced in the Overview, and their administrators, will be used as examples. They combine the equipment and experience of a number of actual businesses. These two scenarios are intended to show some representative problems often encountered when setting up or troubleshooting a server. While you may never see these particular problems, they should give you a feel for the process by which an experienced troubleshooter isolates a problem, determines the solution, and fixes the problem.

## SCENARIO ONE: INSTALLING A NEW SYSTEM

The administrator is installing and configuring a new system. He encounters some typical problems associated with late-model servers using large amounts of RAM and more than one hard disk adapter.

### Snapshot

Is This a New System?

Does It Boot DOS?

Will It Boot under DOS, but Then Fail to Load NetWare?

Does NetWare Load, but Some Devices (Such as Network Cards or Disk Drives) Are Inaccessible?

**NOTE**
For anti-static precautions and other safeguards, see Chapter 5

John, the system administrator for Itsy-Bitsy Inc., has about $25,000 of computer and components sitting in a couple of dozen boxes around his office. They are the parts to put together the new high-performance server that the tech pubs department has been asking for this last year. Being a bright guy, and having read this book before, he's carefully observing anti-static precautions, and recording the settings of all the cards, disks and so forth as he puts the system together.

The server is a 486 ISA (AT-style) bus PC with 32 MB of RAM and an internal 100 MB IDE hard drive, one 3.5" floppy and one 5.25" floppy, two serial ports, one parallel port, and VGA support on the motherboard. It supports shadowing the BIOS in RAM. In addition he has two external enclosures, each with two 1.2 GB hard drives, an 8 mm SCSI tape drive, two SCSI adapters, and two 16-bit Ethernet adapters. He will have two drives attached to each SCSI controller, providing full mirroring—controller, disk drives and power supply will be entirely separate for each set. The tape drive will be added to the daisy chain on the first SCSI controller, the one that the tape drive came with. Of course, the server and enclosures will be plugged into a UPS.

As John installs the boards in the PC, he records the settings of each one on the server configuration form he copied from Appendix B. The first Network Interface Card (NIC) uses interrupt 3 and memory address C000. He sets the second NIC to interrupt 4 and memory address D000. Doing so ensures that there is no interrupt conflict between the cards and makes the LAN configuration easy, too—these are configurations 0 and 1 for the drivers for the NICs.

Next, John installs the two SCSI adapters. He knows that the built-in hard drive adapter uses interrupt 14, so he can choose 10, 11, 12 or 13 for the two cards. He sets them to 10 and 11, records this and then closes the server up. He next makes sure that only the second of the two SCSI drives in the first enclosure is terminated, and that neither is terminated in the other enclosure—he has terminated the tape drive, which will be the last SCSI device in the chain for that controller.

Finally, everything is ready. He plugs everything in to the UPS, attaches and secures all the cables and crosses his fingers. He turns the SCSI devices on, then flips the main power switch on the PC ... Nothing happens. Three hours later, once the UPS's battery has charged, he turns everything on again. This time, assorted fans begin whirring, the PC beeps, and messages begin appearing on the monitor.

John sees several messages, identifying the BIOS, the VGA adapter, and the SCSI adapter. Then DOS is loaded and he's ready to begin the installation of NetWare. He brings the server up to partition the drives. However, when he starts SERVER.EXE, the SCSI adapter won't load its driver. Belatedly, John remembers seeing in the adapter's documentation that the driver must be loaded with a /v switch if the server contains over 16 MB of RAM. A few minutes later, the driver is loaded with the /v switch and the first SCSI adapter driver loads.

However, once the second driver for the other SCSI adapter loads, John is unable to use INSTALL to partition the drives. In fact, none of the drives show up at all. He begins experimenting. He tries removing one of the cards. The other one works fine and its drives are visible to INSTALL. He reinstalls the first and removes the second. The first one works fine too. He tries setting the cards to different interrupt settings, thinking that they might not like being on adjacent disk channels. They still won't work when both cards are installed.

Finally, he goes to a higher authority. He calls CompuServe and asks some questions in the NetWare forum. Within a short while he gets his answer—those two SCSI adapters just won't work with each other. Maybe in the next version of the driver or ROM....

He decides to put all the drives on the single SCSI adapter that came with the tape drive, until he can get another adapter from the same manufacturer. That works fine. He is able to mount all four drives, and mirror the first two to the second two. He does remember to remove the termination from the second drive in each enclosure, so that the daisy chain of two sets of drives and the tape drive will only be terminated at the end. He also makes sure that the SCSI ID is different for all 5 SCSI devices.

**If you can't figure it out, don't spend a lot of time experimenting—try asking someone.**

The drives are mounted and mirrored; now it's time to load the network drivers. John loads the network driver and binds the first protocol to the card. The server hangs. John checks the settings in the LOAD and BIND statements. If the DMA channel or memory segment numbers were wrong, he should get an error message. Instead, the server just freezes. Back to CompuServe. Finally, he discovers that his brand-new NIC should be used with the updated driver supplied on the disk that came with it, rather than the file with the same name that came with NetWare. Once he loads the updated driver and reboots, the NIC works fine.

After a few seconds, the server begins beeping and he sees the message "Router Configuration Error: *Marketing* is claiming my same internet address." Then he remembers he's already used his girlfriend's phone number for the Marketing department server's internal network number. He resolves to use the system he saw suggested in this book—he uses the number of the office the server is in as the first four digits of the network number, and the extension of the phone in the room as the last four digits. Now, once he's implemented this scheme throughout his company, he'll be able to tell where error messages are coming from without having to refer to a long list of numbers and the servers they represent, and will know the phone number of the room the server is in, too.

Once the server is operational, he loads MONITOR to check the basic statistics for the server. When he selects Resource Utilization, the first thing he notices is that NetWare is showing total memory as 16 MB. He downs the server and checks the configuration of the server. The BIOS and DOS programs recognize the whole 32 MB, but when he starts the server again, it still only shows 16 MB. He checks several of the NetWare manuals before he finds the reference to REGISTER MEMORY in the *System Administration* manual. He enters the command and adds it to AUTOEXEC.NCF, and everything is fine.

### Lessons Learned

- ▶ Remember to check the termination and ID of SCSI drives—you may not get an outright failure, but instead an intermittent problem that will drive you crazy.

- ▶ If you can't figure it out, don't spend huge amounts of time experimenting—try asking someone.

- ▶ If you're using over 16 MB of RAM, make sure you know the implications for compatibility with other components and drivers. You may also have to change the default configurations of NetWare to recognize the memory.

- ▶ Get adapters from the same manufacturer whenever possible—even though the standards (Ethernet, SCSI, and so on) are supposed to be the same, they aren't always implemented in quite the same way. Drivers from different manufacturers may conflict with each other too. If you are having a conflict, you can try using the same driver for both cards. Don't expect this to work, though.

- ▶ Make sure your drivers match your devices—check NetWire or your Authorized Reseller to see if you have the latest version of the drivers.

> On a multiserver LAN, be sure to have a scheme for coordinating Internal Network numbers and LAN numbers.

### The Fault Point Chain

In this case there are several chains, from the server to each device, and then on the server itself. The examples below are for the hard disks. Each problem above has its own chain.

### The Disk Drives

> AC power from the wall.

> The power cord.

> The power supply for the disk drive.

> The power cable from the power supply to the disk drive.

> The disk drive mechanism itself.

> The terminating resistors on the disk drive.

> The data cable from the disk drive to the port on the enclosure.

> The data cable from the enclosure to the controller in the server.

> The terminating resistor on the controller (this chain could also continue instead to an internal SCSI drive in the server).

> The controller (hardware).

> The controller (configuration).

> The disk driver installed in NetWare.

### The Server

> AC power from the wall.

> The power cord.

> The power supply for the server.

▸ The motherboard.

▸ The BIOS configuration of the server.

▸ The configuration of the cards in the server (conflicts).

▸ Differences in implementations of SCSI on the two controllers.

▸ DOS.

▸ NetWare (SERVER.EXE).

▸ The disk drivers (AHA1540.DSK, OTHER.DSK).

▸ The formatting and partitioning already on the drives (INSTALL sometimes has problems with drives that were previously formatted with other operating systems. The cure is to format the drives using a DOS formatter, then format them again with NetWare).

Each of these points could have made the disk drives fail to show up as available for partitioning. Some of them could be quickly verified (if the power light on the enclosure is on and you can hear the drive spin up, the first four on that chain are eliminated) before you check the others. In this case, John wasn't initially aware of the possibility that the two controllers might conflict with each other. This may happen to you, too. If you believe you have eliminated all the possibilities, then there is probably something in the chain that you've either overlooked, or weren't aware of.

## SCENARIO TWO: MAINTAINING AN EXISTING SYSTEM

Fran, an administrator for Great Big, Inc., is faced with a server that won't respond to the prompt. She encounters a problem with a faulty NIC and then has trouble with the disk drive—probably caused by the original crash.

### Snapshot—Scenario Two

Is This an Existing System?

Is the Server up?

Can You Reboot the Server?

Will the Server Boot DOS?

Will NetWare Load?

Does NetWare Load, but Some or All Server Functions Cannot
Be Accessed?

Fran, the system administrator for Great Big, Inc., comes back to her desk
after lunch. There are 15 messages from various users, saying that they can't
connect to the server, or that their applications don't work, or that they can't
see drive F. Fran notices that all the user complaints are from people with accounts on the Marketing server, so she decides to check that server first, before
looking at all the users' workstations. She grabs the data sheet she prepared
when she built the server, which lists its hardware and software configurations,
and heads for the office the server is in.

The server is on, and there is text on the monitor
(nothing helpful) but the server doesn't respond to
the keyboard. Even the CapsLock and NumLock keys
don't respond. She checks the connection between
the keyboard and CPU and tries again. Still nothing.
There's a workstation in the room. She tries to connect to the server and gets the message "Server
marketing is unknown at this time."

**A problem that is affecting more than one user is likely to be with the server or networking hardware.**

Fran reboots the server. Both DOS and NetWare
load properly and the server is back on line. Another
crisis averted.... She logs in as supervisor from the workstation and begins
checking the volumes to make sure that everything is accessible again. After
about 5 minutes, the workstation loses the connection to the server, and on
checking, Fran finds that the server has hung again.

After she finishes her primal scream therapy, Fran begins eliminating
possible causes. Since the server will boot, and load DOS and NetWare, and
has been running fine for quite a while, it's almost certainly not a configuration problem. She's the only one with the supervisor password, and she

hasn't changed anything on this server in months, so it shouldn't be a problem with an addition being improperly configured.

She notifies the department members that the server may be down for a while, then reboots the server again, paying particular attention to the messages from the BIOS, DOS, and NetWare. There are no out-of-the-ordinary messages or errors reported. She logs in again from the workstation and quickly goes to the system error log. At the end are a number of messages relating to Ethernet configuration errors. A clue!

She quickly checks the system error log of another server on the same Ethernet segment, and it does not display the same errors. From this she deduces that the problem may be related to Ethernet, but is probably also unique to this server. She tries to log in again, and the server is down. She turns the server off and replaces the Ethernet card with a spare.

The server comes up, but now it can't mount the second volume. Fran ignores this problem for the moment—it may be the result of the freezes and powering off without shutting down properly. She logs in from the workstation and waits anxiously. Five minutes, then ten, then fifteen pass. There are no new messages in the system error log. It seems that the original problem has been fixed.

Now, it's time to get that second volume mounted again. Fran starts up VREPAIR and begins scanning the unmounted volume for errors. It finds errors, says it's repairing them. When VREPAIR finishes, Fran brings the server down correctly, then restarts it. It still can't mount the second volume. Then Fran remembers—VREPAIR should be run over and over again until it doesn't report any errors.

Unfortunately for Fran, with 20 people clamoring outside the door to know when their server will be back on line, the VREPAIR process is taking about 20 minutes per cycle with this 1.2 GB volume. However, on the fourth time through, there are no further errors reported.

When she restarts the server, the volume mounts properly. and everyone is able to log in and get to their files again. Fran reflects that it might have been faster to reformat the drive and restore the disk from last night's backup, but all the work done that day would have been lost. She resolves to talk to her manager about mirroring the drives on the mission-critical servers as insurance against this sort of problem.

Fran then logs the incident in her work log, recording the problems and solutions in case she comes across a similar situation again. She also logs the problems on the data sheet for the server.

### Lessons Learned

▸ Check to see whether a reported problem is affecting more than one user—it will help you tell whether the problem is with the user's workstation or with the server or cabling.

▸ Check the server's system error log regularly. Not only will this enable you to distinguish important messages more easily, you may well be able to spot a potential problem before it results in down time.

▸ Remember that it may be necessary to run VREPAIR several times before all errors are corrected.

▸ Mirror the drives on mission critical servers.

▸ Keep a log, and keep it updated. It will help you solve the problem the next time. There will be a next time.

### The Fault Point Chain

There are several fault point chains in this example. The first one is the original problem with the server.

▸ AC power from the wall (including spikes or brownouts).

▸ The power cord.

▸ The power supply for the server.

▸ The motherboard including RAM.

▸ The BIOS power (if the batteries wear out, configuration information is lost).

- ▶ The BIOS configuration of the server.
- ▶ The cards in the server (each has its own chain of connections, configuration, drivers, and so on).
- ▶ The keyboard and its cable.
- ▶ The monitor, its power, its cable, and the video adapter.
- ▶ NetWare (SERVER.EXE could be corrupted, or could simply have crashed).
- ▶ The NLMs loaded when the server crashed.
- ▶ Applications running on the user's workstations when the server crashed.

In this case, many of these are easily eliminated—if there is text on the screen, obviously the server has power, and the monitor is working. If the BIOS were incorrectly configured or its batteries worn out, the server wouldn't boot correctly. The keyboard responds after rebooting. Since no one has logged in yet, it couldn't be applications running on the server. This trims the list down to the motherboard, the cards in the server, NetWare itself, and the NLMs. The messages in the system error log pointed the way to the first item to check, but if there hadn't been any messages, the order of things to try (easiest to hardest) might have been this: replacing SERVER.EXE, not loading the NLMs, replacing the cards one at a time, and trying another motherboard.

# CHAPTER 2

# Workstations

# SnapShot

The basic purpose of NetWare is to allow personal computers to share resources. The term *PC* has come to be identified with IBM PC-compatibles, which is why the title of this chapter is Workstations. The workstations covered include the IBM PC family and all the clones, Macintoshes, and UNIX workstations.

The quick guide for this chapter covers only PC-compatible workstations and DOS. For other workstations and operating systems, see the appropriate Concepts sections later in this chapter. If problems with a server occur before NetWare loads, treat it as a workstation. Once again, the Real-Life Stories section will lead you through some real problems, showing how they were diagnosed and resolved.

PC-compatibles can be very difficult to troubleshoot, principally because of their enormous variety. There are at least seven Intel processors in use, plus clone processors from other companies such as AMD, many different motherboards and BIOSs for each processor, hundreds of different hard disks, and thousands of different cards. All this variety can make troubleshooting a maze, especially if you don't have the documentation for the PC. However, if you understand the principles of how the PC loads its BIOS, operating system, network drivers, and other software, you should be able to isolate the cause of any problem and figure out what to do about it.

## IS THIS A NEW SYSTEM?

### Does the POST (Power-On Self Test) Finish without Error Messages?

If so, go to the next item. If not, either the system may be configured incorrectly with the SETUP program, or it may have been assembled incorrectly. See the Concepts section on hardware configuration on page 62. Some examples of this type of error message are "RAM configuration error, block 22f," "Kybd Error 301," and "Hard disk not ready."

### Does the Workstation Boot without Error Messages?

If so, go to the next item. If not, the error message should give you a clue as to the problem. Newer video adapters, hard disk adapters, and LAN adapters are examples of possible sources of these messages. See the Concepts section on cards and connections under PC Hardware, on page 59.

### Does DOS Load without Error Messages?

If so, go to the next item. If not, try booting from a floppy disk. If this works, replace the COMMAND.COM file on the hard disk. If DOS still won't load correctly, see the Concepts section on PC software, on page 63.

### Do the Network Drivers Load without Error Messages?

If so, go to the next item. If not, try replacing the IPX and NETx drivers. If this doesn't help, the driver may be configured incorrectly; check the network adapter version and the version of DOS in use. If everything matches, the Network Interface Card (NIC) may be faulty. See the Concepts section on networking software on page 64.

### Can You Log into the Server?

If there are no error messages but you cannot see the server, try to log in to another server, if there is one. Try to log in from another workstation. If the server is up and more than one workstation cannot login, the problem is likely to be with the physical network—either the cabling itself, or one of the devices such as a concentrator or repeater. See Chapter 3, The Physical Network, for more details.

## IS THIS AN EXISTING SYSTEM?

**Is the Display Readable? Does the Cursor Respond to the Keyboard?**

If so, go to the next item. If not, make sure the PC is on—are there any status lights on? Is the fan running? If the PC is on, but won't respond to keyboard input, it is frozen—reboot the PC. A simple test to see if the keyboard is functioning is to try the CapsLock or Num-Lock keys—if the indicator lights come on, the keyboard is functioning, whether the screen responds or not. If the keyboard lights respond, but the screen doesn't change, the PC may still be frozen. This type of hang is typical of software problems, usually with applications or Terminate and Stay Resident (TSR) programs.

The number of possible causes for freezing are practically infinite. If the PC hangs regularly, it may be a hardware or software problem. Check for software problems first, then review the hardware configuration to check for interrupt conflicts. See the Concepts sections below on PC hardware (page 59) and software (page 63).

If the screen or keyboard still won't respond after rebooting, check their connections to the PC. If they are tight, see the section below on PC hardware.

**Does the POST (Power-On Self Test) Finish without Error Messages?**

If so, go to the next item. If not, the chip that holds the setup data may have lost power, or there may be a hardware failure. Check the configuration with SETUP (see the section on Configuration). If everything matches your configuration worksheet, see the Concepts section on PC hardware, on page 59.

### Does the Workstation Boot without Error Messages?

If so, go to the next item. If not, the error message should give you a clue as to the problem. Video adapters, hard disk adapters, and LAN adapters are examples of possible sources of these messages. See the Concepts section on cards and connections under PC Hardware, on page 59.

### Does DOS Load without Error Messages?

If so, go to the next item. If not, try booting from a floppy disk. If this works, replace the COMMAND.COM file on the hard disk. If DOS still won't load correctly, see the Concepts section below on PC software, on page 63—the problem may be with some of the items in the AUTOEXEC.BAT or CONFIG.SYS files.

### Do the Network Drivers Load without Errors?

If so, go to the next item. If not, try replacing the IPX and NETx drivers. If this doesn't help, the driver may be configured incorrectly; check the network adapter version with the command—IPX i and the version of DOS in use, by typing VER, and use WSGEN to create a new driver. If the new driver also doesn't work, the problem is likely to be the NIC. See the Concepts section on networking software on page 64.

If you are using the ODI driver, make sure that the NIC driver is the latest available for your NIC. You may need to update the NIC if it is an older card. The order that the ODI shell drivers load in is: LSL, NIC.COM (the network driver for your NIC), IPXODI, and NETx. Make sure that the NET.CFG file has the proper configuration information for the card you are using.

### Does the Workstation See the Server (SLIST)?

If so, go to the next item. If not, the problem may be in the connection to the physical network, or in the physical network itself, or in the server. If the server is working (screen on, console prompt responds), check the connections from the network adapter to the transceiver (if any) and to the physical network. See the Concepts section below on cards and connections, on page 59, and Chapter 3: The Physical Network.

### Can You Log into the Server?

If not, make sure that the user you are attempting to login as exists, and that the spelling of the user name and the password are correct. Try logging in as another user. If this doesn't work, make sure that a station restriction has not been set up for that PC. Also see BINDFIX in Chapter 1: Servers.

# Concepts

Fault Points

The Basics

PC-Compatibles

  Hardware

  Software

Windows and NetWare

OS/2

PS/2s (Micro Channel)

Macintoshes

  Hardware

  Software

UNIX Workstations

Most workstations attached to Novell networks are currently IBM-compatible PCs of one type or another. However, there are other possibilities: PS/2s, Macintoshes, and UNIX workstations are the most likely. Some of the following principles will apply equally to all sorts of workstations, others will be platform-specific. The basics applicable to all platforms will be covered first, then specifics of IBM compatibles, PS/2s, Macintoshes and UNIX workstations.

## FAULT POINTS

The Overview introduced the concept of fault points as an alternative to the more conventional flow charts. The problem with flowcharts is that they become too hard to use with subjects as complex as a network, or even when covering the possible configurations of a workstation. The basic fault point chain for a workstation includes the same elements for any type of workstation. If you understand the potential fault points for a workstation, you will be able to isolate any problem to a particular part of the system, then apply the concepts below to figure out how to fix the problem.

Figure 2.1 illustrates a typical fault chain for workstations. Each item in the chain depends on the others, and each item has three parts—the part itself, and the connections between it and the preceding and following part. For example, the power at the wall socket can be broken if the power to the socket fails, if the socket itself is faulty, or if the power cord to the PC power supply is defective or not plugged in.

FIGURE 2.1

*The Fault Point Chain for Workstations*

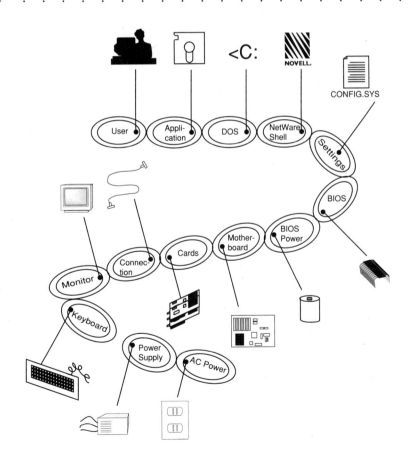

Similarly, the power supply is connected to the wall by the power cord and has connections to the motherboard, the disk drives and its fan. To determine which of the three is causing the problem, you must use deductive logic: if any part of the workstation is receiving power, the power supply and the cable are probably good. If one part of the workstation is not getting power, and the rest are, it's probably the connection for that part to the power supply. If the workstation isn't getting power anywhere, check the power cord and the socket before replacing the power supply.

You might think that the keyboard has only two parts—the keyboard and its connection to the motherboard. However, the third part here is the user—if the wrong keys are pressed, the symptoms may resemble a problem with the keyboard hardware or the connection to the PC. This is also true of the monitor, but it has even more variables: it may be turned off independently of the PC; it has a power connection and a video connection; and it can also be made to seem dead by turning down the contrast and brightness.

The connection to the network is a common failure point, because of the number of possible fault points and their susceptibility to outside interference. The network connection usually consists of the connection from the NIC in the PC to a transceiver, a concentrator or hub, or directly to the server, depending on the type of topology.

> **The connection to the network is a common failure point— often, the only problem is a loose or disconnected cable.**

Take for example the relatively simple case of an NIC with a thick Ethernet connection, connected to a transceiver that converts the thick Ethernet to 10BaseT, which is connected to a wall jack with a second cable. In this chain, the thick Ethernet cable can slip from the NIC, can become defective, or can come loose from the transceiver, the transceiver can become defective, or the 10BaseT cable can come out of its socket on the transceiver, can become defective, or can come out of the wall socket.

The network connection fault points are further complicated by the fact that they are often hard to see, hard to get at, and subject to being kicked by the user or pulled out by a janitor with a vacuum.

Each card in the PC has its own fault point chain including the connections to the bus and to whatever device it supports, its jumper configurations for interrupt, DMA segment and so forth, and the matching configurations in the setup of the PC, whether in hardware or software.

The motherboard has a point of failure where the power supply connects to it, and one for each service it provides, whether on a card, a parallel or serial port, the keyboard interface, the sound interface or the memory. Each of these can typically be diagnosed by the error messages that appear during the boot sequence, or, as a last resort, by eliminating all other possible causes.

The BIOS and the associated CMOS holds configuration information for the PC including the number and types of floppy and hard drives installed, the number of serial and parallel ports installed, the time, and other information. If the battery that provides power to the BIOS wears out, this information can be lost. If the BIOS is out of date, it may not support new floppy drives or hard drives, or it may cause problems with software, such as Windows not running in the enhanced mode with an older 386 BIOS.

The PC's operating system and the NetWare software are configured with several files, including AUTOEXEC.BAT, CONFIG.SYS and NET.CFG. Each of these files contains statements that must be spelled correctly and must also match the settings on the cards they pertain to.

The NetWare shell can fail in its connection with the PC hardware and software, by itself, or in its interface with applications. If the shell isn't configured correctly with SHELLGEN, it won't match the interrupt and memory address used by the NIC, and some shells work better than others with certain applications. For example, if you are running Windows 3.1, you should use NETx version 3.26 or later.

The version of DOS you use can also cause problems in one of three ways—either by not working well with the PC hardware (unusual with versions later than 3.0), or by not working well with applications, extended memory or other added features. Some applications may require a specific version of DOS. Later versions of DOS may also provide services such as memory management, networking support, and file compression.

Applications also have the same three potential problem areas—the interface with DOS, the application itself, and the interface with the user.

If the application is misleading or complex, many users may mistakenly report problems that are due to misunderstanding, rather than hardware or software error. Some applications may also bypass the NetWare shell and access NetWare services directly. For more information on this, see Chapter 9, Network Applications.

Finally, the user is the end point on the workstation fault point chain. Many of the problems that will be reported to you will not be hardware or software problems, but problems caused by misunderstandings—either misinterpretation of instructions, or a lack of knowledge about the software.

## THE BASICS

Often, the only problem with a workstation is a loose or disconnected cable. Never assume that the user has checked seemingly obvious possibilities. Check all the connections; keyboard, mouse, monitor, power and network. The usual workstation has a rat's nest of cables behind it or on the floor under the desk, and especially with network connections that are relatively sensitive to loose wiring, some connections may appear to be okay, even showing a green attachment light on the transceiver, and still cause problems. The first thing to check with any installed workstation that suddenly begins having problems is that all the connections are solid.

> **Never assume that the user has checked seemingly obvious possibilities.**

Unless the workstation is a test or demo machine that is often reconfigured, I highly recommend that you screw all the connections down tight. It's a pain when you have to replace something, but it lessens the chance of a user kicking something loose, or the janitor pulling a connection out while vacuuming.

The error message or behavior may not seem to point directly at the problem. For instance, the symptom might be a monitor that is blank, or showing a fuzzy or distorted display. These symptoms might be the result of a dead motherboard, a dead display adapter, or an extreme software problem. However, the problem might be as simple as a video or power cable that has worked loose. It could also be that another monitor has been placed too close to the first.

This is the place to apply the principle of determining what has recently changed. Has the equipment been moved recently? Has anything new been added or removed? If the user says no, check connections anyway—something could have been accidentally kicked loose by the user, or a connector could have gradually worked out of its socket. You should have a data sheet for the PC—check it to see if the configuration on it matches the current configuration. Check to see if the fan is running—if not, either the PC is not getting power, or the power supply is dead.

Ask the user if they know of any way to make the problem go away. Also ask whether the problem occurs at a particular time, or at certain intervals. Find out what software was running when the PC froze, and what the chain of events leading up to the crash were.

Remember that all connections may not be on the workstation. If the problem is network-related and the connections seem to be okay, check the transceiver or the status light on the network card if applicable. For example, a LatticeNet transceiver has two lights, the SQE Test and the Status lights. If the SQE Test light is out, it indicates that the connection to the PC is out. If the Status light is out and the SQE Test is on, however, it indicates that the connection is broken between the transceiver and the server or concentrator.

If you're troubleshooting a new installation, the same principles apply: Check the obvious before trying the obscure. Make sure that the power is on, and that the connections are tight before replacing the network cards. Check the possibilities that cost you the least time or money first. It doesn't cost much to verify a power connection, but rechecking the entire wiring of a network is relatively expensive.

Ideally, you should use the same workstation throughout the LAN, with the same video adapter, network adapter, and so on. However, in real life this is usually not possible. The next best thing is to standardize on certain brands—if all your network adapters come from the same manufacturer, it will make your life simpler.

## PC-COMPATIBLES

PC Compatibles, and workstations in general, have a uniform underlying structure, as shown in Figure 2.2.

**FIGURE** 2.2

*Basic Workstation Structure*

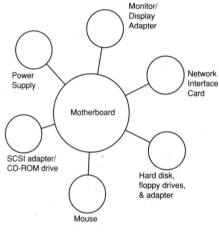

**Hardware**

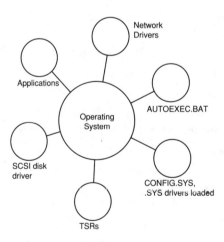

**Software**

No matter what components are used, the underlying structure is similar—the motherboard and operating system tie together all the assorted pieces. No matter what the CPU is, how much memory is installed, or what type of display or network adapter is installed, the basic structure remains the same. In terms of the fault point chain, this is all you need to keep in mind—troubleshooting a problem with the display is the same whether you have a PC with a monochrome display adapter or a 486 EISA PC with a VESA accelerated XGA adapter.

## Hardware

**The Boot Sequence**    To troubleshoot a PC effectively, you should understand the sequence of events that occur when the machine is turned on. The Power-On Self Test (POST) will run diagnostic tests on the motherboard, test the memory, and then tell you that the hard disk adapter is working and how many hard disks are connected to it. Then, before DOS begins loading, you may also see messages from some of the cards installed in the PC. Network adapters, SCSI adapters and video cards are typical examples of cards that produce messages, although not all such cards do.

A missing boot message, or a message like "Error configuring LAN adapter" will give you helpful clues to get a PC working again, but only if you are paying close attention. These messages are often on the screen for a very short time, and there is usually no way to scroll back up the screen and review them. You may have to reboot the PC several times to get the complete text of a message.

This is another time when some advance work will stand you in good stead. If all your PCs have the same configuration, or if you have become familiar with the normal series of messages that appear as each workstation boots, it will be much easier for you to spot anomalies.

**Cards and Connections**    The power is on, the PC boots reliably, the status light on the transceiver is green, but the workstation won't connect to the network. What's the problem? It may still be a loose connection. Network adapters and transceivers vary considerably in the degree of tolerance they have for loose connections. It is entirely possible for the connection to be solid enough to light the status light on a transceiver, for instance, but still be loose enough to prevent the network adapter from connecting properly. Never depend on the status lights; go ahead and crawl under the desk and check the connections.

If the external connections are all solid, try reseating the adapter cards. ALWAYS OBSERVE STATIC SAFETY PRECAUTIONS. Make sure that you are adequately grounded before handling the internals of any workstation. Destroying the parts you are attempting to check is self-defeating to say the least. If you don't have a grounding strap, at least make sure you touch the case of a power supply that's plugged in before handling any cards, memory modules, or the like.

**Always Observe Static Safety Precautions.**

Often the cards are not secured properly, and may have worked loose, especially if the connections are often changed. It may also be that the contacts on the edge of the adapter card are somewhat corroded, causing a faulty connection. If this seems to be a possibility, try rubbing the row of connectors at the bottom of the card, gently, with an ink eraser. Be sure not to get rubber shavings in the PC, and wipe the contacts off with a tissue when you're through. Get a supply of the proper screws and make sure that all cards are screwed down.

If it's a new installation, make sure that the cards are fully seated, and that the connections are fully seated too—it's easy to mistake a good connection for a faulty one in both cases. Install all the supplied screws and cable connectors—it may be a pain initially, but the effort will pay off in the long run. Never assume that two cards will work together, especially in their default settings. In fact, some cards may be impossible to use together, because neither will allow a combination of settings that won't interfere with the other.

Cards may also simply be incompatible with each other, either at a hardware level or because the device drivers necessary to access them conflict. In these cases, you should read the documentation for all equipment you plan to install and make sure that compatibility with anything else you plan to install has been established. The most common instance of this sort of problem occurs with SCSI adapters and their drivers. You should not plan to use SCSI adapters from different manufacturers in the same PC.

If you need to ship a workstation, remove the cards and pack them separately. Use original packing if available. Some manufacturers will not honor the warranty if products are not returned in the original shipping containers.

**Interrupt Conflicts**  This is one of the potentially most confusing areas, but also often one of the most straightforward—it's simply a matter of reading the manuals for the adapters used in the PC (assuming that the interrupts and memory segments are adequately documented). There often seems to be great resistance to reading the manual, but most manuals will, somewhere, discuss getting the card in question to operate with other cards, sometimes even specifically suggesting alternate settings for use with other specific adapters, or certain software. There are two parts to the settings on ISA cards—the memory address (a segment in RAM) and the IRQ (interrupt). The basic requirement to get cards to work together is to make sure that they use different memory segments and different IRQs.

Interrupt conflicts are primarily an issue in setting up new systems, but sometimes a conflict will produce only intermittent problems. This is especially true when the memory segments used by different cards overlap, rather than necessarily using all the same segment. For example, 16-bit video adapters usually use a larger segment than other types of cards, often including memory locations used by Windows. If some software will run, but other programs will not, it may be because these programs are attempting to directly address memory in use by an adapter. This can usually be resolved in Windows by using the EMMEXCLUDE command in the SYS-TEM.INI file. With other programs, it may be necessary to use a memory manager such as QEMM.

The easiest way to resolve interrupt conflicts is to reduce the number of cards in the PC to the minimum, then add the other cards back in, one at a time, until the conflict is found. Resolving it then becomes a matter of using alternate addresses where possible until the problem is solved.

EISA PCs can avoid the interrupt problems entirely, by using the enhanced 32-bit bus mastering mode. However, under certain conditions, such as when the PC needs to have more than 16 MB of RAM, all the cards in the system will have to be EISA-compatible, and EISA drivers must be available for all EISA cards. These cards are often more expensive, but also provide higher performance.

**Configuration—the Setup Program**    Depending on the version of the PC, SETUP may be a program that you'll have to run, or it may be programmed into the PC's BIOS. See your owner's manual for details if you're not sure of how to run it. As an administrator, you should have copies of the SETUP.COM program for every PC that uses it. Be aware that different manufacturers and models will require different versions of the program.

Common problems with SETUP include having a device listed incorrectly, or omitted from the configuration, and loss of stored parameters due to a battery failure. The information you set with SETUP is stored in a chip on the motherboard. If the battery that keeps this chip operating fails, the information will be lost. As a result, the PC may be unable to use its floppy and hard drives, may be unable to communicate with its video adapter, or may lose its connection to serial or parallel ports.

The configuration information necessary to use SETUP includes the size and type of floppy drives installed (double density or high density, and 3.5" or 5.25"), the type and number of hard drives installed, the video adapter installed, and the time and date. The most critical item is the hard drive type. Determine the type of the hard drive(s) installed in the PC and WRITE IT DOWN! In addition to your log sheet, a label in an inconspicuous place on the outside of the PC is a good idea, but at least put a label on the drive itself. Identifying the drive type incorrectly in SETUP may cause the hard drive to be irretrievably damaged and will certainly cause the information on the drive to become unavailable. If you don't know the drive type on existing PCs, use SETUP to determine it and write it down before there's a problem.

## PC Software

PC software comprises several layers: DOS, the basic operating system; DOS extensions such as RAMDRIVE.SYS, which are loaded through CONFIG.SYS; NetWare extensions such as IPX.COM, which may be loaded with AUTOEXEC.BAT; and application software.

**DOS and Its Configuration**    The biggest potential problem in troubleshooting workstation software is variety. Most workstations combine one or more operating systems, various configuration files, and networking software. With PCs, for example, counting all the licensed versions, there are literally hundreds of versions of DOS, and thousands of possible TSRs, device drivers and other add-on enhancements, hundreds of possible configurations of IPX.COM and NETx.COM, and of course millions of possible configurations of AUTOEXEC.BAT, CONFIG.SYS, SHELL.CFG, and so on.

There are some basic principles to resolving software problems. If the problem is with an existing system, go back to the last working configuration. Add the new configuration in a piece at a time until you can determine the problem. It may be necessary to comment out the loading of TSRs or drivers in AUTOEXEC.BAT or CONFIG.SYS to discover which is conflicting with the new software you're attempting to install.

Keeping the old versions of AUTOEXEC.BAT and CONFIG.SYS is not merely a sensible precaution, it's a necessity. Reconstructing old versions is time-consuming and may be impossible, depending on standardization, backups, and how well the system is documented. To avoid these problems, simply rename the old versions AUTOEXEC.OLD, CONFIG.BAK, or something similar. Many programs that modify these files use a similar procedure; all should.

Within an existing LAN, it's a good idea to standardize on a basic operating system. Using the same version of DOS, the same AUTOEXEC.BAT and CONFIG.SYS files, the same network drivers (and the same network cards), and the same basic login script will greatly reduce the record-keeping necessary to document the network, the software necessary to install a new system or re-install a faulty one, and the number of possible problems.

Use a virus detection program on every workstation on your network, run a virus scanner on the network itself regularly, and hold occasional sessions to educate users on viruses; and you will probably only be infected once in a while. The cost of the software and the time you spend configuring it is much less than the time and cost of restoring your server after a virus has corrupted your entire server, assuming that the backups haven't been infected, too.

A workstation with a virus can sometimes be even worse than a server—the time and effort involved in determining the actual problem with an unprotected workstation that becomes infected can be enormous, and it may not be backed up, as your server is.

**Networking Software**   It is handy to keep a set of drivers for each configuration you use on a floppy. This will make configuring new systems easier, as well as replacing drivers that are accidentally erased or corrupted.

Early NetWare drivers were specific to the version of DOS—thus NET2.COM, NET3.COM, etc., collectively known as NETx.COM, NETX.COM (with a capital X) is the latest version of the NetWare driver and is compatible with any version of DOS, as well as being the best driver to use with Windows. Use SHELLGEN to create the appropriate IPX for each network adapter in use and use NETX.COM with all of them. If you don't have a copy of NETX.COM, you can download it from NetWire (see Appendix A).

NETx.COM, EMSNETx.COM, and XMSNETx.COM use regular, expanded, and extended memory, respectively. Using expanded or extended memory will give you more free memory in your base 640K, but may also interfere with Windows, or other programs attempting to use these areas of memory.

SHELL.CFG or NET.CFG is the equivalent of CONFIG.SYS for the shell (IPX.COM/NETx.COM). Below are a number of useful settings for specific circumstances.

    local printers=0

This will keep the workstation from hanging if no ports are captured and the user presses Shift-PrintScreen.

### Preferred Server=servername

This will ensure that the workstation attaches to the correct server, rather than the one that responds the fastest.

### Print Header = 255

This will allow PostScript jobs enough header space to configure the printer correctly.

NET.CFG is the configuration file used for workstations running RPRINTER and is used instead of SHELL.CFG with the DOS Requester under NetWare 4.0, and to effect changes with ODI drivers.

The ODI drivers use a different structure than IPX/NETX. It is more analogous to the way network drivers are supported on a NetWare server. With the ODI driver, LSL (the Link Support Layer driver) is loaded first. This allows you to load different drivers for each protocol such as IPX (IPXODI.COM) or TCP/IP (TCPIP.COM).

The ODI drivers are loaded in the following order: LSL.COM, DRIVER.COM (a NIC-specific driver for your card), IPXODI.COM, TCPIP.COM, NETBIOS.COM, or any other protocol-specific drivers, then finally NETX.COM. There must also be an entry in NET.CFG with the following syntax:

```
LINK DRIVER IPXODI
    INT 3
    MEM C800
    PORT 2E0
```

The first line links the proper driver for your protocol to the NIC. The next three lines, which are indented, specify the interrupt, the memory address, and the port address for the card.

The DOS Requester for NetWare 4.0 uses a group of programs called Virtual Loadable Modules (VLMs) more similar to NLMs on a server. VLM.EXE is loaded first, and it then loads a number of other modules, which control the various aspects of attaching to and using the network.

**Note:** The DOS Requester defaults to Ethernet 802.2, rather than 802.3, as in previous NetWare versions. If you have a mixed network, with some servers that won't initially be upgraded to 4.0, you should ensure that everything is using the same version, either 802.2 or 802.3.

The DOS Requester does not sit on top of DOS and intercept all disk and port traffic to determine whether it is local or intended for the network. Instead, it works with DOS. The principal difference is that the LASTDRIVE entry in CONFIG.SYS should be set to Z:, instead of D: or E:, as is typical with older shells. NetWare and DOS now use the same drive table.

## WINDOWS AND NETWARE

Getting Windows to work can be difficult, particularly with older PCs; getting it to work with NetWare can be even more difficult, for several reasons. Windows normally uses memory in locations generally reserved for DOS or hardware, including video and network adapters. As a result, Windows may interfere with the network adapter necessary to connect to the network. This can be fixed with the EMMEXCLUDE option in the [386Enhanced] section of the SYSTEM.INI file. Some older versions of BIOS in some systems will not run Windows 3.x at all. You can fix this by installing a later version of BIOS, either from the manufacturer or from a supplier such as Phoenix Technologies.

You may also need to update your system to the latest available network driver, a later version of DOS, and perhaps even a newer network card—and that's just to get Windows running on a workstation and able to connect to the network. Running Windows from the network is another question entirely, and best left to a Windows guru, although basic issues will be addressed in Chapter 9, Network Applications.

Some general tips:

▶ Use Windows 3.1—it has much better network support than 3.0.

▶ Use IPX 3.10 or later, and NETX 3.26 or later, or the ODI drivers.

▸ Make sure NETWARE.DRV is about 125 KB—it often doesn't get uncompressed properly.

▸ If Windows is not running, (or not running properly) in the Enhanced mode, try adding the following statement to the SYSTEM.INI file, under the [386Enh] section:

EMMExclude=A000-EFFF

If Windows runs with this setting, it means that some card or other program is using memory that Windows wants. If you can discover which part of the memory is the problem (for example C000–C800), change the statement to that segment.

▸ Another couple of statements to put in the [386Enh] section that may help are

VirtualHDIRQ=FALSE

and

SystemROMBreakPoint=FALSE

These statements control the way Windows uses the hard drive and whether it accesses a potential problem area in memory.

▸ Make sure that the DOS and NetWare environment settings are updated. CONFIG.SYS should have FILES= and BUFFERS= values of at least 30; and STACKS=10 is a good setting. SHELL.-CFG (or NET.CFG) should have SPX CONNECTIONS=60, GET LOCAL TARGET STACKS=5 (or 10 if you'll be using IPX/SPX applications regularly), and a FILE HANDLES= setting of at least 80.

▸ After exiting Windows, you may get a message "Incorrect version of COMMAND.COM—reboot PC." The PC is trying to load DOS from the server, which may have a different version of DOS in the SYS:PUBLIC\DOS directory than is loaded on the PC. Put the statement

COMSPEC=C:\COMMAND.COM

in the user's login script, or make sure that the appropriate version of DOS is loaded on the server. Standardizing on one version of DOS for all PCs on your network is a very good idea.

▸ If your network card uses IRQ 2, 9, 10 or higher with Windows 3.0 or higher, use VPICDA.386, which can be downloaded from NetWire. Replace the statement DEVICE=VPICDA with DEVICE=VPICDA.386 in your SYSTEM.INI file.

These are only a few of dozens of tips necessary to produce a smoothly running Windows environment in conjunction with NetWare. For further information, there are a number of Windows-oriented magazines, forums on CompuServe relating to Windows and NetWare, and several good books on the subject.

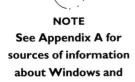

**NOTE**
**See Appendix A for sources of information about Windows and NetWare.**

## OS/2

OS/2 is similar to Windows in that it needs its own network drivers. The only issue addressed here will be getting OS/2 to run on your network. To do that, you need the OS/2 requester program, the equivalent of NETx.COM and IPX.COM. This product is furnished with NetWare, and is available separately for older networks. Again, you should check to see that you have the latest versions of the drivers (available on NetWire or from the CompuServe NetWare forum). The requester files include: LSL.SYS, DDAEMON.EXE, DRIVER.SYS (such as NE2000.SYS), IPX.SYS, SPX.SYS, SPDAEMON.EXE NWREQ.SYS, NWDAEMON.EXE, NWIFS.IFS, VIPX.SYS and VSHELL.SYS. You may also be using NMPIPE.SYS, NPSERVER.SYS, NETBIOS.SYS and NBDAEMON.EXE if you are using named pipes or NetBIOS.

## PS/2 (MICRO CHANNEL)

PS/2s using the Micro Channel bus must initially be configured and set up for each card installed, using the supplied installation utility in a manner similar to the EISA setup utility. However, once this is done, the problem of interrupts is eliminated. PS/2s use the same software as PCs—see the software sections above for information on the software.

## MACINTOSHES

Macintoshes can be added seamlessly to a NetWare network, either with NetWare for Macintosh, or by using MacIPX. In either case, Mac users can access NetWare file server volumes and printers as if they were attached locally.

### Hardware

Macintosh hardware is in general much easier to support than PCs. There is only one brand of system unit, and the add-in cards come in a much more tightly controlled specification which doesn't usually require any physical configuration. In addition, the software is generally easier to install and use.

From the system administrator's point of view, however, there is a big draw-back to the Mac. Much of the system-level operation of the Mac is concealed from the user, and in fact is not accessible at all without special software or hardware. This makes problems more difficult to diagnose. Understanding the basic operation of the Mac as outlined below should make the process easier for you.

**The Power-On Sequence**   When a Macintosh boots up, the first thing it does is run a hardware self-test. This will produce a series of tones instead of a chord if there is a problem. Unfortunately, there are no messages on the screen during this process to give you a clue about what has happened. The length of time this process takes will vary with the speed of the processor and the amount of memory in the system—the more memory, the longer the process. This is particularly noticeable right after a memory upgrade.

After the self-test, the Macintosh looks for a disk to boot from. It will try to boot from any SCSI device attached, in order of SCSI ID from 0 to 6, and then from a floppy. If it can't find a device to boot from, it displays a disk icon with a question mark blinking in the middle. If this happens, try inserting a boot floppy (any of the System 6 Installation disks, or a prepared System 7 boot disk). If the Mac is able to boot from the floppy and the hard drive's icon shows up, try reinstalling the system—it may have become corrupted. Under System 7, this means you should move any system add-ons to another folder and delete the System Folder, then reinstall from the original disks. Under System 6, it isn't necessary to delete the old System Folder, and anything added will be retained.

If the Mac won't recognize that it has a hard disk even when booted from a floppy, try using a formatting utility to locate the drive. These utilities are available as shareware and from a number of manufacturers, and will usually locate any SCSI device attached to the Mac. If the program can't find a device, either the disk is bad or a connection is faulty. Check the connections and try different cables before replacing the drive.

If the formatting utility finds the drive, you will usually have the option of writing a new driver, "refreshing" the disk (rewriting the data on each block of the disk), making a new partition, or reformatting the disk. You can usually also mount the disk manually with the utility. Try this first, then refreshing the disk, rewriting the driver, and if necessary, reformatting the disk.

After the boot disk is found, a Mac icon with a happy face appears, and then the system software is loaded. This part of the sequence is covered in more detail in the next section, Software, but you should be aware that several hardware-related processes occur here too. First, after the boot disk is found, any additional SCSI devices will be mounted. See the SCSI Devices section below for more details. Next, during the boot sequence, any NIC is initialized as its driver is loaded. Thus, a Mac may get partway through its boot sequence and then hang, due to a faulty NIC. This can be determined if the last startup icon that appears before the Mac hangs is the EtherTalk (or other protocol) driver. This icon will be the same icon the driver has when you select the Icon View for the folder it's in.

**Cards**    Macintoshes do not have the problem of interrupts. Simply use any and all cards that will fit in the case, and there shouldn't be any problems in terms of conflicts. However, the Macintosh doesn't use a very secure method of securing cards in the case. It is possible to unseat the card in the process of attaching the cable to it, especially with large external connectors, or those where a fair amount of force is required to seat the cable in the adapter's socket. Reseat the card after attaching the cable in such cases.

**SCSI Devices**    SCSI stands for Small Computer System Interface. It is most commonly used as a disk drive interface, and is the only hard disk drive interface supported on the Mac, but it is also used for many other devices, such as scanners, EtherTalk and color video adapters for Macs with no slots, specialized video applications, additional drives such as CD-ROM drives, cartridge drives, tape drives, etc. See Figure 2.3, below.

FIGURE 2.3
*The SCSI Chain*

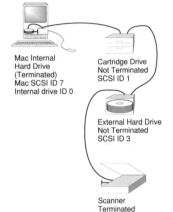

Mac Internal
Hard Drive
(Terminated)
Mac SCSI ID 7
Internal drive ID 0

Cartridge Drive
Not Terminated
SCSI ID 1

External Hard Drive
Not Terminated
SCSI ID 3

Scanner
Terminated
SCSI ID 4

The SCSI bus is a daisy chain, with up to seven devices, each connected to the next. Each device in the chain has its own unique ID, 0–6, with the Mac's motherboard (or the SCSI controller on a PC) having an ID of 7. Although you can put up to seven devices on a Mac, it is not generally a good idea. The more devices, the greater the chance of problems. The PowerBooks should not be used with more than one or two external SCSI devices—they use a lower-power SCSI bus than is normal, which doesn't respond well with too many devices. If you are having problems with a Mac that has more than one SCSI device, make sure that all the devices have unique SCSI IDs. Duplicate

> **The method of removing devices and trying them one at a time to isolate the problem applies here, too.**

IDs will usually cause the Mac to hang right after the self-test, or to display the disk icon with the blinking question mark. Of course, the method of removing the devices and trying them one at a time to isolate the problem applies here, too.

Termination is another major cause of problems with SCSI devices. Often, incorrect termination will cause intermittent problems. Both the first device on the SCSI chain (usually the internal hard disk) and the last device on the chain must be terminated. Problems arise when intermediate devices are terminated, or when the first or last drive is not. Some devices have external switches to enable or disable termination and set SCSI ID; with others, you must add or remove resistor packs on the internal printed circuit board. The simplest way to handle termination is to leave the termination resistors on the internal drive, and remove termination from all other devices. Then use an external terminator on the last device. This allows you to add additional devices or remove devices easily.

**Never disconnect or connect a SCSI device when it is powered up.**

Under no circumstances should you ever disconnect or connect a SCSI device when it is powered up. This can damage not only that device, but any other device in the chain, including the Macintosh. Power everything down before changing connections. This rule also applies to changing termination or manually changing the SCSI ID of a device. (Some devices will allow you to change their SCSI ID with software. This, obviously, must be done while everything is on.)

**Configuration**   Bear in mind that some problems that seem to be related to hardware may be the result of a user having changed a setting in a Control Panel for that device. For example, on a Mac connected to the network with an EtherTalk card, the network connection will be lost if the user switches the Network Control Panel setting from EtherTalk to Built-in. Nothing in the Chooser reflects this

**Check Control panel settings, and check any Init files.**

change in setting; the user (and you) will only see that there aren't any servers or printers available. Other devices may similarly be configured— monitors, scanners, and so on. Also, a device on the Mac such as a scanner, NIC, or CD-ROM drive will often have a Startup document or Init associated with it. Corruption or removal of this file will cause the device not to work. Check these items before assuming hardware failure.

### Software

In the boot process, once the boot disk is located, the system software begins to load. You will usually see a rectangular window with "Welcome to Macintosh" on it, unless the user has added a different startup screen. After a few seconds this screen will disappear, and you will see a series of icons at the bottom of the screen. These each correspond to the extension (control panel, Init, or startup document) being loaded.

**Extensions** Once the "Welcome to Macintosh" screen disappears, the basic system has been loaded. Everything after that is an addition to the system that was created separately. Such extensions add features to the operating system that may do anything from placing a pair of eyeballs in the upper corner of the screen that follow the movements of the mouse, or causing an animated character to appear out of the Trash Can and sing when a document is deleted, to allowing the use of additional fonts or enabling a network connection. A given Mac may have none of these programs, or dozens of them.

System extensions may be carefully developed pieces of software designed by a big software vendor to work within Apple's system specifications, or programming exercises by college students. The important thing to know is that they are common, numerous, and can easily conflict with each other. Mac users also seem more predisposed to adding to their systems than most PC users.

Often the only way to discover which extensions are conflicting with which is to pull everything out of the system folder except for the bare necessities, then put things back until you discover the conflict. In System 6, these files are all loose in the System folder, and will be labeled Chooser document, Control Panel document, Startup document, or simply Document. In System 7 these programs are almost all stored in the Extensions or Control Panels folder.

The easiest way to minimize these sorts of problems is to maintain a standard System folder, containing the system files, printer drivers, extensions, fonts, and so on, and discourage casual additions to it as much as possible. This will be difficult, but will make it easier to recognize "foreign" extensions and resolve conflicts.

The other likely problem you will discover with Macintoshes is that the system itself is subject to becoming corrupted. This can happen more frequently than with a DOS system. If you have an intermittent problem with a Mac and are having a hard time tracking it down, consider reinstalling the operating system. Use the Installer program—don't just copy files into the system folder.

With System 7, it is usually a good idea to boot from a floppy, remove the existing system folder, and reinstall from scratch. If you do this, be sure to save anything that was added to the system folder before removing it.

**Networking**    Getting a Macintosh to attach to an existing network is quite simple. If you are using AppleTalk, simply plug the connector into the printer port on the back of the Mac, turn it on, and you're connected. For EtherTalk, install the network driver, install the network card, make the connections, switch to EtherTalk in the Network control panel, and see what appears in the Chooser.

If you can't see anything in the Chooser, make sure that either Apple-Share or a printer driver is selected. If so, the problem is probably the physical connection, or possibly the AppleTalk driver—either for LocalTalk or EtherTalk. Since the network interface is built into the system at a basic level, there are normally only two things that can go wrong at the workstation: either the system itself or the network driver can become corrupted. These are fixed by reinstalling the system or network driver from the original installation disks. If neither of these work, and other Macs are able to access the devices, it's probably the network connection or the NIC.

**Printing**    The basic setup of printing is as easy as networking—if the network connection works, and the printer driver works, you should be able to print from any application.

Setting up Macintosh print queues and making them available to PCs as well as Macs is considerably more complex, and is covered in Chapter 4.

Make sure that the same version of the printer driver is in use across your entire network, or at least in each segment using a particular printer. Even within a System version, there can be different printer driver versions, each of which can potentially conflict with the others.

## UNIX WORKSTATIONS

UNIX workstations, to an even greater extent than the Mac, tend to be simple to troubleshoot from the NetWare administrator's point of view. (That is, for isolating a problem with the NetWare network—UNIX itself is NOT simple.) This is because a UNIX workstation is usually an integrated package—the hardware, including network adapter, display, system software, and networking software are usually all purchased together and designed to work with each other.

UNIX configuration and system administration are topics outside the scope of this book. There are many books available on every aspect of this subject. For the NetWare administrator, there are basically only two questions with a UNIX workstation: Can it boot? and Can it see the network?

UNIX workstations typically have the basic networking software and hardware built in. They usually use the TCP/IP networking protocol, which is supported in NetWare 3.x and above. The primary troubleshooting tools are PING, IFCONFIG, and NETSTAT, which all come with the operating system. If you can "ping" the server, you should be able to network with it. IFCONFIG will confirm that the Ethernet adapter itself is performing correctly. NETSTAT will give you information about the TCP/IP portion of your network.

If you are unable to mount network drives, but can ping the server, the problem is probably with permissions, either file permissions, or the authorizations in the NFS NLM setup. In fact, 90% of the problems with UNIX probably result from permissions being set incorrectly. These problems are covered in detail in Chapter 8.

**NOTE**
See Chapter 4 for information about troubleshooting NetWare printing operations.

**NOTE**
Configuring a NetWare server to support TCP/IP is covered in Chapter 8.

# Real-Life Stories

This section describes typical problems and how a troubleshooter would go through the process of isolating the fault and fixing it. Once again, the two fictional companies introduced in the Overview and their administrators will be used as examples. They combine the equipment and experience of a number of actual businesses. These two scenarios are intended to show some representative problems often encountered when setting up or troubleshooting a workstation. While you may never see these particular problems, they should give you a feel for the process by which an experienced troubleshooter isolates a problem, determines the solution, and fixes the problem.

## SCENARIO ONE: INSTALLING A NEW WORKSTATION

This scenario describes the process of installing and configuring a new high-powered workstation, and some typical problems that might be encountered with the installation and configuration.

### Snapshot—Scenario One

Is This a New System

Does the POST (Power-on Self Test) Finish without Error Messages?

Does the Workstation Boot without Error Messages?

Does DOS Load without Error messages?

Do the Network Drivers Load without Error Messages?

Can You Log into the Server?

John, the system administrator for Itsy-Bitsy, Inc., is putting together a new PC for one of his users. The system will need to run Microsoft Windows, as well as standard DOS applications, so it's a fairly high-end system. It includes a 33 MHz 386 processor, 16 MB of RAM, a 200 MB IDE hard drive, a Super VGA adapter and monitor, a bus mouse, Novell NE2000 Ethernet adapter, a 5.25" and a 3.5" floppy drive, and a SCSI adapter and external

CD-ROM drive. The user also needs to have one serial port enabled for a modem and the parallel port enabled for a printer.

John, being an experienced administrator, doesn't simply load all the cards into the PC and try to boot it. Instead, he adds the accessories incrementally. This takes a little longer, but makes it much easier to discover where the problems are. Of course, since he keeps a good log of each system he sets up, he could use the log to determine which settings worked for each card if he'd set up one like this before. However, he hasn't used this combination of cards in the past.

The basic system, just the hard drive and video adapter, boots DOS just fine, so John adds the Ethernet card, being sure to record the settings for interrupt and memory segment. The PC boots without errors again. After he uses WSGEN to create IPX.COM and NETX.COM, he tries running them to see if the PC can attach to the server. Instead, the PC freezes. After double-checking the settings on the card and the configuration of the driver, he's ready for the last resort. He reads the documentation.

The documentation doesn't appear to be helpful at first, but then John notices that there is a jumper that should be removed if the NE2000 is installed in a PC that uses the Chips and Technologies chip set. Upon checking, he discovers that the PC does in fact use this chip set. Removing the jumper fixes the problem.

> **Read the documentation. At least look for exceptions to the default configuration—they are often set apart in the documentation or in a READ-ME file on the distribution floppy.**

He next installs the mouse. It uses one of two IRQs (Interrupts)—2 or 5. Since the LAN adapter uses 3 in its default setting, either would do. John chooses 5, and notes on the configuration sheet that IRQ 3 (the NIC), IRQ 4 (the COM1 serial port), and IRQ 5 are in use.

The CD-ROM drive and SCSI adapter are the last items to be added. The default settings for the SCSI adapter use interrupt 11 and a base I/O address of 330h. The NE2000 is using 300h, so there shouldn't be a conflict there. John leaves the settings as is and installs the card, then loads the driver onto the hard disk. He makes sure that the CD-ROM drive is properly terminated.

After loading the driver, John is able to access the CD-ROM. It looks like the hardware configuration is done. He turns the PC off, makes sure all the screws are tight, puts the case on the machine and tightens all the screws down, reinstalls all the cables in the back and then restarts the PC. Halfway through the POST routine, the PC hangs. After several resets, it is clear that whatever is happening is no fluke. He sighs and removes the case, then pulls the SCSI adapter, that being the last item installed.

The PC boots properly with the card removed. He checks the settings on the card and checks the termination of the drive and reinstalls the card. The PC boots fine. John sits and thinks for a minute. The only other thing that changed was putting the case on and screwing it down.

After some experimenting, John discovers that the PC will boot with the case on, but not when it's seated firmly and screwed down. It can be used temporarily with the case unsecured. He calls the retailer. They've never heard of such a problem but say it might be a short to the chassis somewhere. They say they'll be out to replace the PC within a couple of days.

John then runs the SETUP program to configure the ports on the PC. He enables COM1 and LPT1, making sure that COM2, which normally uses IRQ 3, is disabled, so it won't cause conflicts with the NIC. The hardware is all set up.

A few days later, the PC reseller sends a technician out to fix the problem with the case. After swapping the motherboard and hard drive into a new case, the problem goes away.

### Lessons Learned

▶ Keep a log of how each of your PCs is configured. Update it when you change setups. It will pay for itself the first time you are able to check a configuration without having the take the PC apart and remove boards to verify settings.

▶ Read the documentation. The least you should do is look for exceptions—they are often set apart in the documentation or even in a README file on the distribution floppy.

▸ Make sure that neither IRQs (interrupts) nor base I/O memory segments from the different devices installed conflict with each other. Bear in mind that the size of memory used by the I/O segment may vary. Add the size of the segment to the address (remember, the numbers are in hex) to determine the next safe address to use.

▸ A freeze may not be caused by a card or configuration error— it can be something as simple as a sloppily manufactured case, a defective power cord, or a card or cable that isn't seated fully.

▸ Not all IRQs, base I/O addresses, or DMA interrupts are used by cards. For example, the serial ports, which may be on the motherboard, still use IRQs and I/O addresses, and some programs (such as Windows) may access these areas of memory too.

### The Fault Point Chain

Since the PC itself is running, you might think that none of it would be part of the fault point chain for this problem. However, there are a number of possibilities. For example, the motherboard was in this case the actual cause—the NE2000 requires a different setting when used with this type of motherboard. However, other possibilities could include a marginal power supply in an older PC that wouldn't accommodate another board, etc.

The potential faults for the first problem—the PC freezing when IPX.COM loads:

▸ The power supply to the motherboard—wall socket, power cord, power supply, and connection from the power supply to the motherboard. Faulty power can cause intermittent problems. Although it wouldn't usually become apparent at the same point in a software sequence, this could be the result of the actual activation of the Ethernet interface drawing too much power, or something similar.

▸ The motherboard, including the BIOS. The BIOS, especially in older PCs, is often the cause of incompatibilities with software, from network drivers to Windows.

▸ The NIC. This has several aspects—the seating of the card in the bus, the settings on the card, the card's connection to the network, and the version of Read-Only Memory (ROM) on the card.

▸ DOS—the version of DOS will require a specific network driver, but can also cause problems by itself, if it's corrupted or too old. As a rule of thumb, try not to let the standard version of DOS you use get more than two years old.

▸ The network driver—IPX.COM and NETx.COM. Again, don't let these drivers get too far out of date. Older drivers may work fine with DOS, but could cause problems with newer programs, especially Windows.

## SCENARIO TWO: MAINTAINING AN EXISTING WORKSTATION

In this scenario, the administrator encounters some deceptive symptoms, then finds that an existing server is having problems at the workstation level, before NetWare can load.

### Snapshot—Scenario Two

Is This an Existing System?

Is the Display Readable? Does the Cursor Respond to the Keyboard?

Does the POST (Power-on Self Test) Finish without Error Messages?

Does the Workstation Boot without Error Messages?

Does DOS Load without Error Messages?

Do the Network Drivers Load without Errors?

Does the Workstation See the Server (SLIST)?

Can You Log into the Server?

Fran, the system administrator for Great Big, Inc., gets a call from a user in accounting. Something is wrong with his workstation; the application is running too slowly. She takes a look at the workstation. The application that's running too slowly is a word processor. She checks, and the file the user is working on is on the file server. She finds out that the user had tried to save changes to the file and the program hasn't responded to anything since. She tries to cancel the save, and eventually, after several mouse clicks, succeeds. She then saves to the local hard disk. This works quickly and normally. She then exits the program and checks the connection to the server. The server doesn't respond.

She finds the server's screen dark. The server's power light is on, and the fan is running, but the screen won't come on and the keyboard doesn't respond, even to the CapsLock or NumLock keys. She quickly checks the other workstations in the department and discovers that none of them have a good connection to the server. She reboots the server and gets the same result.

She begins eliminating possibilities. The monitor's power light is on, but it could be defective. She pulls a working monitor and video cable off another workstation and tries it. Nothing. She replaces the video card with the good card from the other workstation. Still nothing. In this particular chain of fault points, there is only one link left. The video system consists of the monitor, the cable, the video board, the

> If you suspect component failure, replace the components in the chain, one at a time, with known good components.

motherboard, and the PC's power supply. The only one left is the motherboard. She swaps the server's drives and cards into another PC and starts it up. The server is back on-line.

Later inspection by a technician shows that the motherboard is indeed damaged, probably by a power spike. Fran uses the technician's report to justify UPSes for all servers at the site.

## Lessons Learned

▸ Workstation symptoms may actually result from network problems—either on the server or the connection to it.

▸ If you suspect component failure, replace the components in the chain, one at a time, with known good components.

▸ In an emergency, you can cannibalize one user's workstation (or your own) to replace the parts of a server. No one person's work is more critical than the whole department's. Other resources for quick temporary replacement include rental or leasing through local outlets. See your phone book.

## The Fault Point Chain

Since all the workstations were unable to connect to the server, the fault chain included the physical network (the cabling plant) as well as the server. However, the server is more likely to fail than the wiring, so Fran checked it first. The dark monitor and lack of response to the keyboard established that the problem was with the server. The fact that the problem repeated when the server was rebooted indicated a hardware problem, unless there had been recent changes to the NetWare configuration.

The potential faults were:

▸ AC power from the wall.

▸ The power cord.

▸ The power supply.

▸ The power cable from the power supply to the disk drive.

▸ The disk drives.

▸ The motherboard.

▸ The cards in the server.

▸ The devices connected to the cards (the monitor, the physical wiring, and so on). It's easier to check the connection on the back of a monitor than the electronics inside the monitor, and more likely that the problem is in a loose cable.

▶ NetWare (changes in configuration, corruption of SERVER.EXE, and so on).

▶ Outside interference—brownouts, or a network storm caused by another server or network device overloading the server with bad packets.

## SCENARIO THREE: ANOTHER EXISTING WORKSTATION

In this case, the administrator encounters a situation similar to Scenario Two, but with some critical differences: the administrator listens to a user's diagnosis, jumps to the conclusion that the situation is the same, and doesn't follow some basic precautions.

### Snapshot—Scenario Three

Is This an Existing System?

Is The Display Readable? Does the Cursor Respond to the Keyboard?

Does the POST (Power-on Self Test) Finish without Error Messages?

Does the Workstation Boot without Error Messages?

Does the Network Load without Errors?

Does the Workstation See the Server (SLIST)?

Can you Log into the Server?

Jethro, Fran's new assistant, gets a call from a user in accounting. Her connection to the server is down. She informs Jethro that this has happened before—she's sure it's the server. Jethro investigates and discovers that the server is apparently running, but the screen is dark. He reads the log and notes the similarities to the last incident. He decides he'd better swap the server's drives and cards into the other workstation in the office as quickly as possible, to get the server back on line.

He flips the power switch on the server. Within seconds, cries of consternation drift through the doorway of the server room, quickly followed by the users themselves, asking why the server has gone down. Jethro, a cold feeling in his stomach, turns the server back on. The screen lights up with the normal boot messages, and the server begins to boot.

Once the server is back on line, and he has pacified the users, Jethro makes two discoveries—the screen blanker in MONITOR produces a blank screen in this version of NetWare, rather than the usual bouncing square, and the cable from the first user's NIC to the transceiver has come off at the NIC.

### Lessons Learned

▸ DON'T jump to conclusions and take steps you can't back out of, without trying to confirm your conclusions. If you can't think of some way to confirm your hypothesis, try to at least anticipate what could happen if you're wrong. For instance, Jethro should have checked to see if other users had connections to the server.

▸ Never take for granted that users know what they're talking about. Listen to them, but confirm what they tell you unless you know from experience that they are knowledgeable about PCs and networking, and the setup in their department.

### The Fault Point Chain

A simplified chain would show the main units that could be responsible for the user's PC not being able to connect to the server:

▸ The workstation.

▸ The physical network, including the transceiver, the cabling and connectors, the repeater, the concentrator, and the connectors at the server end.

▸ The server itself.

Each of these fault points would of course have its own fault point chain. The most likely point of failure is at the workstation. Jethro's biggest mistake was not checking the workstation (either by checking the workstation itself or checking other workstations to see if they were also having problems). He should have checked the fault points in order of likelihood of failure—the workstation first, then the server, then the cabling plant.

## SCENARIO FOUR: AN EXISTING MACINTOSH

This scenario covers a common situation encountered with existing Macintosh setups. One of the problems the administrator encounters is in getting reliable information on what the configuration of the system should be, to compare with what it is.

### Snapshot—Scenario Four

Is This an Existing System?

Is the Display Readable? Does the Cursor Respond to the Keyboard?

Does the POST (Power-on Self Test) Finish without Error Messages?

Does the Workstation Boot without Error Messages?

Does the Operating System Load without Error Messages?

Do the Network Drivers Load without Errors?

Does the Workstation See the Server in the Chooser?

When the art department calls about a problem with one of their Macs, Fran brings Jethro along because he is familiar with Macs. One of the artists has a Mac that is hanging about halfway through the boot sequence. The user doesn't remember anything in the system that has changed recently.

They reboot the Mac again and watch the series of startup icons carefully. Just before the point at which the Mac freezes, they see an icon that neither of them recognizes. They restart the Mac from a floppy and open the System Folder in Icon View. They discover the icon is from a public domain Init that is supposed to enhance the usability of the system. The user had forgotten adding it a couple of weeks before.

Since the user isn't wedded to the offending Init, and since its behavior indicates that it may have become corrupted or be interfering with other Inits, they remove it. The system boots properly. Fran makes a note in her log to be on the lookout for this Init in other Macs.

But there's one more thing: the user mentions that some of his fonts are no longer available—as long as Fran and Jethro are there, could they help him get them back?

This problem is aggravated by the lack of a standard for the company's Macintosh font manager—something that has been causing Fran trouble for a long time. The Macs used by the marketing department mostly use one add-on program to control fonts, the art department uses a different program, and other Macs scattered throughout the company may use either, or none.

When Fran checks, she discovers that this Mac is using one of the font control programs to load its fonts. The log for this Mac shows that she installed the latest version of this enhancement program a few days ago. It also shows that this Mac is using the standard set of art department fonts in the appropriately named folder, that this folder is in the proper place, and that the program is set to open the fonts in that folder.

However, the fonts are not loading at startup. Jethro suggests using the program to load the fonts manually. When they try, they get a message saying that some of the fonts they are trying to load are already loaded, Jethro snaps his fingers—the system may have the same fonts installed in it with Font/DA Mover. They check, and some of the fonts in one of the standard suitcases have also been loaded directly into the system.

Once the fonts are removed from the system folder, the conflict goes away, and the fonts all load properly. They reboot the Mac to check and the fonts load automatically. Fran makes another note to check and make sure none of the other Macs she updated have the same fonts in two places.

## Lessons Learned

> ► Macs are easy to use, but not necessarily to administer. They often have more add-ons than comparable PCs, and hide more of the operating system from the user.

> ► When in doubt, return to a basic configuration and add Inits back in one at a time until you discover the conflict. Sometimes, you will be able to tell which Init, startup or CDEV is freezing the Mac by the last icon showing when the Mac freezes during startup. However, this is only one of a pair. The other file helping to cause the conflict may be harder to discover, and the one you find may be necessary to the system. There are programs that can help you isolate and fix Init conflicts—see Appendix A.

> ► Try to standardize on utility programs throughout the site. Use the same virus checker, the same font organizer, and so on. Doing so will cut down dramatically on problems in upgrading and supporting systems. This is important in all systems, not just Macs.

## The Fault Point Chain

Since the Mac was booting at least part way, the indication was that there wasn't any problem with the basic hardware. Further, since the boot sequence from the hard disk was starting, the hard disk and disk driver were probably working correctly. Therefore, the next item to check was the software being loaded during the boot sequence. This is analogous to the AUTOEXEC.BAT and CONFIG.SYS portion of a PC's boot sequence.

The first item (the Init conflict) had the following fault points:

> ► The hardware (power supply, motherboard, any additional cards, and so on).

> ► The hard disk (boot device).

> ► The system software.

> ► The extensions being loaded.

> ► Problems with some of the cards, particularly an EtherTalk adapter— these cards aren't initialized until their extension is loaded; and so the problem might appear to be with the extension, when in reality it is a hardware problem with the card.

In this case, because there was a more or less standard set of extensions in use, and because they were familiar with the normal boot sequence for their Macs, Fran and Jethro were able to identify the icon of the offending Init. However, if this had not been the case, they would have removed all extensions not supplied by Apple, and rebooted. If the Mac had worked then, they'd have added extensions back in until they identified the problem. If the Mac still hadn't booted, they'd have reinstalled the system.

## SCENARIO FIVE: A WINDOWS WORKSTATION

This scenario deals with a Windows installation on an existing PC connected to a NetWare network. The administrator deals with the Windows-related problems, rather than the workstation or its configuration.

### Snapshot—Scenario Five

Is This an Existing System?

Does DOS Load without Error Messages?

Do the Network Drivers Load without Errors?

Can You Log into the Server?

Does Windows Load without Errors?

Can Windows Attach to the Network?

Fran gets a call from a user who has just installed Windows, and now can't attach to the network. Fran discovers that the user has installed a version of Windows 3.0 that is almost a year old. Fran immediately removes this version from the user's PC and gets the user a new license for 3.1. She installs Windows 3.1 and copies the customized SYSTEM.INI file, the latest versions of the drivers, and shell files from the network (through DOS). She checks to make sure that the user's PC matches the standard configuration of NIC, memory necessary for Windows, and so on; then she launches Windows. No problems.

### Lessons Learned

▶ Windows is a complex environment that requires many specialized settings and the latest drivers. Once you get a working setup, record what you've done and try to use the same setup in any other PCs you set up for Windows. Even if this involves changing or updating the NIC, video adapter, or DOS configuration items, it will pay for itself in time saved in troubleshooting and supporting future updates to Windows.

▶ Try to set up a system that lets you control what the users order and install on the network. You are probably much more aware of hardware and software requirements, and the latest versions of programs, than most of your users.

### The Fault Point Chain

The basic units of the fault point chain that could have been causing Windows not to work were:

▶ The processor. Anything below a 386 will probably at least cause Windows to display error messages and run in Real mode; and a BIOS that old may not be compatible with Windows at all. Also, PCs with less than 4 MB of memory should be upgraded before trying to run Windows. Depending on the application you wish to run, you may need as much as 16 MB of RAM.

▶ The BIOS—older BIOSes may not be compatible with Windows 3.*x*.

▶ Any cards in the PC—Windows uses areas of memory that some cards, especially video adapters and NICs, may be trying to use (see EMMEXCLUDE in the Concepts discussion of Windows).

▸ The version of DOS—a minimum of DOS 3.3 is necessary, and in general, the later the version the better.

▸ The network drivers—get the latest version available. This may not be the version supplied with NetWare (even the latest version of NetWare), or with Windows. It's a good idea to check the Novell forums on CompuServe for new drivers once in a while.

▸ The version of Windows. Get the latest—updates are cheap, and usually put out for very good reasons.

▸ The configuration of Windows. There are many items that may have to be specially configured within Windows to get it to run on your network and with your PC, network driver and other software. Once you get this figured out, save the WIN.INI and SYSTEM.INI files and reuse them.

# CHAPTER 3

# The Physical Network

*SnapShot*

The critical aspect to troubleshooting the cabling plant is to first make sure that your problem is not actually being caused by an inoperative or malfunctioning network adapter, server or PC. Second, you must understand the basics of your network topology. What sort of wiring do you have? What are its maximum lengths of cabling, its requirements for termination and grounds? Will one missing connection take out the whole ring? You should understand the various components that make up your cabling system—transceivers, connectors, wiring, concentrators, repeaters, bridges, and so on. See Concepts, below for help in determining these issues if you aren't familiar with your topology.

## IS THIS A NEW NETWORK?

Cabling for a new network should be installed by professionals. For anything larger than a few workstations, this is almost a necessity. Pulling the wire through the walls, crimping connectors, testing circuits, installing concentrators, patch panels and punch-down blocks, and so on are all highly specialized tasks best left to experienced professionals. In fact, when you are planning the network, it is best to get bids and input from several vendors. They may even suggest a better way of networking your workstations. If you want to do it yourself, be very sure that you understand fully the limitations on cable lengths for each type of cable you're using, proper methods of termination and grounding, and the setup and configuration of any networking hardare you will be using. See the Concepts section on cabling, on page 115.

Generally, the company that installs the cable will test all the segments for continuity and polarity. They will often warranty their work for 30 to 90 days. Furthermore, the cabling itself is unlikely to cause problems if installed correctly. You should check other, more probable causes first. However, a basic understanding of your cabling plant will allow you to isolate problems without too much difficulty, if the more likely problems have been eliminated.

The first thing to do is to make sure that the server is running, and that the workstation involved is not having problems. If more than one workstation is involved, and the server is operating correctly, the problem is likely to be in the cabling plant. With a new installation, the first thing to check is that all specified work has been completed. Even with a relatively small network, there may be hundreds of wires, each of which must be properly connected, and dozens of devices which must be set properly, connected, turned on, and so on.

### How Many Nodes Are Affected? Do Some of the Workstations on the Ring Or Segment Work?

If some workstations are able to connect to the server, and more than one is not, the problem can be physically isolated. What do the working nodes or the nonworking nodes have in common? Check to see if a ring is broken, or if all those workstations are on the same card on the concentrator. Bear in mind that it is more likely with new equipment that something has been overlooked, rather than that there is an actual failure. Make sure that all equipment is connected and turned on. See the Concepts section on Topologies on page 100.

### If It Is Only One Workstation That Can't Connect, See If It Can Connect from Another Location.  If So, Then the Wiring Is Faulty Somewhere Between the PC and the Server.

There are several ways to isolate the fault in a wiring system without exotic or specialized equipment, although these make testing easier. Look to see that the colors of the insulation on twisted-pair wiring match at both ends of a connection, that the wiring is neat and the connectors are solidly in place, that coaxial cable connectors are solidly crimped and that the connectors are of good quality, etc.

A continuity tester will allow you to check the physical continuity of the wiring. You can make this yourself if you are familiar with the basics of electrical work, or buy an inexpensive model from an electronics supplier.

Also make sure that there is adequate cable to reach from where it exits from the wall to any point that the user might place the computer. Users can easily overstretch cable or pull the connector from the socket, trying to move their workstation farther from wall socket than the cabling allows. See the Concepts section on cabling on page 115.

## IS THIS AN EXISTING NETWORK?

Often, the administrator may have responsibility for all of the hardware that makes up the network, except for the cabling plant. That part of the network may "belong" to facilities, or corporate MIS. This sort of division of responsibility can make things difficult to resolve. Even when this is not the case, the actual wiring is in the walls, and cannot be visually inspected. In this sense, the cabling plant is the most obscure part of your network. However, you can usually isolate the problem to one of a very few possibilities without specialized equipment, simply by understanding the topology of your network, analyzing its fault point chain, and checking the break points.

Aside from mice chewing through the cabling, it isn't likely that the cable itself will fail. The most likely cause of a failure in the physical plant is that someone has removed, changed, or broken some part of the cabling plant, or that an electronic part of the plant has failed. Problems of this sort can range from construction workers inadvertently cutting cabling, to users removing or changing connectors without realizing the consequences, to someone changing the settings in a router without being sure of all the ramifications, to hardware failure in a repeater or concentrator, to the software in a router freezing up. Check for these sorts of problems first, before you run continuity checks on all the wiring.

### How Many Nodes Are Affected? Do Some of the Workstations on the Ring Or Segment Work?

Once you know which workstations can connect to the server and which can't, you should be able to more easily find the common point. Are they all on one port of the repeater, or one card in the concentrator? Are they all on the same segment or ring? Are they all connecting through a bridge that may have gone down? If there are multiple Network Interface Cards (NICs) in the server, are all the workstations that can't see the server on one of the cards? See the Concepts section on Topology, on page 100.

### If It Is Only One Workstation That Can't Connect, Can It Connect from Another Location?

If so, then the cabling plant is faulty somewhere between the PC and the server. It may be the wiring, or a transceiver, or a board in the repeater, or a faulty socket in the concentrator. What matters is that once you've isolated the problem to one station, you can begin checking the various component parts of the cabling plant between the two points. See the Concepts section on cabling, on page 115.

### Intermittent Faults and Performance Problems.

As with other parts of the network, the most difficult problems to isolate are intermittent ones. In the cabling plant, these may be caused by such varied things as cables that run past fluorescent lights, loose connectors or faulty boards in workstations, servers or other networking hardware such as repeaters, concentrators or hubs.

As with other intermittent problems, the questions to ask are, what parts of the network are affected, what times of day do the problems occur, what other events are associated with the problem, and so on.

Network monitors and analyzers are your best weapon for isolating intermittent problems and increasing performance. Products such as LANalyzer for Windows can quickly find a defective network card or transceiver, locate a component that is sending out faulty packets, monitor the traffic on the network, recording peak and average statistics, and isolate users that are using more than the usual share of resources.

# Concepts

Fault Points

Topology

  Ring Topology

  Star Topology

  Linear Bus Topology

Data Communications Protocols

  IPX/SPX

  IP (TCP/IP)

  NetBIOS

  AppleTalk

  ISO

Hardware Standards

  Ethernet

  Token-Ring

  LocalTalk

  ARCnet

Cabling: Lengths, Termination, Grounds, Connectors. Connection Order

Patch Panels, Repeaters, And Concentrators

Routers, Bridges, and Gateways

Documenting the Cabling Plant

## FAULT POINTS

The approach to troubleshooting introduced in the Overview requires you to identify and isolate the fault points in a system. Using this approach with the physical network can be demanding, because it requires that you understand the basic processes that occur in the system. The possible variations and complexity of the cabling system can make it difficult to approach, but if you take things methodically, once piece at a time, it can be done.

The fault point chain in Figure 3.1 illustrates typical components of the cabling plant. You might not have all of these parts in your system, or you might have others not pictured here. The best way to begin to understand your network is to produce a drawing of a chain like the one below, but specialized for your network. You should also make a map of the topology of your network, showing each workstation and how it is connected to the server.

Each link in the chain can fail itself, or in its connection to a link it's attached to. For example, a cable could break or its connection at either end could fail.

In terms of the physical network, the server's fault points include the network driver for each NIC, the protocol drivers bound to each NIC, and the basic functioning of NetWare itself.

The NIC must be configured correctly, must be seated in the bus connector on the motherboard, and must have a good connection to the network wiring.

There may be one cable directly attaching the workstation to the server, or there may be several lengths of cabling between the two. In every case, the cabling must be connected properly at both ends, and must be physically intact. The connectors must be properly attached to the cabling, and, in the case of twisted-pair cabling, the pairs must be connected in the same order at both ends. You must also be careful to make sure that the cabling does not run too close to possible sources of interference, such as fluorescent light ballasts.

Some systems employ transceivers to translate between two different physical types of cabling, for instance between the thick Ethernet port on a network card, and the 10BaseT jack on the wall. Most transceivers have status lights to allow you to diagnose problems with the connection. If these lights are out, the transceiver is not operating. The connections on both ends of the transceiver must also be solid.

A repeater allows you to extend a network beyond the normal limitations of segment lengths. A typical setup provides one port that connects to the server, and a number of ports that can be connected to different cable segments (legs). A repeater usually has status lights that show network traffic on each leg, allowing you to determine which legs are performing properly. The repeater can fail at each port connecting to the network cabling, and on each internal board that provides a port, or it may fail entirely.

A concentrator, or hub, is similar to a repeater in its basic concept, which allows the total length of cabling in a network to exceed the maximum length for a single cable. A hub is typical of 10BaseT networks or twisted-pair Token-Ring, and will typically have one port that connects directly to the server, and one direct connection to each workstation. Depending on the type, it might fail entirely, or on one port, or on one board that provides a number of ports. The status lights on the hub can help you determine which (if any) of these has happened, as can switching a problem cable to another port or board.

The workstation and its NIC are the last potential fault points in the fault chain, and can fail in the same manner as the server and its NIC—the NIC can fail in hardware or be configured incorrectly, or its connection to the bus of the PC or the network cabling can become loose, causing an erratic connection, or come off entirely.

Figure 3.1 shows a typical fault chain for network cabling and connections.

## TOPOLOGY

Most networks can be broken down into one of three types of topology—ring, linear bus, or star. The type of protocol doesn't necessarily indicate the topology. For example, the three most common types of Ethernet, thick (AUI), thin (10Base2), and twisted-pair (10BaseT), all use different topologies. Thick Ethernet is typically a linear bus, thin Ethernet is typically a ring, and twisted-pair Ethernet is typically a star. See Figure 3.2 below.

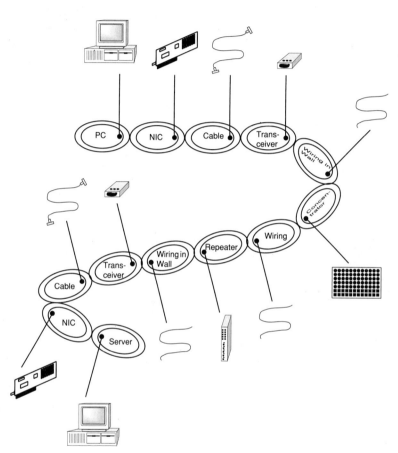

FIGURE 3.1

*The Fault Point Chain for Network Cabling and Connections*

The topology of thin Ethernet can also be described physically as a linear bus, because the T-connector that attaches to the workstation functions in the same manner as the drop cable in a thick Ethernet setup. If the T-connector is disconnected from the workstation, only that workstation loses its connection. If the cable is detached from the T instead, every workstation attached to the cable loses its connection. This is true in a thick Ethernet cabling scheme, as well, but much harder to accomplish—the drop cable is usually all that the user can reach—they don't usually have physical access to the backbone cable.

FIGURE 3.2

*Network Topologies*

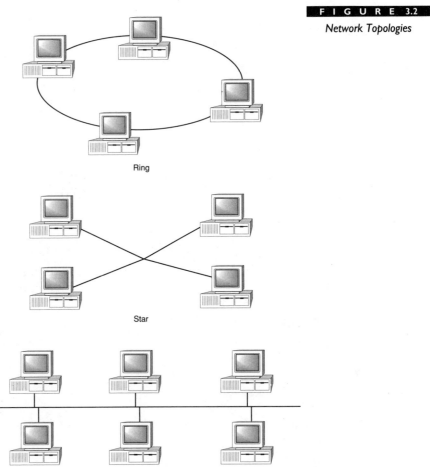

Each type of topology has a different fault point chain. A ring is the most susceptible to interruption—if the physical links are broken anywhere in the ring, the whole ring loses connectivity. To overcome this disadvantage, some ring-type topologies combine star and ring topologies into one.

The figure illustrates physical topology; but we also need to consider logical topology. For example, Token-Ring is usually a star topology physically, but it is a ring topology logically. This means that you must understand the implications of both the logical and physical topologies in order to isolate the probable cause of problems. For instance, a star topology generally prevents a single break in the cabling from interrupting service to all nodes on the network. However, Token-Ring, which relies on tokens passed from workstation to workstation around a logical ring, can fail if one cable breaks, even if the physical topology is a star.

> **You must understand both your logical and physical topologies to isolate the probable causes of problems.**

Topology is the most important part of your network cabling scheme to understand. If you understand the physical and logical topology, you can isolate the fault points, regardless of the protocol running over the wire.

### Ring Topology

In a ring topology, either logical or physical, every physical component of the network is typically a fault point for every connection. If one user on a thin Ethernet network (which can be considered a linear bus) disconnects their workstation by uncoupling the two wires from the T-connector, rather than the connector from the workstation, every workstation on the network will lose its connection. In practice, networks of this type often consist of several rings connected to a repeater, which is then connected to the server. This arrangement provides some redundancy, in that a failure in the ring will usually only affect the users attached to that port of the repeater.

With Token-Ring, the topology is physically a star, but logically a ring, in that a token is passed from station to station. If there is any interruption of the ring, the token will not reach the next station, and the network will go down.

The critical thing to know when troubleshooting this type of network is the location of every place where the connection can be broken by human intervention. Aside from mice chewing through the cabling, it isn't likely that the cable itself will fail. The most likely scenario is that someone has removed a connector, or kicked wiring under their desk and pulled the cabling out of the jack.

### Star Topology

Star topology is the most fault-tolerant topology. Each workstation is connected directly to a concentrator, which means that a break in any part of the fault-point chain up to the concentrator will only affect one workstation. The two exceptions to this rule are the server and its connection to the concentrator, and the concentrator itself.

The biggest disadvantage of star topology is that it tends to be more expensive to install. Cabling has to be pulled from every workstation to the concentrator or MAU; by contrast, a ring network needs cabling only as far as the next workstation. However, the gain in reliability is significant enough that stars are largely displacing the other topologies.

In a star topology, the fault point chain includes only the wiring between that workstation and the concentrator. If more than one workstation is involved, the workstation cabling is unlikely to be the problem—it's most likely that the problem is either with the server, its connection to the concentrator or MAU, or with the concentrator or MAU itself.

### Linear Bus Topology

In a linear bus topology, there are actually two fault chains, the one from each workstation to the bus, and the one from the bus to the server. If a workstation connection fails, it will only affect that workstation. An interruption of the bus will cause every connection to the server to fail. In practice, this isn't any different from a star topology if the concentrator fails, but the concentrator is much easier to diagnose if it fails, through the traffic lights on the concentrator.

## DATA COMMUNICATIONS PROTOCOLS

There are two parts to the method by which computers connect with each other over cabling. The first part is the data communication protocol, which specifies how workstations within a Network Operating System (NOS) communicate. Each protocol is generally associated with a specific NOS, although TCP/IP is used by a wide variety of network operating systems. These protocols divide data to be sent to another computer up into small pieces, called packets, and add a header and trailer that contain information on the sender, intended recipient, and so on. This process is carried out by the networking software.

The second part is the physical layer protocol, which includes Ethernet, Token-Ring, ARCnet, and FDDI. These protocols add further information in a header and trailer that determine which machine gets the packet next. This processing is mostly done by the networking hardware. The physical layer protocol surrounds the data communication protocol, which surrounds the data. If a packet is sent from one protocol to another, the surrounding information must be translated. Since the data communications protocols are inside the physical protocols, converting them is more complex, as you will see below, in the section on routers, bridges and gateways.

### IPX/SPX

The Internetwork Packet Exchange (IPX) and Sequenced Packet Exchange (SPX) protocols are Novell's native protocols. A node address is a hex number, up to 8 digits long. This number must be unique for each server and workstation. Each LAN also has an address, called a network address. With the implementation of the world-wide IPX Internet, IPX addresses will be assigned in much the same manner as TCP/IP addresses are for the UNIX-based Internet. Contact 1-800-NETWARE for more information.

### IP (TCP/IP)

TCP/IP is the standard protocol in the UNIX world. It was developed by the Department of Defense and is also the basis of the Internet, a huge world-wide network of computers from educational institutions, businesses, government and the private sector. Internet addresses are assigned by the Network Information Center of the Defense Data Network. If your TCP/IP network is not connected to the Internet, and never will be, you can use any valid address. However, if there is any chance you will be connected, you should apply for an address. NetWare supports TCP/IP as a native protocol and also allows you to run IPX through a TCP/IP network with a process known as *tunneling,* which surrounds an IPX packet with a TCP/IP header and trailer to allow it to be routed from an IPX network, through a TCP/IP network and back to an IPX network.

### NetBIOS

The Network Basic Input/Output System (NetBIOS), is an application-level interface for networking primarily used by IBM LAN Server and Microsoft LAN Manager networks. NetWare supports NetBIOS. NetBIOS nodes are named with a unique 16-character address.

### AppleTalk

AppleTalk may run over Ethernet (EtherTalk), Token-Ring (TokenTalk) or LocalTalk (Apple's proprietary cabling). AppleTalk devices include servers, workstations and printers. AppleTalk Phase 1 allowed for 254 nodes on a network. Phase 2 allows multiple zones, each with 253 nodes.

LocalTalk only supports 230 Kbps, EtherTalk supports 10 Mbps, and TokenTalk supports 4 Mbps. EtherTalk in particular, is becoming much more prevalent, due to its much higher speed.

### OSI

The International Standards Organization (ISO) has developed a standard called Open Systems Interconnect (OSI). OSI is supposed to resolve the problems existing protocols have with large WANs and high traffic loads. However, implementation has been slow, as existing protocols are deeply entrenched, and most businesses are waiting until the standard catches on before they implement it, which won't happen until more businesses implement the standard.

The OSI model describes standards for communication between network nodes at seven levels. The seven levels of OSI are:

- ▸ The Application Layer

- ▸ The Presentation Layer

- ▸ The Session Layer

- ▸ The Transport Layer

- ▸ The Network Layer

- ▸ The Datalink Layer

- ▸ The Physical Layer

A packet passes through each of these layers on its way from one network device to another. Each layer passes packets to the layer above and below it, but only deals with the information specific to its layer.

A packet arriving at a workstation reaches the physical layer first. This layer processes the signal sent from another network card, interpreting the voltage changes, number of pulses, and so on to provide bits of information that are then assembled and sent to the datalink layer.

The datalink layer is the first layer that handles the packet as such. It may provide error correction to make sure that the packet that is arriving is the same as the one that was sent, discard defective packets, and signal the other workstation to resend the packet if necessary.

The first two layers together make up the hardware standards discussed in the next section. The next two layers, the network and transport layers, in general comprise the protocol layer as discussed above.

The network layer determines the path that a packet takes in going from the sending workstation to the intended recipient. This is the IP part of the TCP/IP protocol, and Novell's IPX also operates at this level.

The next layer, the transport layer, provide error correction for packet routing in the same way that the datalink layer provides error correction for the physical transmission. This is the TCP part of TCP/IP.

The first four layers of the OSI model are clearly defined and usually have clear analogs in any networking setup. The next three layers are not so clearly defined yet, and may not correspond with any particular part of your system.

The session layer deals with making and breaking connections to other systems. Protocols such as SPX and NetBIOS require that a connection to a specific other machine be made at the beginning of a session, and broken at the end of the session. Other protocols, known as "connectionless", don't use this layer.

The presentation and application layers aren't widely used or well defined yet. They both deal with further processing such as compression/decompression and file transfer and conversions that are necessary to allow programs to communicate.

## HARDWARE STANDARDS

Each of the standards listed below, and the many others not covered, has its own advantages. This section is intended only as an overview of the basics. The things to consider when evaluating a new installation are:

▸ Cost of installation—both wiring required and hardware, if necessary.

▸ Upgradability—will you have to rewire your whole building to take advantage of faster technology?

▸ Dependability and fault tolerance—star topology will cost more for the original installation, but will pay for itself in increased fault tolerance.

▸ Throughput—the rated speed of a network is not necessarily what you will experience—load on the network, the quality of the installation, and the protocol will affect throughput. For instance, Token-Ring, rated at 4 Mbps, may be a better choice than

10 Mbps Ethernet network if heavy loads are anticipated and real-time response (for automation or process control) is necessary.

▸ Expandability—how many more workstations can you add to the network before it chokes or you run out of ports?

▸ Standards—make sure that what you buy will work with other LANs in your company, and with planned future purchases. The best way to assure this is to make sure that what you buy adheres to a published standard such as Ethernet (802.2 or 802.3), or a well-established public domain standard such as ARCnet.

### Ethernet

Ethernet is probably the most widely implemented hardware protocol in use for PC-based LANs. It is a broadcast standard, in that each station listens for traffic, and transmits if it doesn't hear anything. If two stations transmit at the same time, it produces a collision, and both stations must retransmit. Ethernet is good for a theoretical 10 Mbps, although that is almost never achieved under ordinary conditions. In addition to the three most common Ethernet standards, thick (AUI or 10Base5), thin (10Base2) and twisted-pair (10BaseT), there are several new 100 Mbps versions, such as 100BaseT and others, implemented either over twisted-pair wire or optical fiber.

The three common types of Ethernet, thick, thin, and 10BaseT, use different topologies. Thick Ethernet is a linear bus, thin Ethernet is a linear bus but has the vulnerabilities of a ring, and twisted-pair is a star. Thick Ethernet is uncommon, partly because with the usual installation, the whole network must be brought down to add another station. Thin Ethernet is common in small installations, because the cabling is simple to install and inexpensive, with no hub required. However, for most business installations, 10BaseT has become the wiring scheme of choice, thanks to its fault tolerance. It does require a hub or concentrator, but the cost of hubs has dropped form over $100 per port to less than $10 in many cases.

Thick Ethernet runs over a thick (nearly ½") coaxial cable with up to five trunk segments, allows runs up to 2500 meters (8200 feet) total, up to 500 meters (1625 feet) per segment, and up to 100 stations per segment. Thin

Ethernet runs over a thinner (about ¼") coaxial cable designated RG-58. Thin Ethernet allows a total run of 185 meters (600 feet) per segment, up to five segments, and 30 stations per segment. 10BaseT uses twisted-pair wiring like phone wiring, but with 4 pairs of wires, two pair of which are used for each connection. The maximum run from workstation to hub should not exceed 100 meters (325 feet). The total number of stations is determined by the capacity of the hubs—these may support anywhere from four to hundreds of connections.

Thick and thin Ethernet allow a maximum of five segments, four repeaters and three segments with workstations on them on any one LAN. This is known as the 5-4-3 rule.

Table 3.1 summarizes the cabling requirements of thick, thin, and twisted-pair Ethernet.

| TYPE | | |
|---|---|---|
| **THICK ETHERNET (AUI, 10BASE5) COAXIAL CABLE** | **THIN ETHERNET (10BASE2) RG-58 CABLE** | **TWISTED PAIR ETHERNET (10BASET)** |
| **Maximum Overall Length** — 2500 meters/8200 feet | 570 meters/3000 feet | NA—number of segments depends on the concentrator |
| **Maximum Segment Length** — 500 meters /1625 feet | 185 meters/600 feet | 100 meters/325 feet (from hub to station) |
| **Maximum Number of Stations** — 100 | 30 | Limited by the hub—anything from 4 to hundreds |

T A B L E  3.1

*Ethernet Cabling*

*Requirements*

### Token-Ring

Token-Ring is known as an IBM standard, although it was originally developed by another firm. It is usually a star topology physically, but a ring logically. A token, a special type of packet, is passed from workstation to workstation around a ring. Each workstation's location on the ring is a function of when it logged onto the network, relative to the others. A station can only send a packet out when it has the token. After it sends its packet, it releases the token to the next workstation.

Each workstation is usually connected by Type 1, 2 or 3 cable to a Media Access Unit (MAU), also known as the Multiple Station Access Unit (MSAU), which may have 8, 12, or up to 50 ports plus the ring-in and ring-out ports. Never connect a workstation to the ring-in or ring-out port— these are only for connecting to another MAU. Some Token-Ring networks are now being implemented over unshielded twisted-pair (UTP), which is much less expensive, although more susceptible to interference. Regardless of the type of wiring, the important thing to understand is that a hardware failure will usually drop a station off the ring, losing only the one connection. However, if a problem occurs that prevents the token from being passed, then the whole ring can fail. This failure can occur if a connection between MAUs is lost, if a LAN adapter fails without dropping its power to the MAU, if electrical interference in the cable distorts signals, and similar situations. A simple protocol analyzer can usually tell you where in the ring a break has occurred.

With type 1 and 2 shielded twisted-pair cabling, Token-Ring supports up to 260 devices, including MAUs and repeaters, although in practice, going much over 100 will cause problems. Cable lengths from the workstation to MAU can be 300 meters (975 feet) if there is only one MAU, or 100 meters (325 feet) if there are multiple MAUs, and MAUs can be up to 200 meters (650 feet) apart. It is wise to keep cable lengths under 100 meters to allow for expansion to multiple MAUs. Both 4 and 16 Mbps Token-Ring can run on types 1 and 2. Type 3 cabling (UTP) supports 96 devices maximum per ring and station-to-MAU cable lengths of 100 meters for single-MAU systems and 45 meters (145 feet) for multiple-MAU systems, with up to 120 meters (390 feet) between MAUs. Type 6 cable is more flexible, and is generally only used for connections from the workstation to a wall jack, or in situations where the cable must be routed around tight obstructions. Table 3.2 summarizes the Token-Ring cabling requirements.

| TYPE | | |
|---|---|---|
| | TYPE I AND 2 COAXIAL CABLE | TYPE 3 UNSHIELDED TWISTED PAIR |
| Maximum Number of Devices (Including MAUs) | 260 | 96 |
| Maximum Cable Length (I MAU) Station to MAU | 300 meters/975 feet | 100 meters/325 feet |
| Maximum Cable Length (Multiple MAUs) Station to MAU | 100 meters/325 feet | 45 meters/145 feet |
| Maximum Distance Between MAUs | 200 meters/650 feet | 120 meters/390 feet |

T A B L E 3.2

*Token-Ring Cabling*
*Requirements*

### LocalTalk

Apple was the first personal computer manufacturer to include built-in networking capabilities. This networking protocol, LocalTalk, is very easy to set up, relatively fault-tolerant, and inexpensive. However, by modern standards it is very slow—230 Kbps, and under normal conditions, as little as 90 Kbps. For networks of more than a few Macs and a printer, this isn't very useful, and has resulted in the development of versions of AppleTalk that will run over Ethernet or Token-Ring.

Before EtherTalk over 10BaseT Ethernet became common, a number of companies implemented unshielded twisted-pair (UTP) Ethernet on their own. LatticeNet is one of the most common of these. LatticeNet is similar to 10BaseT, but not completely compatible. You must either make sure that all your Macs use the same one of the two standards, or get a concentrator that can handle both types.

The theoretical maximum for LocalTalk is 1000 feet total cabling distance and 32 stations per network. However, if you are anywhere close to this number, you should upgrade to EtherTalk or TokenTalk. Cabling specifications and lengths are the same as for Ethernet and Token-Ring, see above.

## ARCnet

Attached Resource Computer Network (ARCnet) is a standard that actually goes back farther than Ethernet. It is not an IEEE standard, as Token-Ring, Ethernet, and the soon-to-be-released FDDI are, but it is widely supported in the industry. Its rated throughput is 2.5 Mbps, and it is a star topology, with a token passing protocol. One advantage to ARCnet is that it doesn't require repeaters or relatively expensive concentrators, as Ethernet does—for larger nets, it uses a combination of inexpensive passive hubs and active hubs, which are less expensive than similar Ethernet concentrators. Small nets require only the passive hubs. The main difference between active and passive hubs is the length of cable they support.

ARCnet requires RG-62 93 ohm coaxial cable, which is cheaper than the RG-58 cable used for thin Ethernet. It allows 256 stations per LAN, a maximum length of 2000 feet between stations or from station to active hub, and 100 feet between stations and passive hubs. The hub-to-hub distance is 100 feet for passive to active, 2000 feet for active to active and up to 20,000 feet in a segment. Passive hubs can't be connected to other passive hubs.

A new ARCnet specification has been developed that allows 20 Mbps. It allows ARCnet installations to be upgraded to provide throughput on a par with

Ethernet or 16 Mbps Token-Ring. It retains existing wiring but requires new NICs. ARCnet over UTP is also possible, but only allows 10 stations per ring, with a maximum distance between them of 6 feet. This gives 80 stations on an 8-port active hub, with a total maximum wiring length of 400 feet.

Some tips for ARCnet setups—set the server to station address 255, always terminate unused ports in a passive hub, ensure that a segment doesn't loop back on itself (don't connect hubs in a circle), and make sure that no two stations use the same station address.

Table 3.3 summarizes ARCnet cabling requirements.

| TYPE | | |
|---|---|---|
| | COAXIAL RRG-62 (93 OHM) | UNSHIELDED TWISTED PAIR |
| Maximum Overall Length | 20,000 feet | 400 feet |
| Maximum Number of Stations | 256 | 10 per ring; 80 per 8-port active hub |
| Maximum Distance Between Stations/Active Hubs | 2000 feet | 6 feet between stations |
| Maximum Distance between Stations and Passive Hub | 100 | NA |
| Maximum Hub-to-Hub Spacing | Active-to-Active: 2000 feet. Active-to-Passive: 100 feet | NA |

T A B L E 3.3

*ARCNET Cabling*
*Requirements*

## CABLING: LENGTHS, TERMINATION, GROUNDS, CONNECTORS, CONNECTION ORDER

It's been said that 90% of all network problems are problems with cabling, particularly with existing networks where nothing has been changed (on purpose). There are three basic things that can give you an edge in tracking down and fixing such problems.

> **Perhaps 90% of all network problems are problems with cabling.**

The first is a good understanding of your cabling setup, both physical and logical. This includes the protocol (Ethernet, ARCnet, or Token-Ring, for example) and the physical and logical topology (how the signals are routed throughout the network). What are the possible effects of breaking the line? Could a bad network adapter bring down the whole network? You should understand not only how the wires are routed through the walls, but where a packet must travel to reach the server. Does it need to be passed on through several intermediate workstations? Does the connection in the office wall go to the server directly, or to a repeater in a broom closet somewhere?

As connectors age, their ability to provide a solid connection may decrease, especially if inexpensive connectors were used in the first place. Be sure to specify high-quality parts, especially in networks where connections are being changed frequently.

> **As network connectors age, their ability to provide a solid connection may decrease.**

A recent study suggests that bit errors caused by electromagnetic interference or faulty wiring can cause many thousands of times the performance drain that collisions do. Make sure that twisted-pair cabling has the correct number of twists, that connectors are solidly crimped, that network wiring doesn't run close to other electrical equipment, and so on.

Check for the correct types of cabling. For example, AG-58 may have been switched with RG-62 (the two types of cable are usually marked with their designation along the length of the cable), or RJ11 (4-pin phone) plugs may have been placed in RJ45 (8-pin 10BaseT) jacks. Silver-satin phone cable may have been used for NIC-to-jack connections, instead of

Ethernet-rated type 5 UTP cable. Are connectors crimped neatly? Terminating resistors of the correct ohmage? Make sure that lengths are not over the rated maximums—it's easy to keep adding "just one more" node until you're past the maximum length. Any of these items can contribute to intermittent problems on your network.

Optical cabling is starting to be seen in networks, especially in high-traffic situations, or as a "backbone." Troubleshooting tools for optical fiber are not especially complicated, but need to be learned. A light meter that will read a light source at the other end of a cable and tell you what the transmission efficiency is, and a simple device to ensure that connectors are properly installed is all you will usually need.

### PATCH PANELS, REPEATERS, AND CONCENTRATORS

Networking hardware should be in a secure area: not just locked up where no one can play with it, but mounted securely and protected from anyone accidentally moving a switch and switching off 20 users. Don't just put a repeater under a desk and forget about it.

The most important thing you can do with a patch panel or punch-down block is to keep it neat. It makes tracing or moving connections much easier, and makes it easier to spot a poorly connected jack.

Repeaters can be thought of as extension cords for networks. If you have, say, 60 workstations on thin Ethernet, spread out over a fairly large area, most cabling cannot connect all of them in one chain—it's simply too many feet of cable, especially if it's run through the walls and up to the ceiling between each office or cube. With a repeater, you can cut the network into several segments, each of which can be 600 feet long. This also gives you some fault tolerance—if one of the segments is broken, it only takes down the workstations on that loop; the other ports on the repeater aren't affected.

Concentrators, or hubs, come in many varieties and sizes, from a small four-port 10BaseT hub to a $50,000 concentrator that will accept fiber-optic lines to a backbone, provide several hundred 10BaseT ports, and allow remote management through Simple Network Management Protocol (SNMP). With the latter, you can use management software and find out what port on the concentrator has lost its connection or is receiving bad packets, without ever leaving your desk.

## ROUTERS, BRIDGES, AND GATEWAYS

A *bridge* looks at the intended destination of a packet and sends it by the most direct route, using the software or Network layer address. A *router* can route packets for different protocols. A *gateway* converts from one protocol to another. Many of the products on the market today combine parts of all of these functions.

The Novell Multi-Protocol Router allows routing between any protocol supported by NetWare, which is just about everything you might find out there. It can replace dedicated boxes that only do one thing well, and do other things in addition such as hub management and backups.

All of these devices are fault points in your network. If you find that traffic on one LAN is normal, but users can't access services on another LAN, check the router, bridge, or gateway. Remember that a server with two LAN cards is acting as a router between the two LAN segments.

**NOTE**
**See Chapter 7:**
**Troubleshooting**
**WANs, for more infor-**
**mation about connect-**
**ing LANs.**

## DOCUMENTING THE CABLING PLANT

The cabling company should provide you with a physical map of the wiring they have installed, as well as locations of punch-down blocks, repeaters, concentrators, and so on. Familiarize yourself with the locations of all the hardware, and identify the workstations/users on each segment of your net. Doing so will make it much easier to isolate faults; for example, if a certain four users who are all on the same loop complain of network trouble, you immediately know where to start looking.

You should also take the time to make a logical map of your network. Identify how a packet actually is routed to get from a workstation to the server and back. Does it have to pass through each workstation on a loop? Which workstations does it pass through, or is that different, depending on which stations entered the net first?

There are many software package and software/hardware combinations being marketed to manage your network. Some of them will create and automatically update a logical map of your network. They can tell you when stations go on or off-line, if network devices fail, and when and where failures occur. If you have a complex LAN or WAN to look after, they can save you many, many hours of time tracing down faults, and will also greatly increase your response time when failures occur—not only will they help you find problems, they will usually alert you when a problem occurs, sometimes long before the users become aware of it.

# Real-Life Stories

This section again uses the two fictional companies and their administrators introduced in the Overview to illustrate typical problems with network connections and the process a troubleshooter goes through to isolate and correct those problems.

## SCENARIO ONE

The system administrator encounters some problems typical of a newly-installed cabling system, and demonstrates some techniques for fault isolation without specialized equipment.

### Snapshot—Scenario One

Is This a New Network?

How Many Nodes Are Affected? Do Some of the Workstations on the Ring or Segment Work?

If It Is Only One Workstation That Can't Connect, See If It Can Connect from Another Location. If So, Then the Wiring Is Faulty Somewhere between the PC and the Server.

John, the system administrator for Itsy-Bitsy, Inc., is halfway through a long working weekend. The marketing department has just moved to a new area and the cabling contractor finished installing and testing the wiring yesterday.

He's gotten the server up and running and is unpacking and connecting the workstations. The network is 10BaseT Ethernet, with a concentrator in a wiring closet and jacks in each work area.

The first few workstations are unpacked and connected to the network with no problems, and they connect to the server without errors. Then John puts his supervisor's PC back together and plugs it in. It boots without error messages, but won't attach to the network. John makes sure that the interrupts are set correctly on the NIC, and changes the cable from the PC to the wall jack. Still nothing. He goes to the wiring closet and makes sure that the jack for his supervisor's office is active. The connection light is on for that jack. He tries changing the cable to another port, with no improvement. He thinks about changing the jack to another port on the concentrator, but he doesn't have the punchdown tools.

To get some diagnostics, he tries another PC in his supervisor's office, one that was able to connect to the network from another jack. It can't see the server either. He is pretty sure now that there is something wrong, either with the jack, the wiring to the punchdown panel, or that port on the concentrator. He observes that other ports on the same card on the concentrator are working—it's unlikely to be a hardware failure in the concentrator. Next, he gets an Ethernet adapter with an AUI (thick) connector, and a transceiver to 10BaseT. The transceiver has monitor lights for connection, transmit, receive, SQE (heartbeat) and collision. When it's installed and the PC is booted, the connection and SQE come on, and the transmit and receive lights blink on and off, indicating that data is being sent to and from the PC. However, the connection still doesn't work.

There is an electrical connection to the concentrator, and data is being transmitted back and forth. The most likely problem seems to be that the data is being sent, but that it's being scrambled somehow. The collision light isn't coming on, and no one is using the network, so traffic is unlikely to be the problem. John concludes that the problem is most likely in the installation of the jack or the punchdown. He calls the cabling contractor and

> **You can isolate seemingly impenetrable problems by taking them step-by-step and eliminating fault points until you have only one or two left.**

asks them to come back and recheck this connection, then moves on to the rest of the workstations.

The cabling installer arrives in a couple of hours, grumbling about being called back in. John explains what he's tried and the installer checks the jack and wiring with a specialized test device. He discovers that two of the wires to the jack have been reversed. He reconnects the wiring to the jack and they try the PC. It connects to the server with no problem.

### Lessons Learned

▸ If you aren't familiar with the cabling company doing the installation, you may want to have the work double-checked. Don't assume that what they say they've checked is perfect—it's very easy to miss a small thing like a polarity error.

▸ You can isolate seemingly impenetrable problems by taking them step-by-step and eliminating fault points until you have only one or two left.

▸ There are some areas that can't be resolved without test equipment. However, if the cabling company hadn't been able to resolve this for John, he could have compared the order of colors of the wiring on both ends of the connection to find or eliminate the issue of the cross-connected wires, and could have punched down the connection on the block again, or replaced the jack, with inexpensive tools. If in doubt, redo it.

### The Fault Point Chain

▸ The driver software in the PC.

▸ The Ethernet transceiver in the PC.

▸ The 10BaseT cable to the wall jack.

▸ The wall jack and its connection.

> ▸ The cabling from the wall jack to the punch-down panel and its connection.

> ▸ The wiring from the punch-down panel to the PC's port on the concentrator.

> ▸ The concentrator.

> ▸ The wiring from the server's port on the concentrator to the punch-down panel.

> ▸ The connection at the punch-down block and the cabling from the punch-down panel to the wall jack in the server room.

> ▸ The wall jack in the server room and its connection.

> ▸ The cabling from the wall jack to the Ethernet card in the server.

> ▸ The Ethernet card in the server.

> ▸ The Ethernet driver software installed in the server OS.

A few minor points, such as the solidity of the connector in the wall jack, could also be included. Many of these can be eliminated right off. For instance, since other PCs can connect to the server, the last seven items can be disregarded. Further, since the PC can connect from another jack, the first two can be eliminated. Trying another cable eliminates the third item. That only leaves three items, a much easier list to test. Traffic lights on the concentrator and the transceiver show that data is being passed through the cable, which leaves only the connections at the jack and the punch-down block.

## SCENARIO TWO

A portion of an existing network goes down. The administrator follows the process of isolating the problem, determining the cause and fixing it.

### Snapshot—Scenario Two

Is This an Existing Network?

How Many Nodes Are Affected? Do Some of the Workstations on the Ring or Segment Work?

Fran, the system administrator for Great Big, Inc., gets a number of calls from users in the engineering department saying that they aren't able to connect to the server. She checks the server to make sure that it is running. Most of the workstations in the department are still able to connect to the server. The workstations are connected with thin Ethernet, in four segments or "legs" to a multiport repeater, which is in turn connected to the server. Fran looks at the wiring diagram for the department and notices that all the affected workstations are on the same loop. The problem could be either of two things—a break in the loop or a problem with the repeater. See Figure 3.3, below.

Fran checks the repeater first, since it is simpler to check than tracing the entire path of the loop, looking for breaks. She finds that the switch that controls the loop in question is turned on. Having found segments switched off by accident before, she had hoped it would be that simple this time, but it isn't. She sighs, then begins tracing the path of the loop, using her network map. The first few connections are all solid and look okay. Then she finds a pair of thin Ethernet cables in an unused cubicle, with no connector connecting them. She finds a spare t-connector, reconnects the two cables, and finds that the workstations in the loop are back on line.

**Check the simple things first, but don't be afraid to do some legwork.**

Further research uncovers a user who borrowed the connector, reasoning that since the cube wasn't in use, the connector wasn't doing anything. Fran refrains from strangling him, but sends out a carefully worded cautionary note to all the users on her networks, emphasizing that users who need networking work done should go through her.

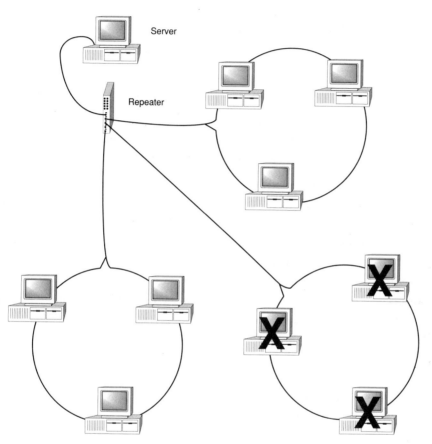

FIGURE 3.3

*Thin Ethernet LAN Using a
Repeater*

## Lessons Learned

▸ Check the simple things first, but don't be afraid to do some leg-work. Even the most daunting task can be handled with a calm and methodical approach.

▸ Break the problem down by isolating the affected elements. In this case, Fran had a network map and was easily able to determine that all the affected users were on the same leg of the repeater. If she hadn't been able to determine that, her job would have been much harder, since there would have been many more elements to eliminate before the fault point was isolated. This is a perfect example of why documenting your network is a necessity, not a luxury.

▸ Never underestimate the users' ability to make your life difficult.

▸ This is a case where a network monitor would have made life easier. Some monitors available now could have sent an alarm as soon as the t-connector was removed, identifying the problem and the most probably location of the break.

### The Fault Point Chain

Since a number of workstations were affected, we can eliminate most points of the chain that are unique to individual workstations, such as the network driver and Ethernet adapter. But we can't eliminate the t-connector connecting each card to the cable, because each one has the potential to affect the entire loop. The fault chain from the server to all workstations could also be eliminated, because if the server's network driver, its Ethernet card, the cable to the repeater, or the repeater as a whole had been damaged, none of the workstations on the rest of the net would have been able to log in, either. The remaining fault points are:

▸ The t-connectors on each workstation.

▸ The cabling.

▸ The port on the repeater to which the loop is connected.

▸ The termination on each end of the loop.

▸ The grounding of the loop.

### SCENARIO THREE

The administrator encounters a problem typical of a Token-Ring network, and you see the process she follows in isolating the fault and fixing the problem.

## Snapshot—Scenario Two

Is This an Existing Network?

How Many Nodes Are Affected? Do Some of the Workstations on the Ring or Segment Work?

The sales department of Great Big uses Token-Ring workstations that access their mainframe through NetWare for SAA. One day, Fran gets a call—no one in the sales department can access the network. Fran knows that with Token-Ring, one workstation can bring the network down if its card fails to pass the token along properly. She checks the server to make sure that nothing is apparently wrong there, then begins checking the workstations. All the workstations reboot without errors and load the Token-Ring driver without error messages about the card's configurations. The network doesn't begin to function when any of the workstations is off-line, which tells us that none of the workstations is failing to pass the token along— otherwise, the network would function with that workstation disconnected from the network.

Fran then checks the wiring closet where the MAUs are located. She discovers that the cable leading from the ring in port on one of the MAUs to the ring out port on the next MAU is disconnected. She reinserts the connector into the ring-in port, and checks the network. Everything is running again. Fran asks around to find out if anyone on her staff disconnected the port on purpose, but no one has, or will admit to it, at least.

> **When you have a single device in your cabling system that can affect the entire network, check it first.**

## Lessons Learned

> ▸ Even though Token-Ring has a physical star topology, it is logically a ring—one card that doesn't function properly may bring the whole network down. If the PC with the faulty card is powered down, it should remove that station from the network, which will then begin functioning properly again.

▸ When you have a single device in your cabling system that can affect the entire network—a repeater, concentrator or MAU, you should check it before initiating a time-consuming process like checking every workstation on the network.

▸ Leave checking the continuity of the wiring in the walls for last, but check connections that users (or janitors) can affect first.

▸ Again, this is a situation where a network analyzer would have helped. It could have told Fran where the connection was broken and which PCs were acting properly, thus pointing her in the direction of the lost connection between the two MAUs earlier.

### The Fault Point Chain

With Token-Ring, a card that goes dead should remove itself from the network. However, a card that remains electrically active, but isn't passing the token along properly will halt the entire network. The relevant fault points are these:

▸ Each card and driver on the ring.

▸ The server, and its card and driver

▸ The MAU, and the connection between each MAU

The wiring and the connections (at each card, the wall jack, and on the MAU) were not as a whole really a factor here. If a connection between one PC and the MAU had been broken either by a faulty connection or a broken wire, it would have deactivated that port on the MAU, and the rest of the network would have been running.

One further possibility, though, would have been a source of electromagnetic interference near one cable that garbled the token as it passed through. This could have caused the same sort of problem.

## SCENARIO FOUR

This scenario addresses the problems typical of a network that has been added to, or which has evolved from several small networks. Some basic recommendations are given for revamping such systems and working within a budget.

### Snapshot—Scenario Four

Is This an Existing Network?

Intermittent Faults and Performance Problems.

Fran has some free time, and since reviews are coming up, she picks an item from her to-do list instead of playing Tetris. The marketing lab has been complaining about the performance of the network in their demo room. It is often slow, and some workstations experience intermittent failures.

Fran begins by inventorying the equipment in the demo room. There are two NetWare servers, and about 50 workstations, including PCs, Macs and UNIX workstations, all attached by thin Ethernet or 10BaseT (twisted-pair) Ethernet. The network and servers were all set up by the marketing people and their system engineer, who quit several months ago and hasn't been replaced. Since then, one of the marketing staff, who has a fair amount of experience with NetWare and Macs, but almost none with hardware, has been maintaining the network.

After looking at the workstations, Fran inspects the cabling. Some of the workstations have 10BaseT Ethernet adapter cards, and are attached to an 8-port 10BaseT mini-hub, which is then attached to another mini-hub, which the server is attached to. Others have a thick Ethernet card (AUI) card which is then connected to a transceiver that is in turn connected to a 10BaseT cable running to one of the mini-hubs. Others are connected by thin Ethernet to one large segment with about 15 workstations and the other server on it (see Figure 3.4). The thin Ethernet loop is not properly grounded, many of the t-connectors in use are old and obviously low-quality, and some of the cables are ARCnet specification (RG-62, 93 ohm

*The Marketing Lab topology*

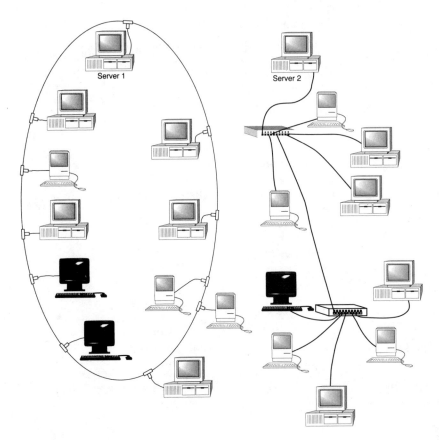

cable), instead of the RG-58A 50 ohm cable required for thin Ethernet. Finally, Fran notices that one of the extra terminators in the box of networking hardware in the room is a 75-ohm terminator, rather than the 50 ohms required for thin Ethernet.

Fran talks with the director of the marketing department and recommends that they install an all-10BaseT network using two 40-port concentrators. This will let them move connections from one server to the other, allowing for easy reconfiguration of the network as necessary, and it will keep everything in the same topology. She shows the manager how easy it is currently for things to get out of whack, and explains how all the things she found can contribute to poor performance. She adds that the two concentrators would give the lab a much more professional appearance than the haphazard look of the current setup.

The director is unwilling to make the investment, so Fran retreats to her prepared fallback plan—some more 8 or 12-port mini-hubs, and the cards or transceivers necessary to get all the workstations running 10BaseT. Even the much more moderate expense represented by 3 mini-hubs and some new Ethernet adapters is more than the director wants to spend. Finally, Fran shows the director the bottom-dollar plan—upgrade the existing thin Ethernet cable and t-connectors to new, high quality ones, including extras for reconfiguring the network as necessary, proper grounding, proper terminators, and a few new transceivers and LAN adapters. And one more item—a half-day training course for the lab administrator in proper cabling techniques and troubleshooting.

The director is happy with the low-cost alternative. After a few hours of work the next evening, aided by the newly-educated administrator, Fran replaces the thin Ethernet cabling and t-connectors with high quality ones, grounds the segment, throws away the old stuff to make sure no one will inadvertently add it to the network, and upgrades some of the transceivers and LAN cards on the 10BaseT network. She goes over the procedures for adding workstations to either network with the administrator, and makes sure they have sufficient additional high-quality cable, connectors, and transceivers to allow for normal reconfigurations.

They also make sure that all the workstations are using the same network driver software, and that the Macs are using the same system version and printer driver software. A few days later, Fran checks back with the administrator. Everyone is amazed at the increase in network performance, and the marketing directory is happy with the minimal expense required.

## Lessons Learned

▸ Don't try to save 25 cents on a connector or a dollar on a cable. It won't be worth it in the long run. This is especially true of the t-connectors used with thin Ethernet. Cheap ones will often become very hard to attach or detach with time, and can cause nasty intermittent problems.

▸ Try to avoid letting users set up their own networks. In this case the systems engineer that did the initial setup knew what he was doing, and the setup was fine, until the administration was handed over to someone who wasn't familiar with cabling.

▸ Watch out for mismatched equipment. Many connectors and cables look similar and will physically interchange with each other, but impedances and other factors can cause big problems.

▸ In a lab environment, the simplest solution is the best. In this case, the marketing personnel sometimes needed to reconfigure the network when the administrator wasn't around. Converting everything to 10BaseT would have substantially reduced the chances of an inexperienced user leaving the ring open, or making a connection that didn't completely lock.

▸ When presenting a plan for an installation to management, try to have more than one scenario: "Plan A will cost more, but will also have the following benefits:... Plan B will sacrifice the following benefits, but reduce costs by this much..."

## The Fault Point Chain

▸ The network card and network software in each workstation.

▸ The connection from the card to the cable or transceiver.

▸ The transceiver (if applicable).

▸ The connection from the transceiver to the network cable.

▸ The network cable.

▸ The concentrator (if applicable).

▸ The connection from the concentrator to the server.

▸ The connection at the server on the thin Ethernet ring.

▸ The LAN adapters and driver software in the servers.

## SCENARIO FIVE

This scenario describes a deceptive problem on an AppleTalk network, and through observation and deduction discovers the solution.

### Snapshot—Scenario Five

Is This an Existing Network?

Intermittent Faults and Performance Problems.

Jethro has one of the toughest assignments possible—someone in the art department is having problems, they think with a virus. Their Mac has been intermittently freezing during startup. He grabs his Mac tool kit and starts tracking down the problem. The virus checker on the affected machine is the latest version, and doesn't report any problems. The user says the problem doesn't seem to occur during any particular type of operation, or when a certain application is open. There aren't any Inits, control panels, or startup documents he doesn't recognize, but he tries removing all the extraneous extensions. The system still freezes up occasionally. He then tries reinstalling the system folder. There are still intermittent problems.

Another person in the department wanders by and mentions that they are having the same problem. Jethro realizes that the problem must be network-related, to be affecting more than one Mac. He checks, and most of the people in the department had been having problems, but hadn't realized they weren't alone.

He begins the tedious process of trying to isolate the common elements of the affected Macs. They aren't all running the same version of the EtherTalk driver, don't all have the same EtherTalk card, and don't even all use the same System version. Then one of the users asks Jethro to take a look at their printer while he's there—it's been jamming. Jethro figures he might as well take a break from thinking about the other problem, so he shuts the printer down and begins cleaning it thoroughly. After he's been working on the printer for about 20 minutes, one of the users comes over and compliments him on having fixed the problem with her Mac freezing.

A light dawns. He finishes cleaning the printer, then turns it back on. Checking with the affected Macs, he discovers that they are freezing again. It must be the printer. He calls the manufacturer to see if they know about this. After climbing up the tech support ladder for a while, Jethro is told that yes, they have seen this behavior on some networks, and they'll have a BIOS upgrade that should fix it within a week or two. Jethro arranges to swap the printer with another PostScript printer currently attached to a parallel port on a PC, which shouldn't be affected by the AppleTalk problem, and takes the offending printer off line. The other PostScript printer is a different brand and works fine.

A couple of months later, the new BIOS arrives, and Jethro upgrades the problem printer. He reattaches it to the network and holds his breath. As each day passes without freezes, he breathes a little easier.

### Lessons Learned

▶ Don't assume that a problem is unique to a user who complains. Check around to see if any others are affected. You won't always hear from some users when they have a problem—there is a certain tendency to take some problems for granted. If Jethro had known from the start that more than one user was affected, he could have saved quite a bit of time working on the system and Inits on the individual Mac. A virus would still have been a possibility, of course.

▶ This is another case where a network analyzer would have been very handy. Jethro would most likely have found that some device on the network was sending out bad AppleTalk packets, and could have at least isolated the cause to AppleTalk hardware or software, and possibly even determined the device causing the problem.

▶ Don't assume that the computers on your LAN are the only devices that can cause problems. It is becoming more common for printers to have networking interfaces built in, not just AppleTalk, but Ethernet as well. Each of these is potentially a problem too.

▶ Never assume that the manufacturer of a device did everything right. It is common for PCs to arrive from the factory with configuration errors, devices installed incorrectly, and of course, occasionally with faulty components. If Jethro had continued with his fault-point analysis, he would eventually have discovered that what all the Macs had in common was the AppleTalk zone that they were on. That would have led to looking at the other devices on that zone—the server and the printer. He might have spent considerable time trying to determine a problem with the server, assuming that it was a result of a configuration error or old driver version, and possibly never even looked at the printer, assuming that it couldn't be causing the problem.

▶ Never assume that the manufacturer will notify you if something you bought from them needs to be updated, or might cause problems under the right conditions. The best place to hear about this sort of thing is on the forums on CompuServe or at user-group or CNEPA meetings.

▶ If he hadn't been lucky, the next step for Jethro should have been to try asking around, either within his department, or at some of the sources listed in the previous paragraph. He might have found someone else who'd already had the same problem.

### The Fault Point Chain

Jethro's initial assumption is that the user's problem is unique to their Mac. This is, of course, incorrect. If Jethro hadn't happened to find out that the problem was actually the fault of the printer, he might have eventually replaced every part of the Macintosh, re-installed its operating system and all the applications. Eventually, with the whole system replaced, and the problem still occurring, he would have had to look at the other factors in the environment that could possibly affect a workstation: the power, electromagnetic interference, and any connection coming into the Mac. The connections might include the keyboard, the printer (network) connection, a serial connection for a modem and the SCSI port.

Jethro would then have replaced the keyboard, and disconnected anything else connected to the Mac. At that point, he would have discovered that the Mac didn't have the problem when not connected to the network. He would then have known that the problem must be caused by something coming from the network, rather than anything in the Mac.

- ▸ The Mac hardware—motherboard, memory, power supply, disk controller, disks, *and ports*.

- ▸ The Mac operating system.

- ▸ The Apple extensions, such as the EtherTalk driver.

- ▸ The non-Apple extensions.

- ▸ Any applications running when the problem occurred.

- ▸ Other devices on the AppleTalk network—the network driver software for each device on the network—this includes the BIOS in the printer, which was of course the actual problem, and the server.

- ▸ The network hardware for each network device.

- ▸ The cabling—this would include problems such as lines that run past transformers or fluorescent light ballasts.

▸ Any other factors in the environment, which might interfere with the electronics in the workstation, from magnets to power cords that run too close to the CPU, to a second workstation.

# Printing

*SnapShot*

**P**rinting from many workstations to one printer was one of the first uses for PC networks, and is still among the most important functions of a network. From a small piece of hardware that lets a few users share a dot-matrix printer to a PostScript print server that can service print jobs from DOS, Windows, Macintoshes, or UNIX, or a queue that stores a thousand-page print job and prints it in the middle of the night when no one else needs the printer, network print services all perform similar functions, but vary widely in cost and complexity. Printing is also more maintenance-intensive than other aspects of network technology. A user may tell you that the printer doesn't work any more, or that they can't print, when the only problem is that the printer is out of paper.

NetWare offers a wealth of features, but with those features comes an attendant complexity that many administrators (and users) find daunting. This need not be the case. If you approach setting up and troubleshooting print services in a systematic manner, and with a basic understanding of the process involved, you will find that problems can be resolved in the same manner as any other problems with the network. See the Concepts section for an outline of the printing process if you aren't familiar with it. In this section the print server may be either a workstation running RPRINTER or PSERVER.EXE, or the server itself. It makes no difference to the troubleshooting process. For clarity's sake, this chapter will always refer to the print server software as *PSERVER*, and the physical workstation to which the printer is connected as the *print server*.

## IS THIS A NEW PRINTER SETUP?

Setting up a printer, its queue, its job configuration, the print server, and PSERVER can be a very complex process. It gets more complicated if you consider PostScript printing, printing to AppleTalk printers, printing to UNIX print queues, and other possible variations. This snapshot guide is not intended to lead you through the process of creating your printer setup, but rather to troubleshoot problems in the process. The NetWare manuals cover the initial setup process well, including some useful troubleshooting hints.

### Can You Print from Any Workstations?

If you can print from some workstations, go to the next item. If you can't print from any workstations, try other printers, on other servers if available.

**Can You Put Print Jobs Directly into the Queue with PCONSOLE? Do They Print?**  If not, go to the next item. If inserting the jobs directly into the queue works, then your problem is likely to be with the capture setup on the workstations, with the print job setup, or with the connection to the server. See the Concepts section on the printing process, starting on page 147.

**Is the Queue Connected to PSERVER?**  Use PCONSOLE to see if the queue is attached to PSERVER. If it is, make sure that the print server running PSERVER is up and running. See the Concepts section on the printing process, starting on page 147. If the print server is running, go to the next item. Otherwise, see Chapter 2: Workstations.

**Can You Print from DOS on the Print Server?**  Try printing from DOS on the print server. If the file server is also the print server, you'll have to down the server first—exiting from NetWare to DOS. Then try printing a DOS file with the command

    PRINT FILE.TXT > LPT1

or whatever port the printer is on. If the printer doesn't respond, you have a problem with the printer itself, or with the workstation configuration. If the printer will print from DOS, then PSERVER or some other part of the print software is incorrectly configured.

### Is Printing Affected on Only One or a Few Workstations?

If the problem is with one or a few workstations, but others can print, then you know that the printer itself, the print server, the queues, and so on are operational. Check the workstations that can't print for common items. Are all the workstations that can print using the same print queue? The same print job? Can you print with a different login?

**Can You Print from DOS on the Workstation?**  Try printing from DOS on the affected workstation. If you can't print from DOS, check the network connection to make sure you have a connection to the server and try printing a DOS text file from PCONSOLE. If that works, the workstation itself is probably causing the problem, rather than the print setup. See Chapter 2: Workstations. Pay particular attention to the printer port configuration, interrupt conflicts, DOS, and the NetWare shell software. Make sure that the print job or capture setup works on other workstations.

**If You Can Print from DOS, It's Probably the Application.**  Try printing from other applications. Make sure that the application is set up to print to the proper printer port or queue. If the program is attempting to print to a NetWare queue directly, and you can't find anything wrong, try printing to the LPT1 port and using CAPTURE to redirect the output to the printer.

## IS THIS AN EXISTING PRINTER SETUP?

With an existing setup, you can have two major things go wrong. One, a user becomes unable to print, or two, no one can access a printer or queue. Isolating the people affected will give you your first clues. One of the first places to check is the printer itself. Printers, more than any other equipment on your network, require maintenance. A large percentage of "printing problems" can be fixed by resetting the printer, cleaning it, installing a new toner cartridge, or adding paper.

Next, make sure that the print server, if you are using one, is running properly. Some versions of PSERVER.EXE and RPRINTER.EXE are more likely than others to lock up the print server, especially with PostScript printers. See the Concepts section for more information on PostScript printers and their special requirements, starting on page 154.

### Is The Printer Operational?

If the printer is apparently running, has paper, and is on-line, go to the next item. If not, see your printer's manual for details on your printer. Check power, cables, connections and other items that users can get to first. Don't forget to check the paper tray and make sure the cover is closed.

### Is The Print Server Operational?

Check the print server for operation—power on, keyboard responsive, and so on. If the print server is running, go to the next item. If not, troubleshoot the print server as a workstation. See Chapter 2: Workstations.

### Can You Print from Some Workstations?

If you can print from some workstations, go to the next item. If you can't print from any workstations, try other printers, on other servers if available. If you can print to another printer, queue, or server, the problem is most likely with the setup of the queue, PSERVER or print server you were attempting to print to, rather than the workstation.

### Can You Put Print Jobs Directly into the Queue with PCONSOLE? Do They Print?

If not, go to the next item. If inserting print jobs directly into the queue works, then your problem is likely to be with the capture setup on the workstations, with the print job setup, or with the connection to the server.

### Is the Queue Connected to PSERVER?

Use PCONSOLE to see if the queue is attached to PSERVER. If it is, make sure that the print server running PSERVER is up and running. If the print server is running go to the next item. Otherwise, see Chapter 2: Workstations.

### Can You Print from DOS on the Print Server?

Try printing from DOS on the print server. If this is the server, you'll have to down the server first exiting from NetWare to DOS. Then try printing a DOS file with the command

```
PRINT FILE.TXT > LPT1
```

or whatever port the printer is on. If the printer doesn't respond, you have a problem with the printer itself, or with the workstation configuration. If the printer will print from DOS, then PSERVER or some of the associated software is incorrectly configured.

### *Is Printing Affected on Only One or a Few Workstations?*

If the problem is with one or a few workstations, but others can print, then you know that the printer itself, the print server, the queues, and so on are operational. Check the workstations that can't print for common items. Are all the workstations that can print using the same print queue? The same print job? Can you print with a different login?

**Can You Print from DOS on the Workstation?**  Try printing from DOS on the affected workstation. If you can't print from DOS, check the network connection to make sure you have a connection to the server and try printing a DOS text file from PCONSOLE. If that works, the workstation itself is probably causing the problem, rather than the print setup. See Chapter 2: Workstations. The items to pay particular attention to are the printer port configuration, interrupt conflicts, DOS, and the NetWare shell software. Make sure that the print job or capture setup works on other workstations.

**If You Can Print from DOS, It's Probably the Application.**  Try printing from other applications. Make sure that the application is set up to print to the proper printer port or queue. If the program is attempting to print to a NetWare queue directly, and you can't find anything wrong, try printing to the LPT1 port and using CAPTURE to redirect the output to the printer. See the Concepts section on the printing process, on page 147, and Chapter 9, Network Applications.

# Concepts

There are a number of ways to make setting up, maintaining and using print services under NetWare easier and more problem-free. Some of these are procedural, some will involve additional software or hardware, but all can make your life easier.

Fault Points

The Printing Process

   The Application

   The Shell: Printer Redirection

   CAPTURE.EXE

   The Print Queue

   PSERVER

   The Print Server

   Serial and Parallel Interfaces

   The Printer

PostScript Printers

NetWare for Macintosh

NFS Printing

## FAULT POINTS

The Overview introduced the concept of a chain of Fault Points as a guide to troubleshooting networks and network components. Within any combination of different types of workstations, Network Interface Cards (NICs), LAN topologies, servers, cabling, software, and so on, there are a limited number of points where problems can occur.

Because a conventional flowchart cannot cover anything close to all the possibilities inherent in a network, it makes more sense to look only at those places where things can go wrong. Figure 4.1 illustrates a typical fault point chain for Network printing.

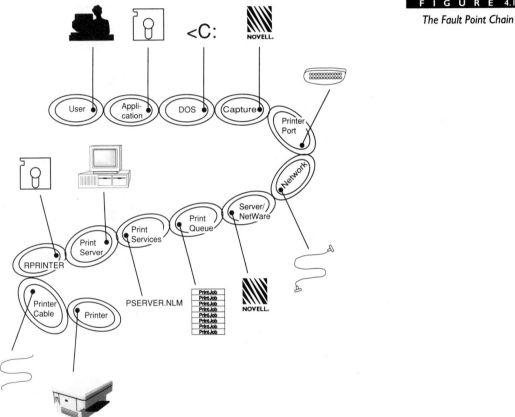

Each of the items in the chain in Figure 4.1 is linked to the preceding and following items. Any one of them can cause the printing process to fail, and if you can determine that the chain works up to any point, all the points before are working.

The printer must have power and a solid connection to the cable, and it must be configured to use the correct interface in the correct manner. It must also have toner or a good ribbon, a supply of paper, and a clear paper path.

The printer cable must be correctly set up to switch the necessary pins to allow both the workstation and the printer to communicate correctly. It should also be within the maximum length limits and well insulated, with properly installed connectors. Of course, the connectors should be screwed snugly into the printer port on the PC and the appropriate port on the printer.

RPRINTER.EXE will only be running if the printer is attached to someone's personal workstation, rather than a dedicated print server or the NetWare server. RPRINTER must be properly configured for the right port on the workstation, and associated with a print queue.

The print server must be properly configured as a workstation to access its drives and NIC, and should also be set up to access the port the printer is attached to, either parallel or serial.

PSERVER provides the connection between print queues and the print server. It must be connected to the print queues with PCONSOLE, and also to the proper print server. PSERVER.EXE can of course also crash, breaking the connection.

The print queue must be set up and attached to a PSERVER. It must also be able to access the directory on the SYS: volume that actually holds the print jobs until they can be printed.

NetWare must be running properly and must support the PSERVER VAP or NLM. If the printer is set up to print to a PostScript printer or provide print services to Macintosh, UNIX or other operating systems, you will also need to have those services set up properly.

The network connection to the user's workstation must be working correctly and allow the shell to provide the normal NetWare workstation services.

The printer port on the user's workstation can also affect the NetWare printing process. The port doesn't necessarily need to be turned on in the PC's configuration, but if a job is printed to the wrong printer port, NetWare won't properly redirect it to the queue.

CAPTURE.EXE must be set up to print to the proper print queue and use the proper print job. This is one of the easiest places for problems to occur in an existing setup, because it is one of the few parts that the user interacts with.

DOS must be working for the workstation to be able to load the NetWare shell, attach to the network and access NetWare print services. If the DOS MODE command has been used to change the settings on a serial port and CAPTURE is set to capture from that port, it may affect the capture process.

Some applications directly access NetWare print services, rather than attempting to send the print job to a port, which is then intercepted and sent to the NetWare queue. Whether the application does this or not, it can affect the print process if it is configured for the wrong type of printer, or if the print menu misleads the user.

The user is the last (and first) link in the printing process, and not one to be forgotten. A user will tell you that the printer is broken when their CAPTURE statement is sending the job to the wrong printer, or tell you that the print server is down when the printer is out of paper. A system administrator recently reported in a computer publication the case of a user who said they couldn't print any more. After investigating a number of possibilities, the administrator discovered that the user couldn't print because the part of the menu that allowed printing wasn't visible on the monitor. After adjusting the horizontal hold, everything was fine.

> **Never forget that the fault point chain begins and ends with the user.**

## THE PRINTING PROCESS

The printing process begins on the workstation, just as it would with a standalone PC. The user prints, either from DOS or from an application. Instead of the job being sent to the port the printer is on (LPT1, 2 or 3, or COM1 or 2), it is redirected by the NetWare shell to a file in a queue directory on the file server. PSERVER checks the queue directory and sends the job to the printer.

PSERVER may reside on the server as PSERVER.NLM, on a dedicated print server workstation as PSERVER.EXE, or on a router or NetWare 2.*x* server as PSERVER.VAP. RPRINTER.EXE is not a software print server—it allows PSERVER to access a printer connected to a user's workstation as if that printer were attached to the PC PSERVER is running on. Wherever PSERVER is located, it looks in the appropriate directory (the print queue) in the file server's SYS:/SYSTEM directory; and when a file is placed there, PSERVER prints it to the assigned printer.

NetWare 4.0 uses a different system. PSERVER is replaced with NPRINTER. NPRINTER.NLM runs on the server and supports up to 256 printers. NPRINTER.EXE runs on a workstation and allows network users to print to the local PC, replacing RPRINTER. There is no software for configuring a dedicated print server workstation, although you can run NPRINTER on a workstation that is only used as a print server.

### The Application

If the program is aware of network print queues, but printing doesn't work when the application tries to insert a print job directly into the queue, try printing to the parallel port (LPT1) and using NetWare's redirection capability instead.

### The Shell—Printer Redirection

IPX.COM and NET*x*.COM, the ODI network drivers, or the VLMs are the first step in the NetWare printing process. When an application attempts to send output to the printer port (LPT1–3), the shell intercepts it and sends it as a file to the queue directory on the server instead. This is the same process used to allow users to access drives on the server as if they were local.

SHELL.CFG is a file in the same directory as NET*x*.COM that controls to a degree how the workstation shell is configured. Think of it as the CONFIG.SYS for the shell. On workstations running RPRINTER, use NET.CFG. There are a number of settings that should be used when setting up printing:

        local printers=0

This will keep the workstation from hanging if no ports are captured and the user types Shift-PrintScreen.

> Print Header = 255

This will make sure PostScript jobs have enough header space to correctly configure the printer.

> PRINT TAIL = 255

This will make sure NetWare has enough space in the trailer to the print job to send reset codes to the printer after the job is finished. Use this setting if the printer is being left incorrectly configured after a user finishes printing.

> SPX CONNECTIONS = 60

This should be used on dedicated print servers running PSERVER.EXE. It is not necessary on workstations running RPRINTER.

## CAPTURE.EXE

This program allows you to specify many options when printing a document. See the *Utilities* or *Print Server* manual for further details. For example, if you were going to print a PostScript document to a queue called LaserWriterI, your capture statement might be:

> CAPTURE LPT1 s=Marketing q=LaserWriterI /NB /NT /NFF

This captures any text sent to LPT1 and prints it to the queue LaserWriterI on the server Marketing, with no banner page, no tabs, and no form feed. The no-tabs setting is standard when printing from an application that (like most) handles the print formatting, and the no-form-feed option prevents the printer from printing a blank page at the end of a document. The only time you need to add a form feed is if the last page of a print job doesn't print when printing from some applications.

You can also specify these parameters with NPRINT, or by setting up a print job with PRINTCON. Using print jobs is a much easier way to set the parameters for complex printing, as it allows you to make choices from menus rather than having to know the exact spelling and syntax for each setting, as with CAPTURE. PRINTCON allows you to designate a default print job, and to set up queues associated with each job. This means that you can switch from printing forms on a line printer, to PostScript on a LaserWriter, and then to text on an HP, with the following simple statements:

> **Set up print jobs with PRINTCON, rather than relying on long CAPTURE statements.**

```
CAPTURE j=line
CAPTURE j=PS
CAPTURE j=HP
```

or even by using PRINTCON to change your default print job. This is much easier for the user and makes troubleshooting the setup much easier.

### The Print Queue

The print queue is actually a directory located in SYS:/SYSTEM with an eight-digit file name that consists of hex characters (0–9, plus A–F), such as 400000BF. This directory contains any files that have been placed in the queue. If jobs are being placed in the queue without error messages, and the PCON-SOLE Print Queue Status Window shows that they are being sent to the printer, but they never print, you should look in the queue directories to see if the files are still there. This will tell you whether the problem is with PSERVER or with the printer. If the files are still in the print queue directory, they aren't actually being sent to the printer, and the problem is likely to be with the software. If the files are gone, then they are being sent to the printer and aren't printing out, perhaps because of a configuration problem with the print server or the printer. You should also make sure that when a print queue is selected in the Print Queue Information of PCONSOLE, the Queue Servers list has at least one PSERVER attached.

## PSERVER

PSERVER.NLM, .EXE or .VAP is the software that controls how the print file is sent from the queue on the server, and to which printer. PSERVER.NLM runs on the server. PSERVER.VAP may run on a 2.*x* server or on a router. PSERVER.EXE runs on a dedicated print server workstation.

The version of PSERVER.NLM shipped with NetWare 3.11 has a bug that can cause garbage to be printed if you are using a fast printer and the print server workstation has a small buffer. If the buffer overflows, the job is killed. This can be fixed by upgrading to the latest version of PSERVER.NLM, which can be found on NetWire.

PSERVER.EXE gives you the advantage of off-loading the PSERVER process from the server to a dedicated workstation. The down side is that it requires an additional dedicated workstation. This does have another additional benefit, though. It allows you to lock up your server and still give users easy access to the printers.

### The Print Server

This is a workstation running PSERVER. It may also be the file server. In either case, the process of troubleshooting is the same, although it may be easier if the file server and print server are separate workstations. The print server itself can usually be treated as an ordinary workstation.

**NOTE**
**See Chapter 2 for more information on troubleshooting workstations.**

### Serial and Parallel Interfaces

PC serial interfaces use the RS-232 interface. This specification is intended to allow a PC to talk to a modem—Data Terminal Equipment (DTE) to Data Communications Equipment (DCE). In the context of printing, however, both the PC and the printer consider themselves to be DTE devices. The means of fixing this problem is to use a special serial cable that "fools" both the printer and PC into thinking that the device on the other end is a DCE. Unfortunately, the way this technique is implemented varies from printer to printer.

The best way to avoid this problem is to use a parallel connection, if at all possible—it's faster and easier to configure. There may be reasons to use a serial printer, such as a requirement for a longer cable than a parallel connection allows, or a printer that has only a serial interface. In that case, you should use a serial cable made as shown in Figure 4.2, rather than a straight-through cable.

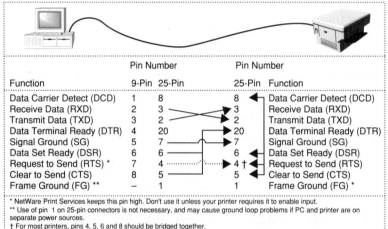

FIGURE 4.2

*Serial Cable Pinouts*

| | Pin Number | | Pin Number | |
|---|---|---|---|---|
| Function | 9-Pin | 25-Pin | 25-Pin | Function |
| Data Carrier Detect (DCD) | 1 | 8 | 8 | Data Carrier Detect (DCD) |
| Receive Data (RXD) | 2 | 3 | 3 | Receive Data (RXD) |
| Transmit Data (TXD) | 3 | 2 | 2 | Transmit Data (TXD) |
| Data Terminal Ready (DTR) | 4 | 20 | 20 | Data Terminal Ready (DTR) |
| Signal Ground (SG) | 5 | 7 | 7 | Signal Ground (SG) |
| Data Set Ready (DSR) | 6 | 6 | 6 | Data Set Ready (DSR) |
| Request to Send (RTS) * | 7 | 4 | 4 † | Request to Send (RTS) |
| Clear to Send (CTS) | 8 | 5 | 5 | Clear to Send (CTS) |
| Frame Ground (FG) ** | – | 1 | 1 | Frame Ground (FG) * |

* NetWare Print Services keeps this pin high. Don't use it unless your printer requires it to enable input.
** Use of pin 1 on 25-pin connectors is not necessary, and may cause ground loop problems if PC and printer are on separate power sources.
† For most printers, pins 4, 5, 6 and 8 should be bridged together.

These cables are commercially available—this diagram is just to show you how the signals are switched from PC to printer. This is a sample configuration that will work for many printers; your printer may use different pins. See your printer manual for details, or contact the manufacturer to purchase the necessary cable.

If you do use a parallel interface, there are still things to look out for—to avoid interrupt conflicts, you can set Use Interrupts to No in the Printer Configuration section of the Print Server Configuration menu of Print Server Information when configuring the printer in PCONSOLE.

## The Printer

There is a huge variety of printers available today—from simple dot-matrix printers that haven't changed much in the last 15 years, to lasers, to dye-sublimation color printers that produce results barely distinguishable from color photographs. In addition to the printers themselves, and their hardware interfaces, there is also a control language for each printer, also ranging from relatively simple dot-matrix control codes to the PostScript language, which is as complex and capable as most programming environments. Both aspects of a printer must be taken into account when connecting it to a network.

The hardware aspect of the connection to the print server has largely been covered earlier in his chapter. However, you should be aware that most printers have a hardware configuration, which may be set using utility software, with DIP switches inside the printer, or from a front panel display. These will tell the printer what type of connection it has, what protocol and speed to expect over the connection, and so on. See your printer's manual for details. If your print server cannot print at all, even from DOS, it is likely to be a problem with the printer's configuration or its connection.

The other aspect of the printer is the software used to control the printer's actions while printing. In the simplest case, an ASCII-only printer (a daisy-wheel or ball printer) can only print ASCII characters. It may have a few escape codes (so called because they all start with the ASCII character for Esc), to allow bold, italic or underlined characters. PostScript, at the other end of the spectrum, not only allows any aspect of text to be changed, but prints exceedingly complex graphics as well.

The application from which the user is printing must understand the language of the printer. In addition, the print job or CAPTURE statement must take into account the special requirements of controlling the printer. This is particularly true when printing graphics or PostScript. The flow to the printer must be set to Byte Stream, rather than Text, when you configure the print job in PRINTCON. This allows the special characters used to control the printer to be sent without being interpreted or removed.

## POSTSCRIPT PRINTERS

PostScript is an extremely versatile printer control language developed by Adobe Systems. It allows text to be printed in any size, any weight, any angle, any color, and more. It is also very good at producing graphics. The drawback to this flexibility is the resulting complexity. If you are interested, try printing a word processing file or art file to disk as a PostScript file, and then open it with a text editor. You will see pages and pages of code describing that document. The PostScript file is actually a program that runs on the controller of a PostScript printer, and tells it how to draw the page. It is not uncommon for a 15 KB word processing document to produce a 100 KB or larger PostScript file.

PostScript printers have also been associated from the first with the Macintosh computer from Apple. Today, most PostScript printers have parallel and serial ports in addition to AppleTalk ports, and you may wish to connect your printer via these ports, even in an all-Macintosh department. A PostScript printer attached to a print server by a parallel port may prove to be quite a bit faster than one connected via AppleTalk, especially if the Macs are using EtherTalk cards.

When printing to a PostScript printer, you should make sure that the following configuration items have been set:

> ▸ Set the print job to Byte stream mode with PRINTCON or use the /NT (no tabs) option in your CAPTURE statement.

> ▸ Other CAPTURE options you should use are /NFF (no form feeds), and /NB (no banner).

> ▸ Set print header = 255 in your SHELL.CFG file.

> ▸ Set PRINT TAIL = 255 in your SHELL.CFG file if your printer tends to hang after printing a job.

**NOTE**
**Configuring NetWare for Macintosh is discussed in Chapter 8: Connecting to Other Systems.**

## NETWARE FOR MACINTOSH

There are a couple of places to check your configuration of NetWare for Macintosh if you have problems:

▸ If a printer isn't showing up in the EtherTalk zone, or if the AppleTalk screen on the Server has error messages like "Can't connect to printer LaserWriter," make sure that the printer name specified in ATPS.CFG has the name spelled *exactly* as it appears in the LocalTalk zone, including upper and lower case. If the name seems to be spelled correctly, make sure that there are no leading or trailing spaces in either the configuration file or the name that was given to the printer with the LaserWriter utility.

▸ If devices are disappearing from zones, or lots of error messages are appearing in the system error log, or if performance is just very slow, make sure that each LocalTalk and EtherTalk zone has a unique zone number. Zone number conflicts can cause many type of intermittent conflicts and really slow down AppleTalk performance.

▸ If you have set up a print job with PRINTCON to print from the PC to an AppleTalk printer, make sure that Mode is NOT set to Reinitialize. This will cause jobs to fail to print.

## NFS PRINTING

NetWare NFS v.1.2b supports bidirectional printing for UNIX printers. This means that PC workstations attached to a NetWare server can print to a printer attached to a UNIX workstation, and the UNIX workstations can print to the NetWare queues. Getting this process to work is more complicated than a standard print server; but approached methodically, it is not any harder. The complication is added by the basic difference between the methods of printing on PCs and UNIX workstations.

Where the PRINT command in DOS simply sends a stream of data to the parallel or serial port, which is intercepted by NetWare and redirected to a NetWare queue, UNIX workstations use a program (called a daemon), **LPD**, to print. **LPD** is a command that is part of the system software in UNIX. It is much more capable than the PRINT command in DOS. It knows what kind of printer it is printing to—for instance, text or PostScript—and where that printer is located, whether on the workstation's printer port, or on another workstation. It also knows the name of the queue that it is printing to, and where that queue is located. This configuration information is stored in a file called **printcap**, usually located in the **/etc** directory.

To set up a UNIX workstation to print to a NetWare queue, the **printcap** file must contain the IP address or hostname of the server, and the information on the name of the queue. The manual for NetWare NFS discusses these requirements in detail. For troubleshooting UNIX-to-NetWare printing, you should be aware that the following fault points are added to the normal ones for NetWare:

> ▸ The **LPD** daemon—is it running?

> ▸ The **printcap** file on the UNIX side—is the information about the NetWare server and the queue to print to correct?

> ▸ The TCP/IP connection to the server—can you **PING** the NetWare server?

> ▸ The configuration of NetWare NFS—is the queue exported? Configured correctly?

> ▸ The PLPD NLM—is it loaded and configured properly?

For printing from a NetWare client to a printer on a UNIX workstation, the fault chain also has the same items, but in reverse order, as the job is going from the NetWare queue to the **LPD** daemon on the UNIX workstation. Additionally, there is a print gateway on the NetWare server that modifies the file after it reaches the print queue, then sends it to the **LPD** daemon on the UNIX host. Of course, in both cases, the normal NetWare printing fault chain also applies, including the workstation-to-printer connection—in the second case it's a UNIX workstation, but you still need to verify that you can print from the workstation to the printer.

# Real-Life Stories

This section describes typical network printing problems and how a troubleshooter would go through the process of isolating the fault and fixing it. The two fictional companies introduced in the Overview and their administrators are again used as examples. They combine the equipment and experience of a number of actual businesses. These four scenarios show some representative problems often encountered when setting up or troubleshooting printers and printing operations. While you may never see these particular problems, they should give you a feel for the process by which an experienced troubleshooter isolates a problem, determines the solution, and fixes the problem.

## SCENARIO ONE

The administrators are setting up a new PostScript printer that will be accessible to both Macs and PCs in the marketing department. They'll be attaching it to a dedicated print server.

### Snapshot—Scenario One

Is This a New Printer Setup?

Can You Print from Any Workstations?

Can You Put Print Jobs Directly into the Queue with PCONSOLE? Do They Print?

Is the Queue Connected to PSERVER?

Can You Print from DOS on the Print Server?

Is Printing Only Affected on One, or a Few Workstations?

Can You Print from DOS on the Workstation?

If You Can Print from DOS, It's Probably the Application.

Fran and Jethro are setting up a new PostScript printer for the marketing department at Great Big, Inc. The printer must be accessible to both Macs and PCs. Further, the server is inaccessible to the users, so they will be using a PC as a print server. The server is running NetWare 3.11, and NetWare for Macintosh version 3.01. In earlier versions of NetWare, they'd have had to set the printer up as an AppleTalk printer, and then set up a queue that PCs could use to print to the AppleTalk printer. With this version of NetWare for Macintosh, they can do it the other way—set up a queue, and allow Macintoshes to print to the PC print queue. This allows the print server to be a PC with a 16-bit Ethernet card, and a parallel interface, which is faster than the AppleTalk interface.

They set up the workstation that will be the print server. Since it is a dedicated workstation that won't be used for anything else, they use a 286 AT clone that has been sitting around. It has a 20 MB hard disk and a Hercules monochrome setup, which is fine—it doesn't need color or much disk space to run PSERVER. The only card in the AT is a Network Interface Card (NIC). The laser printer is attached to the parallel port. The printer is supposed to automatically take input from its serial or parallel port, so there's nothing to configure on the printer.

Before connecting the print server to the network, they want to check the printer setup on the PC for proper functioning. You can't print from DOS to a PostScript printer, so they load an application that will print PostScript to check the printer. Nothing comes out—the printer's data light doesn't even start blinking. After a while, the application shows a message "Printer unavailable."

Since the application is set to print to LPT1, the problem must be between the application and the printer. The possible fault points are the port, the cable, and the software on both ends to enable the ports. The printer is supposed to determine which port is being used, and the cable is the one that came with the printer, so they check the software on the AT first. After they locate and run SETUP, they discover that the parallel port has been disabled. Once they enable it, the application is able to print to the printer.

They leave the application on the disk in case any future debugging is required, then save the existing AUTOEXEC.BAT and CONFIG.SYS files to .BAK extensions. They update the DOS version to the latest, and add the latest versions of IPX.COM and NETX.COM. They create a SHELL.CFG file with the preferred server specified and an SPX CONNECTIONS = 60 entry. They then load the latest version of PSERVER.EXE onto the disk, then set up the AUTOEXEC.BAT file so that it loads IPX and NETX, then logs into the network as a user they've created for printing, then loads PSERVER.

This creates a security loophole in that a user could reboot the print server, and interrupt the AUTOEXEC.BAT with Ctrl-C after it's logged in, but they've carefully restricted the access for the user. They want the print server to connect automatically to the network so that the server can be rebooted or come back up after a power outage, without one of them having to be there to enter a password. This way, any user can specify the PSERVER to load (they've printed instructions and taped them to the printer). The next step is to set up a print server account and queues, using PCONSOLE and PRINTCON.

Fran and Jethro use PCONSOLE to define a print server. They configure the printer as a remote printer, since it is not on the file server. Then they set up a queue, using the AppleTalk Print Services (ATPS) NLM and configure it to use the printer they've defined. Then they use PRINTCON to set up two print jobs—one for printing PostScript from PCs, one for printing text from PCs (PostScript printers won't handle text files as HP-compatible printers do). Finally they reboot the print server, load PSERVER, and start printing test files from several workstations. None of the jobs printed from PCs or Macs come out. They begin rechecking the configuration.

Oops! "Remote printer" means a printer on a user's workstation attached with RPRINTER. They change the configuration to a local printer on LPT1 and reboot the print server. The jobs that were in the queue begin printing. After the second job prints, the print server hangs. They restart the printer, but the print server still thinks it's off-line. They reboot the print server and another job prints, then it hangs again. They look at the configuration of the print server. The Use Interrupts option is set to ON, with interrupt 7 specified. That's the correct interrupt, but they decide to try Use Interrupts set to OFF. This fixes the problem.

The next job in the queue is a Macintosh job. It prints, but the fonts are all Courier, instead of what they should have been. They reread the NetWare for Macintosh documentation and discover that they need to specify a font list for the printer, since it isn't on AppleTalk. They change the configuration of ATPS to look for the font list for the printer in a file instead of through AppleTalk and to download the LaserPrep initialization file with each Macintosh print job, and then reload ATPS. Now the Macintosh jobs are printing with the fonts specified in the document.

### Lessons Learned

▶ Make sure the print server is properly configured with SETUP for the printer. This includes setting the speed, parity and stop bit if using a serial connection.

▶ Follow the configuration instructions in the manuals explicitly. Make sure to check the *NetWare for Macintosh* manual and supplement if necessary, as well as the *Print Server* manual.

▶ If the print server freezes or you have intermittent problems when jobs are printed to a printer on the parallel port, try setting Use Interrupts to OFF.

▶ If you set up a Macintosh queue to print to a printer that isn't on AppleTalk, you must set up a list that contains the fonts native to the printer. NetWare for Macintosh 3.01 comes with default font lists for the LaserWriter, LaserWriter Plus, LaserWriter II NT, LaserWriter II NTX, and HP LaserJet with PostScript cartridge. If you have additional fonts, either installed in the printer's ROM or on a hard disk, you can modify the .FNT file to include them. You must also add a −l option to the queue configuration line in the ATPS.CFG file to download LaserPrep with each Mac job.

### The Fault Point Chain

The fault point chain in this case begins with the users, their applications, and the workstation configurations and connections, but these aren't relevant—in the first step, none of the workstations can print, indicating a problem with the PSERVER or printer configuration. While they are part of the overall fault chain, if the connection from server to workstation, the

NIC in the workstation, or the workstation itself aren't working, they should be addressed as discussed in the previous chapters. Therefore the fault point chain we will consider here is as follows:

▶ The queue. In this case the queue is set up by the ATPS NLM. A standard queue in a PC-only department wouldn't really be any different; it would just be configured with PCONSOLE, instead of the INSTALL NLM.

▶ The print server attached to the queue. This is a software print server that is configured in PCONSOLE and controls the configuration of the PSERVER version running on the server, a bridge or print server workstation.

▶ The copy of PSERVER. It needs to be loaded and attached to a print server that has been configured with PCONSOLE.

▶ The physical print server. This may be the file server, a bridge, or a workstation. In this context, it doesn't matter. If the workstation is running properly, the only aspects to look at in this context are whether it is configured for the port the printer is on, and whether the DOS and NetWare configuration files are properly set up.

▶ The connection to the printer. The cable should be appropriate for the type of printer attached, should have solid connections, and so on.

▶ The printer. It should be properly configured for the type of connection; it should also have paper and a ribbon or toner cartridge, be plugged in, and so on.

## SCENARIO TWO

In this scenario, the administrator sets up a router (known as a bridge in previous versions of NetWare) to act as a print server. This will allow two physically separated groups to use the same file server and both also have a local printer.

### Snapshot—Scenario Two

Is This a New Printer Setup?

Can You Print from Any Workstations?

Can You Put Print Jobs Directly into the Queue with PCONSOLE? Do They Print?

Is the Queue Connected to PSERVER?

Can You Print from DOS on the Print Server?

Is Printing Only Affected On One, or a Few Workstations?

Can You Print from DOS on the Workstation?

If You Can Print from DOS, It's Probably the Application.

John, the administrator for Itsy-Bitsy, has a department that is splitting in two. The sales department is splitting into order entry and shipping, located separately. The shipping department needs to take the line printer with them to do shipping forms, and the order entry department is getting a laser printer. The two departments will be separated by several hundred feet, which exceeds the limit for the type of cabling in use for the current network. John will either have to add a second server for shipping, and move their accounts, or put in a bridge, router, or repeater to extend the network.

John decides to locate a router in the shipping department's new location to handle printing and extend the possible distance from the sales server by allowing two network segments—one to attach to the server, and one for the users in shipping. This extends the possible distance from the server to the maximum for the type of cabling, since the only things on that segment are the router and the server. It does, of course, also require a second NIC in the server as well as the router, to allow the maximum possible distance between the two machines. See Figure 4.3.

The server is running NetWare 2.15c. Both the server and the router will need to run PSERVER VAP. Alternatively, John could add a second router or dedicated print server running PSERVER.EXE for the order entry department, if the load on the server becomes too great and he wants to off-load

*A network connection with two segments and a router*

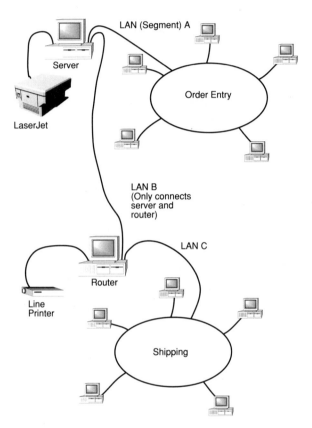

print services from the server. He makes a note to monitor the utilization of the server carefully for the next month or two.

John adds a second NIC to the server to allow the maximum distance between the router and the server, sets up the router, connects the shipping department's workstations to it, and tests the expanded network. When everything is working, he uses PCONSOLE to set up an additional print queue and print server. He reconfigures the existing queue and print server to use the line printer on the router and sets up new ones for the laser printer on the server.

When the configuration is done, he configures the router with PSER-VER.VAP and attaches the printer, then starts PSERVER and tries printing from a workstation in the shipping department. Nothing comes out of the line printer.

John begins tracing the problem with the CAPTURE statement on the PC he's trying to print from. It's set in the user's AUTOEXEC.BAT file to the old queue. (Nothing came out on that printer either.) He resets CAPTURE to the new print server and queue and tries printing again. Still nothing. Next, he tries inserting a job directly into the queue. Nothing comes out of the printer. He reboots the PC running PSERVER as a workstation and tries to print a DOS file to the COM1 port. Nothing.

He uses the SETUP program to see if the PC is configured to use COM1. It is. The only remaining item is the cable. The line printer is serial-only, and the server uses a 25-pin serial cable, while the new router has a 9-pin serial port, so John had picked up a new serial cable at the local computer store. On investigation, it turns out that they have sold him a straight-through, or modem cable. He gets a serial printer cable, and hooks the printer back up.

He can print from DOS to the printer. He loads PSERVER and tries print-ing to the line printer from one of the shipping workstations. Success! John knows that the print job configuration is stored in a file in the user's SYS:MAIL/ID# directory, so rather than use PRINTCON to copy the print jobs to every user, he creates the new set of print jobs for one user and copies the file to everyone's mail directory. Then he creates two groups, one for order entry, and one for shipping, and adds an entry to the system login script like the following:

IF MEMBER OF SHIPPING THEN CAPTURE J=LINE

for each group. This sets the default job correctly for each group.

Then he changes the printer configuration for the order entry department's print server to match their new laser printer. He leaves the queue alone—there shouldn't be any problem there. Testing the printer, he finds no problems from any of several workstations.

### Lessons Learned

▸ Most of the printing problems you will encounter are the results of incorrect setups of the printer, workstation, print server, or queue. Double-check all configuration items before you go to the next step.

▸ Make sure that cabling, interrupts, and printer configurations are correctly set and match the corresponding settings in the workstation.

▸ Take the troubleshooting process systematically—it's complex, but can be resolved if you take it one step at a time.

### The Fault Point Chain

▸ The workstation shell and CAPTURE setup.

▸ The queue on the server.

▸ The print server attached to the queue.

▸ The server or router on which PSERVER is running.

▸ The configuration of the PC.

▸ The connection to the printer.

▸ The printer's configuration.

▸ The printer hardware.

## SCENARIO THREE

The administrator, Fran, encounters a problem with a user who can't print any more. She isolates the problem to a single workstation, then finds the problem on that workstation and fixes it.

### Snapshot—Scenario Three

Is This an Existing Printer Setup?

Is the Printer Operational?

Is the Print Server Operational?

Can You Print from Some Workstations?

Can You Put Print Jobs Directly into the Queue with PCONSOLE? Do They Print?

Is the Queue Connected to PSERVER?

Can You Print from DOS on the Print Server?

Is Printing Only Affected on One, or a Few Workstations?

Can You Print from DOS on the Workstation?

If You Can Print from DOS, It's Probably the Application.

Fran receives a call that one of the printers in the marketing department is not working. On arriving, she checks with the user first, to find out exactly what the problem is. The user says that an application won't print to the PostScript printer any more. Fran begins by checking the printer and print server. The printer is online and has paper, and the print server is operational. She checks around and finds that other people on the network can print, both from DOS and from the application the user is trying to print from. Fran tries inserting a print job with PCONSOLE. It prints fine. She then tries printing from DOS. The job prints to the other printer in the department.

A light dawns. She types CAPTURE and finds that the default capture is to the wrong printer. The system login script is set up so that the default printer is the text printer. If the user is using a program that needs Post-Script, she puts them in a group called PostScript, which uses a line in the system login script like the following:

```
IF MEMBER OF GROUP POSTSCRIPT THEN CAPTURE
J=LASERWRITER.
```

However, this user has a line in their AUTOEXEC.BAT file that sets CAP-TURE J=HP (for the Hewlett-Packard LaserJet), which executes after the user logs in to the network. She looks at the date on the AUTOEXEC.BAT and finds it is over two years old, dating back to before they had a PostScript printer.

Further research shows that the user had been playing with their AUTOEXEC.BAT and accidentally deleted it, then copied an old version off a backup floppy they had kept from long ago. Fran copies the standard AUTOEXEC.BAT file she has created and stored in the SYS:PUBLIC directory onto the PC, and then modifies it slightly for that particular user. She reboots the PC, and everything works as it should.

> **There will always be some way the user can mess things up.**

### Lessons Learned

Fran followed good troubleshooting procedure here. This is a good example of how even an inexperienced user would have been able to follow the proper steps and come to the same conclusion. Some things that Fran might have done to speed the process up are listed below.

- Ask the user if they've changed anything on their system recently. Fran might have been able to save herself some time by discovering first that the user had changed their AUTOEXEC.BAT file. Again, if you don't have to count on the user for information, your life will be easier. If Fran had a configuration worksheet for the user's workstation, she might have noticed right away that the date and size of the AUTOEXEC.BAT file didn't match the standard.

- No matter how much time and effort you spend making sure that every user is configured properly, there will always be some way the user can mess things up. Be on the lookout for the things that the user can affect—their personal login script, the configuration files on their PC, the default print job as set in PRINTCON, and so on.

▸ If you have a standard operating system, set of network drivers, configuration files, and so on, you can make your life easier. For example, in this case Fran noticed that the AUTOEXEC.BAT file had a date that was older than it should have been. If she hadn't been aware of this, she'd have had to reboot the PC and look at the messages on the screen as it booted and the user logged in, or opened the file with a text editor to have found the problem.

### The Fault Point Chain

▸ The workstation shell and CAPTURE setup.

▸ The queue on the server.

▸ The print server attached to the queue.

▸ The server or router PSERVER is running on.

▸ The configuration of the PC.

▸ The connection to the printer.

▸ The printer's configuration.

▸ The printer hardware.

## SCENARIO FOUR

The administrator deals with a problem typical of AppleTalk networks, especially ones with a mixed LocalTalk and EtherTalk environment.

### Snapshot—Scenario Four

Is This an Existing Printer Setup?

Is the Printer Operational?

Is the Printer Connected to the Network?

Does the Printer Show Up in the Correct AppleTalk Zone?

Can You Print from Some Workstations?

Jethro receives a call that one of the Mac users can't see their printer in the Chooser any more. He arrives, and after assuring himself that the Chooser is set to the correct EtherTalk zone, begins to track the problem down. The Mac's Chooser does list the correct number of zones, and shows the server under File Sharing, so Jethro assumes that the Mac's connection to the network is working. He checks on another Mac and the printer isn't visible there, either. Since the printer is supposed to be available (you can

> **With printing problems, first find out how many users are affected.**

hide the actual printer from the Chooser and make only the NetWare queue available), Jethro assumes that the problem isn't related to the queue or printer server.

He quickly takes a look at the printer itself—it's turned on and seems to be working correctly: no error lights, the cover is closed, and so on. Jethro resets the printer just to make sure, and rechecks the Chooser. Still nothing. Then he remembers that the Macs are all connected with EtherTalk, not LocalTalk. That means that the LaserWriter must either be connected to the server with an EtherTalk card, or have a LocalTalk to EtherTalk bridge.

He finds a bridge in the morass of wiring under the printer. He powers it off and on again, hoping to reset its configuration, but when he checks the Chooser, there is still no printer showing. Then he digs up the control software for the bridge, downloads a new control file and restarts it. When the restart finishes, the printer is showing in the Chooser again.

**NOTE**
See Appendix A for information about downloading updated software.

### Lessons Learned

> ► Macintosh networks are no longer the simple creatures they once were. In search of higher performance, many networks now use EtherTalk, rather than AppleTalk. If your network is set up this way, don't forget that any AppleTalk device, including the printers must have some device that makes it available to the

EtherTalk network. This may be an AppleTalk card in the server or Mac, an AppleTalk to EtherTalk bridge, the built-in EtherTalk interface in a LaserWriter IIf or IIg, or a specialized bridge intended only for use with printers. Each of these devices must also have the correct software to enable it to run properly.

▶ Just because the lights are on doesn't mean a device is functioning correctly. It is very difficult to tell the status of a laser printer, especially with LaserWriters, which have no status panel as many other laser printers do.

▶ With printing problems, one of the first things you should do is find out how many users are affected. This will keep you from wasting time checking a workstation's connections and networking software when the problem is actually with the printer or print server. Another way to approach this is to see if the workstation's network connection is still working—is the file server still available? If it is, then the problem is not likely to be related to the connection.

## The Fault Point Chain

▶ The Macintosh AppleTalk and EtherTalk software.

▶ The Mac's connection to the network, including NIC and connections.

▶ The bridge from the print server to the LocalTalk printer.

▶ The printer.

In this case, the queue and print server are not part of the fault chain, since the Macintoshes were printing directly to the LaserWriter, rather than to the queue. If NetWare for Macintosh had been set up so that only the queue was available in the Chooser, and the printer itself hidden, then it would have been necessary to include the queue and printer server in the troubleshooting process, as it would have been if a similar problem had occurred with PCs.

# PART II

# Disasters

The two chapters in this part cover the steps you can take to prepare for disasters or prevent them from happening, and the procedures you should follow once disaster strikes.

Chapter 5: A Pound of Prevention, covers the steps you should take beforehand to prevent or at least minimize disasters. It discusses precautions you can take to make recovery after a disaster less of a problem, as well as the most likely areas to be struck by disaster and the best methods for protecting them.

Chapter 6: Coping With Disaster, discusses methods for dealing with recovery after a disaster strikes. You'll see how to assess which services can be established in-house, and which ones are better handled by outside contractors.

# CHAPTER 5

# A Pound of Prevention

# Introduction

**A**s administrator of even a small network, you can spend most of your time putting out fires—reacting to problems, rather than planning for them. Prevention is a difficult area for most administrators. The time and expense involved are hard to justify, because, if you do it correctly, the problems you prevent will never show up; and it can be hard to convince your supervisors to spend money on something that might never occur. Some preventive measures are becoming easier to justify—when PC-based networks first began cropping up, backup systems were not always included as a matter of course. Now, it would (or at least should) be highly unusual to see more than three or four PCs networked without some type of backup system in place. Uninterruptible Power Supplies (UPSes) are becoming equally common, at least on servers.

Other types of prevention and preventive maintenance will be harder to justify. One plan of attack is to begin small and document the results. The difference between a network with no down time during business hours in the course of a year and one in which several failures interrupt business for hours or even days is not hard to quantify. If you can improve your up time by some quantifiable amount, and show where other preventive measures would have reduced or eliminated down time, you will have less trouble justifying future requests.

The last area to look at is tracking the growth of your LAN, and planning for the future. It may seem that the new high-powered server you just installed should last for a good while, but suppose the department has also grown by 20 workstations, and that the average load per workstation has increased by a factor of four as users begin to be accustomed to their new PCs. Tracking this sort of growth will enable you to justify and install upgrades or additional equipment as necessary to meet the growing needs of your users.

This chapter will cover the following topics:

- Backups
- Power

- ▸ Quality Equipment

- ▸ Preventive Maintenance and Related Precautions

- ▸ Fault Tolerance

- ▸ Network Plans and Logs

- ▸ Baselining

- ▸ Training the User

- ▸ Viruses

- ▸ Security

- ▸ Recovering from Disaster—In Advance

## Backups

Every network that does more than allow printer sharing should have a backup system. You will need backups. Eventually, any LAN administrator who doesn't have a verified backup plan working will regret it. Even mirroring disks is not a substitute for a good backup procedure. Besides the eventual necessity for restoring a drive that breaks, users will occasionally delete files that are still needed. If a server's drive is close to full, the NetWare SALVAGE utility, or similar utilities from other vendors, may not be

**Backups are not a luxury but a necessity.**

able to recover deleted files, depending on how long it's been since the file was deleted.

Thanks to the growing awareness that backups are not a luxury but a necessity, there are numerous systems available from many manufacturers. There are several varieties—¼" tape in several types of cassettes, 8 mm and 4 mm (DAT), even systems that use video cassettes. Usually, there are only a few companies making the actual mechanisms, which are then packaged with different software and sold under brand names. The software is a major part of the difference between different brands, and much more important than a slight difference in speed or transfer rate.

The PC and LAN magazines probably publish half a dozen evaluations a year of backup units between them. Read the latest articles to gain an idea of what's available. You will usually also learn which units to avoid, and why, and which variety of tape is currently considered the best.

When evaluating a backup system, there are a number of factors to consider: capacity, speed, software, cost of media, the cost of the unit, the reliability of the drive, and support from the manufacturer.

## CAPACITY

What is the capacity of the tape drive? It should be enough to support your current configuration, and at least double your current disk drive capacity. Don't buy a 150 MB tape system if you have a 150 MB hard drive—in a year you will probably have 600 MB of hard disk space. Besides, the difference in price between a 150 MB tape drive and an 8GB tape drive is relatively little.

If your backup capacity is limited, back up data first, applications second. Applications, and the NetWare directories, which can be reinstalled and usually don't change after installation, can be backed up once in a while, when new versions are installed. Data, on the other hand, should be backed up regularly, nightly if possible. If backup capacity is an issue, nightly incremental backups of data are better than weekly full backups.

## SPEED

Speed is an issue not because you will be sitting and watching the backup (the software should allow unattended backups), but because you need to schedule the backup for a time of day when nobody will be using the network, and that time may be limited. If you designate 2:00 AM to 6:00 AM as the time when no one will be using the system, your tape drive should be able to back up your system in less than four hours.

## SOFTWARE

The most important thing to evaluate in choosing a tape drive is the software provided with it. This may range from no software at all to a versatile suite of programs that will not only do your backups at 2:00 AM for you, but verify the tape and inform you of any errors. Another issue is whether the program supports any name spaces you may be using. All programs will support the DOS name space, but if you are using Mac, NFS, OS/2, or other name spaces, make sure that your backup program will support them.

## COST OF MEDIA

This will be more important in the long run than the cost of the drive. If you use 20 tapes for your incremental backups, and 2 tapes a month for full backup that are then stored off-site, you will use about 50 tapes a year. In two years, this expense could be more than the cost of the drive. In some cases, lower-cost alternatives exist. For example, in an 8 mm tape drive, you can use 8 mm video tape instead of data-certified tapes, at a cost savings of about half. However, unless your software verifies the backup every time it is made, and is capable of bypassing a bad block on the tape, you may get backups that can't be restored from and never know it. The few hundred dollars a year you save isn't worth it if you can't restore from the tapes.

## COST OF THE UNIT

Tape backup units range in price from a couple of hundred dollars for a 60 MB unit to thousands of dollars for a unit that will do a month's worth of unattended backups on a multi-gigabyte system. Within any standard (such as 4 mm DAT), the mechanisms are often similar or the same. What you'll pay for is the software and support. Determine what capacity you need, double it, and then buy the best software you can afford. Remember, your server's disk contains hundreds or thousands of hours of work, at many dollars an hour. Don't skimp on the backup system.

### RELIABILITY

It does no good to have an extensive backup system in place, and then discover that the tape drive has failed or that the software didn't inform you that the backup tapes had bad blocks and your backups can't be used. Read the magazines for impressions of the internal mechanisms and the various companies that package them. Before you buy a unit, you might also want to ask about it on CompuServe, or at your local CNEPA chapter meeting or Novell User Group.

### SUPPORT

Support can be difficult to evaluate in advance, except by learning what experiences others have had with the company. Ask the company for names of users in your area. In reading reviews, check to see if the reviewers tried to access the tech support or had hardware or setup problems. Check the forums on CompuServe or your local user group meetings.

> **Test whatever backup system you have in place.**

You might also try placing a test call to the backup system manufacturer's support line, to see how easy or difficult it may be to get help when you actually need it, and to get first-hand experience of the support process for the device.

Finally, test whatever backup system you have in place. After the hard disk has disintegrated is no time to discover that those backup tapes you've been making for the last year can only produce an "Error reading from tape" message.

### STRATEGY

Your backup strategy will depend on your users' needs. There are many possible strategies, ranging from a full backup of all files daily to an incremental backup that only adds files that have changed since the last backup. Each strategy has advantages and disadvantages. A daily full backup provides the maximum possible level of recoverability, but uses a very large number of tapes; the incremental systems use fewer tapes, but take more effort to recover complete file systems.

You may also wish to use an off-site storage service for some or all of your backups. This is a typical part of most disaster recovery plans. It allows a business to restore working files to new servers after fire, earthquake, theft or other disasters that could affect any backups stored near the original server.

## WORKSTATION BACKUPS

I strongly recommend that you confine the data on workstations to the operating system and applications. Instruct your users to store their data on the file server. This will ensure that the data is included in the regularly scheduled backups. In almost every case, if the application is on the local drive and the data is on the server, users will not notice any degradation in performance. (The sole exception to this rule might be Macintoshes networked with Local-Talk, but for around $100 per Mac you can convert the network to EtherTalk.) In most cases, performance when accessing applications should actually improve. Unfortunately, with most operating systems, there is no way to prevent the user from storing data on the local hard drive (UNIX being a notable exception). The only way to deal with this problem is education and continuing reminders. Of course, you could have a backup tape device in each workstation, and automatically back up each machine every night—internal tape units for PCs are quite inexpensive. This is a good way to go if users must store data on their workstations.

> **Store applications on workstations and data on the file server.**

There are several other solutions to the problem of backing up workstations. You can create a backup volume on a server, and create batch files that log in and copy everything on the workstation hard drive to that area. For example, if you have 20 users on your network, each with a hard disk of 40 MB, this system would back up every workstation once every 20 days and use 40 MB of disk space on the server. Each day's backup can be deleted from the server after the volume has been backed up to tape, to make room for the next workstation backup.

Another approach is to get a small portable tape drive that attaches to a workstation's parallel port (or a Mac's SCSI port). You can then back up each workstation in rotation with this device. If, as suggested, the workstation has only the operating system and applications, this sort of backup will be necessary only when a system is first configured, and then when significant changes have been made, such as the installation or upgrading of applications or the operating system.

## Power

Given the number of problems that can follow power loss or fluctuation, a good UPS, Standby Power Supply (SPS), or at least a surge protector is a very cheap investment. It doesn't take a lightning storm to damage computer equipment—the spikes caused by some appliances being turned on or off, static discharges from a variety of sources, including users, and older power company equipment may cause enough variation in power to damage equipment.

There are several levels of protection against faulty power. The first level is a surge protector, which will screen out harmful over-voltages, surges, and spikes. It will not protect you if the power goes off. The second level of protection is an SPS. It switches to a battery-powered power supply if it detects problems with your power. It will provide protection against brown-outs and power outages. The third level of protection is a UPS. This type of protection is the ultimate—your computer is always powered by the battery-powered power supply, which is constantly being recharged by your normal AC power. This means that there is no direct connection between your line power and the computer. There is also no switch-over time as with an SPS.

There are several items to check before buying power protection. First look at the manufacturer's warranty. Some manufacturers will replace any equipment damaged by power variations while connected to their system. Another item to look at carefully is whether a battery-powered unit is an SPS or a true UPS. The UPSes tend to be a little more expensive, although both types are much less expensive than they were a few years ago. The last item to look at is the power supplied from the battery—is it true sine wave? Some units simulate sine wave power, which can provide slightly different results that very sensitive equipment might not like.

Evaluating the power requirement of your computer system is fairly simple. Look on the power supply of each unit that will be attached (system unit, monitor, external disk drive, and so on). Each power supply should have a rated capacity in amps. Usual figures are in the neighborhood of 5 to 7 amps for the CPU, 1.5 to 2 for small monitors, 5 to 10 for large monitors, 2 for external hard disks, and the like. If the total is 10, multiply that by the voltage of your system (110 in the US). The total figure, 1100, is the maximum number of volt-amps (VA) your system can use.

For a workstation with a small (14") monochrome monitor, a 400 VA power supply will probably provide 10–20 minutes of backup. For a workstation with a large screen monitor, you might need 600–800 VA. A server with a couple of external hard drive subsystems should probably have 800-1200 VA for a reasonably long duration if the power goes off.

Both the simulated sine wave power supplies and the SPS devices have come a long way in the last few years. It is difficult any longer to say that a UPS is distinctly better than an SPS, or that true sine wave is better than simulated. However, with prices on even the best units dropping as they are, UPSes, true sine wave power supplies, and the premium surge protection systems are the best bets. See the latest reviews in your favorite PC and LAN magazines.

Another issue for the server is the UPS interface. Most UPS and SPS devices provide a serial connection or a card for the server that will allow the server to detect a power outage and shut down properly if necessary before the battery power runs down.

**WARNING**
**Do NOT plug a laser printer into a UPS. Laser printers use a heating element in the fuser assembly that probably draws more power than your server and all its add-ons.**

A reasonable balance of protection and cost is to put a surge protector on every computer, and a UPS on each server. Modems and fax machines should also be protected—phone lines can also transmit potentially harmful variations in current, and surge protectors with phone line filtering capability are available. If cost is not a large factor, or if some workstations are mission-critical, consider using UPSes on workstations as well.

## Quality Equipment

The difference in price between an inexpensive clone server and a high-performance, brand-name server can be double or more—however, 8 hours of down time for a department of 20 can cause a loss of more money, not counting the possibility of deadlines missed, extra costs to rush jobs through, overtime, repairs to the downed equipment, and so on.

This is not to say that even the most expensive equipment will not break down occasionally, but it should be less likely to do so. The service providers should be more responsive as well, and it's easier to find replacement parts for brand-name equipment, although some major brands tend to use proprietary parts, which can mean that replacements can only be obtained from the original vendor, at rather high prices.

Many computer manufacturers and retailers are sensitive to the special requirements of servers. In addition to bigger PCs with extra-high-speed interfaces and more drive slots, they may offer both added features to make their equipment more reliable and service programs that guarantee repair or replacement of defective parts within a matter of hours. The added features may include redundant power supplies or special bus slots that allow swapping cards in and out with the PC still running.

Again, even the most expensive, best-rated equipment can break down. In the case of mission-critical equipment, it's not a bad idea to have a replacement machine, fully configured, ready to replace an existing machine if necessary. The investment can readily be recouped by avoiding the delay necessary to buy new equipment if the existing setup goes down, especially in cases where such orders must be processed by a purchasing department or something similar. In a large wide-area network, having a standard server configuration can make it much easier to provide parts, and of course will also make it easier for the corporate MIS department to support the platform. Also see Fault Tolerance, below.

## Preventive Maintenance and Related Precautions

Regular maintenance is often omitted, either because it isn't seen as a high enough priority to justify the time spent, or simply because it can be a chore. It can save the administrator considerable trouble, however. It is much easier to fix something before it becomes a problem than to wait until it interferes with a user's work, requires the administrator's time for emergency repairs, and costs money to replace parts that might have lasted much longer with good maintenance.

### DUST AND OTHER CONTAMINANTS

It is impossible to avoid dust getting into equipment, and too much dust may have unfortunate consequences. To minimize dust, make sure that slot covers are replaced if cards are removed from a PC, and that the case is completely closed. This can also prevent bugs in the machinery—literally! Insects of many types and even mice have been known to take up lodgings inside computers, often with very strange results. In commercial settings, the normal dust can have a fairly high metallic content, and too thick an accumulation can cause electrical shorts. It can also interfere with ventilation, causing overheating and shortening the life of equipment as well as causing failures. Regular vacuuming and adequate ventilation can extend the life of equipment.

Keyboards are also susceptible to dust, and to many other forms of contamination, from food to eraser shavings. Again, regular vacuuming is a simple way to prevent failures. Keeping monitor screens clean may not increase the life of the monitor, but it will definitely reduce eyestrain among users—the static charge that normally builds up on most monitors collects dust and other airborne particles like a magnet. Mouse devices will also last longer and function better if they are cleaned regularly.

## CONNECTIONS

There are no perfect connections. It is a good idea to schedule some time every six months or so to check all the computers on a LAN for loose connections—power cords, monitor, network, serial and parallel cables, and the cards. A power cord that is loose in the receptacle in the power supply can cause arcing, which can not only cause the eventual failure of the power supply, but can generate interference with the electronics in the PC. Likewise, a network connection that is not fully seated may not simply fail, but may produce intermittent problems that are very difficult to trace. Make sure that all fasteners are screwed down snugly, and that everything is seated properly.

## ANTI-STATIC PRECAUTIONS

Walking across a carpeted room can build up a 50,000 volt charge in your body. Discharging this voltage into electronic equipment designed to deal with a maximum of 12 volts can destroy it. Newer electronics, with their tighter tolerances and lower power requirements, are even more susceptible to static than older equipment. An anti-static mat and professional-quality grounding strap are quite inexpensive—some hardware maintenance courses include a set as part of the cost of the course. In any case, the investment is much less than almost any circuit board.

Not following anti-static precautions may not result in dead equipment—static can cause cumulative, non-fatal damage that has the effect of drastically shortening the life of electronics. Save the anti-static bags that most cards come in; they can make the safe transportation of parts much easier.

## MAINTAINING A RETURN PATH

Another precaution that takes a little extra trouble, but can make the administrator's life much easier, is to provide a simple return path to the old version of anything being changed or upgraded. Rename AUTOEXEC.BAT files to AUTOEXEC.OLD, and save old versions of applications, drivers, and so on. It's much easier to make sure that you have a good copy of a setup that works than to try to recreate a configuration from memory, or track down and reload an application, its updates, new version of printer drivers, and the like, all of which may be in different locations.

Similarly, when upgrading hardware, don't rush to throw the old equipment out. It's much better to be able to get a workstation running again with a monochrome monitor and have at least partial functionality, than to have to either rush out and buy another VGA card, or wait for Purchasing to buy one and forward it to you, if a new card fails.

# Fault Tolerance

In the old days of mainframe and terminals, everything had a backup. There was a generator that took over if power failed, and pretty much any part that failed in the mainframe would have a backup part that took over without interrupting service. As PC networks have begun to be used for the same sorts of things that mainframes were used for—namely, applications in which a few hours without service could literally ruin a company—manufacturers have begun to provide the same sorts of redundancy and fault tolerance. Novell has led the way in providing System Fault Tolerance (SFT) as a part of NetWare.

The first level of SFT provides for protection from disk drive failure in several ways. First, it performs read-after-write verification. Data written to disk is read immediately and compared with the data still in memory. If there is a difference, the block on the disk that was written to is marked as bad. The Hot Fix Redirection area is that part of the disk which is used to provide substitute blocks for any blocks on the disk that fail. If your Hot Fix Redirection area starts getting full, it is a sign that the disk is failing.

Next, SFT allows duplexed and mirrored drives. With both techniques, each logical drive is actually two physical drives—data written to a drive is actually written to two different mirrored drives. This has two benefits: it is a highly effective precaution against drive failure, and it effectively reduces the access time of any physical drive by 50 percent. Technically, the difference between these methods is that a mirrored drive may have two drives connected to the same controller and power supply, while a duplexed drive has separate power supplies, and controllers, so that no one failure will result in a loss of data or access to data. Figure 5.1 illustrates the difference.

FIGURE 5.1

*Duplexing and mirroring*

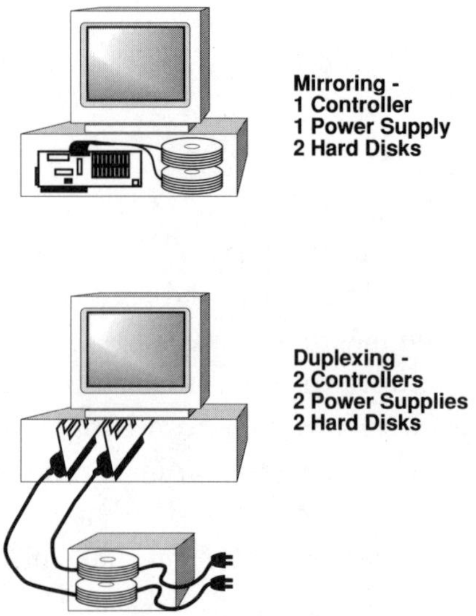

Mirroring -
1 Controller
1 Power Supply
2 Hard Disks

Duplexing -
2 Controllers
2 Power Supplies
2 Hard Disks

Mirroring doubles the cost of data storage, but in mission-critical areas, it can prevent a much more costly loss of time, productivity, and data. If a drive fails in a mirrored system, the users don't even notice—the administrator is notified, and can replace the defective drive when it won't disrupt the network.

The next level of System Fault Tolerance, SFT III, provides complete protection against any failure of any component in a server—the whole server is duplicated. All functions of the main server are duplicated on the mirror server. If anything happens to the first server, the second server takes over and service is not interrupted. The servers can even monitor each other for hardware problems and take over if a fault is causing a slowdown in networking capability. Figure 5.2 illustrates this concept.

FIGURE 5.2
*SFT III—Mirrored Servers*

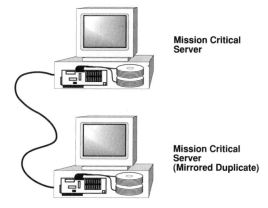

**Mission Critical
Server**

**Mission Critical
Server
(Mirrored Duplicate)**

The cost involved will be double that of a single server, but in mission-critical circumstances, this technique will insure that no single equipment failure can bring down the network. Moreover, because the two servers don't need to be right next to each other, it can also provide insurance against theft, fire, or other catastrophes in a building destroying all networking capability.

# Network Plans and Logs

Keep a record of existing configurations. This not only makes it easier to plan upgrades and determine possible causes without opening PCs, it provides a place to return to if an upgrade or new configuration doesn't work. If you include serial numbers in your log, it will make dealing with most technical support departments much easier—instead of having to trot down the aisle, open a PC and pull a card to get the serial number, you will have it on record, easily accessible when calling tech support.

**The more documentation you have for your network, the less time it will take to recover from a disaster.**

The level of documentation that you have for your network will directly affect the time it takes to recover from a disaster. Ideally, you should document all of the following:

▶ Each server and workstation's hardware configuration, including processor, memory, floppy and hard disk types, installed cards and their settings, and any other hardware additions.

▶ The software configuration of each workstation—OS version, printouts and/or backup copies of configuration files such as AUTOEXEC.BAT, CONFIG.SYS, SHELL.CFG, WIN.INI and SYSTEM.INI, a printout of the directory structure, a list of applications, including version, license number (if applicable), and any other specialized software such as device drivers.

▶ The last goes for the server too—you do have printouts of your AUTOEXEC.NCF and STARTUP.NCF files, don't you? How long would it take you to recreate them if they were lost? Even if you have good backups, you may wish you had a map of the directory structure on all volumes of your server, copies of NET$OS.EXE or SERVER.EXE, and the other .DSK and .LAN drivers necessary to boot the server, and any other configuration files or drivers stored in the DOS partition of the boot drive.

▸ Maps of the physical and the logical structure of your LAN. The physical map will help you with problems in the cabling plant, and the logical map will help you to conceptually isolate the fault points involved in any particular problem.

▸ The backup plan—what tapes are used in what rotation? How often are full backups made, and where are they stored? Remember—your assistant might be the one guessing which tape to restore from.

▸ Procedures to follow in case you aren't there—what do the users do if a print server hangs the day after you leave for a two-week training seminar? You may also need a quick reminder yourself if it's something you haven't dealt with for a long while.

All this information can be collected manually, and should be, if there's no other alternative. However, there are programs that will do all the data collection for you, nicely format the reports, and update the information automatically each time a workstation is logged onto the network.

Using a network analyzer or a statistics program such as FCONSOLE to get an idea of normal traffic on your network will make it much easier to isolate problems caused by abnormal traffic. (See Baselining below.)

Keeping a log of changes to the LAN, and of problems that have come up and the solution, will also save you a good deal of time. Recreating a solution that took 20 hours of work to discover the first time doesn't make sense, especially when a few minutes spent logging the problem and solution can prevent the necessity.

A log can also be useful in other ways. It can allow you to establish trends with problem equipment, situations, or users. It is much easier to justify a more reliable (and more expensive) server if you have documented how many times the current model has failed in the last year. A log can also provide documentation of how you spend your time. Many managers want regular status reports; a well-kept log can provide the basis, or may even be copied and pasted into a template status report. Even if a regular status report is not required, a log can make justifying a promotion or getting additional personnel much easier.

**NOTE**
**The FCONSOLE program is discussed under Baselining, below.**

# Baselining

Baseline information about your network can be invaluable when odd things begin happening. Depending on the level of resources available to you, baselining your network could mean anything from knowing how often collisions show on a transceiver, to maintaining a complete network traffic history automatically created and updated by a sophisticated network analysis package. Such a package can not only show network traffic patterns over an extended period of time, but can be set to warn you if limits are exceeded, or if any of dozens of types of events occur.

Baselining is also essential to being prepared for future growth. Without some idea of how much traffic is increasing over time on your network, you won't be able to spot approaching overloads of servers or LAN segments until it is too late and LAN performance has suffered. Keep records of at least the average server utilization and number of packets received. This can be done with FCONSOLE or MONITOR, although it isn't easy—there are inexpensive programs that can make this much easier, from free programs available on the CompuServe NetWare forums, to LANalyzer for Windows. See Appendix A for resources that can help you learn what's available and best for your network.

## MONITORING THE SERVER

You should at least use the tools built into NetWare to become aware of the normal state of your network. Following the history of certain items can also let you know when it's time to add more memory to your server, or if a hard disk is beginning to fail.

As you saw in Chapter 1, when an existing server begins having problems servicing users, the most common reason is memory. Often, the initial amount of RAM in the server and the settings for memory allocation seem sufficient, but prove otherwise after a period of growth or as users begin to really make use of the network. The second biggest problem of this nature is disk space. Users will expand their disk usage to fill any possible amount of disk space. You can either monitor them and ask heavy users to cut back, or resolve to allow for regular increases in the size of your server's disk space.

NetWare uses as much memory as it can get for cache buffers. When NetWare receives a request for information on one of its disks, it copies the whole block into memory. Then, every time it receives a request for that data, it reads from memory, rather than from the disk. This speeds access to the data by thousands of times. As new disk requests come in, the oldest requests are flushed from memory to make room for the new. Thus, the larger the pool of memory allocated for cache buffers, the more likely that a disk request can be serviced from memory, rather than from the disk. Any memory not necessary for other services is used for cache buffers. Adding RAM for caching is often the cheapest improvement you can make in your server.

### NetWare 2.x

To monitor memory usage, use FCONSOLE to check the Disk Request Serviced From Cache line in the File Server Statistics Summary, and Dynamic Memory Pool Statistics Peak Usage. If less than 93 percent or so of the disk requests are being serviced from disk instead of memory, or if the peak usage is at or near the maximum, add more memory. You should be able to watch these numbers approach the recommended maximum as network utilization increases.

Also check the I/O Error Count under Hot Fix with FCONSOLE. If the error count is not zero, the hard disk is experiencing failures. You should monitor it carefully. One failure may not indicate a hard disk about to fail catastrophically, but a series of errors in a short period, or a small but steady number of errors over time, indicate that the drive should be completely backed up and then replaced as soon as possible.

### NetWare 3.x

NetWare 3.x is capable of dynamically reallocating memory. It will use all available memory not being used for other things such as NLMs for disk cache buffers. Therefore, MONITOR best indicator of your total memory utilization is the Available Cache Buffers line. The other statistics below will also help you monitor the performance of your server.

**Available Cache Buffers**    If the total number of available cache buffers gets too low, it's a signal that the server's memory is almost all in use. Also, the number of disk requests that must be read from disk (rather than from the cache buffers) in memory will increase, slowing the performance of the server down. If the available cache buffers drops below 20 percent, you could experience data loss under some circumstances. This would mean that in a server with 16 MB of RAM, only 3 MB would be available for cache buffers. You should start planning to increase memory if the percentage drops below 50.

**Percentage Of Utilization**    This statistic shows how much of the total processing power of the CPU is in use. It thus gives you a basic indication of the load on the server. If this number is above 75 percent or so on a regular basis, you should consider upgrading to a faster processor.

**Alloc Short Term Memory**    The default size of the pool of Alloc Short Term Memory is 2 MB. As the amount in use gets close to 2 MB, you should increase the size of the pool with the SET command. Also, you should monitor the resource tags for this memory pool. If you see a module (usually an NLM) using an ever-increasing amount of memory, it's likely there's a problem with that NLM. If unloading and reloading the NLM doesn't fix the problem, see if there's an update or bug fix for the NLM.

**Service Processes**    The number of service processes indicates outstanding read requests. If an application issues a read request to the server and the disk can't be accessed immediately, a service process is created that will fulfill the read request as soon as possible. If there aren't enough cache buffers, the number of service requests will go up, since more requests will have to be serviced from the slower disk instead of memory. Further, the disk can only be accessed by one request at a time, whereas more than one cache buffer can be accessed at once.

If you have enough memory and are still getting service processes, you have a problem either with disk I/O or with packet receive buffers. You might consider upgrading to an EISA system and bus mastering controllers for the hard disks, a faster CPU, or spreading disk usage out by using multiple hard disk adapters or spanning volumes across multiple disks.

**Packet Receive Buffers**    Packet receive buffers hold packets from workstations until the server can process them and initiate service requests. The default number of buffers is 100. If the number of allocated buffers gets close to 100, increase the number of buffers with the SET PACKET RECEIVE BUFFERS=xx command in STARTUP.NCF. If you have a large number of packet receive buffers allocated, (it could be up to one for every ISA workstation attached to the server or up to 41 per EISA workstation), the requests to the server from the workstations aren't being serviced fast enough.

You can address this problem by increasing the number of service processes, and by increasing disk I/O, either with faster controllers and disks, or by increasing the memory available for cache buffering.

**Disk-Full Early Warning**    You can have NetWare warn you if the available disk space on any volume drops too low, by setting the Volume Low Warning Threshold, and the Volume Low Warning Reset Threshold. These parameters are specified with the SET command or in STARTUP.NCF. Specify the number of blocks. The default is 256 blocks, which with 4 KB blocks, will warn you when the available space drops below 1 MB. You may want to set this to a larger number—1 MB of space isn't much any more.

### NetWare 4.x

NetWare 4.x adds a number of new tools for monitoring the server. In general, the items above under NetWare 3.x apply to 4.x as well. In addition, NetWare 4.x allows you to monitor the percentage of disk requests that are serviced from cache buffers rather than from the disk. It can also show you the processes currently running and how much of the available processing power they are using, and it can provide early warnings in the event of insufficient memory for cache buffers or full disks.

**Cache Buffer Hits**   Rather than simply telling you what percentage of the total server memory is available for cache buffers, NetWare 4.x will allow you to specifically monitor the percentage of disk requests that have been serviced from memory instead of from disk. MONITOR displays the Percentage of Long Term Cache Hits. Keeping the percentage above 90 will result in optimum performance.

**Processor Utilization**   NetWare 3.x displays processor utilization in its main MONITOR display. In addition to this, NetWare 4.x has a new menu item in MONITOR, Processor Utilization, that will allow you to track the processes and interrupts (I/O—both disk and LAN cards) that are running on the server, and how much of the available processing power they are using.

**Cache Buffer Early Warning**   You can use SERVMAN to set NetWare 4.x to warn you if the number of available cache buffers drops too low. To do so, set the Minimum File Cache Buffer Report Threshold to 100. This parameter is set in the File Caching submenu of the Console Set Commands menu. It can also be set directly in the STARTUP.NCF file.

**Disk-Full Early Warning**   You can use SERVMAN to set NetWare 4.x to warn you if the available disk space on any volume drops too low, by setting the Volume Low Warning Threshold, and the Volume Low Warning Reset Threshold. These parameters are set in the File System submenu of the

Console Set Commands menu. They can also be set directly in STARTUP.NCF. Specify the number of blocks. The default is 256 blocks, which with 4 KB blocks, will warn you when the available space drops below 1 MB. You may want to set this to a larger number—1 MB of space isn't much any more.

## UTILITIES

There are many utilities that will perform monitoring of your network and server. These range from freeware and shareware products available on CompuServe to $20,000+ network monitoring systems that run on UNIX workstations and will provide full documentation and tracking of every element of a complex company-wide WAN. Listing and documenting all the utilities available is far beyond the scope of this book.

The range and scope of utilities available is enormous. You may not need a high-end system that will provide a complete map of your network, an inventory of the software on every workstation on that network, including operating system version, network driver version, and immediate warnings if any of hundreds of problems occur. You may also not have the thousands of dollars in your budget. On the other hand, the administrator of even a small LAN might find it hard to resist a utility that will record and print out the configuration of your server, including all the bindery information, printer setups, and so on, especially if it's free.

The best sources for discovering and evaluating these utilities are (of course) the LAN magazines, your local user groups, and the forums on CompuServe. You can download many utilities (freeware and shareware) from CompuServe. As always, if you find a shareware utility useful, please send a check to the programmer. If the program saves you hours of work, the small fee is more than justified, and besides making you feel good, it will help finance updates and bug fixes on the utility, and will increase your chances of receiving updates.

Baselining and documenting of your network can be a chore, but it could save your hide in a crisis. Find out what utilities are available and use them, or record your configurations manually with the forms in Appendix B, and use NetWare's built-in utilities and simple devices like the PC transceiver's collision light, but whatever you do, get a feel for what's normal, and what things should look like, *before* something goes wrong.

## Training the User

Much of your time as an administrator will probably be used to support users, and most of the problems your users have will not be related to hardware or software failure, but to failures in understanding. From the user who can't find the "Any" key ("Press any key to continue") to the one whose document won't print because there's no paper in the printer, these people have problems that they could probably solve themselves with a little encouragement and a little training.

There are several methods you can use to train your users, and to encourage them to acquire training on their own, without being perceived as unresponsive or condescending. For example, try to put a little time between a user's request for help and your response. Don't delay obviously, just finish what you're working on first. Not only does this improve your chances of completing your regular tasks; users left to themselves for a while will sometimes be able to solve the problem on their own.

Without making the user feel stupid, you can also encourage them to read the manual by prioritizing their requests for help. Rather than jumping up from the dead PC you're working on and showing someone how to print from within their application, tell them you can't get away right now, but the information they need is in their manual.

The converse of these techniques is that if your users get accustomed to your leading them by the hand through every unfamiliar process (and some familiar ones), they will always expect these things of you. As a result, you will spend more and more time in these tasks instead of administering your network, let alone planning for the coming requirements for your organization.

The biggest hurdle you may face in training your users or getting them to be more self-sufficient will be getting support from management. The best approach to take with your supervisor is to document how you spend your time, what support requests you receive, and your proposed future projects. Let them tell you that they'd rather have you working on optimizing network performance than reading the manual for an application to a user.

# Viruses

You've documented everything in sight, you have a UPS on every workstation, you've just finished mirroring the server with SFT III, and you have a thoroughly tested backup system and the best equipment available. Then, one day, a user brings in a disk from home, loads a program onto their PC, and a short while later, your entire network is out of commission. Further, since the virus was replicated in several days of backups, it turns out that you've permanently lost 10 days of work. Sound far-fetched? It has happened. It put a flourishing British investment firm into receivership. Don't take chances. Use a network virus scanning system on your server, and equip *every* workstation with scanning software.

Keep the scanners updated too. I had a user a while ago bypass the virus scanning system on a PC and infect my network. Their reason? The virus scanner on their PC in the other building had "passed" the disk, and they knew therefore that the disk couldn't be infected. It turned out that their scanning software was over a year old...

Software developers are constantly making advances in virus detection and prevention. There are NLMs that monitor suspicious activity on the network, and new hardware add-ons that should prevent viruses from gaining access to the PC. However, the only constant in virus detection is that the virus creators will eventually figure out a way to bypass anything that comes along on the preventive side. Stay abreast of the technology. See Appendix A for some suppliers of virus detection software, and resources for learning more about detectors.

# Security

As in the virus scenario above, it does no good to protect your network against every sort of problem you can imagine, only to have a disgruntled employee or hacker reformat your hard disk or worse. There are several elements to security.

## PHYSICAL SECURITY

Your server should be physically secured. This can be difficult, especially if it is used as a print server and has printers directly connected to it. At least, lock the console on NetWare 3.x and 4.x servers, and use the dedicated mode only

**Your server should be physically secured.**

for 2.x servers and all routers. You may want to use the SECURE CONSOLE command on 3.x and 4.x servers, as well. This prevents the loading of unauthorized NLMs designed to bypass security, and it unloads DOS, so that no one can take the server down and run a DOS program to alter data or bypass security. Once DOS is unloaded, the server must be powered down and back up to reload DOS.

It is still possible to reboot a server from a floppy and load SERVER.EXE or a DOS program designed to bypass NetWare security, then access the server. If this kind of access is a concern, you can disable the floppy drives, or install a hardware password, if your server's BIOS permits it. Most 386 and 486 PCs allow this.

Another aspect to physical security involves every workstation on your network. A hacker, given access to users' PCs and desks, can often break in to their accounts, or even the supervisor account. You can limit the workstations from which the supervisor can log in to yours, and lock it up, but the best idea is to arrange for a guard to walk through the building, and make sure all users monitor unauthorized access to other PCs in their area.

## PASSWORDS

Companies that hire outside consultants to check their security are often astounded at the ease with which the consultants acquire access to their networks. Many users choose passwords that are easily guessed, or even write the passwords down and "hide" them on the bottoms of drawers and similar places. When you set up a user's account, you can set the password and keep them from changing it, set a minimum password length or force password changes at specified intervals and require that new passwords be unique, which keeps them from using the same password they had before.

Other programs will produce passwords that are not in any dictionary, yet are easy to remember. If this kind of security is a serious consideration for you, you might consider using this sort of program to issue passwords, and lock the passwords so the users can't change them.

## RIGHTS

If someone bypasses the physical security, and the login security, and is able to log in as a user, you can still limit their ability to wreak havoc on the network by setting trustee rights and file rights correctly. Trustee rights apply to individual users and define their access to directories and files; file rights apply to the files or directories themselves and define all users' access to those files. These two types of rights can aid you in preventing unauthorized modification or deletion of critical files.

For instance, the files in SYS:PUBLIC and SYS:SYSTEM are normally set read-only, so no one can change them or delete them. When updating some files in these directories, some administrators simply change all files in the directory to read/write. Failure to change them back to read-only afterwards leaves you open to anyone deleting or modifying the files.

You should also set rights carefully on applications and data files on the server. Most applications require only read rights to use them. Some applications, however, require that users be able to modify some files. You can often have separate copies of these files in each user's directory, or at least make sure that all the other files in the application's directory are write-protected.

## LOGINS

The supervisor password should be known only to you and a designated backup person as may be required by company policy. If other users need to have access to supervisor privileges, create a supervisor equivalent account. This prevents someone else from logging in as supervisor and changing the supervisor password. If they change the password on the supervisor equivalent account, you can fix that by logging in as supervisor and changing the password or even deleting the account. Just remember that there's only one supervisor account, and if you're locked out of it, regaining access to the server can be a major problem.

If this does happen, you can sometimes fix it, but it will generally require downing the server and playing games with the binderies—not for the faint of heart. There is always the possibility that you will have to recreate the binderies by hand from your documentation if something goes wrong, too... You do have your bindery information documented by now, don't you?

Many users have their login name in their AUTOEXEC.BAT file—LOGIN SERVERNAME\LOGINNAME. This means they don't have to type their login name at the login prompt, but it also provides a would-be break-in artist with half of the combination to their workstation.

## DIAL-IN ACCESS

As telecommuting becomes a reality for more workers, network administrators are increasingly faced with security problems related to dial-in access.

### Access Servers and Modem Pools

Having an access server on your network is equivalent to having a workstation plugged in at a park bench somewhere, where absolutely anyone in the world can attempt to log in. There are a number of things you can do about this. You can restrict the number of login attempts allowed during any dial-in session. This prevents hackers from dialing in and trying thousands of logins or passwords. You can also use dial-back systems. These range from a (not very secure) system that calls the user back at a number entered during the login attempt, to a system with a separate line for dialing in and dialing out, which won't even allow dialing in on the lines that dial users back.

The only constant in security systems is that anything that someone creates as the ultimate, undefeatable security system, someone else will eventually circumvent. You should make a regular effort to learn about new advances in security (and virus detection), and keep your system updated.

> **Anything that someone creates as the ultimate, undefeatable security system, someone else will eventually circumvent.**

### Modems on Workstations

In addition to the access server, you may have some users with modems on their workstations. If they routinely leave these on, a hacker could gain access to the PC, load a remote control program onto the PC and use that to attempt to log in to the server. You can address this by preventing logins from that workstation during off hours, unless the user needs to be able to access the network. At least, you should make sure that the workstation's AUTOEXEC.BAT file doesn't include the user's login name or password. The important thing is to be aware of the potential hole in your security.

## OTHER ACCESS

There are other possibilities that a hacker could use to gain access to your system. For instance, if you have NFS support on your server, a user with a UNIX workstation could mount the drives on your server that have been exported, and possibly bypass your security. You can fix this issue by setting the NFS NLM up correctly, but the point is that some add-ons may cause potential holes in your system, unless you look for them and find ways to prevent them.

# Recovering from Disaster— In Advance

Finally, you should be prepared to recover from fires, floods, and other kinds of disasters that none of the preventive techniques discussed so far can avoid.

## RECOVERY SERVICES

There are many companies, from large national organizations such as TRW and Wang, to local businesses to freelancers, offering troubleshooting and disaster-recovery services. These services may range from network analysis using a LANalyzer or other protocol analyzer, to hard disk recovery, to companies that specialize in recovering as much as possible from fire or flood-damaged systems. You should develop disaster recovery plans and set up relationships with these services in advance. It will not make things easier for you if you have to spend two days setting up an account and authorizing payment before the service will begin fixing your problems, once disaster strikes.

## THE RECOVERY PLAN

Most areas of the country have their regional disaster. Earthquakes, cyclones or hurricanes, floods, blizzards, they all have potential ramifications to your network. Pipes burst, buildings burn, and thieves steal computer equipment. You can't spend all your time worrying about what might happen, but you should take a little time to think about the possibilities and what you could do to recover from them.

Your plan may be as simple as storing your backup tapes and copies of your network documentation in a different room from the server, or as extensive as detailed lists of what steps you would take, who you would talk to, with their phone numbers and addresses, what services or equipment you'd request and what they'd cost. This will depend on the complexity of your network, and the requirement you have to get back to work quickly after a problem.

## DATA RECOVERY IN ADVANCE

There are programs available for both PCs and Macs that will (sometimes) recover deleted files or data from drives that crash or are accidentally formatted. Most of these programs have a utility that should be loaded on the workstation ahead of time. This utility will keep track of files after they have been deleted, significantly improving the recovery program's chances of getting your data back. You should consider a utility of this type for all your network workstations.

# CHAPTER 6

# Coping with Disaster

If you administer a LAN or WAN long enough, you will experience disaster. This may range from a power surge destroying the motherboard on your server, to the theft of every computer in your building, to a virus that erases your server hard drives and has infected all your backups, too, to a terrorist attack that damages the skyscraper you work in and most of your equipment. The key to surviving disaster is preparedness. See Chapter 5, A Pound of Prevention, for some suggestions on precautions you can take. However, even if you haven't taken the right precautions, there may still be hope, depending on the problem.

The most important part of your network is not the computers, the networking hardware, or the server. It's the data. Obviously, if you have had all your computers stolen, or destroyed in a fire or earthquake, you can't do much with the computers. However, if you have good backups, and logs of what equipment you had and how it was configured, you may be able to get your business back on line. Backups are the single most important precaution you can take against disaster. There is no justification at all for not regularly backing up your server.

> **The most important part of your network is the data stored on it.**

If the server's hard drive has failed, and your backups to the new drive don't work, there may still be options. There are data recovery services that specialize in recovering data from drives that have gone bad. Depending on why the drive failed, it may be possible to get some or all of the data back.

Sometimes it will prove impossible to recover your data. In that case, you will have to reconstruct the system or data. The more documentation you have, the easier this will be. The most expensive part of this, of course, will be the labor. Even a large network is not expensive compared with the cost of recreating thousands or millions of pages of data.

This chapter will cover the following topics:

- ▶ Attitude—Keeping your head
- ▶ Recovering from mechanical failure
- ▶ Recovering from software problems and user errors

- ▸ LAN failures

- ▸ Reconstruction—when all else fails

- ▸ Viruses

- ▸ Prevention

- ▸ Backups

- ▸ Disaster preparedness

- ▸ Documenting your disaster plan and your network

## Attitude: Keeping Your Head

The most important thing to remember in a disaster, however large or small, is to keep your head. Any problem can be broken down into small chunks that can be accomplished. Looking at a widespread disaster, throwing your hands up, and quitting will not solve any problems. It probably won't even make you feel any better. You need to look at the problem realistically, determine its full scope, break it down into tasks you can accomplish, and then forge ahead.

> **Any problem can be broken down into small chunks that can be accomplished.**

Another important thing to remember is that there are always options. If getting a mission-critical server back on line is your goal, for instance, you need to evaluate all possible options, including replacing the server with another workstation (your least critical user's workstation, if necessary), or calling in outside—and probably expensive—consultants in data recovery, PC hardware, or NetWare configuration, as necessary. Don't be afraid that you will look bad if you admit that a problem is beyond you, or that you can't solve it quickly without help. Your boss and colleagues should respect the priority of getting the server back up quickly. A good way to present this is to say, "I can get this done, but it may take several days or a week. Mr. Jones from Harem Guard Consulting says he can have it fixed this afternoon for $1000. That is much less than we will lose by being off-line for a few days."

Similarly, don't hesitate to ask for help from within your organization. Is there someone else who knows the system well? Can some of the users who are sitting on their hands waiting for the server to come back on line take some tasks off your hands? Don't get trapped into thinking that you must accomplish everything yourself. Asking others for help during an emergency will not only off-load some tasks, but possibly even keep users from continually asking you when things will be operational again.

## Recovering from Mechanical Failure or Destruction

If your business depends on your LAN, you should have some level of fault tolerance in place. This might be anything from a UPS and a duplexed hard drive, to a mirrored server under SFT III. Fault tolerance is summarized below in the section on prevention, and discussed in detail in the previous chapter. Your response to damaged or destroyed equipment will depend on your resources. You may be able to replace the equipment with a spare system, or you might have to rent a replacement until your system can be repaired or replaced.

The important thing is to preserve your data. If your server is damaged, for instance, the first step would be to move the hard disks to another PC and see if they work. If the drives don't function, then you can set up a new server and restore from tape. If neither step works, don't panic. There is probably a data recovery service near you that may be able to restore the data on your hard drive. They can sometimes restore data from fire- or water-damaged disks, or disks that have been hit by a power surge. They may even be able to recover some of the data if the heads have crashed. Another consultant might be able to fix the problem with your backups and get your data restored properly. These services can be expensive, but not nearly as expensive as recreating your data.

## YOUR EMERGENCY KIT

Your emergency response kit should consist of the following:

- ► A workstation boot diskette for each type of operating system and each NIC used on your network.

- ► A server boot diskette for each type of server (with NET$OS.EXE or SERVER.EXE).

- ► A spare NIC, and if possible, a set of the standard cards—disk controller, display adapter, and so on.

- ► Tools for opening and working on PCs.

- ► An anti-static strap and mat.

- ► A can of compressed air for dusting off equipment, or a vacuum.

- ► A configuration worksheet for each workstation and server.

- ► A text editor for changing configuration files.

- ► A directory on your server that contains copies of DOS, Windows, or whatever operating system you use, standard configuration files, and any other files, programs, or applications you need to set up a workstation. Make sure you have licensed copies corresponding to everything you download.

## WHAT TO TRY FIRST

Your biggest disasters will generally involve hard disks, especially your server's hard disk. As stated above, your data is the most critical part of your LAN. You can replace workstations and even the server, but your data is much harder to replace. If your server is stolen, or melted into slag in a fire, or crushed by the floor above during an earthquake, you won't be able to recover the data on the drive. Of course, if your backup tapes are lying next to the server, you may not be able to restore from them, either. This is the main reason for off-site storage of backups. (See the section below on disaster planning.) Fortunately, such disasters are rare. The typical problems you are much more likely to face will generally involve malfunctions. For example, your server may stop working;

or it may be working, but the hard disk won't be responding, will be corrupted, or will be missing files or directories.

The first thing to remember when faced with disaster is not to panic, and to never make your first step something that you can't recover from. Make sure that the malfunction is actually in the hard drive. Check the rest of the server or workstation to make sure that the other parts are all okay. If your disk is mirrored, make sure that when you re-mirror the disks, the good disk is mounted. Try running BINDFIX or VREPAIR on a server's hard drive (maybe several times), rather than reformatting or repartitioning the drive and restoring from backup. Try using a disk recovery program or running CHKDSK on a PC's disk before reformatting and reinstalling all the software. The important thing is to consider the results of what you're trying. If you get a warning like "Warning! All Data Will Be Erased!", try other things first.

## PHYSICAL RECOVERY

The first thing to do is to get the hardware functioning again. This may be as simple as replacing a hard disk controller card, or much more involved. Your disaster recovery plan should include vendors to replace nonfunctioning machines and recovery services to get damaged machines back on line. This may include a local service that can remove fire by-products, a service that can get hard drives working again, and specialists in recovery from whatever regional disaster is most likely for your area. In every case, the more planning you do in advance, the less trouble you will have when disaster occurs. Once you have the hardware functioning again, the next step is to get the data back.

### Servers

The server can be broken down into two basic areas. The first is the basic workstation hardware. This hardware is easily replaced—almost any PC clone company can provide you with a 386 or 486 PC that will do in a pinch. It doesn't have to be the latest model, just something that will function until you can get a permanent replacement. The second area is your data storage—the hard drives and associated equipment. This may include SCSI adapters, subsystems to hold the drives, and the like. Again, the basic parts are commodities, easily replaceable. Many companies keep complete back-up servers, preconfigured and ready to replace malfunctioning equipment.

### Workstations

As with servers, you may want to keep a supply of the basic parts—power supply, extra RAM chips or SIMMs, video adapter, NIC, and so on, or simply a spare workstation that you can swap. As the system administrator, you may have to use your personal PC that you can swap a user's hard drive into to get them back on line, if necessary.

### DATA RECOVERY SOFTWARE

There may be times when, even if you have not had a hardware problem, some or all of the data on your hard drive is inaccessible. You may be able to get it back. This will depend on the severity of the problem, and the resources available. The thing that gives a hard disk its structure is the File Allocation Table (FAT). This is a data table at the start of the disk that keeps track of what files are on the disk and where they are. NetWare adds additional information in other data tables. It stores information on rights to the files and ownership in a database known as the binderies, and additional characteristics such as the longer file names used by the Macintosh and other file systems (created when you add name space to a volume) in other data tables.

**NOTE**
**See Chapter 1, Servers, for more information on VREPAIR and BINDFIX.**

### The Server

The basic tools for data recovery on the server are VREPAIR and BINDFIX. Read the manual carefully before using these utilities, to make sure you understand what questions they will ask and what you should do. BINDFIX will (sometimes) repair the binderies, and VREPAIR can fix problems with the FAT, partition information and name space information.

Both of these utilities may need to be run more than once to fix the problem completely. Often, when they fix one problem, they will leave others unresolved. Run them until they report no errors.

### Workstations

Workstations are simpler to recover data on, because they don't have the extended attributes that NetWare does. On the other hand, workstations are seldom protected with mirrored drives, they don't generally have data recovery software built into the operating system, and they aren't often backed up. Some data recovery tools build a duplicate copy of the FAT table and can use this to recover from many disk errors. I highly recommend using one of these utilities. See Appendix A for some sources that you can use to learn more about these programs. Backups are a stickier issue. I strongly encourage you to limit workstation disks to system software and applications. Train users to store all data on the server, which should be backed up. With a good log, you will know what operating system, configuration files, applications, and so on are on the workstation, and you'll be able to restore these fairly easily.

If your data recovery tools can't help, you have exhausted the first level of recovery tools. The next level involves restoring from backups. Your server should be backed up with a documented schedule of tape rotation, and you should consider either a fireproof secure storage area on site, or off-site storage of the tapes. The third level of recovery involves refurbishing the hard drive, and the last level is the recreation of your data from scratch. These are discussed below.

## RESTORING FROM BACKUPS

Chapter 5, A Pound of Prevention, stressed the importance of backing up data and applications, and discussed strategies for doing so in some detail. Here, we'll continue that discussion and focus on what happens when you actually need to restore what you've backed up.

Every server, no matter how small, or how little data is on it, should be backed up. Backup drives are available in a price range from a couple of hundred dollars to many thousands. Even a server being used solely as a print server, with little or no data on it, should be backed up. For one thing, there are probably also mail directories on it that users would be very unhappy about losing; and for another, restoring from an inexpensive 60 MB tape is a lot faster than reinstalling NetWare from scratch.

If you don't have backups of your server, you will wish you had. Eventually, you will need a backup, either to restore the server after a disaster, or to recover files that a user has inadvertently deleted. Fast, reliable and convenient backups are available in capacities from 20 MB to 10 GB and more, and in price ranges from a few hundred dollars to many thousands. There is no excuse for not having backups. The cost is much less than the cost of reconstructing the data on even a small hard disk.

> **There is no excuse for not having backups.**

Be sure of the integrity of your backups. Many backup programs do not adequately warn you if a backup didn't completely finish, or if there were bad blocks on your tape. At a minimum, you should back up your entire system and then restore at least some of the files to test the backup when you install the server and backup device, and whenever you make major changes in the server, such as upgrades. Depending on the nature of the data on your server, you may need to do full backups every night, or incremental backups may fill your needs.

If you weren't able to get the data on your drive back, or if the drive itself can't be repaired, you will have to restore from backups. This may be as simple as restoring a server's drive from the full backup tape made the night before, or as complex as booting from a floppy and downloading a new operating system from the server, reconstructing the user's configuration from your log files, and reinstalling all the user's applications.

If you are using incremental backups, be sure that you know the order in which the tapes were made. You will usually restore first from the last full backup, and then from each incremental tape. If you get one of the incremental tapes out of order, you can overwrite recent files with older versions, so label the tapes clearly, both on the case and the tape cartridge itself. It is a very good idea to have your backup schedule documented and posted.

This can ease the headache if a problem occurs when you are off site. Do you want to have to fly back a week early from your first vacation in two years to restore some data?

### Restoring the Server

A complete restoration of the server will involve three basic components. First the NetWare operating system, NetWare partitions, and additional NLMs and configuration files. Second, the binderies. These are what contain all the information about which users are able to use the server, what files they own or have rights to, and so on. Third, your data files. These include your users' files, applications, and work directories. Most backup software gives you the option to back up and restore the binderies as well as the operating system and data.

Three things to watch out for are restoring to different drives than were originally on the server, restoring to a drive that hasn't been formatted with NetWare yet, and restoring drives that had name space support for other operating systems besides DOS.

If your server's hard drive has failed and you think this is a great time to increase the size of the drive, since it was 98% full anyway, be aware that restoring the partition information will result in errors, because the partition information is based on the size of the drive and its configuration in terms of number of blocks, tracks and sectors. If you wish to do this, you will need to reinstall NetWare from the diskettes, create new partitions, and then restore the binderies and data.

If the drive you are restoring to is new and hasn't been formatted with NetWare yet, most backup software will be able to create the NetWare partition during the restore. You may, however, need to create the partition first with some backup software. Make sure that you have the latest version of the backup software, and of course, that you've read the manufacturer's documentation carefully.

If you have name space support for another operating system such as the Macintosh OS, OS/2, or UNIX, you should be sure in advance that your backup software will handle the name space support. If it doesn't, you may get the files back, but with names truncated to eight characters and a three-character extension.

### Restoring Workstations

As I said above, and as discussed in more detail in Chapter 5, you should attempt to confine the data on workstations to the operating system and applications.

Unfortunately, with most operating systems, there is no way to prevent the user from storing data on the local hard drive (UNIX is a notable exception). The only way to deal with this problem is education and continuing reminders. Of course, you could have a backup tape device in each workstation, and automatically backup each machine every night—internal tape units for PCs are quite inexpensive. This is a good way to go if users must store data on their workstations.

There are several solutions to the problem of backing up workstations. You can create a backup area on a server, and create batch files that log in and copy everything on the workstation hard drive to that area. These backups can be deleted after a daily backup of the server to tape, to make room for the next workstation backup.

Another approach is to get a small portable tape drive that attaches to a workstation's parallel port (or a Mac's SCSI port). You can then back up each workstation in rotation with this device. If, as suggested, the workstation has only the operating system and applications, this sort of backup will only be necessary when a system is first configured, and then when significant changes have been made, such as the installation or upgrading of applications or the operating system.

A third approach is simply to have an area on the server with a standard set of applications and the standard operating system. As long as you have an appropriate license for each workstation, it is quite legal to download the actual files from the server. If your users' requirements are similar enough that you can standardize on one or two operating systems and a standard suite of applications, this makes restoring a workstation or setting up a new one quite simple—just boot from a floppy with a networking driver on it, log in to the server, and install the standard OS and applications. This is also much faster than installing everything from floppies, and can usually be done as a batch operation—the OS and all the applications with one command, such as NCOPY G:/SETUP/*.* /S.

This approach also makes updates easier—you can simply copy the new version from the network to each users' workstation, observing license requirements, of course. This is a good way of keeping the versions on your network in sync, another practice I recommend. In some cases, as with the Macintosh operating system, having different versions on the network can cause printing problems, network protocol routing conflicts or file system errors.

### Restoring Applications

Since all your applications are legally acquired and registered copies, you can if necessary reinstall them from the original disks. I suggest that you have a central repository (perhaps fireproof and lockable) to hold these applications. It will make your life much simpler than trying to find everything in various areas, and discovering that someone from another department has "borrowed" the manuals and disks. Of course, if you have adopted one of the schemes described above for backing up workstations, you can also restore from tape, or restore from the server's tape drive to the data collection area on the server and then copy everything back onto the workstation, after reinstalling enough of the operating system to boot and connect to the network. You should have boot diskettes for this purpose for every type of workstation on your network.

### RECOVERY SERVICES—HOW MUCH IS ALL YOUR WORK WORTH?

If your disk is not responding, and backups are not available or aren't working, your next step is a data recovery company. A good recovery service can repair or replace the electronics on a damaged hard drive, and may be able to open the drive itself in a clean environment and replace damaged components, enabling you to recover some or all of your data. Some companies employ a software-only approach and are experts with data recovery software. They may be able to get better results than you can, or be able to reassemble scrambled data that is beyond most data recovery software. Their services may seem expensive, but are likely to be much less than the cost of recreating all your data from hard copy or from memory.

## Recovering from Software Problems and User Errors

The most common problems you will have that aren't related to hardware are caused by incorrect software configuration, inadvertent changes in permissions, and user errors. Users setting up their own programs and workstation utilities will often have an incomplete understanding of your network, and may make settings that are not correct for use on a network. Unfortunately, even with an effective user-education program, you will often only find out about these problems after the fact.

Short of becoming an expert on every application in use on your network, your best option is to become aware of the methods applications use to directly access the network. These are the most common problems with network applications. The most probable service they will access will be print services or file services. If the application has problems accessing print queues or file permissions directly, set the program to a non-networked mode, and use the standard NetWare redirection utilities to access print and file services.

If a user has problems using data files on the network, the most common reason is permissions. If a file is still there, but is not opening correctly, check first for other things that may be affecting it. For example, if the permissions were mistakenly altered, a user might be getting messages that imply that the file is damaged, when the problem is actually that they don't have the proper access. Similarly, if a file is shared, or being worked on by several users, permissions might be altered by one user; or if the file is being worked on by one user, it may be locked (perhaps with good reason), so that others are temporarily unable to access the file. Here, again, the application's messages may be misleading.

Your biggest use for your backups will be restoring files that have been scrambled by programs that were incorrectly terminated or are simply buggy, or accidentally deleted by users. If the files were accidentally deleted, you may be able to recover them with SALVAGE, which is much simpler than restoring from backup, unless you don't have much free space on the volume, or you have turned the "purge immediately" feature on. See the *System Administration* manual for details on SALVAGE and the PURGE options.

## LAN Failures

**NOTE**
**Chapter 7 discusses
the issues involved in
troubleshooting
WANs.**

Failures in networking hardware other than servers can be catastrophic, because they can affect everyone on the LAN, or even everyone on a WAN. The failure will not necessarily be total, and tracking the problem can be very difficult without some sort of network analyzer. For example, a router could become defective and begin sending out extremely large packets, which could cause every server or workstation receiving those packets to freeze or be unable to communicate with the network. With a protocol analyzer, a log of normal traffic and a table of all network devices and their ID numbers, diagnosing this type of problem is easy. Without such tools, you can only try to isolate your WAN into LANs, find the LAN that still has the problem when cut off from other LANs, and then take devices off the LAN until the problem device is found.

There are a number of routers and other types of networking hardware that allow you to swap boards in and out of the device without powering off or affecting other connections. Many devices also support Simple Network Management Protocol (SNMP), which allows you to remotely diagnose and control them using an SNMP management console. See Chapter 4, The Physical Network, and Chapter 8, Connecting to Other Systems, for more details on finding and fixing network problems.

# Reconstruction—When All Else Fails

Your ability to reconstruct your network in the event of physical destruction or unrecoverable data loss will be completely dependent on the extent of the records you have kept. If you have hard copy of documents, you can probably have them rekeyed, either by in-house staff, or by a company that specializes in such work. Replacing, reinstalling, and reconfiguring your network without documentation may not be possible, and at least will require much longer. See Disaster Planning, below, for suggestions on what you should record.

The recurring theme of this chapter applies here too. The two parts of your network you will need to reconstruct will be the physical network and the data. You may or may not need to reconstruct both parts. Obviously, getting the hardware back in place will be relatively simple—a matter of buying, leasing or renting whatever is necessary. Next, you will have to reinstall the components and software and reconfigure the network. The time involved will be a function of how complex your network was and how well it was documented. Finally, you will need to recover your data. If your backups were lost, too, you will have to reenter everything. Hopefully, you will be able to rekey much of your data from hard copy, but if not, it will have to be recreated in other ways. One factor here is time. The longer you have to wait before people can begin recreating their work, the less they will remember.

Another factor that shouldn't be overlooked is alternate sources of data. For examples, an employee manual could be rekeyed from a copy an employee had at home, and accounting records could be reconstructed by contacting your accounting or tax firm, and asking the companies you do business with for their records of transactions with your company. The critical thing is to make a list of all the data that was on the network, and then work out methods to recover as much as possible of the data. I suggest you have a group meeting of all employees who used the affected network, and brainstorm on both what was there and possible methods for recovery.

# Viruses

There are virus checkers that check for over 1400 viruses. Some virus scanners run as NLMs, some as TSRs on workstations, and others as standalone programs that will scan local and network drives. Many are free or low cost; and all are less expensive than recreating all your data and reinstalling all your applications, to say nothing of trying to figure out what has been scrambled and what hasn't, and what to do about that.

The three important parts to dealing with viruses are using virus detection software, keeping it updated, and using virus recovery programs if necessary. Ideally, you should have virus scanning software covering every workstation on your network, and every server. Given the cost versus the potential for damage, there is no excuse for not doing this. Educate your users on the necessity for virus scanning and the importance of not disabling the software to save two seconds when inserting a floppy disk. The one time that you may need to disable virus checking software is when using some software installation programs.

> Given the cost versus the potential for damage, there is no excuse for not having virus scanning software covering every workstation and server on your network.

Keeping your virus scanning software updated is critical. Having a virus checker in place can give you and your users a false sense of security, since people tend to assume that having a virus checker will automatically prevent any viruses from infecting your system. The sad fact is that there are a small number of asocial criminals who are constantly devising new viruses that can bypass existing scanning software.

For example, I once had a user who disabled a virus checker that was automatically ejecting an infected disk. The reason they gave was that they had a virus checker of their own, and it didn't report any problems, so they knew there couldn't really be a virus on the disk. As a result, I had over 15 workstations infected with a virus (fortunately easy to detect and remove), and that user lost all privileges on my network, permanently.

If you do have workstations or servers that become infected, there are a number of programs which may be able to remove the virus and possibly repair any damage. These programs are definitely a good investment. They will often tell you in an introductory message that you should really delete the infected application and reinstall it, and this is usually the best way to recover from a virus; but the program will always tell you whether the virus removal was successful, and if the program runs properly afterwards, you may wish to leave it alone.

The most critical thing on your network to protect from viruses is your server. I wholeheartedly recommend that you get an NLM that will scan your server for infected applications and files and warn you if anyone attempts to place an infected file on the server. The worst thing about having a server infected is that it can corrupt your backups, making it difficult or impossible to recover from the damage. The key if this happens is to determine the latest backup that is not infected, and restore from that. If you don't catch the virus for

> **The most critical thing on your network to protect from viruses is your server.**

a while, this could cause to you lose all recent data. If you can isolate the infected files, you can sometimes restore earlier versions of just those files, and recover everything else.

## Prevention

The following items are covered in more detail in the previous chapter, A Pound of Prevention; they are summarized here simply to reiterate the importance of preventive measures. All of them can prevent disaster by shielding your network from the things that can cause you problems in the first place.

### UPSes AND SURGE PROTECTORS

Power spikes and surges, brownouts and blackouts all have the potential to cause disaster. Whether the disaster is a motherboard destroyed by a surge, or a NetWare volume damaged by powering the server off without downing it first, a good surge protector or UPS would have prevented the problem.

### QUALITY EQUIPMENT

Hardware failures are in general less likely with quality equipment. Many manufacturers also offer on-site service. When purchasing equipment, saving a few hundred dollars may cost you many times that much later, if you can't find compatible hardware to repair the PC with, or if a hardware failure causes an unrecoverable loss of data.

### PREVENTIVE MAINTENANCE

Proper preventive maintenance can prevent hardware failures from oc-curring in the first place. Too much dust in a PC can cause shorts on circuit boards, or read or write errors on floppy drives, and it can cause filters to clog on hard drives, making them run hotter and reducing their life. Similarly, keeping the disk drive heads clean can prevent floppy drive failures, and keeping connections tight can prevent failures of several kinds.

### PRECAUTIONS

Not observing static precautions can damage the parts you are inspecting or trying to repair. Your body can hold a static charge of many thousands of volts, more than enough to damage the circuitry in your PCs. Units that aren't properly grounded can be affected by static discharges even when the cases are closed.

Other precautions include following the manufacturer's directions when dealing with hardware or software. For example, most programs should be exited before the workstation is turned off. Another example is waiting five minutes after a Mac has been turned off before removing or adding cards.

### FAULT TOLERANCE

SFT II or III can protect you from what would otherwise be disaster. SFT II is disk duplexing or mirroring, which can protect you from hard drive failure. If a mirrored drive fails, users won't even notice. The system will notify you that a drive has failed, and you can down the server and replace it at your leisure. You won't even need to do a restore. SFT III carries fault tolerance to a level unique in the LAN world. It creates a duplicate of your entire server, which can be in another part of the building, or even at a remote location, as long as a high-speed data link is available. With SFT III, even the total destruction or theft of one server won't bring the network down.

### BASELINING

Baselining can not only help you isolate the problems with LANs, it can prevent disaster by allowing you to identify trends in advance and expand the capacity of your network in time to deal with increased demands before they cause your system to shut down. For example, if your percentage of available cache buffers is gradually declining, you can add more memory to your server before it gets to a state where you have to remove services to get it to run at all.

### TRAINING

Training your users has a number of advantages. It can lighten your workload, by reducing the number of requests you receive for support. User training can also reduce or eliminate some types of failures by getting users to observe proper procedures and even do some preventive maintenance on their own equipment.

### SECURITY

Some of the potential disasters that could befall your network can be prevented by proper security. This has a number of levels. For example, in addition to breaking into your building, thieves should also have to defeat the lock on the server room door before they can walk off with your server. Anti-theft registration stickers, cables that secure the server to something immobile, or video surveillance could also deter thieves from walking off with your equipment. Another step to take is to lock software and backups up in a cabinet, perhaps in another room.

# Disaster Preparedness

It is a sad fact that over 95% of businesses that experience a disaster and don't have a disaster plan will be out of business within two years. To get a feel for the scope of disaster preparedness, image what would happen if your building was bombed and you were unable to even enter your facilities for several months. What would happen to your business? Similar effects could result from fire, earthquake, flood, or simply a virus that isn't caught until it's too late. You only need to look at recent news to find examples of businesses forced into receivership as a result of any of these.

## DISASTER PLANNING

Your disaster plan may include many elements not germane here, such as evacuation plans, a relationship with a real estate broker to get new facilities, and arrangements for employee counseling after the disaster. This section will only deal with recommendations for areas involving your network. These may be more extensive than you imagine.

Pipes burst, buildings burn, and thieves steal computer equipment. You can't spend all your time worrying about what might happen, but you should take some time to think about the possibilities and what you could do to recover from them.

Your plan may be as simple as storing your backup tapes and copies of your network documentation in a different room from the server, or as extensive as detailed lists of what steps you would take, who you would talk to, with their phone numbers and addresses, and what services or equipment you'd request and what they'd cost. This will depend on the complexity of your network, and how long your business can survive without the network.

Sit down, maybe with other members of your staff, and list all the things you would need to do to get your system back on line if your building were completely destroyed. Lesser disasters will be a subset of this, but don't skimp here. You may later decide that some measures will be too expensive to keep on-line, but if you at least have an idea of what will be needed, you will have a place to start should anything happen.

You've just entered the parking lot Monday morning, and there's a hole in the ground where your building used to be. Where do you start? You should have both soft and hard copies of your network documentation and disaster plan, in several locations. Give a copy to each manager to keep at home. Store a copy with your off-site backup tapes. Now you have a list of what equipment you need to replace (your complete disaster plan will also include other equipment—from office furniture to phones and copiers). You should include in the plan a list of your standard suppliers, your customer representative's name and phone number, and so on.

If your business couldn't run without your network and the data on it, which is very probable, then you should have backup tapes stored off-site. Many disasters will either destroy on-site tapes or render access to them impossible for extended periods of time. For example, some buildings have not reopened for months or even years after fires; and even if your equipment or backup tapes weren't harmed, you might not be able to get to them.

If you can recreate your hardware setup and your data, you can probably survive most disasters. Having a plan is not enough. You should test your plan, at least on a small scale. Rent some space, or set up a small network at home, using rented equipment, and get backup tapes from your off-site storage company, and restore to a test server. You will uncover flaws in your plan and areas you hadn't considered. Modify your plan to accommodate these, and test it again. Finally, document the whole thing and make sure that your management is familiar with the plan, and have copies at home.

> **Having a plan is not enough. You should test your plan, at least on a small scale.**

## DATA RECOVERY IN ADVANCE

There are programs available for both PCs and Macs that will (sometimes) recover deleted files or data from drives that crash or are accidentally formatted. Most of these programs have a utility that should be loaded on the workstation ahead of time. This utility will keep track of files after they have been deleted and significantly improve the recovery program's chances of getting your data back. You should consider a utility of this type for all your network workstations. See Appendix A for suggested ways to learn more about these products, and which ones may be right for you.

# Documenting Your Disaster Plan and Your Network

As suggested above, you should have a documented disaster recovery plan. This doesn't need to be a formal, 100-page document, but it should be thorough, and cover all aspects of your network. Your company as a whole should have a more comprehensive plan that includes every aspect of recovering from disaster, from new buildings to employee counseling, but yours need only cover your network.

Include copies of all of the following:

- ▸ The hardware and software configuration worksheets for your workstations and servers.

- ▸ The documentation of your network wiring plan and networking hardware.

- ▸ Your backup plan.

- ▸ The address, contact name, and authorization code for your off-site storage facility.

- ▸ The names of your hardware and software suppliers and their customer representative's phone numbers.

> ▸ The number of your local phone company's networking services representative.

Include similar information as needed, and as time permits. It's impossible to make this plan too thorough or complete, although time will be your limiting factor.

The two prevailing themes of this chapter have been "back up, and document everything." Easy to say, but hard to do? Not really. The forms in Appendix B can be used as-is, or customized as you wish. Make a copy for each workstation and server on your network. Fill out as much as you can from your own knowledge. Lots left, isn't there? Take the remaining items a few at a time. Do one workstation or server a day until you have them all done. Then you can start updating.

Create a network map, showing every workstation and server on your network and how they're connected. Print out a copy of your directory structure. Get network and file server management packages and use them to create complete inventories of what's on every workstation and server on your net. Whether you do it manually or with software, create the documentation, keep it updated, and spread lots of copies around.

Another step that will help you is to keep a diary. This task doesn't need to be onerous—use a word processor and keep the file open. Update it with what you're doing during the day, or make it the last thing you do before you go home. Keep copies of this document around, too. Not only can it be helpful in reconstructing your network in case of disaster, but it can show your boss that the user you've been griping about asked for your help with the same problem eight times in the last two months, and it also makes a great place to start when writing up your job description, doing a job review, or showing your boss just why you need an assistant or some new equipment.

# PART III

# Large Networks

The chapters in this section discuss aspects of large networks and connecting multiple LANs to form WANs, as well as connecting different operating systems and topologies together to form a unified network.

Chapter 7: Troubleshooting WANs, covers connecting multiple LANs to form MANs and WANs, considerations of networking over long distances, and isolating problems on large internetworks.

Chapter 8: Connecting to Other Systems, discusses the approaches to connecting various other network protocols and operating systems to NetWare, the advantages and disadvantages of each alternative, and troubleshooting methods relevant to the connecting software.

# Troubleshooting WANs

**M**any companies are no longer limited to single Local Area Networks (LANs), but have multiple LANs connected to form Wide Area Networks (WANs), or internetworks; these connections considerably increase the difficulty of isolating problems. This chapter will discuss how LANs are interconnected, troubleshooting methods and tools, and user services, both on multiple LANs within a single building or campus, and on WANs over multiple sites which may span a city, a continent, or the entire globe. To help you get through the large number of standards and acronyms in WAN technology, there is a glossary at the end of this chapter.

This chapter will cover the following items:

- ▸ How LANs are connected to form WANs
- ▸ Additional Fault Points of WANs
- ▸ Diagnosing WAN-related problems
- ▸ Network Management Tools
- ▸ Diagnostic Tools
- ▸ Managing without Diagnostic Tools
- ▸ Services across WANs
- ▸ NetWare Directory Services (NDS)

# How LANs Are Connected to Form WANs

A basic definition of a LAN is a group of workstations connected to a server with a single type of wiring. This can be as simple as a few PCs connected by Token-Ring to a server, or as complex as PCs and PS/2s running OS/2, both using IPX, Macintoshes using EtherTalk, and UNIX workstations using TCP/IP, all connected by Ethernet to a server. As long as there is only one network number and one server, it is still one LAN.

The simplest method of connecting two existing NetWare networks is to put two Network Interface Cards (NICs) in a single server, and connect each of the existing networks to one of the NICs in the server. In this case the server with two network cards is acting as a router. You can also make this type of connection with a non-NetWare router or a gateway. The section below will not attempt to cover every possible variation used to connect LANs—there will be new ones released between the time this book is finished and when it is published. Instead, I will try to give you the basic principles of connecting and troubleshooting LANs; these principles will be applicable no matter what specific hardware or topology you use.

## MULTIPLE LANS AT ONE SITE

There are several reasons you may have multiple LANs at one site. The first is that the LANs may have been created separately, at different times, in response to the varying needs of different departments and only later hooked together to form an internetwork. In fact, this is typical of the development of networking at many companies. Another reason is that different departments may be using differing types of LANs. For example, an engineering department might be using Token-Ring, the accounting department Ethernet, and the marketing and art departments LocalTalk. A third

> **Splitting a network into several LANs will reduce traffic and server overhead, improving performance for everyone.**

reason is to reduce network traffic or provide more services than a single server could handle. Too many workstations on a single LAN, or too many users on a single server, can cause the entire network to bog down. Splitting the network into several LANs will reduce traffic and server overhead, improving performance for everyone.

### Bridges

Bridges are the least complex method of connecting two LANs (although once they are connected, they are actually one LAN, with one network number). Versions of NetWare before 3.x called the function built into NetWare a bridge.

> **A bridge can be used to divide a LAN with too much traffic into segments, substantially reducing traffic on both sides of the bridge.**

Actually, the NetWare product has attributes of both a bridge and a router; and thus in later versions of Net-Ware, it is referred to as a router. A bridge generally connects similar types of networks—Token-Ring to Token-Ring, and so on—but it can connect different types of cabling, such as thick Ethernet to 10BaseT. A bridge can be used to divide a LAN with too much traffic into several segments, because it only passes traffic from either side through if the packet's destination is on the other side. This can substantially reduce traffic on both parts of the LAN.

Bridges are designed to handle specific protocols—IPX/SPX, AppleTalk, TCP/IP, and so on. They look at the hardware address of every packet and send it to the other side if the address is on that side. Since the hardware address is always in the same place in a packet, their function is relatively simple, and they are generally the fastest type of connection between two LANs, for a given cost or speed of processor. A bridge generally learns the addresses of all the workstations on either side by polling them occasionally to find out their addresses.

### Routers

A router differs from a bridge in that it can handle multiple protocols; also, the network on each side is a different LAN, with differing network numbers. A router doesn't just read the destination hardware address, but can read the packet to find out its eventual destination, rather than just the next one identified by the destination hardware address. It can add further information to a packet to enable it to go through a LAN that uses a different hardware standard, such as Ethernet to Token-Ring, or take that information off a packet it receives from the other side of such a LAN.

Another difference is that routers don't handle every packet on the LAN. (They aren't "transparent.") Instead, a packet that is to be passed through the router must be addressed to it. NetWare handles this automatically, but some protocols (TCP/IP, for instance) require you to tell a workstation the address of the router to which it should send packets for forwarding.

A router is more capable than a bridge, but requires more processing, which, all other things being equal, makes a router either slower or more expensive than a bridge. There is also an in-between class of devices called brouters, which combine the functionality of bridges and routers, generally by examining every packet on the LAN (transparency), but only being able to handle some protocols.

### Gateways

A gateway is the most complex type of device for connecting LANs, and is typically very specialized. It doesn't just transfer packets from one LAN or one protocol to another; it usually translates between two dissimilar standards. For example, a gateway might act as a file translator, to allow your Macintoshes to access files on a UNIX server, or as a mail gateway, translating between the NetWare mail protocol MHS and another such as X.400.

Gateways are typically complex to configure. You should understand the basics of configuring both sides of the gateway. For instance, for a file and print services gateway that translates between AppleTalk and UNIX (TCP/IP), you should understand how to configure both AppleTalk and TCP/IP.

## CONNECTING LANS BETWEEN BUILDINGS

LANs in buildings that are close enough together to be linked with a cable or by a beam of light can be connected by either repeaters or bridges, depending on the requirements of the network. Buildings can be connected with wire or fiber-optic cable, or linked with wireless means such as an infra-red laser or a pair of radio transceivers.

### Repeaters

A repeater is a device that simply passes everything it sees to every segment hooked up to it. It may support several types of cable—for instance, thick, thin, twisted pair and fiber-optic Ethernet—and is primarily used to extend the maximum length of cable possible. The primary disadvantage to a repeater is that it passes everything through; this can make for a very high traffic load if too many workstations are connected. There are two basic types of repeaters, single- and multi-port. A single-port repeater is used simply to extend the possible length of cabling for a network segment. A multi-port repeater allows several "legs" on the same segment. A repeater with many ports may also be known as a hub, or a concentrator. Repeaters are relatively inexpensive and easy to set up.

### Bridges

A bridge provides the same type of extension as a repeater, with the added benefit of traffic isolation, since only the traffic destined for the other building is passed across. Bridges do cost more, and require software configuration, but are also much more flexible.

## CONNECTING LANS ACROSS LONG DISTANCES

Once you go beyond the range that can be spanned by physical cabling, your options become much more limited. You can set up a satellite or microwave link, lay your own long-distance cable, or use the facilities provided by your local telephone company.

### Telephone Company Services

Transmitting data over a phone line intended for voice has its limitations. Because the line is only engineered to support voice communications, it will only support a data communications rate of about 9600 bits per second (Bps). (A rate of 14,400 Bps can be achieved with special equipment, and up to 57,600 Bps with data compression.) The basic division between the types of services is between dial-up connections that can connect to any other phone line and leased lines that connect two specific sites, and between analog and digital connections. All-digital connections can allow speeds of up to 622 million bits per second or more (Mbps).

**Analog Dial-up Connections**   Dial-up connections are almost all analog, offering limited speed, but also offering the flexibility to connect to anyone with a phone. The typical problems are the limited speed available through lines intended for voice, the relatively high levels of line noise, and the rates charged for standard phone service.

**Leased Analog Connections**   If you are using a dial-up line to connect regularly with another site, you may save money by leasing an analog connection. This won't typically offer higher speed, but can give you a cleaner, more reliable connection, and with usage over a certain point, will save money over a standard connection.

**Digital Dial-up Connections**   As phone companies convert from equipment intended only for voice transmission to digitally based equipment designed to handle data and even video as well as voice, high-speed dial-up connections are becoming available. These range in speed from 56 thousand bits per second (Kbps) to 100 Mbps or more. The problem with these services is that they are currently available only within metropolitan areas, and then only in some areas. The areas served by all-digital services will expand, and eventually, you will be able to get a dial-up digital connection anywhere that you can now reach with a standard phone line. Check with your local phone company for availability. Digital connections generally require equipment much more expensive than a simple modem, although ISDN (Integrated Services Digital Network) adapters can now be found for under a thousand dollars. The equipment you will need will depend on the type of connection. For every type of high-speed connection, there are many vendors who can help you get connected.

**NOTE**
See Appendix A for magazines and other sources of information about communications equipment.

**Leased Digital Connections**   If you need a connection with a throughput of over 64 Kbps to another site, you will probably need to lease a digital line. Digital services that may be available to you include T-1, which provides 1.544 Mbps, T-3, which provides 45 Mbps, ISDN at 64 Kbps and up, FDDI at 100 Mbps, and ATM, which can provide 622 Mbps or more. These types of services tend to become more expensive as the distance between sites increases. There are also services called fractional T-1 and fractional T-3, which divide the channel into several sub-channels, at a reduced cost and speed. Your phone company representative can provide you with rates. Again, you will also need special equipment to access these services.

## Other Options

Other options for connecting LANs include satellite communications, microwave relays, and independent providers of services similar to those available from the phone companies. Satellite services can provide widespread communications for organizations with many sites across a continent. However, the drawback is that satellite communications are more expensive than leased lines for distances of less than a thousand miles or so, and also tend to be slower than land-based communications, at least unless large, expensive antennas are installed rather than the usual 6-foot dish.

Microwave relays can provide high-speed, secure communications between sites, but are generally so expensive that they are reserved for highly specialized applications and those with unlimited budgets, like the government. Some organizations such as railroads, television networks or cellular phone companies may lease some of their extra capacity. Within limited ranges (three to five miles), inexpensive microwave equipment can provide 1.5 Mbps connectivity to a large number of sites for a one-time investment with no monthly fees. The drawbacks are that the range is limited, and that all sites to be connected must be in line-of-sight.

There are a number of companies now laying fiber-optic cable of their own and competing with the phone companies. These include railroads, which are laying cable along their rights-of-way, television cable companies, and others. The most common service available is FDDI, which offers 100 Mbps of throughput. The rates are typically similar to those offered by phone companies. Be sure that you can add locations and that the company has agreements with other service providers in case you need to route a line to an area not covered by their normal service.

## CONNECTING LANS AROUND THE WORLD

Beyond WANs and MANs (Metropolitan Area Networks) are world-wide networks. Depending on the country you need to connect to, you may find that standard services range from some that are more sophisticated than U. S. services, to some that are barely above the level of carrier pigeons. Western Europe, for example, has large areas already networked with ISDN and ATM, and Eastern Europe has areas in which the line quality is so bad that special modems are required to support any speed over 300 Bps.

### X.25

X.25 is a standard maintained by the CCITT, an international telecommunications standards organization. Illustrations of X.25 typically show a number of different types of installations, all with lines ending in a cloud in the center of the picture. This is meant to illustrate the very large variety of ways that users can access X.25 services, and the large number of possible routes that the data can take from one end to the other. X.25 services can be accessed by dial-up lines or leased lines, at speeds from 1200 Bps to 1.544 Mbps or higher. The primary advantage to this type of service is that it is very widespread and widely supported by many vendors. The biggest disadvantage is that it is relatively slow. It is an excellent way of forwarding e-mail between LANs, but would not be appropriate for a regularly used data connection.

### Telephone Company Services

Typically, any service that can be had across town can be had around the world, but the cost will be much higher. For instance, T-1 lines typically double in cost as distances increase from 500 miles to 2000 miles, so New

York to Japan will increase the cost considerably. Where a 1000-mile T-1 (1.544 Mbps) line might cost $10,000 per month, a T-3 (45 Mbps) line would cost $100,000 per month. For longer distances, especially overseas, these prices go up much further.

### Other Options

As distances increase, satellite communications may become more practical. If you have heavy traffic between LANs on different continents, a satellite link can provide reliable, relatively inexpensive high-speed throughput. The initial installation can be expensive, but with enough use, it can save you money over a leased line that continues to cost you money every month.

# Additional Fault Points of WANs

As is sometimes the case within buildings, the actual hardware and wiring used to connect your LANs will seldom belong to you or be under your control. The positive side of this is that the service provider is responsible for maintaining, troubleshooting, and upgrading this hardware. The down side is that it can be difficult to get a response from some companies as quickly as you would like in an emergency. This chapter won't deal with equipment that is typically outside your installation, but should help you determine whether it's your equipment or the phone company's that is causing the problem.

### HARDWARE

The basic WAN hardware is a device that sends traffic from your LAN to another LAN. This may be as simple as a repeater on either end of a few hundred feet of coaxial cable, to link two buildings, or a T-1 bridge attached to a leased line that connects two sites in different states. From a troubleshooting standpoint there is very little difference in the basic approach to either of the extremes. First determine whether traffic is getting to the WAN link device, then whether the device is operating correctly, and finally whether the device is able to read signals coming or going on the link. If these conditions are all met, the problem is probably elsewhere. Of course, determining these items can be difficult, especially without a LAN analyzer or similar equipment.

### Repeaters

Repeaters are the simplest type of device used to link LANs. Depending on the distance, you could use a repeater to link two buildings with either thin or thick Ethernet. Thin Ethernet would allow you a maximum distance of 185 meters (about 600 feet), and thick Ethernet would allow 500 meters, or over 1600 feet. It is relatively simple to tell whether most repeaters are operating—if the activity lights on the front are blinking, the device is probably working. The additional fault points for this type of setup would include the repeater at each end of the long cable and the long cable itself. With a multiport repeater, the separate ports can be isolated, usually with switches. This can make isolating parts of the network for troubleshooting easier, but it can also cause problems if a port is shut off accidentally.

### Bridges

A bridge can be used for something as simple as the situation above—a few hundred feet of cable linking two buildings—or for an application as complex as a T-1 leased line linking a New York office to a Los Angeles office. As with any other network connection device, the elements for troubleshooting are to determine whether the traffic is getting to the bridge, whether the bridge is operational, and whether the traffic is getting from the bridge to the other side of the link.

Bridges, routers, and gateways usually can be accessed through remote management or monitoring software, which means you can make sure that the device is operational without having to physically go to it and use its console. You should also be able to examine the routing table to determine what network devices the bridge knows about.

▶ · · · · · · · · · · ◀

> **The simplest way to isolate a bridge as a break point is to try to attach to a server that is on the other side of the bridge.**

A simple way to isolate a bridge as a break point is to try to attach to a server that is on the other side of the bridge. If you know that the server is up (if workstations on that side of the bridge can attach to it), but you can't reach it from the far side of the bridge, you have isolated the break point to the bridge, or the physical connections attached to the bridge.

### Routers

A router may be internal to a server (a server with two NICs that routes between the two LANs), or it may be a standalone product, running either proprietary software on proprietary hardware, or generic software on a PC platform. Novell has two products, the standard router included with Net-Ware, and the MultiProtocol Router (MPR), both of which run on a standard PC platform.

The troubleshooting process described above for bridges applies equally well to routers. The biggest difference is that because routers handle multiple protocols, a router may be routing one protocol (perhaps IPX) correctly, but not another (such as TCP/IP). To isolate such problems, you will need to check each protocol to see if it is being forwarded through the router.

### Gateways

Gateways can be more difficult to troubleshoot because they generally involve a service as well as protocol translation. For instance, a gateway that allows Macintoshes to print to a UNIX printer might seem to be inoperative when the actual problem was that the LPD daemon on the UNIX host wasn't working. To troubleshoot gateways, you must understand the process on both sides of the device. Whether file, print or mail services, you should be able to determine that the process is functioning properly on both sides of the gateway.

## Dial-in/Dial-out Servers

With more and more services accessible through modems, dial-in/dial-out servers are allowing users to connect with a network from home or a portable computer, or dial out to a service from their office, without having to have a modem for each workstation on the LAN. One such server, with up to 16 modems, can serve the needs of dozens of users, at a much lower cost than a modem for each workstation. Consolidating the modems on a network in this way can also enhance security, and make upgrades to hardware and software much easier. Some network modems also provide fax services.

The biggest difficulty in troubleshooting dial-in and dial-out connections lies in the lack of standardization in the telecommunications world. There are many protocols and standards, such as V.32, V.32bis, V.42, and so on, "Hayes-compatible" and others. The problem is that different manufacturers do not always implement these standards in the same way. Even modems that claim to be Hayes-compatible may have different default command sets than other modems that also claim Hayes compatibility. The modem world very much resembles the PC world before the IBM PC became the dominant standard. There are many manufacturers offering enhanced performance, but their equipment may only work with the same modem on the other end.

There is also no set standard for communication protocols. The simplest protocols specify only data bits (7 or 8), parity (odd, even, or none), stop bits (1, 1.5, or 2) and speed (50–57,600 baud). There are also several data compression schemes, some "standard" and some proprietary. Further, the serial port that connects the modem to the server may be a standard COM port, or an enhanced port such as is offered by the Novell WNIM+ adapter. The only way to ensure that these settings match is to speak with the user on the other end and ascertain what settings they are using.

Setting up the server itself will not require that you confirm that both sides of a connection are using the same speed, protocol, and so on, but you cannot troubleshoot problems with such connections without understanding the settings. There are several parts to a dial-in/dial-out server. The easy parts are the ones that are the same on any server—the workstation, NIC, COM port or WNIM+ adapter, OS software, and server software. You may also need to troubleshoot the user's software that is accessing the server. The hard part comes when everything up to the modem is working correctly.

The great number of possible settings makes it imperative that you know exactly what both sides of the connection you are trying to set up expect. Dial-in/dial-out servers include software for the workstation that allow the user to configure the modem for the protocol that is used on the other end. Many modems will negotiate automatically with the modem on the other end until they determine a common setting that they both understand. Unfortunately, this may be much slower than what could be achieved if the modems were both set properly to begin with. This can mean the difference between requiring a few minutes to send a file of several hundred KB, or a few hours.

> **The great number of possible settings makes it imperative that you know exactly what is expected on both sides of a dial-up connection.**

Another factor in the smooth operation of a dial-in/dial-out server is the line quality. If there is a fair amount of traffic, you will probably want to use a line that doesn't pass through your PBX system. Check with your phone company for other options that may be available. You may already have such a line for your fax machine.

> **You will not usually have access to the equipment that belongs to your telecommunications service provider. However, you will get faster service if you do your best to eliminate all other possibilities before contacting the provider.**

## TELEPHONE COMPANY SERVICES

In general, you will not be able to troubleshoot the problems that originate with your telecommunications service provider. However, you will get faster service if you do your best to eliminate all other possibilities before contacting the provider. If you have a good idea of the topology of your network, you should be able to isolate the problem to the other side of the interface with the telecommunications network.

Of course, in some cases, you will have a clear symptom such as no dial tone, but usually you will only have a situation in which traffic is getting as far as the T-1 bridge, but not to the other end of the T-1 line. Try to establish a relationship with a particular customer representative. Once you've established mutual trust, you won't have to prove to the telephone company that you know what you're doing every time you call.

## SOFTWARE

There are two typical problems with software on a WAN. The first is with incorrect configuration and the second is with corruption or freezing. Incorrect configuration is symptomatic of a lack of planning or management on a WAN. This kind of problem is usually caused by two workstations or servers using the same address or network number, or two servers on the same cable segment not having the same number for that cable. In either case, the ultimate cause is a lack of documentation or standards for that network. Corruption of files or software freezes can be caused by many different things, such as hardware problems, user errors, bugs in the software, or configuration problems.

### Planning and Management

At a minimum, you need to coordinate the internal network numbers, IPX numbers, and similar configuration settings for other protocols such as TCP/IP. You may need to coordinate these numbers with an outside agency. TCP/IP, for example, is regulated by the Defense Data Network's Network Information Center. If you have a site that is not connected to the Internet, and never will be, you can use any numbers that are valid. If you want to be able to connect to the rest of the world, you must have an assigned address. The same will shortly be true of IPX addresses.

Management software will quickly compile and show you all the addresses in use on your network. If you don't have such software, use the forms in Appendix B to document your network manually. This not only ensures that you won't have address conflicts, it will also make troubleshooting easier when you receive a message like: "node at 140.11.138.244 has caused a bindery error."

Bridges, routers and gateways will come with some sort of configuration utility. This utility will usually allow you to monitor and troubleshoot the device as well as establishing the initial configuration. The exception to this is a NetWare server that is also acting as a router. In this case there are several utilities available with NetWare—MONITOR, FCONSOLE, and TCPCON—that enable you to track packets sent and received, and so on. With both standalone devices and servers, you should have some idea of what the normal traffic looks like and what normal statistics are for the device. If nothing more, occasionally open the device with the configuration utility and look at the information. This will familiarize you with what things should look like. Unless you know this, you won't know what is out of whack when you're trying to troubleshoot the device.

Baselining, as discussed throughout this book, is one of the cornerstones of troubleshooting. It is very difficult to know if something is wrong unless you know what it should look like. The items to look for at the most basic level will tell you that traffic is moving in and out of your device. The specifics will vary with the type of device, the protocol, and so on, but you should see items such as number of packets received, number of packets sent, and the number of bad packets (often subdivided into different types of bad packets, depending again on the type of protocol).

The causes of bad packets, and how to isolate and fix the problem, are the subject of numerous books. LANalyzer for Windows offers a distinct advantage is this area, as it has a help facility called the Network Advisor that will tell you not only that bad packets are being received, but also what typically causes that sort of error and where it is coming from. I highly recommend this product or something similar for anyone with a large LAN or multiple LANs. LANalyzer for Windows also includes a very good book on the subject, *Novell's Guide to NetWare LAN Analysis*, by Laura Chappell, from Novell Press, which covers using LANalyzer for Windows to diagnose problems on Ethernet.

**NOTE**
**See Chapter 5 for a complete discussion of baselining.**

If you know that you are usually receiving about 10,000 packets a day, and the number drops to 1,000, or jumps to 100,000, you will have a start on finding the problem. If you are receiving a larger number than you are sending, this may also indicate a problem. Of course, large or steadily increasing numbers of bad packets will also indicate a problem. The NetWare *System Administration* manual discusses the statistics that MONITOR tracks, and the manual for your device or monitoring software may also have further details.

### Configuration

Once you get a configuration that works for a network device, server, or whatever, record it! Keep copies of the information with the machine, and in a central area. It will be useful in reconstructing a device after the configuration is lost, in identifying conflicts with other devices, and in determining the best settings for new devices. If you have your configurations documented, you can also avoid discovering conflicts after they have caused every server on your network to crash or caused a "Router Configuration Error" message. Solving a conflict problem quickly won't make you look good if you could have avoided it in the first place.

### Address Conflicts

A major problem with LANs is also one of their benefits. They are not terribly complex (compared with a mainframe) and can be administered by local personnel, rather than requiring a centralized IS department. However, as companies and their networks grow, some level of coordination becomes critical. With two or three servers, the chances that two will use the same internal IPX number seem minuscule, but that's exactly the time to begin coordinating information, not when there are 50 servers. With an IPX address conflict, you will get a "Router Configuration Error" and an annoying beep on the server's console. With a TCP/IP address conflict, you may have every workstation on your network crash. The only way to avoid address conflicts is to document configurations and coordinate with other administrators.

# Network Management Tools

As networks grow in complexity, the need for management and diagnostic software becomes greater. With a single LAN, it's relatively easy to determine whether network traffic is getting to a device or not. Once you have several LANs, perhaps running different or multiple protocols, the situation is much harder to troubleshoot. The software necessary to help you determine and fix problems is becoming less expensive and more capable all the time. For example, the original Novell LANalyzer product retailed for around $15,000. LANalyzer for Windows offers 90% of the functionality, plus some great features the original product lacks, and has a street price of under $1000. One of the new features is a help facility called the Network Advisor that will not only tell you what's wrong, but will tell you the usual causes for that sort of error and where it is coming from.

> **If you have a WAN, or even multiple LANs, you should have some level of network monitoring capability.**

If you have a WAN, or even multiple LANs at a single site, you should have some level of network monitoring capability. You can usually diagnose most WAN problems without such capability, eventually; but given the cost of having dozens or hundreds of users off-line for hours, the software will quickly pay for itself.

There are network management and/or analysis products ranging in price from less than $100 to about $100,000. The capability you will need will depend on the complexity of your network. The basic bottom-line capability is to track the packets flowing on your network. How much the program can tell about the packets, and the other diagnostic tools included, will depend on the product. Most products can only cover one LAN—you will need a basic tool for each LAN segment, or a more capable (and expensive) product that can cover the WAN. Top-of-the-line packages include a workstation (usually a UNIX workstation) and may include services such as network mapping that will alert you if any configuration on your WAN changes.

## WHAT'S AVAILABLE

It would be futile to try to list every product available in a field as wide as this one. For one thing, there would be new products, and revisions to old products, released between the time the book was finished and the time it reached your hands. What I'll give you here is a list of the basic features that you may want. You can then use the information resources listed in Appendix A to determine the best program for you.

### Packet Monitoring

This will include information on the various types of packets moving on the network, including numbers of good and bad packets and their sources. It may also include the ability to look at the header information for each packet, or to decode the packet completely and look at the contents. You will usually be able to set thresholds for certain types of events and the software will notify you if the limits you set are exceeded.

### Trend Analysis

Some programs will allow you to save information about your network's normal traffic, and establish trends over time. This can be enormously helpful in both identifying problems and upgrading your network before performance degrades significantly.

### On-line Help

You can have megabytes of decoded packets, but unless you understand what the information in the packet header means, the data won't do you much good. You can have an alarm that tells you that your token-ring network is beaconing, but unless you know what beaconing is and what the likely source of the problem is, there isn't much you can do with the information. You can either learn this information in a class such as the Basic and Advanced LANalyzer classes available through Novell Authorized Education Centers, or you can get a book on the subject and learn the information yourself, or you can get a program that will help you figure it out. The Network Advisor in LANalyzer for Windows is a great example of how such help should work.

### SNMP Management

The Simple Network Management Protocol (SNMP) is a standard for managing networking devices that many manufacturers incorporate into their software and hardware. If your management software and your network devices support SNMP, you will be able to manage many different devices, from different manufacturers, with one management tool.

### Network Mapping

Management programs offer many levels of network mapping, from simple logical maps of your network that tell you how many workstations are on each segment and provide some basic information about them, to programs that either discover or allow you to enter physical data on location, distance between devices, types of connections, and so on, and can then help you isolate faults caused by changes in the physical network.

### Network Inventory

Network inventory programs also span a wide range of functionality, from programs that can tell you what kind of workstation is at each network address, to programs that can tell you all the software on every workstation's disk, the operating system version, the contents of the AUTOEXEC.BAT and CONFIG.SYS files, and more, to programs that will allow you to track usage of applications and how many valid copies of each you have, and even update software remotely on every workstation.

### Server Management

NetWare provides some basic tools for managing your server and keeping track of users, and so on, but the tools are limited. There are a number of companies offering extensions to NetWare that will allow you to print out reports of all users, the files and directories they own and have trustee rights to, the setups of printers, print servers and print queues, the basic configuration files and the ones for any additional NLMs you may have installed, and other aspects of your server. If you have more than one server, or even one that has a lot of disk space or many users, this sort of utility can make your documentation chores much easier. Some programs will even monitor CPU utilization, disk access, and memory usage and alert you if you need to upgrade your processor, NIC, or disk system.

## COST ANALYSIS

It can be difficult to justify spending money on preventive measures and "conveniences." However, you can estimate the cost of down time per hour on your LAN, and then measure that against the cost of a tool that could save you hours in getting your network fixed and back on line. The larger your network or internetwork, the easier it is to justify management and diagnostic tools, and the more you need such tools.

# Diagnostic Tools

Diagnostic tools range from a simple volt meter or continuity checker to a $100,000 package, preinstalled on a UNIX workstation, that can monitor your entire WAN and alert you if problems arise or are about to arise. The two basic categories are hardware-based products and software-only products. Hardware-based tools are generally faster, and often more capable than software-only tools, and usually more expensive, as well.

Many diagnostic tools include management functions, and some management tools can be used for diagnostic purposes—it depends as much on how you are using the tool as what it is intended for. The two functions should be tightly integrated: if you manage your network well, and document it well, you will often be able to avoid problems before they arise.

## HARDWARE-BASED PRODUCTS

Most hardware-based tools for WAN troubleshooting include protocol analysis. They may be referred to as sniffers, protocol analyzers, or packet decoders. These are all descriptions of the same basic function—intercepting the packets flowing through your network and gathering information about them. The difference between products lies in how much they will do with the packets and how much information they can collect, sort, generate reports on, and watch over a period of time to establish trends.

### Protocol Analyzers

A protocol analyzer consists of two parts—the hardware that collects the packets that are traveling along the wires of your network, and the software that provides you with information about those packets. The hardware may be a special NIC for your workstation, or a complete (sometimes portable) workstation. The need for dedicated hardware is decreasing as LAN adapters grow in power. Many modern LAN adapters include a CPU with more power than PCs had a few years ago, as well as on-board RAM. If you have a large internetwork, or very high levels of traffic, the hardware-based products will still provide an advantage. At the high end of the scale, products are available that provide much more than capturing and decoding packets—they may be able to monitor every device on your network at once, or build both physical and logical maps of your network, or even allow you to simulate different network configurations so you can plan upgrades in advance.

Hardware-based protocol analyzers range in price from a few hundred dollars to $50,000 or more for some workstation-based integrated network management and analysis tools. The level of capability you will want (or need) will depend on the complexity of your internetwork, and its stability. If you seldom or never have new networks or servers added to your network, you may not need much management capability at all. If you have a dynamic, growing internetwork, or are supporting hardware or software development, for instance, you will probably want more capability.

The basic items you should look for include:

- ▸ What protocols are supported? Even if you are only using one protocol now, you may want to leave room for expansion or upgrades in the future.

- ▸ How much information will the product gather? This may range from simply telling you how many packets of each type are coming through the network, to providing specific information such as the original sender of the packet, its intended recipient, the purpose of the data in the packet, and the contents of the data part of the packet.

- ▸ Some products will save greater or lesser amounts of information, and may allow trend analysis over periods from days to years. You should also look at what data formats the product will export to—can it save your network information in a spreadsheet or database format?

- ▸ One of the problems that you will face in trying to troubleshoot WAN problems is that some of them will occur sporadically or periodically. Some protocol analyzers will also allow you to simulate a number of users producing various levels of traffic to stress the network, hopefully reproducing the conditions that caused your problem.

- ▸ Can the product gather information about the networking devices that connect your LANs, or is it limited to gathering information about the single LAN segment it's attached to?

- ▸ Does the product support SNMP or CMIP (Common Management Information Protocol)? If so, you will be able to remotely manage any devices that also support these protocols.

- ▸ How portable is the product? Many protocol analyzers can only see the LAN segment they are attached to. If you have to carry the machine from segment to segment, it's nice to have a fairly small package.

▶ Time Domain Reflectometry (TDR) allows you to isolate cable breaks to a particular distance from your location, or the nearest node. This can be invaluable in tracing cabling problems.

▶ Packet filtering allows you to select only packets that fit certain parameters, for instance all the packets being sent by a certain workstation or server. The number of filters a product has, the degree of flexibility in combining filters to provide Boolean searches, and in some cases, the ability to create your own filters are all useful gauges.

### Other Hardware Tools

There are other types of diagnostic tools that serve specialized functions. For instance, there are standalone products that perform the TDR function mentioned above, to determine the location of breaks in your cabling. Other types of useful tools include continuity testers, which can check cabling for breaks, and in some cases, also check polarity, to make sure that the two wires in a twisted pair connection haven't been crossed, and voltage checkers, which can help diagnose a LAN adapter that is defective and unable to maintain the proper voltage.

### SOFTWARE-ONLY PRODUCTS

The only real difference between hardware-based products and software-only products is that software-only products rely on the standard networking hardware already installed on your workstation to gather the packets off the wire. These products will usually require a special LAN driver for your card, and they may not support all NICs. These products are usually much less expensive than hardware-based products, but may be less capable, or slower.

### Tools in NetWare

NetWare comes with some basic tools that can be used for diagnosing problems on your networks, and these should not be underestimated. Using MONITOR, FCONSOLE or TCPCON, you can determine traffic flows for each of the LAN cards in your server, and you can monitor some common problems, such as packets that are outside the normal size or improperly formatted. The only problem with these tools is that they have no data-gathering or reporting features—the numbers are reset every time you bring the server up or down, and there is no easy way of printing the information.

There are a number of inexpensive programs, some created but not supported by Novell, that can provide you with the ability to save these statistics and format them nicely for printed reports. If you can't get anything more into your budget, I highly recommend that you at least get one of these programs. Most are available as shareware from NetWire.

### LANalyzer for Windows

LANalyzer for Windows not only has the advantage of being a Novell product, designed to work well with NetWare; it is also an extremely capable package that includes almost all of the features listed above for hardware-based products, as well as the Network Advisor, a tool that is almost a product in itself. It can not only recommend actions for any problem you are likely to run across, it can explain the underlying principles of networking involved, and teach you the specialized terminology and concepts you need to know to really understand your network. Furthermore, the price is $1495 list, and you can buy it for a good deal less than that. Recommended for anyone managing more than two small LANs.

### Other Products

There are many other software-only products available, designed to support various combinations of software platforms and many different LAN adapters, and offering widely varying capabilities. Most of the features in the list above for hardware-based products are available, with the possible exceptions of load simulation and TDR. There may even be software-only

**NOTE**
See Appendix A for sources of information about available software.

products with these features coming soon. Use the sources listed in Appendix A to determine what's available and what will suit your needs. Your fellow administrators will generally be happy to tell you about their experiences with products they've used (sometimes in greater detail than you will want).

## Managing without Diagnostic Equipment

All of the products described above can make your life easier, greatly speed up the process of finding and resolving problems, and enable you to manage larger networks with fewer people. However, it is very rare that a problem will be unsolvable without such equipment. If you have the problem now and don't have the equipment, you will simply need to follow the basic principle of troubleshooting: identify the fault points, check them one at a time, and approach the problem systematically.

For example, if you have a problem with a network card that has gone bad, it may be "jabbering" or sending out large numbers of bad packets. This may not only affect network performance in general, it may cause servers or workstations to freeze. In this case, something like LANalyzer for Windows could identify the problem in seconds. However, you could identify and isolate the problem by checking LANs with MONITOR, and isolating them physically, until you find the LAN that is producing the faulty packets, then take workstations off-line one at a time until you find the one that has the faulty NIC. You might not be able to identify the NIC as the problem immediately, but you can isolate the problem to the workstation, which will then give you a limited number of fault points to check: the motherboard, the OS, the LAN driver, the NIC, and the transceiver, if any.

# Services across WANs

LANs were originally conceived of as a way to share resources such as files, printers, and modems within a department. Providing these services to many users across multiple LANs is a growing concern as companies grow or replace mainframes with LANs (commonly known as downsizing or "rightsizing"). Setting up, maintaining, and troubleshooting a print queue can be complex on a single LAN with a few dozen users. Trying to give users on other servers or at other sites access to your printer can become an enormous headache. These issues have become enough of a concern that NetWare 4.x contains many new features specifically designed to address the needs of users across WANs. These services are known collectively as NetWare Directory Services, or NDS, and are discussed a little later in this chapter.

## PRINTING ON WANS

Giving users outside your LAN access to your printer can be relatively simple. Just give the user GUEST and/or the group EVERYONE access to the print queue. However, a user in another state who needs to print a document to your printer (saving considerable time over mailing the printout) will need to know the exact name of your server, how to attach to it, the exact name of the print queue and print job, if any, and how to set up CAPTURE to print to that queue. They may also need other information, if the printer is specialized (PostScript, a color printer, or the like). Things can be further complicated if you need to restrict use of the printer and cannot grant GUEST or EVERYONE access to the queue. In this case, you may need to create a special user with access to the queue.

Coordinating all these details once may not be too much of a problem, especially if you have taken the time to set up print jobs, are familiar with the NetWare utilities PRINTCON, PCONSOLE and CAPTURE, and have fully documented the configuration of the printer, print server, and print queue. However, if you aren't prepared, or if this is a common way of exchanging information within your organization, there are some things you should do to be prepared.

First, document your configuration. As I have said many times before, you cannot overdo documentation. In this case, it is especially true. If a user in another state is on the phone, waiting for the information necessary to print to your printer, it will be much faster to open a binder and read the information off, than to log in, run three or more different programs to obtain the configuration information, and try to present it in an orderly manner. If this is a frequent request, you might want to write up instructions on how to accomplish the process, which would also be very useful as part of a manual for new users on your LAN.

Another thing that will make your life easier is to use PRINTCON to define print jobs, rather than depending on long CAPTURE statements. It is much easier to explain, and document, CAPTURE J=LW, than CAPTURE Q=PostScript F=1 NB NFF K. Similarly, having a print job set up allows you to configure it as the default job for the guest account, letting anyone logging in as guest print without further effort. You can also set up queues on other servers that print to the print server on your LAN. If you have users on other servers who regularly send jobs to your printer, you may want to consider this. It will require coordination between the supervisors of both servers, as you must be SUPERVISOR to create the queues, and SUPERVISOR on the other server to attach the queue to that server's print server.

## MANAGING MULTIPLE LOGINS

Depending on a user's requirements, they may need to attach to more than one server. With NetWare 2.*x* and 3.*x*, you can LOGIN to only one server at a time. If you need to connect to more servers, you must use ATTACH, which does not execute a login script. This means that users attaching to multiple servers must manually execute the additional commands to map drives, set up default print queues, and so on. NetWare 4.0 fixes these problems, but you can make life easier for users by putting a batch file in the login directory that will execute the appropriate MAP and CAPTURE statements.

# NetWare Directory Services

NetWare 4.0 is the first version of NetWare designed specifically with the needs of large company-wide WANs in mind. Its principal new feature is the NDS database, which is the equivalent of a network-wide bindery that encompasses all the servers on your network. You can organize your network by logical groups, rather than being confined by the physical structure of your system.

## THE NEW STRUCTURE OF NETWARE 4.0

NetWare Directory Services uses a completely new paradigm for network structure. Instead of a group of servers, each with its own bindery, containing information on the users, printers, volumes, and so on for that server only, there is a single distributed Directory, with multiple copies replicated throughout the network, which contains information on all the resources, users, groups, and so on, on that network. Users, resources, and rights to those resources are managed on a network-wide basis, rather than by individual server. Each user has one login, and can log in from any workstation, on any LAN, and have the same access to resources that they would have on their own workstation.

A company-wide internetwork is organized in a tree-like structure, as illustrated in Figure 7.1. The root is the total directory that encompasses the entire company. It is divided into "containers," which are logical units such as divisions, organizations, workgroups, and so on. Containers may contain other containers. Each container contains "leaf" objects, which are entities such as users, printers, print queues, volumes, and so on. Leaf objects do not contain other objects. For example, you might be a user *admin*, in a container *engineering* (Organization), in a container *explosives* (Organizational Unit), in a container *road runner traps* (Organizational Unit), in a company *Acme* (Root).

Every container and leaf in the database has properties, which hold the information about the object. These include, for example, login name, phone number, address, and so on for a user object, and printer type, print

**NOTE**
For more information on other new features in NetWare 4.*x*, see the Concepts section of Chapter 1, Servers.

Root (ACME)

O=Production    O=Legal    O=Finance    O=Sales    O=Engineering

OU=Explosives    OU=Anvils    OU=Jet_Skates    OU=Disguises

OU=Traps    OU=Excavation    OU=Fireworks    OU=Rockets

CN=Roadrunner
CN=Porky
CN=Bugs
CN=Speedy
CN=LW_Printer_1
CN=HP_Plotter_1
CN=Traps_Server
CN=AFP_Server_4
CN=VOL_Bang
CN=GRP_Bombers
CN=OR_Chief_Eng
CN=PQ_PostScript_3
CN=PQ_Plotter_1
CN=PS_Room_1442
CN=Alias_Anvils_Server

queue, Access Control List, and so on for a printer object. An Access Control List is associated with each object, and lists which users have access to that object.

Every part of the network, whether container or leaf, is an object. There are essentially three types of objects—the root object, container objects, and leaf objects. There can be only one root object in a tree structure. If you have two organizations, and make each a separate tree, with its own root, you will have great difficulty later merging the two trees into one. It is also painful to change the names of existing organizational (container) objects. For these reasons, you should consider very carefully both your existing organization and possible growth or changes in structure, before planning your network. I strongly recommend that you read the April 1993 *NetWare Application Notes*, published by Novell, before planning a NetWare 4.0 network.

There are two types of container objects you will usually see, Organization, and Organizational Unit (OU). Each allows you to set defaults for a user, and the Organizational Unit allows you to setup a login script for every user in that container. Thus, you can give every member of a department access to the same resources, whether they are attached to the same server, or in different states.

There are many different leaf objects, organized into user-related objects, server-related objects, printer-related objects, informational objects, and miscellaneous objects. User-related objects include users, groups, organizational roles, and profiles. An organizational role is a set of rights that can be assigned to different users. For instance, if the manager of a group changes, you would disassociate the former manager as a user from the "Manager" object, and associate the new manager with that object. A profile is a type of login script that can be associated with a group of users who may not all be in the same Organizational Unit. Login scripts are executed in the following order: system login script (associated with the OU), profile, and then user login script.

Server-related objects include servers, volumes, and directory maps. Servers and volumes are what you would expect. Directory maps can be thought of as aliases for a directory. If you map a search drive to a directory in your user's login scripts, and then later change the name of the directory, you will then have to change each login script. With a directory map, you would map the search drive to the directory map in the login scripts, and if the name of the directory changes, you would modify the directory map, and wouldn't need to change the login scripts.

Printer-related objects include print queues, print servers, and printers. These are handled in the same manner as with previous versions of NetWare, but can be managed through the NDS system as well. Informational objects include AFP servers and computers. AFP servers are separate objects holding information on servers running the AppleTalk Filing Protocol. These may include NetWare servers represented by server objects. They will need a separate AFP server object to describe their AFP-related information. Computer objects store information about the computers on your network. They are not required, but are an easy way to store, maintain, and access the information you should have about the workstations on your net.

Miscellaneous objects include aliases, bindery objects, bindery queues, and unknown objects. Aliases are pointers to other objects in the NDS. They make it appear as if the object referred to is located where the alias is stored. Aliases are a simple way to give users in one container access to resources in another container. Bindery objects and bindery queues are used to provide backward-compatibility with previous versions of NetWare. They represent resources that are to be made available to users with previous versions of NetWare. Unknown objects are objects that cannot be classified as a known type of object.

## THE NEW MANAGEMENT TOOL

The most welcome addition to the management tools provided with NetWare in version 4.x is NWADMIN. This is a graphic-interface utility that runs under Windows. It can show you the entire network, if you have the rights to view the whole network, and allow you to inspect, modify, create or delete objects on any part of the network. It allows you to perform tasks that previously required switching between a half-dozen different programs such as SYSCON, FILER, PCONSOLE, PRINTCON and PRINTDEF.

> ► · · · · · · · · · · · · ◄
>
> **The biggest problem users will have with NDS will be in understanding the new structure, especially contexts.**

## TROUBLESHOOTING NDS

NetWare Directory Services will be harder to troubleshoot than older versions of NetWare, simply because it allows a more complex structure to be built. Some things to watch for are:

- ► Make your directory structure as flat as possible—try not to have more than 3 or at most 4 levels of organization.

▸ Don't have too many copies of the directory. The directory is updated regularly, and every copy is also updated. If there are too may copies, your network traffic may become unmanageable.

▸ Remember to think globally. Don't have more than one account per user. Similarly, login scripts from multiple accounts on prior versions of NetWare must be consolidated. Be sure that you resolve any potential conflicts in the new scripts.

▸ You may find that you will have different EVERYONE groups and GUEST accounts in different partitions. This can happen if you use the server upgrade system to upgrade to NetWare 4.0. Each server has a different membership for EVERYONE, and this forces the creation of a new group.

▸ The biggest problem for users with NDS will be in understanding the new structure, especially contexts. Make certain you understand the contexts on your network completely. I recommend setting the user's context at login to their usual work area. This will allow them to type:

login username

instead of:

login .cn=username.ou=widgets.o=marketing

In general, the differences between NetWare 4.0 and NetWare 3.x are in the organizational structures allowed, rather than in the underlying protocols used. Of course, there will be an adjustment period as vendors upgrade their products to conform to the requirements of NetWare 4.0, but your biggest problems will probably reflect the items above.

# Glossary

**ANSI**   American National Standards Institute. American body that sets standards, and is a voting member of ISO.

**ATM**   Asynchronous Transfer Mode. A protocol designed to send parts of a transmission over different routes as they become available. Works very well with mixed video and data transmissions. Allows up to 622 Mbps.

**Baud**   The number of transitions per second in a signal on a line. Commonly, but not always accurately, equated with bits per second. For instance, 9600 baud with compression can produce 19,200 or more Bps.

**CCITT**   Consultative Committee for International Telephony and Telegraphy. An international organization headquarters in Geneva that sets telecommunications standards, including X.25, V.22, V.32, and V.42, X.400 and X.500.

**DQDB**   Distributed Queue Dual Bus. A proposed IEEE standard (802.6) for MANs, it uses multiple channels to achieve very high speeds—from hundreds of Mbps to 1 Gbps. It is also designed to provide service over a greater area than is possible with FDDI, which is limited to about 60 miles.

**FDDI**   Fiber-optic Data Distribution Interface. An ANSI standard for fiber-optic networks. Allows transmission at 100 Mbps.

**IEEE**   Institute of Electrical and Electronic Engineers. U.S. national standards organization with over 100,000 members. IEEE standards include 802.2 (Ethernet), 802.4 (includes ARCnet) and 802.5 (Token-Ring).

**ISDN**   Integrated Services Digital Network. International standard for telecommunications including voice, video and data over one digital line. Generally provides 64 Kbps. Developed by the CCITT. Broadband ISDN (B/ISDN), which will soon be available, uses broadband transmission and fiber optic cables to provide speeds up to 150 Mbps.

**ISO**   International Standards Organization. An international standards organization with over 75 member countries. ANSI is the U.S. representative to ISO. ISO developed the OSI model.

**MAN**   Metropolitan Area Network. A network linking more than one site, but limited to a metropolitan area. (In cases such as Los Angeles or New York, these can, of course, be quite extensive.) Generally offers public access and high performance (100 Mbps or greater). MANs are beginning to grow up in most large cities.

**Multiplexer**   A device that allows you to send several streams of data over one high-speed connection. This allows you to make full use of a T-1 or higher-speed line.

**OSI**   Open System Interconnection. The ISO standard for communications. Defines a seven-layer protocol model in which each layer handles a different aspect of communications on networks. Chapter 3, The Physical Network, describes the OSI model.

**VSAT**   Very Small Aperture Terminal. A satellite dish up to approximately 6 feet. Generally limited to 56 Kbps.

**WAN**   Wide-Area Network. Originally, a network that spanned more than one site. Now, generally refers to an interstate network.

**X.25**   The CCITT standard for a terminal interfacing with a packet-switching network. Implemented world-wide in many public and private networks.

# CHAPTER 8

# Connecting to Other Systems

**F**ew companies more than a few years old have a homogeneous comput-ing and network environment. More typically, there are departments that were automated with mainframe technology many years ago, and different sorts of PCs and topologies and network operating systems in use in dif-ferent departments throughout the company. Integrating all these services into one network provides a number of benefits such as easy communica-tion and data exchange between groups, but it requires a much more com-plex network structure.

A large company might include an office using a mainframe or minicom-puter for order entry, connected to another building through high-speed leased lines. The second building might have an IBM AS/400 serving workstations connected via Token-Ring, a UNIX server connected to workstations and ter-minals with Ethernet, Macintoshes connected to a NetWare server with Ether-Talk, and PC workstations connecting to a NetWare server with IPX.

There are two basic ways of allowing all these disparate types of com-puters to exchange data and access databases, and share services such as modems and printers. You can either use a specialized gateway to connect each system, or extend NetWare with software such as NetWare NFS, Net-Ware for Macintosh, NetWare for SAA and the NetWare Access Server to allow the different systems to access the same data and services.

Since a gateway is required between every two systems, a network with three different systems would require three gateways-—one from A to B, one from B to C, and one from A to C. In a similar setup using NetWare, assuming that NetWare is one of the three systems, only two packages are required, to allow the other two systems to access NetWare services. See Figures 8.1 and 8.2, below. Additionally, the NetWare approach is often cheaper than standalone gateways, offers higher performance, has more fea-tures, or all three.

You will notice that in the second example, Figure 8.2, there is no direct connection between the Macintosh network and the UNIX network. Users on both LANs can share files by placing them on the NetWare server, or take advantage of the routing capabilities of the server to communicate with the other LAN. For instance, the Mac users could use MacTCP to send files to the UNIX workstations through the server.

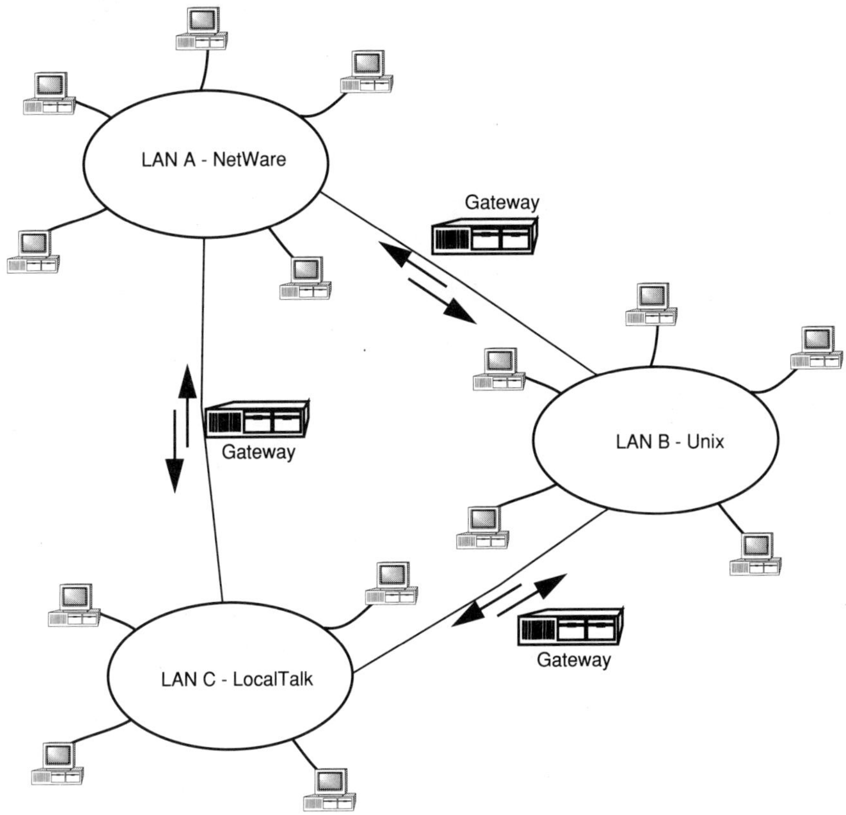

FIGURE 8.1

Three LANs Connected
with Gateways

These additional capabilities bring with them additional complexity, whether they are implemented within NetWare or with external devices. This chapter will guide you towards understanding the mechanisms involved in an internetwork and troubleshooting it. The primary difficulty from a troubleshooting point of view is that you must understand the basics of both networks and of whatever hardware or software you are using to translate between them. The sections below outline the basics of other operating systems and suggest possible problem areas in the interface between the two systems.

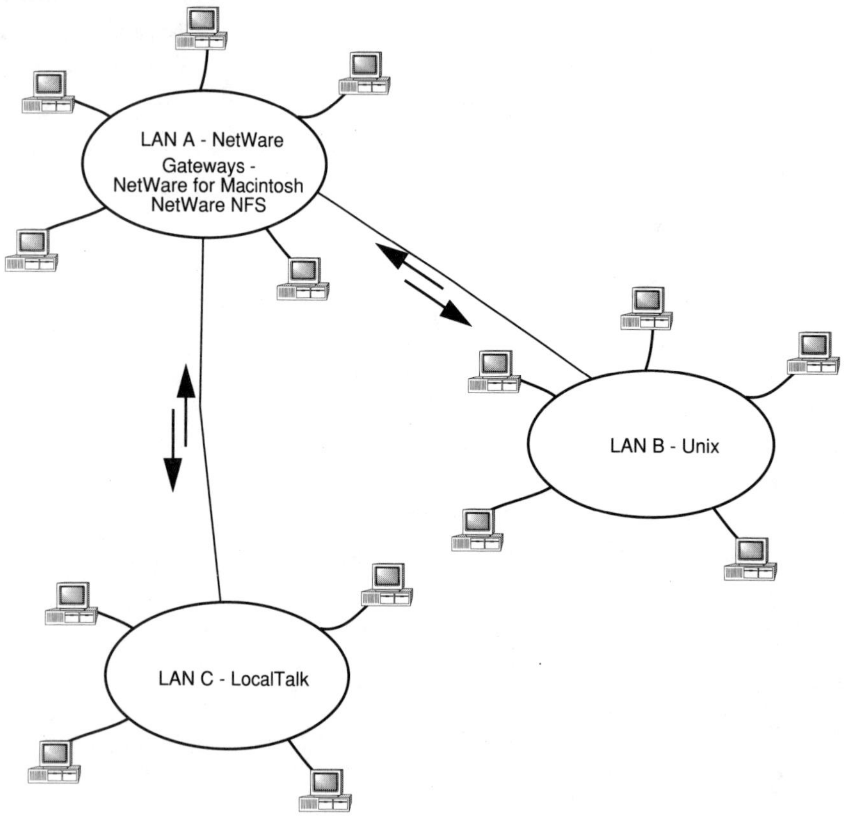

FIGURE 8.2
*Three LANs Connected
through NetWare*

# Other Systems

Say you have two networks, one consisting of PCs running DOS and connecting to a NetWare server, and the other containing UNIX workstations connecting to a UNIX server. There are three ways to allow two different systems to connect:

- On one of the servers, you can run software that allows the other network's workstations to access files on that server. In this case, that would mean running NetWare NFS on the NetWare server or Portable NetWare on the UNIX server.

- You can add software to the workstations that allows them to communicate with the other network server, which would be LAN WorkPlace for DOS or the NetWare UNIX Client.

- You can add a gateway between the two systems that allows them to exchange files. One gateway can be run on a NetWare server— the NetWare NFS Gateway. It allows DOS and Windows users to access UNIX volumes as if they were native NetWare drives.

Each option has advantages and disadvantages. Running software on the server takes advantage of the processing power of the server, and is generally the most transparent to the user. Software on the workstations allows you to keep the server free for more important tasks if it is already running near capacity, and can be cheaper if there are only a few of one type of workstation. A gateway doesn't require any software on either servers or workstations and may provide services beyond what the software solutions have, but will produce a bottleneck that all traffic between the two systems must funnel through, which can become onerous on systems with lots of traffic.

NFS for NetWare and Portable NetWare are both fairly expensive. With few users, you may find it more economical to use a gateway or client software. However, if you have more than 10 or so users, or want to allow for expansion, you should consider the server-based solutions—they'll be less expensive in the long run. Using a server-based solution also makes upgrades much simpler—a gateway will require at least a BIOS upgrade, and possibly the whole system will have to be replaced. Workstations, of course, must all be updated individually when a new version is released.

# Other Operating Systems on PC Workstations

There are a surprising number of operating systems other than DOS that run on PC-compatibles. OS/2 is perhaps the most prominent of these. Windows also needs to be mentioned here—although it runs on DOS (until Windows NT is released, at least), it requires additional setup to work with NetWare. Several varieties of UNIX, from a number of vendors, run on PCs. These will be covered in a general way in the section on NFS, below. Some versions of PC-based UNIX also provide direct support for IPX and Net-Ware. Two of these are NeXTStep for PCs, and UNIXWare.

For client software that allows DOS workstations to connect to another environment, see the section below on that environment. If you want to be able to access more than one environment at a time from a DOS workstation, you can run the Open Data-link Interface (ODI) driver. This allows you to run IPX and other protocols such as TCP/IP at the same time, providing simultaneous access to both NetWare and UNIX servers from the same workstation.

## OS/2

NetWare versions 2.15c and above support access by OS/2 workstations. OS/2 requires additional software to access NetWare services. The OS/2 requester is supplied with NetWare, and is also available on NetWire. OS/2 also requires a directory on the server equivalent to the SYS:\PUBLIC\DOS directory, to supply the OS/2 files corresponding to LOGIN.EXE, SLIST.EXE, SYSCON.EXE, and so on. These files are supplied on the OS/2 Requester disk. If you are running the High Performance File System (HPFS), you must also have OS/2 name space support on the server.

Two things to remember: First, when you log in or attach to another server, that server must also have the OS/2 directory, or you must have LOGIN.EXE or ATTACH.EXE on your local drive, as well as any other NetWare utilities you might want to run, such as SLIST, SYSCON, or PCONSOLE. Second, you must make sure that the DLLPATH to the NetWare requester files is in the

DLLPATH set up for your environment, or edit the AUTOEXEC.BAT file and add the path to the NetWare DLLs to your DLLPATH statement.

## WINDOWS

When you install Windows, it will detect existing NetWare drivers and automatically install NetWare support. If you install NetWare drivers at a later time, you must run the Windows INSTALL.EXE program again. For Windows to work well with NetWare, you should have the latest NetWare drivers available. Updates to these drivers are available on NetWire. Once the latest NetWare drivers are installed, Windows 3.1 offers a high degree of compatibility with NetWare and can directly access NetWare drives and print queues.

## NEXTSTEP

NeXTStep is the first PC-based UNIX operating system to include the NetWare UNIX Client (NUC). It provides direct access to NetWare file servers through the normal login and authentication process. It allows you to print to NetWare queues as well as standard UNIX queues. NeXTStep must be configured to use the NUC. This can be done during installation, or afterwards. Once the NUC is installed, it automatically provides access to any available NetWare servers.

File names are automatically translated into the DOS eight-character-plus-three-character-extension format when they are moved to a NetWare server. In fact, the file names are automatically truncated even if the NetWare server supports the NFS name space, unless the server is also running NUC.NLM. Other than file translation problems and the ubiquitous permission problems that occur when NetWare and UNIX collide (see the section on UNIX, below), you are unlikely to encounter problems with this setup. The Ethernet interface and driver software are built-in and supported by the operating system itself.

**NOTE**
See the section on Windows and NetWare in Chapter 2, Workstations, and the section on Windows in Chapter 9: Troubleshooting Network Applications, for details on troubleshooting Windows.

### UNIXWARE

UNIXWare, being a Novell product, supports NetWare and IPX automatically. In fact, that is the default configuration. To get support for the UNIX standards TCP/IP and NFS, you must add an additional support package. Be sure that the installed NIC is supported by UNIXWare and that the PC meets the minimum standard for UNIXWare, and there shouldn't be problems with this setup. Unless you have NFS name space and are running NUC.NLM on the server, only DOS eight-character file names will be supported on the server. Both UNIX and NetWare printers and print queues are fully supported.

# AppleTalk and Macintoshes

There are four basic ways to connect a Macintosh network with a Net-Ware PC-based network:

- ▶ You can run NetWare for Macintosh on the NetWare server. (Note that there is no equivalent for an AppleShare server, as there may not even be a server in the AppleTalk environment.)

- ▶ You can run AppleTalk on the PC workstations, which would be expensive—it requires an AppleTalk network adapter in addition to the regular NIC that connects the PC to the NetWare server.

- ▶ You can run IPX (the NetWare protocol) on the Macs, as long as they are connected to the network with EtherTalk, rather than AppleTalk. This can be an inexpensive solution, especially if you have a number of NetWare servers and don't want to have to install NetWare for Macintosh on all of them.

- ▶ Finally, you can run a gateway that translates between the PCs and Macs.

## NETWARE FOR MACINTOSH

All versions of NetWare from version 2.1 on support AppleTalk. The method is different for 2.x than for later versions. NetWare 2.x servers use the Value Added Process (VAP) to add AppleTalk support and allow Macintoshes to access NetWare volumes. The VAPs function as an AppleTalk gateway. That is, AppleTalk is converted to IPX, file or print requests are processed by the server, and the results are converted back to AppleTalk.

Under 3.x and 4.x, this functionality is provided by NetWare for Macintosh. This product is a series of NLMs that provide direct support for the AppleTalk Filing Protocol (AFP) and AppleTalk Print Services (ATPS). With NetWare for Macintosh, there is no gateway—the NetWare server is running AFP and ATPS as if it were an AppleShare server.

Servers running NetWare for Macintosh should have a minimum of 5 MB RAM, plus the RAM required for name space support, which you can calculate by multiplying the number of MB on the volume by .032 and dividing the product by the block size, (the default is 4 KB blocks—divide by 4). For example, a server with one 660 MB hard drive that has Mac name space loaded and 4 KB blocks would need (660 × .032) / 4 = 5.28 MB. Add the 5 MB minimum and you have 10.28. The server will probably allow you to install 8 MB or 16—it would need 16, assuming no other memory requirements.

Configuring AppleTalk support requires that you understand the basics of AppleTalk networking. AppleTalk is a protocol that can run over LocalTalk, which is the built-in interface provided on every Macintosh. Or it can be run over Ethernet or Token-Ring, using EtherTalk or TokenTalk, respectively. An AppleTalk network is theoretically limited to 254 nodes, although 100 nodes is a more practical maximum in real-life conditions. AppleTalk Phase II provides support for large networks, allowing up to 1024 zones, each with up to 254 nodes. If you run AppleTalk Phase II on your network, every server or router must also be running Phase II; don't mix it with Phase I. This can be done with transition routing, but isn't worth it—upgrading everything on your network

> **Try to avoid mixing AppleTalk Phase I and Phase II networks.**

to Phase II requires changing only the software drivers, and is very much worth the trouble.

When configuring your server, remember that the zone name may contain spaces. If you can't get access to a particular zone, try inserting a leading or trailing space in the configuration entry—it's easy to accidentally put a space at the beginning or end of a zone name. This also applies to printer names. A simple way to test for spaces is to use ATCON.NLM to do a lookup test in the suspect zone or on the suspect printer. If the lookup fails with the name spelled as it looks, try adding spaces before or after, until the lookup succeeds. If you have control over the zone and printer names, you should change the names to remove the spaces, to prevent further problems.

If you set up NetWare print queues that print to Macintosh printer, you will see both the NetWare queue and the printer itself in the Macintosh Chooser. You may wish to hide the printer itself, to keep users from printing directly to the printer, which can insert their print jobs ahead of those in the queue. See the *NetWare for Macintosh Installation and Maintenance* manual for details.

If NetWare for Macintosh is running, you will have an additional status screen on your server. Check this screen occasionally—it will show jobs printed through ATPS, and any problems encountered, and will also identify any problems with file services.

A fairly common problem is that the directory used to maintain the Macintosh "Desktop" becomes corrupted or out of sync. The Macintosh desktop file holds information on each file on the disk, including what program it was created by. The corresponding directory, DESKTOP.AFP, contains three files: ICONINDX.AFP, which links each file to its creator application; ICONDATA.AFP, which holds the bitmap image for each icon; and APPLDATA.AFP, which has the location of each application so it can be started if the user double-clicks a document icon.

If the desktop files become corrupted, Mac users may be unable to access files on that volume by double-clicking on them, or they may not be able to access the volume at all. In this case, you should unload AFP.NLM by typing

unload afp

at the server console. Then reload it with the CDT option, which recreates the three files:

```
load afp cdt
```

Finally, rebuild the Macintosh desktop by first highlighting the server's drive in the Chooser and then holding down the Option and Apple (flower) keys together while clicking on the Open Button. Hold the keys down until you see the dialog box that asks "Are you sure you want the desktop rebuilt on the disk *rebuilt diskname*? (This could take a few minutes.)" Rebuild the desktop for each volume that supports the Macintosh name space. This will update the information .AFP files to match the files on the disk.

## ADDING APPLETALK SUPPORT TO PC WORKSTATIONS

You can add AppleTalk support to a PC workstation in either of two ways, depending on the type of network—LocalTalk or EtherTalk. With LocalTalk, you must add an NIC to the PC that will allow it to access the LocalTalk network. Then you must add the driver software that allows the PC to access the NIC. Using an AppleTalk board in a PC is usually an either/or situation—you can access the AppleTalk network or whatever network you use to communicate with your NetWare server, but not both at once.

If you have PCs networked with Ethernet, and Macs networked with EtherTalk, you could add an ODI driver on the PCs that would allow you to simultaneously access NetWare services over Ethernet and AppleTalk services over EtherTalk.

## IPX FOR MACINTOSHES

NetWare *on* Macintosh uses MacIPX to provide Macintosh users with full access to NetWare services on NetWare servers that aren't running NetWare *for* Macintosh. If you have only a few Mac users in a large PC group, this can be more cost effective. Remember, though, it is a one-way link. If you have Macintosh resources such as printers that you want to make accessible to PC users, you will have to use NetWare for Macintosh. If the Macs are running LocalTalk, you will also need a LocalTalk NIC in the server and the gateway NLM provided with MacIPX.

### APPLETALK GATEWAYS

There are gateways available between LocalTalk and Ethernet, and between AppleTalk and TCP/IP. The simplest gateways are small devices used to connect Macs or printers that don't support a direct Ethernet interface into an EtherTalk network.

The AppleTalk-to-TCP/IP gateways are useful if you are trying to connect a Mac-only network to a UNIX network, but such networks are beyond the scope of this book. If NetWare is also being used, you will probably find that NetWare for Macintosh plus NetWare NFS gives you greater flexibility and easier upgrades, at roughly the same cost as the gateways.

### ACCESSING OTHER ENVIRONMENTS FROM APPLETALK

There are many products that provide Macintoshes with the ability to communicate with other systems. One example is the Apple Coax/Twinax card and software that provides access to IBM 3270 services. These sorts of products are generally not necessary in the NetWare environment. It is simpler to provide an Ethernet connection to the NetWare server, which then provides connectivity to the 3270 host, without the need for a second network adapter. Of course, you will still need the software on the Macintosh that allows the Mac to access the services on the 3270.

# TCP/IP and UNIX Connectivity

TCP/IP was originally developed in the early 70s and has been the standard for the Department of Defense and many other government agencies and educational institutions since the 80s. TCP/IP is associated with Ethernet and UNIX, but it will run on Token-Ring, ARCnet, FDDI, and other topologies, and is supported on DOS, OS/2, Windows, Macintosh and other operating systems. The now world-wide Internet started by the Defense Advanced Research Projects Agency (DARPA) is based on TCP/IP.

Since the focus of this book is NetWare, and connecting NetWare into existing systems, TCP/IP itself will not be covered in great detail. If you are setting up a TCP/IP network from scratch, there are a number of good books devoted to the subject.

A TCP/IP address is a 32-bit number specifying the network and machine sending or receiving a message. In UNIX systems, a file usually called HOSTS allows users to specify another UNIX workstation or server by name, rather than by a number like 192.42.133.244. What you should know about TCP/IP is that each workstation and server must have an address, and each address must be unique.

If your network is attached to the Internet, you will have a network address and a range of workstation addresses assigned to you by the Defense Data Network Network Information Center. If you are not on the Internet, and *never will be*, you can assign any valid address you wish, although even then you should keep in mind that as your company grows, you will need to provide for growth in your TCP/IP network as well.

The other standard associated with UNIX is NFS, the Network File System standard developed by Sun Microsystems and used by most UNIX vendors. NetWare NFS supports the NFS file standard, allowing UNIX users to access NetWare drives as if they were on their own system and includes name space support, which means that the longer file names supported by NFS can be used on a NetWare drive.

If your NetWare servers aren't running NetWare NFS, you can also provide NetWare users with access to UNIX services by running NetWare for UNIX on a UNIX server. This software is available for many different UNIX platforms and allows NetWare users to access files on a UNIX server and print to UNIX printers.

To allow PC users to access UNIX services, Novell markets LAN WorkPlace for DOS, LAN WorkPlace for Windows, and LAN WorkPlace for Macintosh. These packages allow users on these workstations to access

TCP/IP network services. LAN WorkGroup for DOS or Windows allows this software to be loaded from the server and provides additional services, outlined below.

For users on UNIX workstations, there is the NetWare UNIX Client. This software is supplied with the NeXTStep operating system and is, or will soon be, available for a number of other systems. It allows a UNIX client to log in to a NetWare server and access NetWare services as if from a PC running IPX.

## NETWARE NFS

NetWare NFS allows UNIX workstations to access NetWare volumes and print services using the TCP/IP protocol. Differing protocols can even share the same network interface card (NIC), so that one NIC can support IPX/SPX, TCP/IP, EtherTalk and others. IPX packets can also be sent through a TCP/IP-only segment via a process known as *tunneling*, which encapsulates the IPX packets within a TCP/IP packet.

TCP/IP transport services are available for NetWare 3.11 and above. They require at least 4 MB of RAM. You should also have the Maximum Physical Receive Packet Size set to 1514 bytes on Ethernet, and whatever size is in use on ARCnet or Token-Ring networks (may be up to 4 KB). The Maximum Packet Receive Buffer Size should be set to at least 200. Use MONITOR to see how many packet receive buffers are in use and increase this parameter beyond 200 if necessary.

The NFS name space must be loaded to support UNIX files on your NetWare server. This will use additional RAM. The amount may be calculated by multiplying the size of the disk to which you are adding name space by .032, and dividing the result by the block size. The recommended minimum block size for disks with NFS name space support is 8 KB. For a 660 MB hard disk with NFS name space loaded, this would be $(660 \times .032) / 8 = 2.64$ MB of RAM, in addition to the 5 MB minimum and any other requirements.

The configuration files for NetWare NFS are located in the SYS:ETC directory, and correspond to the files with the same names located in the /etc directory on a UNIX system. Each is a text file containing the UNIX parameter and its associated NetWare parameter. They are:

- ▸ HOSTS: Contains the TCP/IP addresses for the workstations, servers and printers that the server can identify.

- ▸ NETWORKS: Associates names with the TCP/IP addresses for networks the server can identify and forward messages to.

- ▸ EXPORTS: Controls what directories or volumes are made available to UNIX workstations.

- ▸ USERS: Maps UNIX User ID numbers to NetWare user names.

- ▸ GROUPS: Maps UNIX Group ID numbers to NetWare groups.

NetWare NFS supports the following UNIX services:

- ▸ Network File System (NFS) version 2. The file system developed by Sun Microsystems, this allows UNIX workstations to use NetWare drives as if they were standard UNIX volumes and supports the NFS name space.

- ▸ External Data Representation (XDR). Implements a standard UNIX data transfer syntax.

- ▸ Mount Protocol. Allows UNIX workstations to mount the NetWare volumes as they would UNIX volumes.

- ▸ Line Printer Daemon (LPD). Enables UNIX workstations to access NetWare printing services as if they were native. UNIX workstations can print to NetWare queues, and NetWare workstations can print to UNIX queues.

- ▸ File Transfer Protocol (FTP). Supports the standard UNIX file exchange protocol, which allows UNIX workstations to get files from a server without having to mount the volume (the equivalent of attaching to a server). This allows even UNIX workstations that don't support NFS to access files on the NetWare server.

- ▸ Telnet. Allows UNIX users to log in on the NetWare server, using XCONSOLE.NLM and perform remote management of the server.

▸ LOCKD (Lock Daemon). The UNIX record-locking utility that prevents two or more users from trying to change the same file at the same time.

### Permissions

Because of the difference between the NetWare permission structure and the UNIX permission structure, permissions tend to get out of sync with what was originally intended. Additionally, the mapping between UNIX and NetWare rights cannot be mapped perfectly because the rights don't correspond perfectly.

> **The mapping between UNIX and NetWare rights cannot be maintained perfectly because the rights don't correspond perfectly.**

NetWare 3.x has both trustee rights, which can be granted to a user or a group, and file attributes, which are the same for any user or group. In contrast, UNIX grants three access rights to three entities—the file or directory's owner, its group, and everyone else (the world). A common problem occurs when UNIX users have mounted a NetWare volume and can access it, but are not defined as users on the NetWare server.

A typical default file-creation mask for UNIX users is to give the owner of a file all three rights, and to give the group and the world the rights to read the file and execute it, but not to write to it. When a user with this setup writes a file to a NetWare server on which they don't have an account, the server identifies them as user −2 (nobody) and group −2 (nogroup). If they then try to change their own file, they don't have access rights, because a user identified as user −2 or with the group −2 isn't given rights to files created by unidentified users or groups, for security reasons. This means that the UNIX user is effectively locked out of their own file or directory.

The way to avoid this problem is to make sure that every UNIX user who will be accessing a NetWare server has a login on that server. Also, if your users will be accessing files from the UNIX side and will need to modify the permissions of files, be sure that the option "Modify DOS attributes" in the export entry is set to Yes. Otherwise, you will only be able to change the permissions on the files from DOS.

Another problem with versions of NetWare NFS prior to version 1.2 is that every time a directory or file is created or the permissions on an existing directory are modified from the UNIX side, another trustee entry is created. This can result in hundreds or thousands of trustee entries, especially in the EVERYONE group. In version 1.2, you can turn this off, but you should then create the file TRUSTEES as described in the *NetWare NFS Administration* manual.

Troubleshooting TCP/IP connections from a NetWare server can be difficult. There is no equivalent to the PING command found in UNIX, which allows you to query another UNIX workstation to see if it is up and its network interface is working. TCPCON will allow you to track packets that are reaching the server, and what happens to them. Add-on utilities to NetWare such as LANalyzer for Windows will allow you to do this, and you can also PING the server from a workstation running LAN WorkPlace or a UNIX workstation.

You may also be routing TCP/IP through your NetWare server. If so, there will be two NICs in the server, each with a different TCP/IP address, such as 192.42.172.4 and 192.42.173.60. To check connectivity between a workstation on your network and one on another network, first PING the board that connects your network to your NetWare server. If the PING shows that the server is responding, then PING the other board. If it doesn't respond, make sure that the LOAD TCP/IP command in AUTOEXEC.NCF ends with FORWARD=YES. The first board should also be identified as the router in the NET.CFG file for LAN WorkPlace, or in the /etc/hostconfig file for a UNIX workstation. If the second board responds, PING a workstation on the other TCP/IP network. If it responds, then the TCP/IP forwarding is working correctly. Any UNIX workstation that needs to communicate with other workstations on the other side of a TCP/IP router must have the router identified in its host configuration file or NET.CFG file.

## NETWARE ON UNIX SYSTEMS

NetWare for UNIX (formerly Portable NetWare) allows UNIX servers to run NetWare 3.0 or higher as a process. This provides the users on that network with full access to NetWare services, and allows interconnectivity with other NetWare servers and networks. A major difference from standard NetWare is that NetWare for UNIX is running as a process (an application) on top of the standard UNIX operating system. This adds an extra level where things can go wrong. The UNIX operating system may have other processes running on it that could cause NetWare to crash, or disrupt services.

# PART IV

# Advanced Topics

**T**his section covers topics beyond the scope of basic NetWare services: troubleshooting network applications, and applications running over the network; upgrades to NetWare, hardware and other software; and a chapter on tips and techniques.

Chapter 9: Troubleshooting Network Applications, covers applications that access network services, applications that run from the server, and getting Windows to work with NetWare and even run on the server.

Chapter 10: Upgrades to NetWare, Hardware and Software, covers upgrading NetWare from 2.x to 3.x and from 3.x to 4.x. It discusses planning considerations and ways to make the transition easier, as well as methods for troubleshooting problems with the upgrade process. It also presents the basic theory of troubleshooting upgrades to workstation hardware and software.

Chapter 11: Tips and Techniques, is a collection of pointers that aren't easily classified into topics. You'll find special methods for dealing with problems that aren't well documented or intuitively obvious.

# CHAPTER 9

# Troubleshooting Network Applications

This chapter addresses three types of network applications: applications that need access to NetWare services, which may either be "NetWare aware"—providing direct access to NetWare services such as print queues—or simple DOS applications that don't have any provision for the existence of a network; applications that run from the server; and applications such as e-mail and fax servers that provide additional network services.

Network applications produce some additional fault points for troubleshooting. First, they are accessible to users, who have occasionally been known to misunderstand the proper usage of applications or network services. Second, they interface with NetWare, to one degree or another. Finally, they are themselves a fault point. Of the three, the second fault point is the most difficult to diagnose. Users can (usually) be educated, and buggy software can be upgraded or replaced. Discovering how the software is attempting to access NetWare services, and what's going wrong, can be complex. Also, some programs that run from the server require a configuration file for each user or workstation that will be accessing the software. You may get one user running, and have to do the whole thing over again for the next user. This is another good reason to keep records and default configuration files.

## Applications Accessing NetWare Services

The essential network services that applications need to access are file services, print services, networked modems, and sometimes fax services. Almost all applications save files, but the NetWare drivers make this process essentially identical to accessing the local drive on the workstation. Some programs will allow you to select a server's drives by volume name, rather than having to remember that, for example, drive G: is mapped to VOL1.

Accessing print services directly, rather than through CAPTURE, allows users to select a print queue from a list, rather than having to set the printer configuration before starting the program, or having to quit the program and restart to change to a different queue.

Networks are beginning to provide users with a common fax and/or data modem. These services are covered in more detail in the section on networked modems below, on page 299. For network applications to access these services, they may need to use drivers provided by the modem manufacturer, or the manufacturer may allow you to set up a print queue that will print to the fax modem instead of to a regular printer.

## FILE SERVICES

The most basic network service is storing and managing files, a fact that is reflected in the name *file server*. In the most basic case, a user can send a file to the server instead of his or her hard disk by simply changing the entry in the Save dialog box in the application from C: to H:. There are several considerations that can confuse the user, even in this most simple case.

The primary use for a network is file sharing, not simply storing files on some other workstation's disk. The problem is that if a file is shared, two people may try to access it at the same time; and even if this doesn't actually cause a crash, it will generally mean that one of the two will lose their work. The way to fix this problem is to lock the file, either through the use of the NetWare file services, through the application, or with the existence of a lock file, which lets the application know that the file is in use.

NetWare services allow an application to lock a file by designating the file as *locked exclusive*, or *locked shareable*. Locked-exclusive files cannot be accessed by anyone else while they are in use. Locked-shareable files can be read, but not changed. Some network applications can keep track of what files are in use by authorized users, and return an error message if a second user attempts to access the file. The last common method of locking is the use of a temporary lock file, which is deleted when the file is closed and typically has the same name as the file being locked, but with a .LCK or similar extension. If a user attempts to access a file for which there is an equivalent lock file in the same directory (that is, a file currently in use), the application will either deny access or warn the user that the file is in use, and that changes will not be saved. This method of locking is typical of UNIX applications, and can also be seen in network-oriented applications that run on other networks besides NetWare. Of course, in all of these types of locking, you can use the Save As command and save the file to another location or filename.

The problems that arise from file locking are generally of two sorts. If users don't understand the message received, they may think that the reason they can't access a file is a system problem, rather than that another user has the file open. Network novices (who aren't necessarily computer novices) need to be educated about the implications of working with files to which others have access; and particularly cryptic error messages may need to be translated for them. The second problem is with files that are in use when an application crashes. If the application doesn't exit cleanly, the files may remain locked, or the lock file may not be deleted. In this case you will need to determine that no other user has the file in use (MONITOR can tell you what files each user has open with Connection Information), and then reset the file's status with ATTRIB or FILER, or remove the lock file.

## PRINTING FROM APPLICATIONS

In general, any application that can print to the local PC's printer port can be made to print to a NetWare queue. The most common sticking point is with applications, such as Windows, that attempt to bypass the DOS LPT port device and send data directly to the physical printer port. If this occurs, the NetWare shell cannot intercept the data and send it to the queue. The problem can often be avoided by instructing the application to print to a file, and when prompted for a file name, entering LPT1. This doesn't actually print to a file, but to the DOS device LPT1, which is then intercepted by the Net-Ware shell and sent to the queue.

The print utilities provided with NetWare have never been famous for stability. Even the utilities provided with NetWare 3.11 and 2.2 are not perfect. There are updates to the utilities NPRINT, CAPTURE, and ENDCAP, and to PSERVER (.NLM, .VAP, and .EXE) available on NetWire.

You may have several different printers on your network—perhaps one PostScript printer, one PCL (HP LaserJet compatible), and one dot-matrix for multipart forms. A user who needs to print from an application first to

**NOTE**
See Appendix A for information on downloading software from NetWire.

one of these printers and then to another must typically enter the CAP-TURE statement for the first printer, open the application, print the first document, exit the application, enter the new CAPTURE statement for the next printer, reopen the application, and print the second document.

The NetWare print utilities normally intercept any TAB characters (ASCII 09) and convert them to spaces (the default is eight). This is fine when printing a text file to a text printer. However, if you are printing graphics, either to an HP LaserJet or compatible, or PostScript, this is not what should happen. In order to prevent the tabs from being replaced, you must use the /NT switch in the CAPTURE statement, or set File Contents to Byte Stream when configuring the print job in PRINTCON.

When printing PostScript, you should also have the banner page turned off with the /NB switch for CAPTURE, or in the print job configuration. Leaving this on can confuse the printer by sending ASCII text before the PostScript initialization commands.

### Accessing NetWare Print Queues Directly

If the application can directly access NetWare queues, then the user can simply tell the application to send the first job to one queue, and the second job to the other queue. This method may even give the user a list of queues that can be printed to, rather than requiring the user to remember their names. The problem with this approach is that, from a programmer's point of view, it further complicates an already complicated subject. Programs that handle this process without errors deserve your respect.

> **If a program cannot print directly to a print queue, try printing to LPT1 and using CAPTURE to send it to the queue.**

There are several common problems you may encounter with programs that are attempting to access NetWare print services directly. The first is that programs can detect the print queues, but not print to them. If this happens, try printing to LPT1 and using NetWare's redirection capability instead. If that works, make sure that the program is compatible with the version of NetWare you are using—

it may be trying to use an outdated method of accessing the NetWare queue. If printing to LPT1 doesn't work either, or you get garbled text, it may be that the application is not configured correctly for the printer you are using. Many users don't understand that you can't print a text file to a PostScript printer, or a PCL graphics file to a dot-matrix printer.

You should also make sure that the queue name entered is correct. If the application allows the user to specify the queue name, but doesn't allow selection from a list, the user may have misspelled the queue name. If the queue name is longer than eight characters, some older programs may truncate the name, which will cause printing to fail.

### Fonts

Fonts are another potential problem area, particularly using fonts beyond what the printer provides. Most programs can access the standard fonts fairly easily. However, if you want to add another font, every program that you want to use it with will probably have different requirements for loading it, and different ways for getting the printer to use it. One of the real advantages of Windows is that it provides a unified way for loading and using fonts, although adding fonts to Windows isn't simple either. If your users need additional fonts, there are several good books on what fonts are available and how to get them to work with your system.

### ACCESSING NETWARE SERVICES FROM WINDOWS

Windows has its own section here because it is almost a separate operating system. Unlike true operating systems, it loads on top of DOS, but it does offer a unified approach to menus, fonts, file services and other system services such as fax modems. For that reason, it's often called an "operating environment." If you are using Windows with NetWare, get Windows 3.1 or later. Chapter 11 offers some tips for getting previous versions to work with NetWare, but given the low cost and the added functionality of upgrading to 3.1, it is very difficult to think of any

> ► · · · · · · · · · · ◄
>
> **If you are using Windows with NetWare, use Windows 3.1 or later.**

valid reason to stay with older versions. This chapter will only discuss Windows 3.1.

Getting Windows to run on a PC under NetWare can be troublesome. Chapter 2: Workstations provides detailed suggestions on appropriate settings. Once it is running on the workstation and connecting with NetWare, Windows offers convenient access to NetWare print services through the Printers Control Panel. You should also get the NetWare Tools for Windows (NWTOOLS.EXE) program, which allows you to use the MAP, ATTACH, CAPTURE, USERLIST, VOLINFO, SETPASS, SEND, MESSAGES and SESSION utilities from within Windows, instead of having to exit Windows to reconfigure your NetWare environment from DOS.

Be sure to use the latest IPX and NETX (or NETx), or the ODI drivers if you are running Windows. If you are having problems accessing a queue from Windows, try exiting and setting the default queue with CAPTURE or PRINTCON, then restarting Windows.

Another problem you may run into is the result of a difference between the ways DOS and NetWare display files and directories. If you type DIR on a DOS drive, the first two items will be a period and double period, representing the current directory and the parent directory. Windows allows you to double-click on the double period to move back up the directory tree in the File Manager or in file menus. On a NetWare drive, you won't get the period and double period in Windows dialog boxes or the File Manager, unless the entry SHOW DOTS = ON is in the SHELL.CFG or NET.CFG file. This doesn't hurt, so I recommend you use it in your default configuration files.

When installing Windows on a workstation connected to an ARCnet network, be sure to run INSTALL with the /I switch. This prevents the automatic hardware detection feature of the Windows installation routine from running, and so prevents the ARCnet network driver from being accidentally unloaded.

**NOTE**
**See Chapter 2:**
**Workstations for**
more details on IPX,
NETx, and other
recommended
settings.

### Printing from Windows Applications

Printing from a Windows application is not like printing from a DOS application—with Windows, the application does not handle the printing itself, it passes the job on to Windows. This means that you only need to configure Windows, instead of every application, for your printer, print queue, and fonts. While the installation and configuration of a printer in Windows can be complex, it is generally a matter of following the directions carefully. The same is true of adding fonts to Windows.

The most common problems in printing from Windows are related to incorrect configuration settings, incorrect paths to directories, and incorrect permissions. These are the items to check first if a printer configuration doesn't work. If all else fails, set Windows to print to LPT1 and set CAPTURE before starting Windows, rather than printing directly to a queue.

If you are using the NWTOOLS program (and you should be), you will be able to set configuration options such as No Tabs, No Banner, and Timeout from within Windows, instead of needing to use CAPTURE before starting Windows.

# Applications Running from the Server

Getting an application to run from the server may be as simple as copying the APP.EXE file to a network drive and running it, or as complex as separate installations for each server and workstation, plus configuration files for each user. Applications written to run on DOS can be run from the server, as long as you understand the implications.

Some applications maintain configuration information within the program code. On a workstation, this isn't a problem. However, if two users try to simultaneously use a program on the server that operates this way, they can both attempt to change the same data at the same time, resulting in a crash for one or both of them. Fortunately, most major applications are available in network versions, which allow multiple users to run the application at once.

Many applications have configuration files that contain information on user preferences and the setup of the workstation. Programs designed to run on a network typically have an installation program that installs the program files, and a user installation program that creates the configuration files. If the application isn't started from the directory that contains the configuration files, it may use a default configuration and save a new configuration file in the directory that the application was started from. This can cause crashes because the user doesn't have permission to write a file in that directory, or result in the proliferation of configuration files in many different directories.

Be sure that the application is marked as shareable. This should be the default with a network-aware installation, but in some cases it may not happen correctly. You may also need to make sure that any user who will be using the application has adequate rights to configuration files, and possible copy-protection files as well. Check with the application documentation for information on network installation. If you use NCOPY to copy the directory structure for the user's files, use the /E switch in addition to the /S switch, to copy empty directories as well as directories containing configuration files; some applications look for files in a specific default directory, which may not initially have any files in it.

If you can't get an application to run from the network, try setting it up as a local application. Most applications offer you the option of either type of installation. If it works from the workstation, this should give you clues about why it won't work from the server. As always, ask yourself, "What's different?" Also try to run the application from another workstation or as another user. This can isolate problems with rights or with configuration files.

Be cautious about checking the installation of applications as Supervisor—this user has access rights to everything and trustee rights everywhere, so the application may work for you and not for anyone else. Of course, this is a clue in itself—it may mean that the user needs additional permissions that they don't have, or that the Supervisor has permission to write to the root directory of the volume and the user doesn't.

Some applications expect to be located in a directory directly off the root of a drive—for instance C:\APPDIR. If your standard setup on the network is to have an APPS directory with applications under that, some applications may not run correctly. You can fix this by using the fake root, which makes the application think that the directory is a root directory. A directory set up as a fake root won't allow the user to CD past that level toward the real root. See the NetWare documentation on the MAP command for more details.

## RUNNING LAN WORKGROUP

Because LAN WorkGroup runs from the server, it is liable to the problems affecting networked applications in general. Specifically, you need to make sure that the configuration files for each user and workstation are correctly set up, and that the correct search drives are set up for each user with the MAP command. A simple way to do this is to set up a group (called WGUSERS, perhaps) and put a statement in the system login script such as:

```
IF MEMBER OF GROUP WGUSERS
MAP S16:=SYS:/APPLICATIONS/LANWG
```

This statement will set up the appropriate mapping for anyone placed in the group. This method allows you to add or remove this functionality for users without having to go to their workstations.

## RUNNING WINDOWS FROM THE SERVER

Running Windows from the server reduces the space necessary on local workstation drives by up to 10 MB, and makes updates to Windows much easier, especially in large departments. You can also exercise control over the Windows environment, preventing users from changing the configuration of Windows, including program groups, the screen saver and colors, and so forth by denying permission to the appropriate configuration files.

You can also prevent users from adding unauthorized (and possibly buggy or virus-infected) programs or utilities to Windows.

On the other hand, it increases network traffic and can be difficult to set up and manage, and most users will want some control over their Windows setup. If you have different types of workstations, with differing monitor types, different types of mouse, or different versions of the NetWare LAN drivers, you will need to have different configuration files on the server for each type of workstation.

You will need about 17 MB free on a server drive to install Windows, and it will take up about 11 MB after it's installed. Windows 3.1 is considerably easier to install on the server than previous versions. Just run SETUP with the /A option. Installing the workstation files is also easier—log in on the user's workstation and run SETUP /N. If you create one User Definition File (UDF) directory on the server, and then copy it to everyone else's directory, be sure to change the trustee rights and ownership of the directory and files afterwards. You will also need to make the appropriate changes to CON-FIG.SYS and AUTOEXEC.BAT. You can also create the UDF directory on the user's local drive and configure Windows to look for it there, but this makes updates to Windows more complex.

If you are going to be running the SETUP program from a number of workstations that all use the same configuration, you can use the SETUP /H option with an Automatic Installation File (AIF) to automate the installation. Running SETUP this way doesn't require you to answer the questions for configuration. It allows you to set everything up in the AIF in advance. You will need a different AIF for each different workstation configuration. See the Windows documentation for more details on this option.

The UDF directory contains the files that control how Windows is configured for each user. The files include WIN.COM and the .INI and .GRP files. WIN.COM is not the Windows executable file; it simply starts Windows. The .INI files control various aspects of Windows, and the .GRP files control what applications are shown in each window on the desktop. If you set these files to Read-Only for the users, they won't be able to change their Windows configuration.

The UDF directory must be in the user's directory search path, and must be found before the Windows directory. This will happen automatically if Windows is started from the UDF directory. Otherwise, make sure that the UDF directory is before the Windows directory in the DOS path.

The WIN.COM file in the user's UDF directory assumes a certain video configuration, mouse driver, and version of NetWare. If the user logs in from another workstation and any of these items are different, Windows may hang, drop back to DOS, or give error messages about configuration files not being found. The solution is to create a version of WIN.COM for each display, etc., that the user might need to use, and rename them along the lines of WINVGA.COM, WINEGA.COM, WINHERC.COM, as seems appropriate. Since this program just starts Windows with the specified configuration, having several such files in the UDF directory won't hurt anything.

You can also have several default UDF directories—one for each type of workstation on your network. This would require that the user replace their UDF directory with a different default directory to change configurations. You could also put the UDF files in a default location such as C:\UDF on every workstation. If a user changed their configuration and moved to another workstation, it wouldn't reflect their configuration, but whatever configuration had been installed on that workstation.

# Electronic Mail Applications

The standard for e-mail on NetWare is MHS. MHS is a store-and-forward system that holds a message until it can be forwarded to the recipient. Each user has a mail directory, which is a numbered directory in SYS:MAIL. You can get each user's number with SYSCON (User Information/Login Name/Other Information). SUPERVISOR always has the directory number 1.

The most common problems with e-Mail fall into two areas: not attaching correctly to the mail server, and permission problems. The mail server may not be the same server the user normally uses. If it isn't, the user's login script should attach them to the mail server and set up a mapping to the appropriate directory. See your e-mail application's documentation for details. If the user doesn't have the correct permissions in their e-mail directory, they won't be able to access their mail.

## Networked Modems

As networking becomes an integral part of computing, the need to access other systems becomes greater. The simplest way to accomplish occasional access is with a modem. Rather than have a modem on every workstation, you can set up a modem on the network that anyone on the network can access, and that can also be used to access the LAN from another location. A fax machine is essentially a specialized modem with a scanner and a printer attached. It is relatively simple to convert a data modem to send the proper signals to a fax modem as well.

Using networked modems requires additional software beyond the standard NetWare shell. This may be software similar to CAPTURE that sends a print job to the fax modem instead of a printer, or software that allows a modem connected by Ethernet to simulate a modem connected to the serial port of the PC. This software is specific to the manufacturer of the modem and is not part of NetWare, with the exception of LAN WorkPlace, which can be used to access the NetWare Access Server.

The typical problems with this software are incompatibility between the printer driver of the application and the fax modem software, and interrupt conflicts or COM port access problems with data modem software. Make sure that the printer driver used by the application is supported by the fax modem software. With data modem software, the terminal application must be using the DOS port calls, rather than trying to send data directly to the physical port, or the software won't be able to intercept the data and forward it to the network modem.

## NETWORKED DATA MODEMS

Novell has solutions such as the NetWare Access Server, which supports up to 16 simultaneous modem connections; and there are many products available from other vendors, such as the Shiva NetModem/E, which provides one modem connection accessible from both PCs and Macintoshes. In addition to the hardware and software running on the networked device, you will need to install software on each workstation that needs to access the modem. There is usually one program that allows users on the LAN to dial out, and a second program that allows users elsewhere to access the LAN.

The additional fault points for a networked modem are the software that intercepts the data that would otherwise be sent to the serial port and reroutes it to the network modem, and the connection to the network modem. If the terminal application you are using supports the networked modem, the first fault point is eliminated. If the terminal application is set up to use a COM port, you should make sure that it uses the DOS COM port driver, rather than sending data directly to the physical port—which makes it impossible to intercept the data and route it to the network modem.

## NETWORKED FAX MODEMS

**NOTE**
See Chapter 4: Printing, for an illustration of the printing fault point chain.

The additional fault points for a network fax modem are the software that simulates a print queue or replaces CAPTURE and sends the data to the fax modem, the connection to the fax modem, and the fax modem itself, especially in the degree to which it is compatible with a standard fax machine. You may find that a fax modem produces cleaner outgoing faxes than a standard fax machine, because it reduces the number of times the page must be reproduced—the page doesn't have to be printed and then scanned by the fax machine. On the other hand, fax modems may have trouble with incoming faxes, especially if line quality is not good.

Since NetWare doesn't provide direct support for fax modems yet, you must rely on the manufacturer's documentation for troubleshooting information. When possible, test all other parts of the process. For instance, say that the process for faxing is as follows: the application prints PostScript, but to a queue established by the fax modem software, which then sends the output to the fax modem. Make sure that the application can produce Post-Script output that prints on a regular PostScript printer. Also make sure that the network fax modem shows up as a node on the network (that it is accessible as a network device). This would then leave only the fax modem software and its configuration as potential fault points.

# CHAPTER 10

# Upgrades to NetWare, Hardware, and Software

**U**pgrading computer systems is a process every administrator must go through. The computer industry is advancing at such a rate that two-year-old systems are often obsolete. Upgrades to hardware or application software are generally a matter of removing the old version and installing the new one. NetWare differs in that the data on the server and all the configuration information about your users must be preserved during the upgrade. This chapter discusses practices that can make upgrades easier and decrease the potential for disaster.

# Planning an Upgrade

Upgrading a system, whether the NetWare operating system, a PC workstation, or application software, can be a traumatic experience. However, this is often because the administrator tries to combine several upgrades at once, rather than taking them one at a time. For instance, when you upgrade a server from NetWare 2.*x* to 3.11, it is also the ideal time to upgrade the server hardware. However, if you aren't cautious, this can make it very difficult to track down problems—if you change several things at once, figuring out which one is causing the problem is harder. Always make sure that you can trace your steps back—upgrade the hardware first and make sure it's working, then install the new version of NetWare.

Upgrading a system may require that you upgrade related parts. If you change a workstation NIC to a new, faster NIC, you will also need to upgrade the network driver. Save the old configurations and software, just in case—that way, you will always be able to go back to a working configuration. If possible, this practice should even be followed with servers—you will probably want to set up a new server, to take advantage of advances in speed since the last one was installed. Set up the new server and install the new version of NetWare on it, debug any problems, and then transfer the data drives from the old server to the new server, or restore the data from the old server's drive to the new server's drive.

**Save the old configuration and software, just in case.**

# Upgrading NetWare

Upgrading NetWare within a version (2.15 to 2.2, for instance) is a relatively trivial operation. If you ensure that you have good backups, there should be few challenges. Upgrading between versions can be another story. You may find that the new version requires a different network organization or more powerful hardware, or that it has a different permission structure. Be very sure that you understand the differences between versions before you upgrade. Resources for getting more of this information include the NetWare forums on CompuServe, the local chapter of the CNEPA, *NetWare Application Notes*, and your local NetWare Users Group.

One thing that can make your upgrades much easier, and can make your server more stable as well, is to strictly limit your server's boot drive, the SYS volume, to NetWare directories and applications. Put your user directories and all data directories on other drives. This allows you to upgrade to a new server by changing only the SYS volume. You can set the new server up in advance, then add it to the network and test it, and finally, move the data drives from the old server to the new. Of course, you should still have backups of the data drives before you begin, just in case. This approach also adds fault tolerance—if the server fails, you can take any workstation, install NetWare on the internal drive, add the external drives, and have a server back on line quickly.

## UPGRADING WITHOUT DISRUPTING WORK FLOW

One of the facts of life for most administrators is working before or after normal hours to minimize network down time for users. To minimize the time you need to spend outside normal hours, plan the upgrade ahead of time. If you do update the server hardware at the same time as the software, you have the luxury of installing the new version of NetWare any time you wish. The only part you need to do after hours is swapping drives from the old server to the new one. If you are using the same hardware, write down all the configuration steps you will need to do: don't just use a check list, write the steps down. This procedure is more likely to help you spot problem areas in advance,

**NOTE**
**See Appendix A for details about the sources of information listed here.**

and it lets you refer to a written configuration sheet while you are actually upgrading the server.

Allow twice the time you think you will need for the upgrade, and then about the same time for testing. Make sure that you can test logins from a couple of different users, particularly users who don't have supervisor privileges, to make sure that trustee rights have been restored properly.

### PLANNING THE UPGRADE

When you plan the upgrade, you need to keep three basic questions in mind: What do you have now? What do you want to end up with? And How are you going to get there? To know what you have now, you should print out a complete directory map of all existing directories on all volumes, including ownership information. Also print out all the configuration information about the server, including user information, trustee rights, login scripts, and so forth.

> **Keep three basics in mind: What do you have now, what do you want to end up with, and how are you going to get there?**

Next, determine what you want to end up with. If permission structures are different, how will that affect the upgrade? If you are going to install NetWare 4.x, what do you need to change to fit in with the company tree structure? Will user login scripts on different servers conflict with each other? Are printer or print queue names unique throughout the company? Decide how the server will be configured—write out what the new AUTOEXEC.NCF and STARTUP.NCF files should look like. Finally, plan how you will make the changes. In some cases, such as the NetWare 3.x to 4.x upgrade, you should spend a good deal of time consolidating the existing user login scripts, deleting unnecessary files, and planning how your user names, print queues, groups, and other network resources will fit into the new overall network plan.

The most common upgrades will be from NetWare 2.x to 3.1x, and from 3.x to 4.x. Each of these has special considerations, some of which are covered in the examples below. A complete discussion of all considerations

**NOTE**
See Appendix A for information about obtaining *NetWare Application Notes.*

is impractical—the *NetWare Application Notes* April 1993 issue covers some of the considerations of the 3.*x* to 4.*x* upgrade in 240 pages. Depending on the complexity of your network and server configurations, you should consider taking the appropriate System Manager or upgrade course at your local Novell Authorized Education Center.

### File Structure

As long as you are going to do the upgrade anyway, it is an ideal time to consider your file systems. Is there anything you'd like to do differently? Do you wish your Users directory wasn't on the SYS volume? Now is the ideal time to change it. However, making changes in your file structure will entail some additional steps in the upgrade. You can either use UPGRADE and then move the file structure around, or use the RESTORE method for the upgrade—back up the files, upgrade the server to the new version and then restore the files into their new directories.

You can make your life simpler by using the SYS volume only for NetWare files and applications. It doesn't hurt to have lots of free space left on SYS—with the prices of hard drives dropping constantly, it's an inexpensive precaution to ensure that you'll always have lots of room for print queues, mail directories, and the NetWare files themselves. The NetWare 3.*x* to 4.*x* upgrade requires as much as 30 additional MB on the SYS drive, and printing PostScript files can create very large temporary queue files—10 to 50 MB is not uncommon when printing books or color PostScript files.

Limiting the files on SYS in this way also reduces the backups necessary on this volume—the only files that will change are the mail files. Applications and the NetWare directories will normally only change when you update the system or add users or new software.

### Documentation

If you don't have good documentation of your network now, create it before you upgrade. Not only does it give you a better feel for what you have and what you should change before or during the upgrade, it gives you a hedge against disaster. If the server freezes while UPGRADE.EXE is running, and you can't restore the binderies, you should have enough documentation to recreate every user's environment and trustee rights. Look at your server and gather all the information you would need to recreate the server if you had to start from scratch with just the basic NetWare installation and your data files.

This information would include documentation of all the NetWare configuration items—the startup files, system login script, print configuration and any additional configurations such as NetWare NFS or NetWare for Macintosh. It would also include documentation of every user—their login script, trustee rights, group memberships, and so forth. Accumulating this information using only NetWare tools can be cumbersome in the extreme. There are a large number of utilities that can create reports with all the necessary information, ranging in price from nothing to several hundred dollars. See Appendix A for resources to find the utility that's right for you.

There are three utilities, PRINTUSR.EXE, PRINTGRP.EXE, and DUP-BIND.EXE, that you can download from the CompuServe NetWare forum. PRINTUSR produces a report on the user's group memberships, security equivalencies, trustee assignments, login script and disk utilization. PRINTGRP provides similar information about groups. DUPBIND reports any duplicate names in the bindery—a user and a group with the same name, for instance. These utilities are provided by Novell, but not supported.

### Backups

*Always* back the server up before starting an upgrade. If you are going to use UPGRADE.EXE to upgrade the server, you should have *two* backups—the one you did for safety, and the one you'll be working from. It may take a few hours to back the server up again, but it would take much longer to reconstruct it from scratch if something happens to the only tape you have. Verify the tapes by performing test restores of at least some files—many backup programs don't tell you if the backup is any good or not.

> **Always back up the server before planning an upgrade; and verify the tapes by performing test restores of at least some files.**

If you are upgrading the server hardware at the same time, install the new version of NetWare on the new server. You can then restore the data from the backups of the old server to the new server. If you only have one drive in the old server, back it up and then restore the data to the new server's drive, being careful *not* to restore the binderies—they are specific to the old drive's partition information. Of course, you won't restore the SYSTEM or PUBLIC directories. You will then have to recreate the trustee rights and ownerships for the restored directories. This is more work than simply using UPGRADE, but makes sure that everything ends up with the correct rights, particularly when upgrading from 2.x to 3.1x or 4.x.

**Once your new server is running smoothly, back it up.**

Finally, once you have your new server installed, configured and running smoothly, back it up. This new backup will give you a reference point to which you can return if trouble occurs.

### Hardware

The hardware requirements of the new version of NetWare may be different. NetWare 3.x requires a minimum of a 386 processor and shouldn't be run with less than 4 MB RAM. NetWare 4.x shouldn't be run with less than a fast 486 and 16 MB RAM. Depending on the size of your network and the amount of additional network traffic that NetWare Directory Service database updates will produce, you will probably also want to upgrade the network adapter to a faster model.

### Support Files

In addition to NetWare itself, you will need to consider the workstations. If you are upgrading to NetWare 4.x, you will need to upgrade the workstation NetWare files to the VLM drivers. This should be done before the server is upgraded—it won't interfere with users' access to the 3.11 server, and it lets you approach the relatively time consuming operation over a period of time. If you're upgrading to 3.11 from 2.x, you should upgrade your workstation drivers, unless you are already using the latest IPX and NETX or ODI drivers. If you are performing an incremental upgrade, from 2.15 to 2.2, for instance, you probably won't need to update anything on the workstations.

## METHODS

The methods available for upgrading NetWare depend on whether the change is from 2.*x* to 3.*x* or from 3.*x* to 4.*x*. The upgrade from 2.*x* to 4.*x* actually encompasses both—you must upgrade from 2.*x* to 3.*x* (you don't have to buy 3.*x*) and then from 3.*x* to 4.*x*.

### Upgrading from 2.*x* to 3.*x*

There are two basic methods of upgrading NetWare from 2.*x* to 3.*x*. The first is to use the UPGRADE utility to move data from an existing 2.*x* server to a new 3.*x* server (the transfer method). The second is to use UPGRADE to back the server up, remove the existing version of NetWare, install the new version of NetWare, then restore the data with UPGRADE (the backup device method). Each has advantages and disadvantages.

The transfer method is simpler, but does have disadvantages—it can produce errors in the translation of user rights and other bindery elements, and it requires that you have a new server to install 3.*x* on. If the server should crash during the upgrade, you will have to restore the old server from tape to its original state, reinstall NetWare on the new server, and begin from scratch. It is a more secure method, though, because you will normally have the old server to fall back on if necessary, and it is often necessary to upgrade the server anyway to support the new version of NetWare.

The backup device method can be more cumbersome, because you must recreate the users, groups, and trustee rights after the data is restored, but it has the advantage of letting you start from a clean slate. If you are planning changes in the directory structure at the same time, the disadvantage becomes much less significant. If you are planning to use this method, make sure that you understand the MAKEUSER utility thoroughly before you start—it can make this process much simpler.

The biggest problem you might face with the backup device method is that your data is deleted from the hard drives, forever—if the restore doesn't work, your data is gone. You can reduce the risk by upgrading one hard drive at a time—if the first restore works, you can feel more comfortable about the rest, and if it fails, you have only lost some of your data.

If you decide to use the backup device method, it is critical to test your backups by restoring at least some files from them. If several files from different directories can be restored, the tape as a whole is likely to be good, although there is always the chance of a bad block on the tape causing the corruption of a file. This is the reason you should have two backups.

### Upgrading from 3.x to 4.x

There are three methods of upgrading a server from 3.1x to 4.x. They are: migration to an existing 4.x server, migration to a workstation and back to the same server after an upgrade, and upgrading the server with the files in place.

The first method moves the users, groups, files, print queues, and so on from the existing server to a NetWare 4.x server. This method allows you to set up the new server in advance, and only the transfer itself needs to be done while no one else is on the network. There is no risk of data loss, because the data still exists on the old server. Moreover, you can choose what data goes where in the new directory structure, even consolidating several old servers into one new server, or the reverse. The basic disadvantage is that you must have all new hardware for the new server.

The second method is to move all the data to a workstation, using the migration utility. The workstation must have enough disk space to hold all of the server's files. Then you install NetWare 4.x on the server, and migrate the files back to the server. This method has many of the advantages of the first (migrating to a new server), and requires only a workstation with enough hard disk space, rather than a complete new server. You could even accomplish this without any additional hardware by unmirroring your server's drives, installing the mirror drives on the workstation, migrating the files, upgrading the server, migrating the files back, and then remirroring the drives. The risk with this method is slightly higher, because the data is not maintained on a server while the old server is upgraded. If the workstation hard disks fail, the data would have to be restored from tape.

The third method, the in-place upgrade, requires that the server be running 3.1x or higher. If the server is a 2.x server, you must first upgrade to 3.1x, then to 4.x. This doesn't incur additional cost—the upgrade facility will perform this upgrade first. The server is then upgraded from 3.x to 4.x. The advantage to this method is that it is the cheapest—it doesn't require any additional hardware. However, it is the least secure—if the process fails, you will have to restore from tape and begin again. It also requires the most time, especially with a 2.x server, which requires two steps, and has the least flexibility.

Since there is a good chance you will be upgrading the server hardware at the same time, I strongly recommend the server-to-server migration if you can get the equipment. It provides complete security of data (you should still make backups first, of course—just for luck), gives you the most flexibility in restructuring the network, and requires the least time outside of business hours. You could even make the change while users are working on the network, although I would strongly recommend against it.

## EXAMPLE: 2.15 TO 3.11

There are many considerations involved in planning the upgrade from 2.x to 3.x. The NetWare 3.x *Installation* manual covers the process in detail. What will be covered here are the typical problem areas and the most important considerations.

### Planning and Preparation

There are a number of differences in the structure of NetWare from 2.15 to 3.11. Changes include the partition information on NetWare volumes, the format of the binderies and the number of bindery files, the way rights are assigned and inherited, the format and assignment of user numbers, and the method of password encryption.

The most important changes are those in partitions and rights. The partition changes mean that drives must be repartitioned, which destroys all data on the drive. There is no way of upgrading a NetWare 2.15 volume to a NetWare 3.11 volume without erasing the volume and restoring the information from tape or setting up a new server and moving the data from the old server. The new rights structure means that there is no exact way to translate rights between the two systems—there will be effective changes in the access users have to files. These changes may be minimal or extensive, depending on what rights users had before.

NetWare 3.11 will require more memory than 2.15, and at least a 386 processor. If you have older NICs, backup tape drives, or other devices in the server, you may need to get updated drivers or change to newer hardware. Of course, if the old server was a 286 PC, you'll need to upgrade to at least a 386, and at least 4 MB of RAM (I recommend a minimum of 8). Given the relative differences in price, it makes good sense to get the highest-performance server you can—the difference between a 386/16 with 8 MB RAM and an ISA bus and a 486/66 with 16 MB RAM and an EISA bus is unlikely to be more than a couple of thousand dollars, but the performance difference could be several hundred percent.

Another consideration is applications. If you use the transfer method, you may need to reinstall some applications—if the application manual recommends that you always install from the original floppies, it's a good indication that you may have to reinstall after the upgrade. If the application is copy-protected, you may need to uninstall it and then reinstall after the upgrade. Some applications that access the NetWare binderies may need to be upgraded to versions that support 3.11.

You should update the workstation network drivers to the version that comes with NetWare 3.11. You can do this before the server upgrade. If you are running the Mac VAPs, you'll need to have Mac name space loaded on the new server before the upgrade. Run BINDFIX to ensure that the 2.15 bindery is error-free. Back up NET$OS.EXE and the binderies too—if necessary, you can boot the server from a floppy and restore to it. Print out copies of the printer configurations and any other configurations you will need to transfer to the new server.

### The Upgrade

You can either install 3.11 on an entirely new server, and then connect the old and new servers and run UPGRADE.EXE from a workstation (the transfer method), or back up your old server to a Novell Device-Independent Backup Interface (DIBI)-compatible device, reformat the drive and install 3.11, and then restore the files from the backup. The transfer method is faster, and less chancy—you'll always have at least one operational server. It does, of course, require a new server, but given the speed with which PCs are growing in capability, this is probably a good idea anyway.

You can perform most of this upgrade piecemeal, before the actual transfer. If you upgrade the workstations at the users' convenience, and get the new server on line during normal hours, the only part that you'll need to do after hours is migrating the files from the old server to the new server, and checking user rights on the new server. It's easiest to do this over a weekend—plan on at least one day for the migration, and one day for checking. If you finish early, fine. If not, you'll have more leeway before the users are banging on your door. Once the upgrade is finished, make a backup of the new server.

### Troubleshooting the New Installation

If you have problems after the installation, you will need to determine what has changed, and how that change is causing the problem. This may seem simplistic, but the biggest problems I have seen resulting from upgrades were the result of the administrator either failing to understand the implications of some change in the features of NetWare or in the default configuration of some part of the system software, or leaving some part of the upgrade undone, such as failing to update login scripts to a new path or syntax.

Ensure before and after the upgrade that your users are aware of the changes you'll be making. At the least, you should provide them with a directory map

> **The biggest problems with upgrades arise when the administrator has failed to understand the implications of some change in the features of NetWare or in the default configuration of some part of the system software.**

of the server, showing changes, and a summary of the differences in trustee rights and the new inherited rights mask. Creating this document may also help you solidify your understanding of the differences. Make sure that the syntax of every user's login script and the system login script is correct for the new drive mappings, if you make changes.

Some areas that could create problems if you aren't aware of them are naming conventions, System and Hidden directories, and directory depth. If you used the 14-character filename capability of NetWare 2.15, the file names will be truncated to the DOS standard of eight characters and a three-character extension. This may not be a problem unless you have paths set to directories whose names become truncated.

Any directories that are marked as System or Hidden will not be migrated during the upgrade process. If you have any such directories other than the SYSTEM and PUBLIC directories, or have additional files or applications in the PUBLIC directory that users need, you will have to transfer them separately, or make sure the directories are unmarked before the upgrade.

NetWare 3.11 has a default maximum directory tree depth of 25 levels. If you have directory structures deeper than this on your 2.15 server, you will need to reduce the directory depth before performing the upgrade, or set the maximum directory depth to more than 25 levels in STARTUP.NCF on the 3.11 server before beginning the upgrade. I recommend reducing the directory depth. Excessive directory depths can cause problems with the backup software, and may also cause PATH statement line lengths in configuration files to exceed the maximum permissible length (256 characters). Some applications may also have problems with excessively long paths.

### Example: 3.11 to 4.x

Upgrading a network from NetWare 3.11 to NetWare 4.0 is a much more complex proposition than previous upgrades. Because of the WAN-oriented, global nature of NetWare 4.0, your entire corporate internet must be considered when upgrading. You must coordinate nomenclature for users, printers, volumes, groups and other network resources, with the other administrators to ensure that no two objects on your corporate tree use the same name. You will also need to ensure that users with login scripts on more than one server consolidate the login scripts to avoid conflicts in mappings. Ideally, you should have an overall coordinator responsible for the corporate upgrade. This person should plan the corporate tree structure, install and administer the master server for the root level, and coordinate all the information necessary to bring the other servers in your company into the NetWare Directory Services structure.

### Planning and Preparation

The *NetWare Application Notes* April and May '93 issues cover many of the issues you should consider before the upgrade. You might also want to read *Novell's Guide to NetWare 4.0 Networks*, available from Novell Press. Some issues you will want to pay special attention to are addressed below.

The server will need to have at least 60 MB free on SYS and a minimum of 16 MB RAM (technically, it's 8 MB, but this isn't a place to save $200); and it should be the fastest PC you can obtain. Desirable options include fast hard drives, an EISA bus, and 32-bit NICs.

If possible, I recommend the server-to-server migration upgrade. This gives you the maximum in safety and control and allows you to do most of the upgrade at your leisure, without affecting network services. It also gives you good justification to request a new fast server.

Once the new server is ready, run BINDFIX until the binderies are clean. Then use the PRINTUSR, PRINTGRP, and DUPBIND utilities and the NetWare utilities, or the aftermarket utility of your choice, to document all your users, groups, printers, print queues and print servers, binderies, applications, and directory structure.

Consider how your server, the users and your network resources will fit into the overall corporate structure. Some items to look for:

> ▸ Are user login scripts consolidated? If the users log in to more than one server, make sure that at least there are no conflicting commands in the different scripts.

▸ Make sure that the user names for the same users are the same on all servers.

▸ Run PUPGRADE to upgrade printer definitions, and jobs.

▸ Are all 2.*x* and 3.*x* servers using 802.2? (802.3 is the default for 2.*x* and 3.*x*.) If not, upgrade the whole network, including workstations, to 802.2 before migrating to 4.0.

▸ Does your server keep accurate time? Time synchronization across the network is an important part of NetWare 4.0. See the *Installation* manual for more details.

▸ Review the upgrade plan with users, department managers, and your management—especially with regard to training the users on the requirements of the new system and the new network structure.

▸ Do you have tested backups of the old server?

▸ Have you cleaned out obsolete accounts, printer definitions, junk files, and other files you no longer need? The simpler the bindery and file structure of your server is beforehand, the easier the upgrade will be.

▸ Have you run BINDFIX? Until there were no errors?

▸ Is there a new backup that reflects the cleaned-up status of the server?

▸ Do you have a record of the old server configuration, including BIOS settings, STARTUP.NCF and AUTOEXEC.NCF?

▸ Are all clients updated to the VLMs? Are any other necessary updates on the workstations made?

▸ If you have Macintoshes on your network, you will have to run bindery emulation on the 4.0 server, until NetWare for Macintosh 4.0 is released.

▸ If you currently have dedicated print servers running PSERVER.EXE, have you planned what to do with them?

These are only some of the more important issues you will face. The most important thing you can do to prepare for the NetWare 3.x to 4.0 upgrade is to fully understand the new features you will be implementing. Whether you get the information from a class, a book, or just the manuals, you should understand what you have, what you want to achieve with the new network structure, and the steps you will take to implement the new system.

After you understand the implications of the upgrade, make sure that the users and managers in your department also understand. Clarifying the issue for them will not only make the possibility of problems due to user errors less likely, it may raise issues that you haven't considered, and force you to be completely clear on all aspects of the upgrade yourself.

### The Upgrade

Once you have planned the new network structure and how your new server will fit into it, you can begin the actual process of the upgrade. Assuming this is not the first 4.0 server in the company tree (it shouldn't be—the master server should be a new, fast server with no other function than maintaining the master database), you should know where in the tree you will be—which organizational unit and organization.

The upgrade itself should be relatively simple, if you have prepared properly. The migration utility will move the designated files, users, and other bindery objects into the new structure of your NDS tree. If you have already updated the user's workstations to the new VLM network drivers, you will need only to switch some configuration items such as the login command syntax used in AUTOEXEC.BAT to reflect the new syntax for organizational unit and organization, rather than server names.

Be sure to allow time to log in as different users and test access to applications and data files, printers, and other network resources. You may spot problems that won't show up for the supervisor object, with its more extensive permissions.

### Troubleshooting the New Installation

Some troubleshooting may be needed even before you upgrade the server. For instance, you might find that some applications don't work well with the VLMs. You will need to identify each of these applications and either develop methods for fixing the problem, or upgrade the applications. Once the server is upgraded, your most common complaint initially will probably be from users who don't understand how NDS has changed the way they access resources on other servers.

If a user can't access network services at all, it may be because the upgrade process has changed their username to prevent conflicts with an existing user name in the tree. Similar problems can occur within login scripts. If a user had login scripts on more than one server before the upgrade, their usual directory mappings may have been changed, depending on which server was upgraded to NetWare 4.0 first. If the workstation can't see any servers, make sure that the Ethernet frame types on server and workstation match—the default for the VLMs is 802.2.

# Upgrading Hardware

If you are upgrading hardware, give yourself a way to return easily to what you had before. Save the old version of the operating system and the configuration files on a floppy before you replace them. Save the old cards, in case you discover conflicts that you can't resolve immediately. You don't need to stockpile the old equipment indefinitely—just long enough for any problems that may arise to show up—say, a couple of weeks.

As with any other upgrade, make sure that you understand the implications of the upgrade beforehand. For example, if you upgrade a workstation from a monochrome display to Super VGA, most applications will need new display drivers, and may have to be reinstalled. The new display adapter may use additional memory that could cause problems with Windows or other applications. You may also find that display updates are noticeably slower with the new display, because of higher processor overhead to display color instead of monochrome.

**NOTE**
**See Chapters 1 and 2 for more information about troubleshooting servers and workstations, respectively.**

You handle troubleshooting an upgrade to hardware in the same manner as troubleshooting a new system. First, make sure that all new configuration settings match the hardware configuration. If the problem persists, return to the most basic configuration possible, and once that works, add the rest of the system back in a piece at a time until you discover the problem. Often, this approach will lead you to the problem by forcing you to methodically compare configuration files with the actual hardware as you verify settings.

Say for instance that you are upgrading one of the workstations on your network to the VLM networking software in preparation for installing NetWare 4.x. You decide at the same time to upgrade the old NE1000 NIC to the faster 16-bit NE2000. The ideal process for ease of troubleshooting would be to install the new hardware first and get it running with the old shell, then upgrade the shell, but you decide to save time and do both at once.

You save the old IPX.COM, NETX.COM, AUTOEXEC.BAT and CONFIG.SYS on a floppy, then install the new card and reboot the PC. The existing IPX and NETX produce error messages, because they aren't configured for the new adapter, but you were expecting that. You then run the NetWare 4.0 Workstation Installation program, which installs new ODI and VLM requester files, creates a new NET.CFG, creates a batch file to start the network services with, modifies CONFIG.SYS and AUTOEXEC.BAT, installs the appropriate Windows network drivers and modifies the Windows .INI files.

Once the installation program is finished, you reboot the PC and execute the STARTNET.BAT file to attach to the network. The message that appears on the screen is "No Servers Available." Going over the configuration in NET.CFG, you notice that the frame type is Ethernet 802.2, and you're still running 802.3 on your 3.11 server. You change the frame type and restart. The login process begins to run, and then the whole workstation hangs.

After several reboots, the workstation freezing each time, but at different points in the boot sequence, you pull out the configuration worksheet for the PC. You note that the original NIC was set to an alternate configuration, to avoid an interrupt conflict with the serial ports. When you installed the new NIC, you used the default configuration. You pull the card out, set it to the same interrupt as the old card, and change the configuration parameters in NET.CFG. The system works.

## Software

With software, you should also maintain a path to return to your old configuration. This can be simple on a network—copy the old software (or the entire workstation disk, if necessary) to a network drive. Make sure you have a floppy disk that you can boot from, attach to the network, and copy the old system back to the workstation, if necessary.

### Networking Software and Operating Systems

If you are updating the networking software or system software on your network, you can take two approaches. If you update all the workstations on the network at once, you may find that some unanticipated incompatibility will affect your entire department. This procedure will also require a fairly large block of time, probably on a weekend or after hours, when you can go from workstation to workstation, making the necessary changes. Updating one workstation at a time, on the other hand, while it doesn't require the same large block of time all at once, may produce conflicts between OS versions.

For instance, updating some Macintoshes on your network to System 7, while others are still using System 6.0x, or even from one incremental version of the System to another, will cause conflicts between the differing LaserWriter drivers. You can fix this by updating the LaserWriter drivers on all systems, using the driver from the new system version with the older systems.

Updating PC operating systems will often require new versions of the NetWare shell as well. For instance, upgrading from MS-DOS 4.0 to 5.0 will require that you upgrade from NET4.COM to NETX.COM, unless you are already running it, or something newer, such as the ODI drivers or the

VLMs. You may also find that the DOS version reported to NetWare will cause problems, if you have upgraded to MS-DOS 5.0 to 6.0.

You can fix this by using the DOS command SETVER.EXE on the NETX.COM and then including SETVER in your CONFIG.SYS file. When you run SETVER.EXE you will want to set NETX.COM to 5.0:

```
SETVER NETX.COM 5.0
```

then, in CONFIG.SYS, add the line:

```
DEVICE=C:\DOS\SETVER.EXE
```

This makes NetWare think that you are using the version of NETX.COM appropriate to the version of DOS.

## APPLICATIONS

Be aware that updating software can affect other software on the workstation. For example, if you update the operating system, you may need to update utilities, TSRs or Inits, and applications. Upgrading system software or an application to a new version that uses more memory may affect the operation of other applications on the system. The new version may also produce conflicts with existing hardware—read the hardware requirements for the new version carefully, noting any changes from the old version, and checking them against the hardware installed in the workstation.

For example, many users are asking for Windows 3.1. However, the minimum configuration that users will need to be happy with Windows is a 386SX, with 4 MB of RAM, a 100 MB hard disk, a mouse, and a VGA monitor. While Windows may run on lesser workstations, the users won't like the performance. Depending on the applications the user will run, the minimum recommended RAM can be as high as 16 MB (for programs such as FrameMaker, from Frame Technology).

# Tips and Techniques

**T**he previous chapters have emphasized the need for a systematic approach to problem-solving, and they have shown how such an approach can be implemented in various situations. Some of the problems you are likely to encounter as a NetWare administrator, however, don't fit easily into the categories discussed so far. This chapter contains information on various problem areas and presents tips or techniques that may be necessary to get things to work. The topics are as follows:

- ► PCs

- ► Windows

- ► Macintoshes

- ► UNIX Workstations

- ► NetWare Utilities

- ► 2.*x* Servers

- ► 3.*x* Servers

- ► 4.*x* Servers

- ► Printing

# PCs (DOS Computers)

The biggest problem with PCs is their variety and variability—the processor, the type of memory, the bus, the display; virtually every part of a PC can differ completely from other PCs, and the same is true of the configuration files and software. The tips below may help you better understand or fix some part of your system.

### BOOT ERRORS

- ► If you have a problem reading the messages that appear as your PC boots, try hitting the Ctrl-NumLock or the Pause key on a

101- or 102-key keyboard. This should pause the boot process until you press another key.

▸ If your PC's manual doesn't tell you what the POST messages mean, try to find an old IBM XT or AT hardware reference manual. It might be useful for determining whether an error code is hardware related and what part of the system it relates to.

## AUTOEXEC.BAT AND CONFIG.SYS

▸ The single most common cause of problems in system configuration through the AUTOEXEC.BAT and CONFIG.SYS files is spelling and typographical errors. Double-check every line you add to these files.

▸ Add a PAUSE command in the AUTOEXEC.BAT file before a command if you are trying to trace a problem and aren't sure whether the problem is occurring before or after that command.

▸ Errors in CONFIG.SYS usually produce an error message that identifies the problem line in the file. If not, the message should at least identify the driver causing the problem. You might see an error message like "Bad or Missing C:\BOOT\ANSI.SYS." If you get a message like this, check spelling and make sure that the path in the file matches the actual path to the directory. Don't rely on the PATH command in AUTOEXEC.BAT—put the whole path to the driver or command in the file. If you can't resolve an error, you can temporarily add REM at the beginning of the line to prevent the error message and see if the rest of the lines execute properly.

▸ With MS DOS 5.0 or later, you can boot without using CONFIG.SYS or AUTOEXEC.BAT by holding down the F5 key when "Loading MS-DOS" appears. If the PC boots without errors, then you can reboot again, holding down F8 at the same time. DOS will step through the commands in CONFIG.SYS one at a time, asking you to confirm, for each statement, that you want to load

the driver named there. You can get the same result with
AUTOEXEC.BAT by using the PAUSE command suggested above.

## IRQs

▸ PCs use IRQs (Interrupt channels) to access physical devices. Unfortunately, the number of IRQs can be smaller than the number
of devices that you want to attach to your PC. Trying to use an
IRQ for two things can lead to problems. Table 11.1 shows how
IRQs are mapped to memory segments and devices. The memory
segment is the reserved area of memory used by DOS to hold information about the device. Two devices attempting to use the
same memory segment can scramble the data so that neither
device can function.

| IRQ | MEMORY SEGMENT | DEVICE |
|-----|----------------|--------|
| 2 | N/A | Actually served by IRQ 9— use with caution in an AT; IRQ 9 may be in use. |
| 3 | 2F8 | COM 2—usually the default for LAN adapters. If you aren't using the COM 2 port, this should be safe. |
| 3 | 2E0 | COM 4 |
| 4 | 3F8 | COM 1 |
| 4 | 2E8 | COM 3 |
| 5 | 3F0 | PC-XT hard drive controller |
| 5 | 278 | LPT 2 |
| 6 | 3F0 | Floppy disk drive controller |
| 7 | 378 | LPT 1 |

► The default IRQ is the IRQ that a PC card is set to at the factory. The installation program for the software that comes with the card will usually assume that you want to use the default settings unless you change them during the installation. Unfortunately, many cards are set to the same default; if you have two cards with the same default, one will have to be changed to avoid conflicts. For example, a system with an ARCnet adapter and a mouse would be a potential source of interrupt conflict, because the default IRQ for both the mouse and the ARCnet card is 2. Ethernet cards default to IRQ 3, as a rule. Token-Ring adapters may be either 3 or 4 as a default.

# Windows 3.1

► If you are running Window on a NetWare network, use Windows 3.1 or later, and NetWare 2.2, 3.11, or 4.0 or later. Download the NetWare Workstation Kit for DOS/Windows from CompuServe to make sure that you have the latest NetWare drivers.

► If you used NWSETUP from the NetWare Workstation Kit for DOS/Windows to install your network drivers, and Windows now hangs, check your Windows directory for a file called WINSTART.BAT and delete it.

► If you can't get Windows to run in Enhanced mode, try running it in Standard or Real mode. Determining the last mode in which it will run should give you clues about what is preventing it from running properly. For example, if Windows will run in Real mode, but not in Standard or Enhanced mode, there may not be enough memory available to Windows, the memory handler (HIMEM.SYS) may not be loading, or the TEMP directory environment variable may not be set to a directory that exists. Similarly, if it will run in Real and Standard modes, but not Enhanced, you may need to install the VPICD.386 driver, WINA20.SYS or

EMM386.EXE might not be running correctly, or (most obviously), you might not have a 386 or higher processor.

▶ Two common problems are a video configuration that doesn't match the video card installed in the PC, and memory conflicts resulting from hardware such as NICs or TSRs loaded before Windows trying to use the same parts of memory that Windows uses. See the EMMEXCLUDE command in Chapter 2, Workstations, for more details.

▶ If a user opens a DOS window from within Windows, and there's no prompt, no path and no environment variables set, Windows is probably not configured for NetWare. Check the configuration with the Control Panel, and if necessary, use SETUP.EXE to add NetWare support.

## WINDOWS VERSIONS BEFORE 3.1

▶ The original SMARTDRV.SYS supplied with Windows 3.0 can corrupt disk partitions created with utilities other than FDISK, including SpeedStor from Storage Dimensions, Disk Manager from OnTrack, InnerSpace from Priam Systems, and VFeatures Deluxe from Golden Bow.

▶ With Windows version 3.0, beware of using CHKDSK /F or any utilities that directly access the File Allocation Table (FAT) or write directly to disk, rather than using the DOS programming calls from within Windows. If you need to use these utilities, exit Windows first, or you may corrupt files or the FAT.

▶ Running Windows with NetWare versions before 2.2 (2.15c at the very earliest) or 3.11 is possible, but not recommended. Both the workstation network drivers and some of the utilities on the server must be upgraded; and even with a small budget, the time it will take you to get everything working will probably justify the expense of an upgrade, which will also get you a better version of NetWare.

▶ Get the latest version of the NetWare DOS/Windows Client Kit from your reseller or from NetWire. It includes the latest network drivers, including the ODI drivers, as well as the NetWare Tools for Windows utilities, which allow you to use the MAP, ATTACH, CAPTURE, USERLIST, VOLINFO, SETPASS, SEND, MESSAGES and SESSION utilities from within Windows, instead of having to exit Windows to reconfigure your NetWare environment from DOS.

▶ There is a difference between the ways DOS and NetWare display files with the DIR command. If you type DIR on a DOS drive, the first two items will be a period and double period, representing the current directory and the parent directory. Windows allows you to select the double period to move back up the directory tree. On a NetWare drive, you won't get the period and double period unless the entry SHOW DOTS = ON is in the SHELL.CFG or NET.CFG file. This setting doesn't affect performance or cause any other problems, so I recommend you use it in your default configuration files.
WARNING! If you use SHOW DOTS=ON and you are running a version of NetWare prior to 2.2, you must replace BINDFIX.EXE with the updated version in the DOS/Windows Client Kit. Otherwise, running BINDFIX could result in the SYS volume being erased.

▶ If you're planning to use a Windows workstation with a remote printer (running RPRINTER), make sure that you have the latest version of RPRINTER or are using NPRINTER. Older versions can cause the workstation to lock up when anyone attempts to print, and have even been known to cause ABENDs on the server.

# Macintoshes

▸ If a Macintosh is not booting and you suspect the problem may be caused by Init conflicts, restart the Mac while holding a Shift key down. This prevents all Inits from loading with System 7, and deactivates most under System 6. If the Mac boots without the Inits, remove them all from the System Folder or from the Extensions Folder in the System Folder with System 7. Then add them back in, one at a time, rebooting after each one, until you identify the problem. A simpler solution is to use a utility such as InitPicker, which allows you to designate the order in which Inits load, or lets you deactivate them without removing them from the System Folder.

You can identify the order in which Inits load by watching the icons that appear along the bottom of the screen as the Mac boots. If you aren't sure which icon is associated with which Init, open the System or Extensions folder and select Icon View.

▸ If you can't see any volumes once you log in to a NetWare server, the Macintosh name space may not be loaded. Check on the server by typing VOLUMES at the console. If the volumes don't have Mac name space listed, you will have to load MAC.NAM and add Macintosh name space to the volumes.

▸ If the volume names are dimmed in the login window of the Chooser, the Desktop files may be corrupted. To rebuild the desktop files, go back to the server, unload AFP and then reload it using the CDT option—LOAD AFP CDT. Then log in to the server from a Macintosh, as supervisor, highlight each volume that needs to be rebuilt, hold down the Command (flower or apple) and Option keys, and click on OK. Confirm that you wish to rebuild the desktop when prompted.

▸ During backups, Macs running System 7 may lose their connection to the server, while Macs running System 6 are fine. This is because the binderies are closed for a while during backups; and

System 6 simply queries the server until the binderies are opened again, while System 7 quits after a few retries. AFIX2.ZIP in NOV-LIB1 on CompuServe works with v.3.0 and v.3.01 NetWare for Macintosh and allows the server to respond to the Macs even while the binderies are closed.

▶ If you have Macintoshes using System 7 connecting to a NetWare server that has volumes that support UNIX name space, you may find that the Macs freeze when attempting to access certain volumes or folders. Check to see if the option to calculate folder size automatically is set to On in the Views Control Panel. If it is, the Mac may be attempting to calculate the sizes of folders that were created with UNIX, or that contain files created with UNIX. Attempting to get these sizes can cause the Mac to freeze. Set the automatic folder size calculation to Off.

▶ Insufficient memory can only be solved in one of two ways—unload any unneeded applications, if any exist, or add RAM to the Mac. Fortunately, adding memory to most Macs is a simple matter of installing more or higher capacity SIMMs. Macs with more than 8 MB of RAM must be running 32-bit addressing to take advantage of the extra memory. If you use this feature, be aware that older applications that are not 32-bit compatible may not run until you switch 32-bit addressing off again and reboot the Mac. If you install more memory, and the About the Macintosh—Finder shows that the System is using more than about 1.5–2 MB (probably the amount of memory over 8 MB installed), it means that 32-bit addressing is not switched on. Remember that you must reboot after switching it on.

▶ If you see an "Insufficient Memory" message while using an application, and there seems to be sufficient memory in the Mac, use the Get Info command in the Finder while the application's icon is selected, to see what the Suggested Memory Size is and how much is allocated in Application Memory Size. You may need to increase the Application Memory Size beyond what is suggested, particularly if you are working with large files.

▸ When configuring your server, remember that the zone name may contain spaces. If you can't get access to a particular zone, try inserting a leading or trailing space in the configuration entry—you may have accidentally put a space at the beginning or end of a zone name when it was initially assigned. This also applies to printer names. A simple way to test for spaces is to use the ATCON NLM to do a lookup test in the suspect zone or on the suspect printer. If the lookup fails with the name spelled as it looks, try adding spaces before or after, until the lookup succeeds.

▸ If you set up NetWare print queues that print to a Macintosh printer, you will see both the NetWare queue and the printer itself in the Macintosh Chooser. You may wish to hide the printer itself, to keep users from printing directly to the printer, which can insert their print jobs ahead of those in the queue. See the *NetWare for Macintosh Installation and Maintenance* manual for details.

▸ On a NetWare 3.x server running NetWare for Macintosh, if you get an error message "ATPS can't login ####," you need to delete ATPS with PCONSOLE. Go to Print Server Information, select ATPS, and press the DEL key. Confirm the action and exit. When you load ATPS, the server will be recreated.

▸ With the Macintosh VAPs on 2.x servers or bridges (routers), the AppleTalk address is assigned based on the last two digits of the Ethernet address of the NIC. If those digits are FE, the AppleTalk ID assigned is 254, which is an invalid AppleTalk ID. The only solution is to swap the Ethernet card. PCs don't care about this, so you can swap the card for one from another system.

# UNIX Workstations

▸ If UNIX workstations can mount a NetWare server's drive but
cannot access the files, it may be that the entire volume is not exported (set in the NFSADMIN NLM), but the problem is more
likely to be with permissions. A user who doesn't have the execute permission on a directory won't be able to see the files in
that directory. Don't rely on having set trustee rights from a Net-
Ware workstation—the translation of permissions between UNIX
and NetWare may not be what you expect, since there is not a
one-to-one correspondence between the two permission schemes.
Appendix B of the *NFS Supervisor's Guide* gives information about
what the UNIX permissions will be, given specific NetWare trustee assignments.

▸ If UNIX users will be saving files to your NetWare server, make
sure that the Modify DOS Attributes From UNIX option is set to
Yes in the Exports information in the NFSADMIN utility. Otherwise, users may be unable to modify their own files or place files
in directories they create.

▸ If you export NetWare volumes with NetWare NFS, users on
other systems can access the files without ever having a login account on your system, assuming that the directory trustee rights
give the group Everyone or the user Nobody access. However,
the user will have a UNIX user ID of −3, and will have the Net-
Ware name of Nobody. Nobody cannot access files created previously by that user (it might not have been the same Nobody),
unless the group (Everyone) is also allowed access to the files.
Since the typical UNIX file-creation mask turns the Write permission off for the group and the world, users will not be able to
open and then save the files they just put on the server. Similarly,
they won't be able to delete the files, and may not even be able to
put files into a directory they have just created! The solution is to
give a NetWare account to each person who needs to access the

server through UNIX, or set the file-creation mask on the user's system to give the group write permission.

▶ If you are using a version of NetWare NFS prior to v.1.2, and have many users accessing volumes on the server through UNIX, get version 1.2b or later. With the older versions, every time that a user accesses a directory, a trustee entry is created for that directory. This can result in thousands of trustee entries, especially for GUEST or EVERYONE. This is not just inconvenient—if the number of entries gets too large, you may not be able to access the binderies with NetWare utilities such as SYSCON, the binderies might become corrupt, or the server could ABEND. With version 1.2 or later, you can turn Create Trustee Rights to OFF. You will need to create a file in each directory hierarchy that lists what the trustee rights should be. See the NetWare NFS 1.2 documentation for details.

# NetWare

The following are tips that apply generally to several or all versions of NetWare. Version-specific information follows.

### BINDFIX

▶ Run BINDFIX until no errors are reported. It will fix some problems each time, but the next time through it may find more problems.

▶ *Don't* run BINDFIX from a Windows workstation if NET.CFG contains the statement SHOW DOTS=ON and you are running a version of NetWare prior to 2.2. Running BINDFIX could result in the SYS volume being erased. Replace BINDFIX.EXE with the updated version in the DOS/Windows Client Kit.

► When updating to a new version of NetWare, run BINDFIX until no errors are reported. This ensures that the binderies are clean before the upgrade.

## PRINTCON

► PRINTCON creates a job definition file named PRINTCON.DAT for the user in their SYS:MAIL directory. You can define a default print job for one user and then copy that file to everyone's mail directory, to set everyone's default print job. If you want a user to be able to change the default, make sure to give that person rights to the file (only SUPERVISOR will initially own and have rights to the file).

## AFTER ABENDS OR POWER FAILURES

► You should run VREPAIR any time the server is not properly shut down. Unless the volumes are properly dismounted before the server is downed, it's possible for the binderies and FAT tables to become corrupted. This damage may not show up when the server is brought back on-line, and if left untended, can cause permanent data loss. If the FATs are corrupted, even the backups may not be recoverable.

## LOGIN SCRIPTS

► Each user's login script is stored in a numbered directory in SYS:MAIL, based on a unique user ID number that is assigned by NetWare when a new user is created. You can get each user's number with SYSCON (User Information/Login Name/Other Information). The login script is a text file called LOGIN. If you need to make changes to many scripts, it can be faster to use a text editor on these files directly, instead of using SYSCON.

# NetWare 2.x

▶ Users upgrading from NetWare v.2.15A to v.2.15B or v.2.15C may have severe performance problems if they have two internal MFM drives on the same controller. Use the ATDISK.DSK driver instead of the ISADISK.DSK driver. Make sure its date is 11/11/88 or later, and the ATDISK.OBJ is dated 10/12/88 or later.

▶ NetWare 2.2 will use a maximum of 12 MB of RAM on a dedicated server. If you have more installed, it will be recognized but not used. If you are running out of memory, upgrade to NetWare 3.x or 4.x.

▶ If you run VREPAIR and the screen blanks and nothing further happens, you should try booting the server with a DOS 3.x diskette before running VREPAIR. If you have upgraded the DOS version that the server boots with to a later version, you will need to download a patch from NetWire (see Appendix A for more details) or reboot the server with DOS 3.x.

# NetWare 3.x

▶ To load NetWare without using STARTUP.NCF or AUTOEXEC.NCF, use the following command-line options: SERVER –NS (to skip STARTUP.NCF), SERVER –NA (to skip AUTOEXEC.NCF), or SERVER –NSA (to skip both). These commands allow you to manually load hard disk drivers, LAN drivers, and so forth, bypassing the usual settings. This can be extremely useful for troubleshooting problems that you can't trace during the normal boot sequence, or for occasions when you've changed the hardware configuration in advance of software, and the new configuration won't boot.

- Load MONITOR with the –p option to get more statistics on your server utilization. It will show you what processes are running and how much of the available processor capacity they are using.

- A typical server setup may have two or more external drives in enclosures. If one of these drives fails, you will receive a message saying that drive 1 on adapter 1 has failed. This doesn't tell you anything about the physical location of the drive, however. In some cases, you can use the Disk Information menu item in MONITOR to set the Drive Light Status for each drive to "Flashing" until you have identified all the physical drives by their drive number and volume segment. Of course, if you label the drives before you start, this won't be a problem; the drive numbers generally correspond to the SCSI ID number—the drive with the lowest SCSI ID has the lowest drive number, and so on.

# NetWare 4.x

- Upgrade workstations to the VLMs before you upgrade the server—this will let you debug any problems with applications or TSRs on the workstations before you need to use them to attach to the server.

- If you're having trouble logging in to a server, try including the entire context in the login command:

  LOGIN .CN=login_name.OU=organizational_unit.O=organization

  If this works, it means the context you've specified in the NET.CFG file may be incorrect, or misspelled.

- If you are running the VLMs and attaching to both NetWare 4.x and 3.x servers, and the 3.x connections are unexpectedly dropping out, look at your NET.CFG file. If CONNECTIONS=## is set to more than 8, connections may be dropped when you run

NetWare utilities (such as ATTACH, WHOAMI or SLIST) on a 3.*x* server.

▸ DON'T delete the Admin object unless you have given supervisor rights to another object; doing so will leave you with a tree that can't be administered. You will have to either restore the partition from a backup or reinitialize the directory and start from scratch. You won't lose data, but all the structural information would be lost.

▸ If you can't create, delete, or modify objects, first make sure that you have sufficient rights. Then, if you do, run DSREPAIR. It's a good idea to run this utility every few months, to make sure that everything in the database is optimized and that all entries match actual objects.

▸ Make sure that everything on your LAN is using either Ethernet 802.2 or 802.3—they don't mix well. The default for the NetWare 4.0 and the VLMs is 802.2, while older systems use 802.3.

▸ Don't try to define objects such as printers for a domain before you upgrade the server to 4.0. This can cause problems with the upgrade that will result in the print queues, print jobs, etc. on the old server being lost during the upgrade.

▸ DON'T use SBACKUP to back up and restore a partition (the NDS information, not the volume) with the initial release of NetWare 4.0. Using SBACKUP can result in the corruption of the partition, which will require that you redefine users, groups, and so on. If you have recorded this information, it shouldn't be too much of a problem to reconstruct, but doing so will cause lots of work, disrupt the network, and waste time. Cheyenne Software's ARCSERVE 5.0 is a better choice for backups.

# Printing

- ▶ If you have a printer attached to the parallel port of a workstation running NPRINTER, RPRINTER or PSERVER.EXE, and print jobs are not printing, try setting the printer configuration in PCONSOLE to Don't Use Interrupts.

- ▶ As with the LOGIN files in each user's SYS:MAIL\######## directory, print queues are numbered directories in SYS:SYSTEM. You can identify the directory associated with any queue by looking up the print server's ID number in PCONSOLE. Go to the Print Server Information menu, select the print server you are looking for, and then select Print Server ID. Each directory contains hidden files named FILESERV, PRINT, QUEUE, and NOTIFY. You can either change the file attributes or use FILER to view them. FILESERV lists the file servers serviced, PRINT has configuration information for the printer, QUEUE contains information on the print queue, and NOTIFY lists the users to be notified of problems. There may be several versions of each file except FILESERV—one for each printer attached to the print server. The extension will be the same for each defined printer, beginning with 000. If you are having problems with printing, and you have deleted print server definitions, check to see if there are queue directories that don't correspond to any existing print server. If there are, delete the directories.

- ▶ If you are having problems with a printer on a workstation running RPRINTER, try adding the following items to SHELL.CFG or NET.CFG:

```
IPX RETRY COUNT = 35
SPX ABORT TIMEOUT = 700
```

▸ If you are running PSERVER.EXE, make sure that you use the latest available network drivers. Older drivers can cause PSER-VER to hang the workstation on occasion. Also, make sure that NET.CFG includes the entry:

SPX CONNECTIONS = 60

# APPENDIX A

# Resources

**T**he more you know about your system, the easier it will be to solve any problems that arise. This appendix lists resources that can help you learn more about your system, or get good advice if you're stumped. Some sources for utility software that can make your life easier are included at the end.

The following topics are covered:

- ‣ The NetWare Manuals and README files

- ‣ Other Novell Publications

- ‣ Magazines

- ‣ Books

- ‣ Tech Support

- ‣ The CNEPA and NUI

- ‣ Aftermarket Support Services and Consultants

- ‣ Training

- ‣ Software

## The NetWare Manuals and README Files

It is often laughingly said that real administrators don't read manuals. In fact, the opposite is true. It is impossible to get a complete grasp of the Net-Ware software without reading the manuals. Be sure that you also read the README files on the distribution disks—the information there can be critical to getting your system to work.

A manual set of 1500 pages can be daunting to approach. I don't suggest that you read through the entire set before installing NetWare. The most efficient way to approach the manuals is to first decide what you need to accomplish with your network and your server, then research those particular topics in the manuals. Having an idea of what you need to know will tend to make those topics stand out in your mind, and will also allow you to bypass irrelevant information.

Bear in mind that with the standard manual sets, the information you want may be in several places—some in *Installation*, some in *Concepts* and some in *System Administration*. If you have a chance to install the Electro-Text on-line documentation (ET), do so. You may wish to consider installing it on your workstation, if you have enough disk space—that way you will have access to the documentation even if the network is down. ET will let you jump between the different manuals by clicking on a cross-reference, rather than having to dig out the other manual and page through it.

## Other Novell Publications

Novell publishes *NetWare Application Notes*, *Novell Research Reports*, and *Novell Technical Bulletins*. These publications can be ordered from Novell, and some can be downloaded from NetWire. Some are also available in the *NetWare Support Encyclopedia*.

### NETWARE APPLICATION NOTES

*NetWare Applications Notes* is a monthly publication that covers several topics a month relating to troubleshooting or optimizing NetWare, as well as information on new products, bug fixes, and a tips-and-techniques section. I heartily recommend the April and May 1993 issues to anyone contemplating the move to NetWare 4.0. They cover new features, NDS, migration to 4.0, installation of 4.0, planning issues, and so forth. *NetWare Application Notes* is available in subscription, on the NSE disk, and on-line on NetWire. Call (800) 377-4136 for subscription information, or write to Novell Research Order Desk, 1601 Park Avenue West, Denver, CO 80216-5199. The current cost is $95/yr., which also includes *Novell Research Reports*. Probably the best deal around.

## NOVELL RESEARCH REPORTS

Recent *Novell Research Reports* cover topics such as *Integrating NetWare and Windows 3.1*, *Inside NetWare for UNIX*, and *NetWare Security: Configuring and Auditing a Trusted Environment*. These are specialized reports that cover topical issues in depth. They can be ordered through your reseller or from: Novell Research Order Desk, 1601 Park Avenue West, Denver, CO 80216-5199.

## NOVELL TECHNICAL BULLETINS

Novell publishes these bulletins on the NetWare Support Encyclopedia disk, and on NetWire—the NOVLIB forum, Technical Bulletins section, on CompuServe. Recent topics include: *TCP/IP across Access Server*, *Printing and NetWare for Macintosh*, and *Using DR DOS LANPack*.

# Magazines

In addition to a dozen or so magazines dedicated to networking, most magazines that cover the workstation of your choice cover networking products from time to time. All of these magazines can provide you with helpful information, with the specialization that is appropriate for your network. If you have a largely Macintosh network, for instance, you should scan *MacUser*, *MacWeek*, and *MacWorld* for network-related articles. In general, the weekly magazines will provide information in a more timely manner, so you should pay special attention to reported bugs and their fixes. The monthly magazines usually provide more in-depth coverage of issues, and are appropriate for researching additions to the network that you are considering.

The magazines mentioned below are only some of the many available. This list is not meant to be all-inclusive, nor to recommend one over another.

## WEEKLY

Weekly or biweekly magazines include *LAN Times* and *LAN Computing*, the workstation-specific *MacWeek* and *PC Week*, and *InfoWorld*. All of these contain useful information on recently released or soon-to-be-released products.

For subscription information contact the following:

### LAN Times

1900 O'Farrell St. Suite 200

San Mateo, CA 94403

(800) 525-5003

### LAN Computing

Cardinal Business Media, Inc.

101 Witmer Road

Horsham, PA 19044

(215) 957-4269

### MacWeek

c/o JCI

Customer Service Department

P.O. Box 1766

Riverton, NJ 08077-7366

(609) 461-2100

### PC Week

Customer Service Department

P.O. Box 1770

Riverton, NJ 08077-7370

(609) 461-2100

### Infoworld

P.O. Box 1172

Skokie, IL 60076

(800) 457-7866

## MONTHLY

There are many monthly magazines dedicated to networking topics, as well as more general computing-oriented magazines that produce articles related to networking. *Network News* is produced by the CNEPA, and is dedicated to NetWare-specific topics. It is a benefit of CNEPA membership—one of many.

*Corporate Computing* covers networking topics from a manager's point of view—details of cost justification and considerations that may affect other areas of your network, rather than a deep level of technical specifications. It generally offers a couple of case studies showing how a business has upgraded its network to meet changing requirements.

Among the technically oriented magazines are *Network Computing*, *LAN Technology*, *LAN Computing*, and *LAN Magazine* which cover client-server applications from many companies, including, of course, Novell. They generally have one or two comparison tests featuring products from a number of manufacturers that may relate to your network, such as protocol analyzers or fax modems. They review new products, feature commentary on industry trends, and predict trends that you will eventually have to deal with. Get a couple of issues of each at the newsstand before subscribing—

they all take a different approach to the issues, which you may or may not find relevant to your network.

*Networking Management* and *Beyond Computing* are two Information Services-related magazines that take a more corporate approach. They tend to cover WAN issues and systems management more than LANs.

For subscription information contact the following:

### Network News (CNEPA)

Included with CNEPA membership

CNE Professional Association

122 East 1700 South

MS E-31-1

Provo, UT 84606

(800) 926-3776

### Corporate Computing

950 Tower Lane, 19th Floor

Foster City, CA 94404

(800) 827-7556

CompuServe ID: 72631,73

### Network Computing

CMP Publications

600 Community Dr.

Manhasset, NY 11030

(516) 562-5882

### LAN Technology

M&T Publishing

411 Borel Ave.

San Mateo, CA 94402

(800) 456-1654

### LAN Magazine

600 Harrison St.

San Francisco, CA 94107

(800) 234-9573

### Networking Management

PennWell Publishing Company

1421 South Sheridan

Tulsa, OK 74112

(918) 831-9424

### Beyond Computing

P.O. Box 3014

Northbrook, IL 60065-9984

(708) 564-1385

## NEWSLETTERS

In addition to the magazines, you can find newsletters, which may cover topics as specialized as packet analysis or workgroup publishing. These newsletters may have 10 subscribers or 10,000. They tend to be more specific and more opinionated than the larger-circulation magazines.

## COMPUTER SELECT

If you don't have the budget to subscribe to a dozen or more magazines, or the time to flip through them, consider Computer Select. This is a fabulous research tool, containing articles from over 170 different periodicals in the computer industry on CD-ROM. You can search for a topic, and have every article written in the last year at your fingertips. For more information, call Computer Library at (212) 503-4400 or 1-800-827-7889. You will need a PC-compatible system with a CD-ROM drive, 640K RAM, and at least 500K of hard disk space or a Macintosh with System 6.0.7 or later, 1 MB of RAM, and a CD-ROM drive.

# Books

For more depth than magazine articles, and a different perspective than manuals, you can turn to books. There are perhaps a dozen publishers with lines of computer-related books. Some are consistently good, others are best in certain areas or are oriented to a certain kind of user. There is only one publisher that concentrates specifically on Novell products: Novell Press.

## NOVELL PRESS

Novell Press selects authors based on their expertise with some aspect of NetWare. Books currently available include:

- *Novell's App Notes for NetWare 4.0*

- *Novell's CNA Study Guide*, by David James Clarke, IV

- *Novell's Guide to Integrating UNIX with NetWare Networks*, by James E. Gaskin

- *Novell's Guide to Managing Small NetWare Networks*, by Kelley J.P. Lindberg

- *Novell's Guide to NetWare 3.11 Networks*, by Cheryl Currid & Company

- *Novell's Guide to NetWare 4.0 Networks*, by Cheryl C. Currid with Stephen Saxon

- *Novell's Guide to NetWare 4.0 NLM Programming*, by Michael Day, Michael Koontz, and Daniel Marshall

- *Novell's Guide to NetWare LAN Analysis*, by Laura Chappell

- *Novell's Quick Access Guide to NetWare 3.11 Networks*

- *Novell's Quick Access Guide to NetWare 4.0 Networks*

- *The Official Novell DR-DOS 6 Instant Reference*, by Robert M. Thomas

- *The Official Novell NetWare Lite Handbook*, by Edward Leibing

## OTHER BOOKS

Other books that I have found helpful include:

- *NetWare, The Professional Reference*, 2nd Ed. by Karanjit Siyan, from New Riders Publishing, 1993. This is a very thorough encyclopedia that covers the details of NetWare 2.*x* and 3.*x*.

- *Running Windows on NetWare*, by Stephen Saxon, from M&T Books, 1992. A good guide to getting Windows and NetWare to work together. Covers Windows through 3.1 and NetWare through 3.11.

- *LAN Connectivity*, by Drew Haywood, Janos Jerney, Jon Johnston, et al., from New Riders Publishing, 1992. A thorough coverage of LAN basics from the most popular vendors, including Novell. Covers protocols, topologies, and internetworking. Not specific to NetWare, but contains lots of useful information.

# Tech Support

Once you've purchased NetWare you will be entitled to tech support, either from Novell or from the dealer you purchased it from. When your initial support agreement lapses, you will have to pay for support. Novell offers tech support over the phone at an hourly rate. There are other options. You may wish to purchase an extended support plan from your Novell Authorized Reseller, or from another firm. You can also get information from on-line resources such as CompuServe or NetWire, from tech support databases, from tech support companies, from consultants, or from your local chapter of the CNEPA or NetWare Users International.

Each possible avenue for tech support has advantages and disadvantages—cost, speed of response, expertise, convenience of access, and hours of availability are the most important considerations to keep in mind as you evaluate each option.

## ON-LINE RESOURCES

NetWire has so many features and so much information available that books have been written on it (see below). Other on-line resources include manufacturer's bulletin boards, forums on the Internet, and other bulletin boards such as BIX. All you need is a modem and a communications program.

### NetWire

*Using Novell's NetWire,* by Laura Chappell and Brent Larson, from Know, Inc., 1992, P.O. Box 50507, Provo UT 84605-0507, deals solely with the NetWire services available on CompuServe. NetWire is accessible from anywhere in the country through CompuServe. You can even try it out for free: call (800) 848-8199 and ask for representative #58. You'll get $15 of usage credit. If you're already a member of CompuServe, type GO NOVELL at the prompt.

Not only can you converse on-line with many different experts on Net-Wire, including some of the engineers who created NetWare, you can download the latest versions of NetWare drivers and software, and patches that will fix specific problems.

My CompuServe ID is 75600,2175. I welcome feedback on this book and suggestions for the next edition.

**NOVLIB**    NOVLIB is the forum that contains files you can download. The following are the libraries of files you can download:

1 · Novell NEW Uploads

2 · General Information

3 · NetWare 2.X Specific

4 · NetWare 3.X Specific

5 · Client/Shell Drivers

6 · NetWare Utilities

7 · Btrieve/XQL

8 · Mac/NFS/MHS

9 · Communications Products

10 · NetWare Lite

11 · Techinfo/IMSP's

12 · NDSG/DRDOS

13 · Other Patches/Drivers

14 · Independent Development

15 · Shareware/Demos

16 · Public Domain/Text

17 · Miscellaneous Novell Uploads

Other forums on NetWire are devoted to discussions of different Net-Ware topics, general information and some special and private forums. Novell (**GO NOVELL**) is a general information area. NOVA, NOVB, NOVC, NETW2X, NETW3X and DRFORUM are conference forums which feature discussions of various topics. Two forums, NOVDEV and NOVG, are restricted-access forums for developers. Summaries of the topics discussed in each of the forums are given below:

**NOTE**
The titles of forums listed here are subject to change, depending on demand for certain topics. You can get a listing of current forums available when you log into one of these areas.

**NOVA**   The NOVA forum topics are as follows:

1 · ELS NetWare

2 · Async Communications

3 · Mini/Mainframe Links

4 · LAN/WAN Links

5 · NetWare for Macintosh

6 · NetWare for VMS

7 · Portable NetWare (NetWare for UNIX)

8 · NetWare NFS, TCP/IP

9 · NetWare Lite

10 · NetWare Support Encyclopedia

11 · LANalyzer/LANtern

12 · LAN WorkPlace for DOS & OS/2

**NOVB**   The NOVB forum topics are as follows:

1 · Servers and Workstations

2 · Backups

3 · Printing

**4** · Disk Drives, Controllers

**5** · K-12 Networking (Education)

**6** · Closed at this time

**7** · Closed at this time

**8** · Power Monitoring

**9** · Ethernet

**10** · ARCnet

**11** · Token-Ring

**12** · Other LAN Types

**13** · Cabling Media

**14** · New Shells

**15** · Windows

**NOVC**   The NOVC forum topics are as follows:

**1** · General Information, Miscellaneous

**2** · Upgrades

**3** · Applications and Utilities

**4** · Btrieve, XQL, SQL

**5** · E-mail, MHS

**6** · Programming NetWare

**7** · Network Management

**8** · Product Suggestions

**9** · User Groups, Training

**10** · The OS/2 Requester

**11** · VARs and Dealers

**12** · CNEs

**13** · Developers

**14** · On Your Soapbox

**15** · The Lighter Side

**16** · CNIs, NAECs (Private)

**NETW2X**    The NETW2X forum topics are as follows:

**1** · Printing

**2** · Utilities

**3** · Disk Drives, Controllers

**4** · Clients, Shells

**5** · LAN Drivers, Cards

**6** · NetWare 2.1x and Below

**7** · NetWare 2.2 Specific

**NETW3X**    The NETW3x forums are as follows:

**1** · Printing

**2** · Utilities

**3** · Disk Drives, Controllers

**4** · Clients, Shells

**5** · LAN Drivers, Cards

**6** · NetWare 3.x Specific

**DRFORUM**   Contains forums for conversations on a variety of topics pertaining to DR DOS and other Digital Research products and libraries of programs, utilities, patches, etc.

### Bulletin Boards

Many companies maintain bulletin boards that can allow you to ask questions on problems you may be having, or to download patches or new versions of software. Some of these bulletin boards are listed below. Every effort has been made to make sure that the information is current. However, these numbers are subject to change.

| | |
|---|---|
| 3Com | 408/980-8204 |
| Adaptec | 408/945-7727 |
| Advanced Systems Support (modems) | 800/874-2937 |
| AST Technical Support | 714/727-4723 |
| AT&T Support (PCs) | 201/769-6397 |
| AT&T/NCR (Ethernet and Token-Ring drivers) | 612/638-2854 |
| ATI Support (modems & video cards) | 416/756-4591 |
| BMUG (Mac support) | 510/849-2684 |
| Book (info on 2000 computer books) | 215/657-6130 |
| Capital PC User's Group (5500 members) | 703/750-7809 |
| Cheyenne (ARCSERVE) | 516/484-3445 |
| CompuCom Customer Support | 408/738-4990 |

| | |
|---|---|
| Computer Business Services (John Dvorak) | 714/396-0014 |
| CrossTalk Technical Support | 404/740-8428 |
| CTC IEEE Employment Database (resumes) | 508/263-3857 |
| eSoft Product Support | 303/699-8222 |
| IBM National Support Center | 404/835-5300 |
| Intel | 503/645-6275 |
| JOBBS (job listings technical) | 404/992-8937 |
| LANtastic (support) | 602/293-8065 |
| Maxtor Technical Support | 303/678-2020 |
| McAfee Associates (virus info) | 408/988-4004 |
| The Micro Foundry (software support) | 415/598-0398 |
| Micro Design International (SCSI Express) | 510/793-3491 |
| Micro Message Service (news magazines) | 919/779-6674 |
| Microrim Technical Support (R:Base) | 206/649-9836 |
| Microsoft Product Support | 206/646-9145 |

| | |
|---|---|
| Microsystems Software Inc. (support) | 508/875-8009 |
| Net (windows, OS/2) | 203/246-3747 |
| Network World Bulletin Board (LAN, WAN) | 508/620-1178 |
| NIST Computer Security (virus issues) | 301/948-5717 |
| Online With Hayes | 404/446-6336 |
| Oracomm Support | 619/346-1608 |
| PacComm (packet radio equipment supplier) | 813/874-3078 |
| PKWare (PKARC and PKZIP Utilities) | 414/354-8670 |
| PowerNet (REMOTE ACCESS software) | 407/834-3326 |
| Practical Peripherals (support) | 818/706-2467 |
| ProComm Support | 314/474-8477 |
| Qualitas, Inc. (support) | 301/907-8030 |
| Remote Access HQ | 619/389-8048 |
| Seagate Technical Support | 408/438-8771 |
| Searchlight (support) | 516/689-2566 |
| SemWare Support (QEdit, shareware) | 404/641-8968 |
| SMC (Network Interface Cards) | 714/707-2481, 516/434-3162 |

| | |
|---|---|
| Society for Technical Communications | 703/522-3299 |
| Star-Link Network (75,000 programs) | 718/972-6099 |
| The Business (Microsoft Windows) | 213/477-0408 |
| The Well (popular— hourly charges) | 415/332-7190 |
| U.S. Robotics | 708/982-5092 |
| Ventura Professional Forum | 408/227-4818 |
| Western Digital Technical Support | 714/753-1068 |
| WordPerfect Customer Support | 801/225-4444 |
| XTree | 805/546-9150 |
| XyQuest Technical Support (XyWrite) | 508/667-5669 |
| Zenith Technical Support | 800/888-3058 |

## BIX

The Byte Information eXchange is an online database of computer knowledge from BYTE magazine, designed to help users fix problems and obtain info on specific hardware and software products. For information on joining BIX, call 800/227-2983, or 603/924-7681.

## The Internet

If you have access to the Internet, you can join the discussions in Comp.Sys.Novell, as well as many other computer-related forums. Topics in the Comp forum include a huge variety of computer manufacturers, and the Comp.Sys section includes most of the popular operating systems in existence, as well as some pretty obscure ones. A large number of Novell employees, including many of the engineers who wrote various parts of NetWare, participate in these forums. If you want to get all of the messages in Comp.Sys.Novell, you can subscribe to the list server by sending mail to novadm@suvm.acs.syr.edu, or novadm@suvm on BITNET, with the following text in the body of the message (the subject doesn't matter):

subscribe NOVELL *Your Full Name*

This will forward all the messages posted on Comp.Sys.Novell to your e-mail account. Additionally, the FAQ (Frequently Asked Questions) is available via anonymous FTP from 129.65.43.132. It is an extremely useful document full of the answers to the most often-asked questions in the comp.sys.novell forum. Kevin Wang (kwang@gauss.elee.calpoly.edu) does a tremendous job of maintaining this document.

I am also frequently on comp.sys.novell, and can be reached by UNIX mail at logan@sjb.novell.com, if you have comments on this book or suggestions for the next revision.

**USENET**　　USENET (USEr NETwork) is a public access network on the Internet that provides user news and e-mail. It is a giant, dispersed bulletin board maintained by volunteers willing to provide news and mail to other Internet sites.

## TECHNICAL SUPPORT DATABASES

Several databases that you can purchase provide technical support information from either Novell or many different manufacturers.

### NetWare Support Encyclopedia

You can subscribe to two versions of the *NetWare Support Encyclopedia*—the *Standard Volume* and the *Professional Volume*. Both contain Novell

Technotes, hardware and software test bulletins, product documentation, the *NetWare Buyers Guide*, and a listing of all files available on NetWare. The *Professional Volume* also includes NetWare patches and fixed versions of software, new network drivers and enhanced products, as well as the *Novell Application Notes*.

If you access the NSE frequently on CompuServe, you may find it more economical to purchase a subscription to the CD-ROM distribution. The *Professional Volume* has a list price of $1395, which can be a real cost saver compared to the time necessary to access the same information on Compu-Serve. It's also much more convenient.

### Support On Site for Networks

*Ziff Desktop Information* produces a bimonthly CD-ROM that contains the manual sets and support documentation from many software and hardware vendors. If the sources included are ones that you use, it can be a real boon, especially in a heterogeneous networking environment, where you would otherwise need dozens of manuals from many different vendors. Unfortunately, some major companies haven't yet contributed to the database. Novell has, to the tune of over 13,000 documents, but Apple, for example, has not. At $1495 per year, it can be an expensive investment if it doesn't cover the products you use, so you may want to try it before you buy.

## The CNEPA and NUI

The Certified NetWare Engineer Professional Association is open to CNEs and anyone who is trying to become a CNE (anyone who has taken one of the tests that lead to the CNE certification). Membership in the CNE has many benefits, including labs that can show you how to configure and troubleshoot Novell products, discounts on software and admission to networking-related events such as NETUCON, and a subscription to *Network News*.

The local chapter of the CNEPA is a great place to learn more about networking, and to make contacts with other CNEs who may be able to help you (for a fee, or not) in times of need.

NetWare Users International is the world-wide organization of NetWare User Groups. In addition to meetings that can help you learn more about NetWare and make contacts with other users, NUI provides a united front that can influence Novell to make changes in NetWare that users want. Membership also includes a subscription to *NetWare Connection*, a bimonthly newsletter that focuses on user (administrator) issues.

# 900 Numbers and Consultants

Check your local Yellow Pages and the network-related magazines for technical support specialists and consultants in your area. These companies can often provide service at a lower price or in a more timely manner than resellers or Novell's tech support department, because they are smaller and have far fewer customers. Be aware, though, that there is a wide variation in expertise and levels of service. Ask about a company or consultant at your local CNEPA or NUI before spending money on their services.

# Training

Novell Authorized Education Centers can provide you with a complete program that will train you in administering every aspect of NetWare. There are three levels of certification available—Certified NetWare Administrator, Certified NetWare Engineer, and Enterprise Certified NetWare Engineer. CNA certification means that you have taken the System Manager and Advanced System Manager courses for one version of NetWare, or at least passed the tests for those courses. A CNE has demonstrated good general knowledge of NetWare. An ECNE has taken additional coursework in WAN-related subjects.

Other sources may provide courses that can provide you with enough knowledge to pass the same tests, or may offer specialized training in some aspects of NetWare networking. Companies such as Data-Tech Institute offer courses in many other computer-related subjects, including maintaining, setting up and troubleshooting PCs, Macintoshes or UNIX workstations, setting up and maintaining Windows by itself or on NetWare, and disaster recovery for LANs.

Another source for training on NetWare may be your local community college, adult education center, or university extension program. As NetWare becomes steadily more entrenched as the preeminent LAN operating system, more colleges are offering courses on it. In some cases, the universities may work with Novell to ensure that students who pass the courses are also eligible to obtain CNE certification.

# Software

Throughout this book, I have mentioned types of software that can make your life as an administrator easier. A few of the programs that I've worked with are listed below.

### VIRUS DETECTION SOFTWARE

McAfee's NetShield works well with NetWare. It's shareware (not freeware), it's fast, it maintains a log of scans, and it can scan all incoming files and move infected files to a protected directory. You can specify users who should get notifications of viruses found. You can designate directories or files to scan regularly. Also, McAfee's virus software is updated regularly and you can easily get updates from the Internet or CompuServe. To contact McAfee Associates, call (408) 988-3832.

LanProtect is a NetWare Loadable Module (NLM) manufactured by Intel that scans for viruses on file servers and workstations on LANs. It reads DOS or Macintosh files in real time before they are written to or read from the file server. When LanProtect detects a virus, the user is given the option of renaming the file to prevent execution, deleting and purging the file, moving it to a protected area for inspection, or leaving the file alone. LPSCAN is the corresponding utility that scans workstations logged into the server. Get information at (503) 629-7354 or (800) 538-3373.

Untouchable Network, from Fifth Generation Systems, is an NLM that can scan for both known and unknown viruses (by looking for executable files that have changed in size or content). It can also scan both compressed and archived files. Fifth Generation can be reached at (504) 291-7221.

Central Point Software Inc.'s Anti-Virus for NetWare is a DOS or Windows utility that can scan network drives as well as local drives. It creates a checksum database for applications that lets it detect applications that change in size or contents. Contact Central Point at (503) 690-8090 or (800) 445-4208.

Cheyenne Software Inc. produces InocuLan 2.0, an anti-virus NetWare Loadable Module (NLM) that has a wide variety of tools to deal with viruses. Some of InocuLan 2.0's useful tools include its Delete File Option, as well as its Purge option, which enables users to delete an infected file so that it is not able to be recovered. In addition, the application includes some time-saving options for managers, and it has some useful administrative tools, such as the ability to administer the NLM remotely from a workstation, and view the activity log. Cheyenne can be reached at (516) 484-5110.

There are many other virus scanning utilities available both as NLMs or VAPs, and as workstation utilities (TSRs or Macintosh INITs). Check your favorite PC or Networking magazine for recent reviews.

## WORKSTATION UTILITIES

Help! examines your Mac's hardware and software configuration, notifies you of any problems it detects, and suggests corrective action. It even prints configuration and diagnostic reports. For information, contact Teknosys at (813) 620-3494.

INITPicker helps isolate problems with conflicting Inits on Macs by allowing you to change the order that Inits load in, or whether they load or not. Contact Inline Design at (203) 435-4995.

Micro 2000's Micro-Scope is one of the oldest diagnostic programs available. It has a full set of features and can diagnose problems with PCs as well as compiling information on cards installed and their settings. For information, contact Micro 2000 at (818) 547-0125.

Norton Utilities is a disk management utility program for the PC and Macintosh from Symantec Corp. It includes programs to search and edit files, undelete files, and restore damaged files, among others. For information, contact Symantec at (800) 441-7234.

PC Tools Deluxe is a comprehensive package of PC utilities from Central Point Software that includes a DOS shell as well as file management, communications, disk caching, backup, and data-compression utilities. Contact Central Point at (503) 690-8090 or (800) 445-4208.

PKWARE (PK stands for Phil Katz) makes the popular PC shareware compression programs. PKZIP compresses files into a ZIP file and PKUNZIP decompresses them. PKSFX compresses files into a self-extracting EXE file that decompresses when loaded and doesn't require the PKUNZIP program. ZIP2EXE creates the self-extracting file from an existing ZIP file. These utilities are necessary to uncompress many of the patches and utilities you may wish to download from NetWire or other on-line services. To contact PKWARE, call (414) 354-8699.

QEMM-386 (Quarterdeck Expanded Memory Manager-386) is a popular expanded memory manager from Quarterdeck Office Systems, for 386 and higher machines. It has a well-engineered configuration/installation program that does a good job of detecting TSRs and other programs you may want to load, and accommodating them in upper memory. Contact Quarterdeck at (310) 392-9851.

SAM (Symantec AntiVirus for Macintosh) is the most popular Macintosh antivirus program. It can be configured for various levels of protection, depending on your estimation of the danger of infection on your network. It also allows you to password-protect the configuration options, so users can't bypass the system. SUM II (Symantec Utilities for Macintosh) is a set of Macintosh utilities that provides hard disk optimization, analysis, and repair and security capabilities. For information, contact Symantec at (800) 441-7234.

SpinRite II is a nondestructive, low-level formatting program for PCs from Gibson Research Corp. that reformats the hard disk without erasing the data. It rewrites only the sector ID, which may have drifted over time. You can contact Gibson Research at (800) 736-0637.

WinSleuth is a diagnostics and system-information program that runs under Windows, and checks the system setup. WinSleuth is particularly useful for users who want to optimize their hardware to work with Windows. For information contact Dariana Technologies Inc. at (800) 892-9950.

XTree provides PC disk management and a DOS shell. Introduced in 1985, it was the first program to help users manage hard disks by providing a hierarchical display of directories. XTreePro added a built-in text editor, and XTreePro Gold added application launching, split windows, and file viewers. There is also a version available for the Mac. For information, call XTree at (800) 395-8733.

## NETWARE UTILITIES

Brightworks Development offers a number of NetWare utilities. LAN Server Watch monitors your servers and informs you if parameters exceed set levels. It can even correct some conditions automatically, NETremote+ allows you to take over another Windows workstation on the LAN. LAN Tachometer is an inexpensive tool that maintains a watch on network traffic and server utilization. LAN Automatic Inventory (LAI) keeps a history of changes to a user's configuration files, new boards that may create interrupt conflicts with network hardware, and new or virus-infected software that a user installs in a network directory or on a local hard disk. For more information, contact Brightworks at (800) 522-9876.

Frye Computer Systems offers a suite of network management programs for NetWare. They are fairly expensive, but very complete. They include a server-monitoring program, an automatic workstation software updating and inventory program, and a mapping utility that will generate a logical map of your network. For more information, contact Frye at (617) 451-5400 or (800) 234-3793.

Intel's LANDesk Manager runs under Windows and provides a wide variety of Server and LAN monitoring and control. It can show you packet traffic on the LAN, monitor what applications are running on your server, log peak and average statistics for server and LAN, and inventory workstation hardware and software configurations remotely. Contact Intel at (800) 538-3373.

BVEquip, from the LAN Support Group, Check-It LAN from TouchStone Software Corp., LANlord from Microcom, and Fresh Technology's Node-Vision are all LAN inventory packages that provide inventories of each workstation's hardware and software, and benchmark performance as well.

You can download a number of free or shareware programs from NetWire's NOVLIB. These may allow you to produce reports on all of your users and their file utilization, login scripts, and so on, or print out the contents of AUTOEXEC.NCF. There are many other commercial utilities of varying cost and capability. Check your favorite magazines for product reviews, and then ask around at your CNEPA or NUI meetings.

# Forms

This appendix contains forms that you can use to record the configuration of your network and its components. They can be copied and used as is, or serve as the basis for forms that you design. The worksheets are:

- ► Figures B.1 and B.2: Server Configuration Worksheet (two sides). Figures B.3 and B.4 illustrate a worksheet filled in for a hypothetical server.

- ► Figure B.5: Workstation Configuration Worksheet. Figure B.6 illustrates a worksheet filled in for a hypothetical user's workstation.

- ► Figure B.7: Network Configuration Worksheet.

- ► Figure B.8: User Configuration Information Worksheet.

- ► Figure B.9: Printer Configuration Worksheet.

- ► Figure B.10: Print Queue and Print Server Configuration Worksheet.

These forms are available as Adobe Illustrator files (Macintosh and PC) on NOVLIB, Library 2. You can download them and make any changes you like. The collections are named macforms.sit and pcforms.zip. My CompuServe address is 75600,2175, and my UNIX email address is logan@sjb.novell.com. I welcome any input on this book or suggestions for the next revision.

# Server Configuration Worksheet
## Side One

Name: _____ Location: _____ Date: _____

Internal IPX Number: _____ Department: _____

Brand/Model: _____

Support Phone Number: _____ Serial Number: _____

Memory Installed: _____ Possible: _____ Type: _____

**Board** : _____        **Board** : _____
Brand: _____             Brand: _____
Support #: _____           Support #: _____
Model #: _____           Model #: _____
I/O Port: _____          I/O Port: _____
Memory Address: _____           Memory Address: _____
Interrupt: _____           Interrupt: _____
DMA: _____             DMA: _____
Slot Number: _____           Slot Number: _____
Driver: _____            Driver: _____
BIOS Version: _____          BIOS Version: _____
Network Number: _____           Network Number: _____

**Board** : _____        **Board** : _____
Brand: _____             Brand: _____
Support #: _____           Support #: _____
Model #: _____           Model #: _____
I/O Port: _____          I/O Port: _____
Memory Address: _____           Memory Address: _____
Interrupt: _____           Interrupt: _____
DMA: _____             DMA: _____
Slot Number: _____           Slot Number: _____
Driver: _____            Driver: _____
BIOS Version: _____          BIOS Version: _____
Network Number: _____           Network Number: _____

Disks - see other side

**F I G U R E  B.2**

*Server Configuration*
*Worksheet, Side 2.*

# Server Configuration Worksheet
### Side Two — Disks

**Controller:** _____     Int: ____ DMA: ____ Slot #: ____
Support #: _____     Driver: _____
Port: ____ Mem. Address: ____     BIOS Version: _____

| Disk | Size | Heads | Cylinders | Device Code (5-digit) | Logical Device | Physical Partition | Mirrored With |
|------|------|-------|-----------|-----------------------|----------------|--------------------|---------------|
|      |      |       |           |                       |                |                    |               |
|      |      |       |           |                       |                |                    |               |
|      |      |       |           |                       |                |                    |               |
|      |      |       |           |                       |                |                    |               |
|      |      |       |           |                       |                |                    |               |
|      |      |       |           |                       |                |                    |               |
|      |      |       |           |                       |                |                    |               |

**Controller:** _____     Int: ____ DMA: ____ Slot #: ____
Support #: _____     Driver: _____
Port: ____ Mem. Address: ____     BIOS Version: _____

| Disk | Size | Heads | Cylinders | Device Code (5-digit) | Logical Device | Physical Partition | Mirrored With |
|------|------|-------|-----------|-----------------------|----------------|--------------------|---------------|
|      |      |       |           |                       |                |                    |               |
|      |      |       |           |                       |                |                    |               |
|      |      |       |           |                       |                |                    |               |
|      |      |       |           |                       |                |                    |               |
|      |      |       |           |                       |                |                    |               |
|      |      |       |           |                       |                |                    |               |
|      |      |       |           |                       |                |                    |               |

# Server Configuration Worksheet
### Side One

Name: __Asmodeus__    Location: __Office 1141__    Date: __2/29/90__

Internal IPX Number: __C11412385__    Department: __Marketing__

Brand/Model: __ACMA 486/66 EISA Tower AMI BIOS 4.25__

Support Phone Number: __408 555-1491__    Serial Number: __A11093B31__

Memory Installed: __32 Mb__  Possible: __64 Mb__  Type: __16x4 SIMM__

Board : __LAN Adapter__
Brand: __Eagle__
Support #: __801 555-8872__
Model #: __NE3200__
I/O Port: _____
Memory Address: _____
Interrupt: _____
DMA: _____
Slot Number: __3__
Driver: __NE3200.LAN__
BIOS Version: __1.21__
Network Number: __1A114100__

Board : __LAN Adapter__
Brand: __Eagle__
Support #: __801 555-8872__
Model #: __NE3200__
I/O Port: _____
Memory Address: _____
Interrupt: _____
DMA: _____
Slot Number: __2__
Driver: __NE3200.LAN__
BIOS Version: __1.21__
Network Number: __2B114100__

Board : __SVGA__
Brand: __On Motherboard__
Support #: _____
Model #: _____
I/O Port: _____
Memory Address: __B000-B7FF__
Interrupt: _____
DMA: _____
Slot Number: _____
Driver: _____
BIOS Version: _____
Network Number: _____

Board : _____
Brand: _____
Support #: _____
Model #: _____
I/O Port: _____
Memory Address: _____
Interrupt: _____
DMA: _____
Slot Number: _____
Driver: _____
BIOS Version: _____
Network Number: _____

Disks - see other side

*Server Configuration*

*Worksheet, Side 2—Filled In.*

# Server Configuration Worksheet
### Side Two — Disks

**Controller:** <u>Adaptec 1742B (EISA)</u>     Int: <u>—</u> DMA: _____ Slot #: <u>4</u>

**Support #:** <u>510 555-3201</u>    Driver: <u>AHA1740.DSK</u>

**Port:** <u>—</u> **Mem. Address:** <u>—</u>    BIOS Version: <u>6.02</u>

| Disk | Size | Heads | Cylinders | Device Code (5-digit) | Logical Device | Physical Partition | Mirrored With |
|------|------|-------|-----------|----------------------|----------------|--------------------|----------------|
| Maxtor PO-12S | 1 Gb | 15 | 4196 | 21100 | 1 | 0 | 1 |
| Maxtor PO-12S | 1 Gb | 15 | 4196 | 21200 | 2 | 1 | — |
|  |  |  |  |  |  |  |  |
|  |  |  |  |  |  |  |  |
|  |  |  |  |  |  |  |  |
|  |  |  |  |  |  |  |  |

**Controller:** <u>Motherboard</u>    Int: <u>E</u> DMA: _____ Slot #: _____

**Support #:** <u>415 555-8195</u>    Driver: <u>ISADISK</u>

**Port:** <u>1f0</u> **Mem. Address:** _____    BIOS Version: _____

| Disk | Size | Heads | Cylinders | Device Code (5-digit) | Logical Device | Physical Partition | Mirrored With |
|------|------|-------|-----------|----------------------|----------------|--------------------|----------------|
| Quantum IDE 105S | 100 | 8 | 995 | 11000 | 1 | 0 | — |
|  |  |  |  |  |  |  |  |
|  |  |  |  |  |  |  |  |
|  |  |  |  |  |  |  |  |
|  |  |  |  |  |  |  |  |
|  |  |  |  |  |  |  |  |

# Workstation Configuration Worksheet

User: _____   Location: _____   Date: _____

Network Node Address: _____   Department: _____

Brand/Model: _____

Support Phone Number: _____   Serial Number: _____

Memory Installed: _____   Possible: _____   Type: _____

Ports Enabled: LPT1☐   LPT2☐   LPT3☐   COM1☐   COM2☐   COM3☐   COM4☐

Floppys: 3.5"- DD ___ HD ___ 5.25"- DD ___ HD ___   Mouse: _____

Hard Disk 1: Brand _____ Controller _____ Type ____ Heads ____

       Cyl ____ PreComp ____ LZ ____ Partition _____ Size _____

Hard Disk 2: Brand _____ Controller _____ Type ____ Heads ____

       Cyl ____ PreComp ____ LZ ____ Partition _____ Size _____

**Boards:**

Brand/Model _____ Support # _____

Int ____ DMA _____ Port _____ Mem. Addr. _____ Slot ___ BIOS Ver. _____

Brand/Model _____ Support # _____

Int ____ DMA _____ Port _____ Mem. Addr. _____ Slot ___ BIOS Ver. _____

Brand/Model _____ Support # _____

Int ____ DMA _____ Port _____ Mem. Addr. _____ Slot ___ BIOS Ver. _____

Brand/Model _____ Support # _____

Int ____ DMA _____ Port _____ Mem. Addr. _____ Slot ___ BIOS Ver. _____

Operating System Version: _____

Networking Software: _____

TSRs and Other Drivers: _____

Comments: _____

       _____

*Workstation Configuration*
*Worksheet—Filled In.*

# Workstation Configuration Worksheet

User: _Bosco Ninnyhammer_   Location: _Cube 1510_   Date: _3/10/92_

Network Node Address: _FC3010014C13_   Department: _Engineering_

Brand/Model: _ACMA 486/33 ISA with AMI BIOS v. 4.26_

Support Phone Number: _415 555-7717_   Serial Number: _A551C-30-1147_

Memory Installed: _16 Mb_ Possible: _32 Mb_ Type: _4 Mb x 9 SIMMs_

Ports Enabled: LPT1☐ LPT2☐ LPT3☐ COM1☐ COM2☐ COM3☐ COM4☐

Floppys: 3.5"- DD ___ HD _A:_ 5.25"- DD ___ HD _B:_ Mouse: _Logitech Bus_

Hard Disk 1: Brand _Conner_   Controller _IDE_ Type _45_ Heads _8_
   Cyl _960_ PreComp _0_ LZ _960_ Partition _MS DOS 5_ Size _210 Mb_

Hard Disk 2: Brand _____ Controller _____ Type ____ Heads ____
   Cyl ____ PreComp ____ LZ ____ Partition _____ Size _____

**Boards:**

Brand/Model _Orchid SVGA 1150_   Support # _703 555-4491_
Int ____ DMA _____ Port _____ Mem. Addr. _____ Slot _5_ BIOS Ver. _1.31_
Brand/Model _Eagle NE2000 10BaseT_   Support # _408 555-7171_
Int _3_ DMA _____ Port _300_ Mem. Addr. _____ Slot _3_ BIOS Ver. _4.6_
Brand/Model _____ Support # _____
Int ____ DMA _____ Port _____ Mem. Addr. _____ Slot ___ BIOS Ver. _____
Brand/Model _____ Support # _____
Int ____ DMA _____ Port _____ Mem. Addr. _____ Slot ___ BIOS Ver. _____

Operating System Version: _DR DOS 6.0_

Networking Software: _NETX v 3.26, IPX 3.1, NET.CFG_

TSRs and Other Drivers: _SMARTDRV.SYS_

Comments: _Runs Windows 3.1, NE1000 failed 11/28/91, Bosco eats over the keyboard - vacuum regularly._

# Network Configuration Worksheet

Server Name _____  Network Type and # _____

(One Worksheet per protocol.)

User _____ Node # _____ Protocol Addr: _____
User _____ Node # _____ Protocol Addr: _____
User _____ Node # _____ Protocol Addr: _____
User _____ Node # _____ Protocol Addr: _____
User _____ Node # _____ Protocol Addr: _____
User _____ Node # _____ Protocol Addr: _____
User _____ Node # _____ Protocol Addr: _____
User _____ Node # _____ Protocol Addr: _____
User _____ Node # _____ Protocol Addr: _____
User _____ Node # _____ Protocol Addr: _____
User _____ Node # _____ Protocol Addr: _____
User _____ Node # _____ Protocol Addr: _____
User _____ Node # _____ Protocol Addr: _____
User _____ Node # _____ Protocol Addr: _____
User _____ Node # _____ Protocol Addr: _____
User _____ Node # _____ Protocol Addr: _____
User _____ Node # _____ Protocol Addr: _____
User _____ Node # _____ Protocol Addr: _____
User _____ Node # _____ Protocol Addr: _____
User _____ Node # _____ Protocol Addr: _____

▶ . . . . . . . . . . . . . . . . . . . . . . . . . . ◀

*User Configuration*
*Information Worksheet.*

# User Configuration Worksheet

Date: _____

User Name: _____    Location: _____

Workstation: _____    Phone: _____

Groups: _____

Managed Users & Groups,
Security Equivalences:         _____

Time, Station, Volume
Restrictions:               _____

Login Script:                    Trustee Assignments:

_____        _____
_____        _____
_____        _____
_____        _____
_____        _____
_____        _____
_____        _____
_____        _____
_____        _____
_____        _____
_____        _____
_____        _____
_____        _____
_____        _____

# Printer Configuration Worksheet

Date: _____

Printer Name: _____  Type: _____

Manufacturer: _____  Phone: _____
(Tech Support)

Location: _____  PSERVER Name: _____

Parallel ☐  Interrupt: _____  AppleTalk ☐  Ethernet ☐  Addr: _____

Serial ☐  Baud: _____  Data bits: ___  Stop bits: ___  Parity: ___  XON/XOFF: ___

Hard Disk ☐  Size: _____

Mode: _____
(Text, PostScript, PCL, etc.)

Forms Defined:          Queues Serviced:          Notify List:

_____          _____          _____

_____          _____          _____

_____          _____          _____

_____          _____          _____

_____          _____          _____

_____          _____          _____

Notes: _____

_____

_____

**FIGURE B.10**

*Print Queue and Print Server Configuration Worksheet.*

## Print Server and Print Queue Configuration Worksheet
### Print Server

Name: _____ File Server(s): _____

ID: _____          _____

Printer 0: _____   Queue(s) Attached: _____

Printer 1: _____   Queue(s) Attached: _____

Printer 2: _____   Queue(s) Attached: _____

Printer 3: _____   Queue(s) Attached: _____

Printer 4: _____   Queue(s) Attached: _____

Printer 5: _____   Queue(s) Attached: _____

Printer 6: _____   Queue(s) Attached: _____

Printer 7: _____   Queue(s) Attached: _____

Operators: _____

Users: _____

### Print Queues Attached to this Print Server

Queue: _____ ID: _____    Queue: _____ ID: _____

Operators: _____    Operators: _____

_____    _____

Users: _____    Users: _____

_____    _____

Queue: _____ ID: _____    Queue: _____ ID: _____

Operators: _____    Operators: _____

_____    _____

Users: _____    Users: _____

_____    _____

# Glossary

**T**his glossary is intended to supplement the glossary in the *Concepts* manual of your NetWare documentation.

# A

### ACTIVE HUB
See *hub*.

### ACTIVE STAR
Network topology that provides regeneration of signals in the central hub. See *passive star*.

### ADDRESS RESOLUTION PROTOCOL (ARP)
A process in Internet Protocol (IP) and AppleTalk networks that allows a host to find the physical address of a target host on the same physical network when it knows only the target's logical address. Under ARP, a network board contains a table that maps logical addresses to the hardware addresses of the objects on the network.

### AFP
See *AppleTalk Filing Protocol*.

### AIX
(Advanced Interactive eXecutive) IBM's version of UNIX for 386-based PS/2s, RTs and mainframes. It is based on AT&T's UNIX System V with Berkeley extensions.

## APPLESHARE

Networking software from Apple that enables a Macintosh computer to function as a file server in an AppleTalk network.

## APPLETALK FILING PROTOCOL (AFP)

A network file-system model from Apple that allows workstations to share files and programs on an AppleShare file server.

## APPLETALK PROTOCOLS

The underlying forms and rules that determine communication between nodes on an AppleTalk network. These protocols govern the AppleTalk network, from the network board to the application software.

### The Link Access Protocol (LAP)

Works at the Data Link Layer (the bottom layer of the network), receiving packets of information and converting them into the proper signals for your network board. Examples of LAPs include LLAP (LocalTalk LAP), ELAP (Ethernet LAP), and DTLAP (Token-Ring LAP).

### Datagram Delivery Protocol (DDP)

Works at the Network Layer and prepares packets of data to send on network cables. These packets, called datagrams, include network address information and data formatting. They are delivered to one of the Link Access Protocols (LLAP, ELAP, or TLAP), according to the hardware in the computer.

### Name Binding Protocol (NBP)

Each network process or device has a name that corresponds to network and node addresses. AppleTalk uses a Name Binding Protocol (NBP) to conceal those addresses from users.

### Routing Table Maintenance Protocol (RTMP)

When many small networks are connected, a router connects them together in an internetwork. Information about other networks is stored in routing tables. Routers update routing tables by using the Routing Table Maintenance Protocol (RTMP) to communicate with each other.

### Zone Information Protocol (ZIP)

In a large internetwork, all AppleTalk nodes are divided into zones, for ease of locating an object. The NBP uses a Zone Information Protocol to assist in finding the correct network and node addresses from a Zone List.

Zones are referred to by names, which can be up to 32 characters each. The zone names are converted to addresses on the internetwork by the Name Binding Protocol and the Zone Information Protocol. In a network without routers, only one zone exists, and the zone name is invisible to users.

Zone names and addresses are maintained in a Zone Information Table within each router. A NetWare server acts as a router for AppleTalk nodes connected to it.

### Printer Access Protocol (PAP)

When a network node prints to a network printer, the Printer Access Protocol (PAP) prepares a path to the requested printer using NBP.

### APPLICATION LAYER

See *OSI model*.

### ARCNET

(Attached Resource Computer NETwork) Local area network introduced in 1968 by Datapoint Corp. It was the first LAN. It uses a token-passing access method at 2.5 Mbps with a distributed star topology for up to 255 nodes.

## ARP

See *Address Resolution Protocol.*

## ARPANET

(Advanced Research Projects Agency NETwork) Research network funded by DARPA (originally ARPA) and built by BBN, Inc., in 1969. It pioneered packet switching technology and was the original backbone and testbed for the now-gigantic Internet. In 1983, the military communications part of it was split off into MILNET.

## AS/400

(Application System/400) IBM minicomputer series introduced in 1988 that supersedes and advances the System/36 and System/38.

## ASCII

(American Standard Code for Information Interchange) A 7-bit binary code providing 128 possible character combinations, the first 32 of which are used for printing and transmission control. Since the common storage unit is an 8-bit byte (256 combinations) and ASCII uses only 128, the extra bit is used to hold a parity bit or special characters such as foreign language and graphics symbols.

## ASYNCHRONOUS TRANSMISSION

Asynchronous transmission is transmission of data in which each character is a self-contained unit with its own start and stop bits. Intervals between characters may be uneven. It is the common method of transmission between a computer and a modem. Asynchronous communications protocols include ASCII, TTY, Kermit and Xmodem. See *synchronous.*

## ATM

(Asynchronous Transfer Mode) High-speed packet switching technique suitable for MANs and broadband ISDN transmission.

# B

### B/ISDN
(Broadband/ISDN) See *ISDN*.

### BACKBONE
The part of a network that handles the major traffic. It may interconnect multiple locations, and smaller networks may be attached to it. It often uses a higher-speed protocol than the LAN segments.

### BASE ADDRESS
Location in memory where the beginning of a program is stored. The relative address from the instruction in the program is added to the base address to derive the absolute address.

### BASEBAND
Communications technique in which digital signals are placed onto the transmission line without change in modulation. It is usually limited to a couple of miles and does not require the complex modems used in broadband transmission. Common baseband LAN techniques are token passing ring (Token-Ring) and CSMA/CD (Ethernet).

In baseband, the full bandwidth of the channel is used, and simultaneous transmission of multiple sets of data is accomplished by interleaving pulses using TDM (Time Division Multiplexing). See *broadband*; *TDM*.

### BAUD RATE
The signaling rate of a line. It's the switching speed, or number of transitions (voltage or frequency changes) that are made per second. Only at low speeds are bauds equal to bits per second; for example, 300 baud is

equal to 300 Bps. However, one baud can be made to represent more than one bit per second. For example, the V.22bis modem generates 1200 Bps at 600 baud.

## BIOS

(Basic Input/Output System) A set of routines, usually in firmware, that enables each computer's central processing unit to communicate with printers, disks, keyboards, consoles, and other attached input and output devices. It searches for other BIOSes on the plug-in boards and sets up pointers (interrupt vectors) in memory to access all BIOS routines. It loads the operating system and passes control to it.

## BISYNC

(BInary SYNChronous) Major category of synchronous communications protocols used in mainframe networks. Bisync communications require that both sending and receiving devices be synchronized before transmission of data is started.

## BNC

Commonly used connector for coaxial cable. The plug looks like a cylinder with two short pins on the outer edge on opposite sides. After the plug is inserted, the socket is turned, causing the pins to tighten the plug within it.

## BRIDGE

A device that retransmits packets from one segment of the network to another segment. It will only forward a packet if it is intended for the other segment. A router, on the other hand, is a device that receives instructions for forwarding packets between topologies and determines the most efficient path.

## BROADBAND

Technique for transmitting large amounts of data, voice and video over long distances. Using high frequency transmission over coaxial cable or optical fibers, broadband transmission requires modems for connecting terminals and computers to the network. Using the same FDM (frequency division multiplexing) technique as cable TV, several streams of data can be transmitted simultaneously. See *baseband; FDM*.

## BROUTER

Communications device that performs functions of both a bridge and a router. Like a bridge, the brouter functions at the OSI data link level (layer 2) and remains independent of higher protocols, but like a router, it manages multiple lines and routes messages accordingly.

# C

## CACHE

A reserved section of memory used to improve performance. A disk cache is memory on the disk controller board. When the disk is read, a large block of data is copied into the cache. If subsequent requests for data can be satisfied in the cache, a slower disk access is not required. If the cache is used for writing, data is queued up in memory and written to the disk in larger blocks.

A memory cache is an extra high-speed memory bank between memory and the CPU. Blocks of instructions and data are copied into the cache and instruction execution and data updating are performed in the higher-speed memory.

## CCITT

(Consultative Committee for International Telephony and Telegraphy) An international organization for communications standards. It is one of four organs of the International Telecommunications Union, founded in 1865, headquartered in Geneva and comprised of over 150 member countries.

## CD-ROM

(Compact Disc Read Only Memory) Compact disc format used to hold text, graphics, and audio. It's like a music CD, but uses a different track format for data. CD-ROMs hold about 660 MB. Audio and data reside on separate tracks and cannot be heard and viewed together. See *CD-ROM XA*.

## CD-ROM EXTENSIONS

Software required to use a CD-ROM player on a PC running DOS. It usually comes with the player and includes a driver specialized for the player and Microsoft's MSCDEX.EXE RAM-resident program.

## CD-ROM XA

(CD-ROM eXtended Architecture) CD-ROM enhancement introduced in 1988 by Philips, Sony and Microsoft that allows concurrent audio and video. It provides up to 9.5 hours of AM-quality stereo or up to 19 hours of monophonic audio.

## CHANNEL

The logical location of hard-disk controller hardware for the flow of data. For instance, a hard-disk controller in a PC is installed in a channel. An HBA (Host Bus Adapter) and its disk subsystems also make up a disk channel. Available channels are usually 0 through 4. Channel 0 is normally used by internal controllers and hard disks.

## CHECKSUM

A value used to ensure that data is transmitted without error. It is created by adding the binary value of each alphanumeric character in a block of data and sending it with the data. At the receiving end, a new checksum is computed and matched against the transmitted checksum. A non-match indicates an error. Just as a check digit tests the accuracy of a single number, a checksum tests a block of data. Checksums detect single-bit errors and some multiple-bit errors, but are not as effective as the CRC method.

### CLIENT

A workstation accessing the network. Under NetWare, client types include DOS, Macintosh, OS/2, UNIX, and Windows. With the respective client software, users can access network drives, printers, and applications.

### CMIP

(Common Management Information Protocol) The OSI protocol that defines the format for network monitoring and control information.

### CMIS

(Common Management Information Services) The OSI standard functions for network monitoring and control.

### CMOS RAM

(Complementary Metal-Oxide Semiconductor RAM) Random-access memory used for storing system configuration data (such as number of drives, types of drives, and amount of memory). CMOS RAM is battery powered to retain data while the computer is turned off. If the batteries die or are disconnected, the configuration information is lost.

### COAXIAL CABLE

High-capacity cable used in communications and video, commonly called coax. It contains an insulated solid or stranded wire that is surrounded by a solid or braided metallic shield, which is wrapped in an external cover. Coax provides a much higher bandwidth than twisted-pair wire.

## CONCENTRATOR

A device that joins several communications channels together. The central unit that ties a star topology together.

## CONNECTION NUMBER

A number assigned to any workstation that attaches to a NetWare server; it may be a different number each time a station attaches. Connection numbers are also assigned to processes, print servers, and applications that use server connections.

## CONNECTION-ORIENTED

A protocol that requires a direct connection or established session between two nodes before communication takes place. See *connectionless*.

## CONNECTIONLESS

A protocol in which the source and destination addresses are included within each packet so that a direct connection or established session between nodes is not required. See *connection-oriented*.

## CONTENTION

Condition that arises when two devices attempt to use a single resource at the same time. See *CSMA/CD*.

## CRC

(Cyclic Redundancy Check) A numeric value derived from the bits in a message. The transmitting station uses a formula to produce a number that is attached to the message. The receiving station applies the same formula and should derive the same number. If the numbers are not the same, the receiving station signals an error.

### CSMA/CD
(Carrier Sense Multiple Access/Collision Detection) Baseband communications access method that uses a collision-detection technique. When a device wants to gain access to the network, it checks to see if the network is free. If it is not, the device waits a random amount of time before retrying. If the network is free and two devices attempt access at exactly the same time, they both back off to avoid a collision and each wait a random amount of time before retrying. Typical of Ethernet.

# D

### DAEMON
A program that waits in the background ready to perform some action when a certain event occurs. Used in OS/2 and UNIX.

### DARPA
(Defense Advanced Research Projects Agency) See *ARPANET*.

### DAT
(Digital Audio Tape) A magnetic medium suitable for mass storage of digital data. The most common format is a 4mm, helical-scan DAT drive that holds 1.3 Gb or more, with extended-length tapes or compression.

### DATA FORK
See *Macintosh files*.

### DATA LINK PROTOCOL
The protocol that controls the transmission of a unit of data from one node to another (OSI layer 2). It ensures that the bits received are the same as the bits sent.

## DATAGRAM

TCP/IP message unit that contains internet source and destination addresses and data.

## DCE

(Data Communications Equipment or Data Circuit-terminating Equipment) A device that establishes, maintains and terminates a session on a network. It may also convert signals for transmission. Typically, a modem. See *DTE*.

## DEVICE DRIVER

Software that forms the interface between the operating system and devices such as hard disks or network boards. See *disk driver*.

## DEVICE NUMBERING

A method of identifying a device, such as a hard disk. Devices are identified by three numbers:

- ▶ *Physical address.* Set with jumpers on the boards, controllers, and hard disks. The physical address is determined by the driver, based upon those jumper settings.

- ▶ *Device code.* Determined by the physical address of the board, controller, and hard disk. In the device code #00101, for example, the first two digits (00) are reserved for the disk type. The third digit (1) is the board number; the fourth (0), the controller number; and the fifth (1), the disk number.

- ▶ *Logical number.* Determined by the order in which the disk drivers are loaded and by the physical address of the controller and hard disk.

All physical partitions are assigned logical partition numbers. These numbers are assigned to both the mirrored disks and the DOS partition.

Mirroring messages use the logical partition number to record which hard disks are being remirrored or unmirrored.

### DIRECTORY TABLE

A table that contains basic information about files, directories and directory trustees. The directory table occupies one or more directory blocks on the volume. Each block is 4 KB. A directory entry is 32 bytes long, so each block can hold 128 directory entries.

### DISK DRIVER

The software that forms the interface between the operating system and the hard disks. The disk driver talks to an adapter that is connected to the disk drives.

### DISK DUPLEXING

Disk duplexing consists of duplicating data on two hard disks, each on a separate disk channel and with a separate power supply. This protects data against the failure of a hard disk or the channel between the disk and the server. The hard disk channel includes the disk controller and cable. If any component on one channel fails, the other disk can continue to operate without data loss or interruption. See *disk mirroring*.

### DISK MIRRORING

Two or more hard disks on the same channel that hold the same data. Blocks of data written to the original (primary) disk are also written to the duplicate (secondary) disk. The disks are constantly storing and updating the same files. Should one of the disks fail, the other disk can continue to operate without data loss or interruption. See *disk duplexing*.

## DISK PARTITION

A logical unit for dividing hard disks. A PC may have a DOS partition and another partition such as OS/2 or UnixWare.

## DMA

(Direct Memory Access) Specialized circuitry or a dedicated micro-processor that transfers data from one place in memory to another without using the CPU. Although DMA may periodically steal cycles from the CPU, data is transferred much faster than using the CPU for every byte of transfer.

## DNS

(Domain Naming System) E-mail addressing system used in networks such as Internet and Bitnet.

## DOS BOOT RECORD

A record containing information that the BIOS uses to determine which device to boot from. The boot record can be on either a floppy diskette, a local hard disk, or a remote boot chip. The BIOS determines from the boot record the disk format and location of system files and directories. The BIOS then loads the system files and COMMAND.COM.

## DS

(Digital Signal) Speed measurements:

| | |
|------|-------------------|
| DS-0 | 64 Kbps |
| DS-1 | 1.544 Mbps (T1) |
| DS-2 | 6.312 Mbps (T2) |
| DS-3 | 44.736 Mbps (T3) |
| DS-4 | 274.176 Mbps (T4) |

### DSR
(Data Set Ready) RS-232 signal sent from the modem to the computer or terminal indicating that it is able to accept data. See *DTR*.

### DSU/CSU
(Data Service Unit/Channel Service Unit) Communications device that connects an in-house line to an external digital circuit (T1, DDS,...). The DSU converts data into the required format, while the CSU terminates the line and provides signal regeneration and remote testing.

### DTE
(Data Terminating Equipment) Communications device that is the source or destination of signals on a network. It is typically a terminal or computer. See *DCE*.

### DTR
(Data Terminal Ready) RS-232 signal sent from the computer or terminal to the modem indicating that it can accept data. See *DSR*.

# E

### ENCAPSULATION
In communications, inserting the frame header and data from a higher level protocol into the data frame of a lower level protocol.

### ETHERNET CONFIGURATION
The setup that allows communication using an Ethernet environment. In an Ethernet environment, stations communicate with each other by sending data in frames along an Ethernet cabling system. See Chapter 3 for details on cabling types.

Different Ethernet standards use different frame formats. NetWare 4.0 uses the IEEE 802.2 standard by default. In addition to 802.2, you can use one of the following frame types:

▸ *Ethernet 802.3.* The default frame type used in NetWare 3.11 and earlier. This frame type is also referred to as the raw frame.

▸ *Ethernet II.* The frame type used on networks that communicate with DEC minicomputers, and on computers that use TCP/IP or AppleTalk Phase I.

▸ *Ethernet SNAP.* The IEEE standard 802.2 frame type with an extension (SNAP) added to the header. Use this frame on networks that communicate with workstations that use protocols such as AppleTalk Phase II.

Using Novell's Open Datalink Interface (ODI) technology, NetWare allows stations with different Ethernet frame types to coexist on the same Ethernet cabling system.

### ETHERTALK

The AppleTalk implementation that runs over Ethernet. See *AppleTalk Protocols.*

# F

### FAKE ROOT

A subdirectory that functions as a root directory. Some applications can't be run from subdirectories; they read files from and write files to the root directory. However, for security, don't assign users rights at the root or volume directory level. Instead, load the files in a subdirectory and designate it as a fake root directory.

## FAT

See *File Allocation Table.*

## FAULT TOLERANCE

A means of protecting data by providing data duplication on multiple storage devices. See *System Fault Tolerance (SFT)*.

## FDDI

(Fiber optic Data Distribution Interface) ANSI standards for fiber optic local area networks. It deals with OSI layers 1 and 2 and transmits at 100 Mbps.

## FDM

(Frequency Division Multiplexing) Method used to transmit multiple signals over a single channel. Each signal (data, voice, etc.) is modulated onto a carrier of a different frequency and all signals travel simultaneously over the channel. See *baseband, TDM*.

## FIBER CHANNEL

Future ANSI standard under development for a high speed computer channel that incorporates IPI, SCSI and HiPPI command sets. Speeds range from 12.5 to 100Mb/sec using coax and optical fiber.

## FILE ALLOCATION TABLE (FAT)

An index table that points to the disk areas where a file is located. Because one file may be in any number of blocks spread over the disk, the FAT links the file together. In NetWare, the FAT is accessed from the Directory Entry Table (DET). The FAT is cached in server memory, allowing the server to quickly access the data.

## FILE LOCKING

The means of ensuring that a file is updated correctly before another user, application, or process can access the file. For example, without file locking, if two users attempt to update the same word processing file simultaneously, one user could overwrite the file update of the other user.

## FOIRL

(Fiber Optic Inter Repeater Link) IEEE standard for fiber optic Ethernet.

## FRACTIONAL T1

The division of a T1 channel into subchannels that provide between 64 and 768 Kbps. See *T-carrier*.

## FRAME

A packet data format for a given media. Some media support multiple packet formats, such as Ethernet 802.2, Ethernet 802.3, Ethernet II, Ethernet SNAP, Token-Ring, or Token-Ring SNAP.

## FRAME RELAY

High-speed packet switching protocol that provides faster transmission than X.25. It is suited for data and image transfer.

## FTAM

(File Transfer Access and Management) Communications protocol for the transfer of files between systems of different vendors.

## FTP

(File Transfer Protocol) TCP/IP protocol that is used to log onto the network, list directories and copy files. It can also translate between ASCII and EBCDIC.

# G

### GATEWAY

A link between two networks. A gateway allows communication between dissimilar protocols (for example, NetWare and UNIX networks) using industry-standard protocols such as TCP/IP, X.25, or SNA. See *bridge*; *brouter*; *router*.

### GOSIP

(Government Open Systems Interconnection Profile) Government mandate that after 8/15/90, all new network procurements must comply with OSI. Testing is performed at the NIST, which maintains a database of OSI-compliant commercial products. (TCP/IP protocols can also still be used.)

# H

### HALF-DUPLEX

Transmission of data in both directions, but only one direction at a time. See *full-duplex*.

### HANDSHAKING

The initial exchange between two data communication systems prior to and during data transmission to ensure proper data transmission. A handshake method (such as XON/XOFF) is part of the complete transmission protocol.

### HBA

See *Host Bus Adapter*.

## HDLC

(High-level Data Link Control) ISO communications protocol used in X.25 packet switching networks. It provides error correction at the data link layer. SDLC, LAP and LAPB are subsets of HDLC.

## HEADER

The first part of a packet that contains controlling data, such as originating and destination stations, message type and priority level.

## HFS

(Hierarchical File System) Macintosh file system. Currently supports NetWare volume sizes up to 2 GB.

## HOP COUNT

The number of network boards a message packet passes through on the way to its destination on an internetwork. The destination network can be no more than 16 hops (NetWare servers or routers) from the source.

## HOST

Mainframe computer in a distributed processing environment. It typically refers to a large timesharing computer or a central computer that controls a network.

## HOST BUS ADAPTER (HBA)

The HBA relieves the host microprocessor of data storage and retrieval tasks, usually improving the computer's performance time. An HBA and its disk subsystems make up a disk channel.

## HUB

A device that modifies transmission signals, allowing the network to be lengthened or expanded with additional workstations. There are two kinds of hubs:

- ▶ *Active hub*. An active hub amplifies transmission signals in network topologies to allow additional workstations on a network or to extend the cable distance between stations and the server.

- ▶ *Passive hub*. A device used in certain network topologies to split a transmission signal, allowing additional workstations to be added. A passive hub can't amplify the signal, so it must be cabled directly to a station or to an active hub.

# I

## IEC

(International Electrotechnical Commission) The organization that sets electrical and electronics standards founded in 1906 and headquartered in Geneva. It is made up of national committees from over 40 countries.

## IEEE

(Institute of Electrical and Electronic Engineers) Membership organization that includes engineers, scientists and students in electronics and allied fields. It has over 300,000 members and is involved with setting standards for computers and communications.

The Computer Society of the IEEE has over 100,000 members and holds meetings and technical conferences on computers.

For networking, the most important IEEE specifications are the following:

802.1      Covers network management and other aspects related to LANS. The IEEE standard for local area networks.

802.2      Specifies the data link layer for the following three access methods.

802.3      Specifies CSMA/CD, popularized by Ethernet.

802.4      Specifies a token passing bus.

802.5      Specifies a token passing ring, popularized by IBM's Token-Ring.

## THE INTERNET

The huge network of military, business, and university computers that stretches around the world and reaches millions of people. The Internet is based on the TCP/IP protocol. See *ARPANET*.

## INTERNETWORK

Two or more networks connected by a router. Users on an internetwork can use the resources of all connected networks.

## IPX

(Internet Packet eXchange) NetWare communications protocol used to route messages from one node to another. Application programs that manage their own client/server or peer-to-peer communications in a Novell network can access IPX, or NetWare's SPX protocol, directly. IPX does not guarantee delivery of a message as does SPX.

### IPX external network number

A network number that uniquely identifies a network cable segment. An IPX external network number is a hexadecimal number from one to eight digits (1 to FFFFFFFE). The number is assigned when the IPX protocol is bound to a network board in the server.

### IPX internal network number

A logical network number that identifies an individual NetWare server. Each server on a network must have a unique IPX internal network number. The internal network number is a hexadecimal number from one to eight digits (1 to FFFFFFFE), and is assigned to the server during installation.

### IPX internetwork address

A 12-byte number (represented by 24 hexadecimal characters) divided into three parts. The first part is the 4-byte (8-character) IPX external-network number, the second is the 6-byte (12-character) node number, and the third is the 2-byte (4-character) socket number.

### IPXODI

(Internet Packet eXchange Open Data-Link Interface) A module that takes workstation requests that the DOS Requester has determined are for the network, packages them with transmission information (such as their destination), and hands them to the LSL.

IPXODI attaches a header to each data packet. The header specifies information that targets network delivery, announcing where the packet came from, where it's going, and what happens after delivery.

Because IPXODI transmits data packets as datagrams (self-contained packages that move independently from source to destination), it can only deliver the packets on a best-effort basis. Delivery is assured by SPX.

## ISDN

(Integrated Services Digital Network) International telecommunications standard for transmitting voice, video and data over a digital communications line. It uses out-of-band signaling, which provides a separate channel for control information. ISDN services come in two forms: Basic Rate Interface (BRI) and Primary Rate Interface (PRI).

BRI provides 144 Kbps service, which includes two 64 Kbps "B" channels for voice, data or video, and one 16 Kbps "D" channel for control information. PRI provides 1.54 Mbps, allowing 23 64 Kbps "B" channels and one 64 Kbps "D" channel.

Broadband ISDN(B/ISDN) should become available in the near future. It uses broadband transmission and fiber optic cables to jump transmission speed to 150 megabits per second.

## ISO

(International Standards Organization) Founded in 1946 and headquartered in Geneva, this organization deals with all fields except electrical and electronics standards, which is governed by the older International Electrotechnical Commission (IEC). With regard to information processing, ISO and IEC created JTC1, the Joint Technical Committee for information technology.

ISO carries out its work through more than 160 technical committees and 2,300 subcommittees and working groups and is made up of standards organizations from more than 75 countries, some of them serving as secretariats for these technical bodies. ANSI is the U.S. member body.

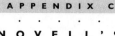
# L

### LAN

See *local area network.*

### LARGE INTERNET PACKET (LIP)

(Large Internet Packet) Allows the internetwork packet size limit to be increased from the default 576 bytes. By allowing the NetWare packet size to be increased, LIP enhances the throughput over bridges and routers.

### LINK SUPPORT LAYER (LSL)

An implementation of the Open Data-Link Interface (ODI) specification that serves as an intermediary between the NetWare server's LAN drivers and communication protocols, such as IPX, AFP, or TCP/IP. The LSL allows network boards to service one or more protocol stacks.

### LOCAL AREA NETWORK (LAN)

A network located within a small area or common environment, such as in a building or a building complex. A LAN has only one network address.

### LOCALTALK

LAN access method from Apple Computer, Inc. that uses twisted-pair wires and transmits at 230,400 Bps. Third-party products allow it to hook up with bus, passive star, and active star topologies.

### LSL

See *Link Support Layer.* See also *Open Data-Link Interface.*

# M

## MACINTOSH FILES

A Macintosh file contains two parts, the data fork and the resource fork:

► The *data fork* contains data specified by the user.

► The *resource fork* contains file resources, such as the windows, icons or fonts used with the file.

When a Macintosh client accesses the file stored on the server, it accesses both the data and resource forks. When a non-Macintosh client accesses the file, only the data fork is used.

## MAN

(Metropolitan Area Network) Communications network that covers a geographic area such as a city or suburb. See *LAN* and *WAN*.

## MAU (MSAU)

(Multi-Station Access Unit) Central hub in a Token-Ring LAN.

## MHS

(Message Handling Service) E-mail system from Action Technologies, Inc., licensed by Novell for its NetWare operating systems. It allows for the transfer and routing of messages between users and provides storage and forwarding capabilities. It also provides gateways into PROFS, All-in-1, X.400, and other message systems.

## MLID

See *multiple layer interface driver* and *Open Data-Link Interface*.

### MULTIPLE-BYTE CHARACTER

A single character made up of more than one byte. One byte allows 256 different characters. Since the number of ASCII characters equals 256, a computer can handle any ASCII character with one byte. Asian character sets, however, include more than 256 characters; for this reason, a computer must use two bytes for each character in an Asian character set.

### MULTIPLE LAYER INTERFACE DRIVER (MLID)

A device driver written to the ODI specification that handles the sending and receiving of packets to and from a physical or logical LAN medium.

### MULTIPLEXING

Transmitting multiple signals over a single communications line or computer channel. The two common multiplexing techniques are FDM, which separates signals by modulating the data onto different carrier frequencies, and TDM, which separates signals by interleaving bits one after the other.

### MULTIPLEXOR (MUX)

A device that merges several low-speed transmissions into one high-speed transmission and vice versa.

### MUX

(MUltipleXor) See multiplexor.

### MULTI-SERVER NETWORK

A single network that has two or more NetWare servers operating. A multi-server network isn't the same as an internetwork, where two or more networks are linked through a router; an internetwork has at least two network numbers, a multi-server network has one.

# N

### NAME SPACE

A special NLM that allows you to store non-DOS files on a NetWare server. Files appear as they would on the workstation. File types such as Macintosh or OS/2 must have a name space NLM linked with NetWare before the server can store such files.

### NBP

See *Name Binding Protocol* under the entry *AppleTalk protocols*.

### NCB

(Network Control Block) Packet structure used by the NetBIOS transport protocol.

### NCP

See *NetWare Core Protocol*.

### NDIS

Network Driver Interface Specification. See *ODINSUP.*

### NETBEUI

(NetBIOS Extended User Interface) Implementation of the NetBIOS transport protocol used by LAN Manager and LAN Server. It communicates to the network adapter via NDIS.

### NETBIOS.EXE

NetWare's NetBIOS emulator program that allows workstations to run applications written for peer-to-peer communication or distributed processing on IBM's PC Network or MS-Net and LAN Manager. The INT2F.COM file is used with NETBIOS.EXE.

### NET.CFG

A workstation boot file, similar to CONFIG.SYS, that contains configuration values for the network shell that are read and interpreted when the workstation boots. These configuration values control the operating parameters of the NetWare DOS Requester, IPX, and other workstation software. Also called SHELL.CFG.

### NETVIEW

IBM SNA network management software that provides centralized monitoring and control for SNA, non-SNA and non-IBM devices. NetView/PC interconnects NetView with Token-Ring LANs, Rolm CBXs and non-IBM modems, while maintaining control in the host.

### NETWARE CORE PROTOCOL (NCP)

Procedures that NetWare follows to accept and respond to workstation requests. NCPs exist for every service a station might request from a server. Common requests handled by an NCP include creating or destroying a service connection, manipulating directories and files, opening semaphores, altering the Directory, and printing.

### NETWARE EXPRESS

Novell's private electronic information service that provides access to Novell's Network Support Encyclopedia. NetWare Express uses the GE Information Services network and software and requires a connection through an asynchronous modem.

## NETWARE LOADABLE MODULE (NLM)

A program you can load and unload from server memory while the server is running. (Some NLMs that are depended on by other NLMs are loaded automatically.) NLMs link disk drivers, LAN drivers, name spaces, and other NetWare server management and enhancement utilities to the operating systems.

The NetWare server allocates a portion of memory to the NLM when the NLM is loaded. The NLM uses the memory to perform a task, and then returns control of the memory to the operating system when the NLM is unloaded.

## NETWARE MANAGEMENT AGENTS

A group of NLMs that bring together software, hardware, and data components of a NetWare server and an external network management software package. When NetWare Management Agents are loaded, they create a hierarchical representation of all managed objects and their attributes.

## NETWARE REQUESTER FOR OS/2

Software that connects OS/2 workstations to NetWare networks, allowing OS/2 users to share network resources. The NetWare Requester directs network requests from the workstation to the network and allows application servers (such as SQL Server) and their workstations to communicate on the network without using a NetWare server. DOS and OS/2 users can access data on OS/2 application servers without using a NetWare server.

## NETWARE RUNTIME

A single-user version of NetWare. It supports front-end or back-end applications as well as basic NLM services such as communication services, database servers, electronic mail, and other third-party applications.

## NETWIRE

Novell's online information service, which provides access to Novell product information, Novell services information, and time-sensitive technical information for NetWare users. NetWire is accessed through the CompuServe Information Service. It requires a modem and a communications program.

## NETWORK DRIVER INTERFACE SPECIFICATION (NDIS)

See *ODINSUP.*

### Network Interface Card (NIC)

A board installed in each workstation to allow stations to communicate with each other and with the NetWare server. NetWare documentation uses the term *Network board* instead of *Network Interface Card.*

## NETWORK NODE

A device connected to a network by a network board and a communication medium. A network node can be a server, workstation, router, printer, or fax machine.

## NETWORK SUPPORT ENCYCLOPEDIA (NSE)

Novell's electronic information database containing comprehensive information about network technology. The NSE is available as a CD-ROM subscription, or through NetWare Express. (See Appendix A.)

## NETX

The latest version of the shell for NetWare 2.*x* and 3.*x* networks. Under NetWare 4.*x* , a VLM (NETX.VLM) under the NetWare DOS Requester that provides backward compatibility with NETX and other older versions of the shell.

## NFS

(Network File System) Distributed file system from Sun that allows data to be shared with many users in a network regardless of processor type, operating system, network architecture or protocol.

## NIC

See *Network interface card.*

## NIST

(National Institute of Standards & Technology) Standards-defining agency of the U.S. government, formerly called the National Bureau of Standards.

## NMI

(NonMaskable Interrupt) High-priority interrupt that cannot be disabled by another interrupt. It is used to report malfunctions such as parity, bus, and math coprocessor errors.

## NODE NUMBER

A number that uniquely identifies a network board. Every node must have at least one network board, by which the node is connected to the network. Each network board must have a unique node number to distinguish it from all other network boards on that network.

Node numbers are assigned in several ways, depending on the network board type:

- ► Ethernet boards are factory set. (No two Ethernet boards have the same number.)

- ► ARCnet and Token-Ring board numbers are set with jumpers or switches.

### NSE

See *Network Support Encyclopedia.*

### NUI

(NetWare Users International) NetWare user groups.

# O

### ODI

See *Open Data-Link Interface.*

### ODINSUP

(Open Data-link Interface/Network driver interface specification SUPport) An interface that allows the coexistence of two network driver interfaces: the Network Driver Interface Specification (NDIS) and the Open Data-Link Interface (ODI) specification. ODINSUP allows you to connect to dissimilar networks from your workstation and use them as if they were one network. ODINSUP also allows NDIS protocol stacks to communicate through the ODI's LSL and MLID. This way, NDIS and ODI protocol stacks can coexist in the same system, making use of a single ODI MLID.

### OPEN DATA-LINK INTERFACE (ODI)

An architecture that allows multiple LAN drivers and protocols to coexist on network systems. The ODI specification describes the set of interface and software modules used to decouple device drivers from protocol stacks and to enable multiple protocol stacks to share the network hardware and media transparently. The major components of the ODI architecture are described in the following sections.

### Multiple Layer Interface Driver (MLID)

The MLID is a device driver written to the ODI specification that handles the sending and receiving of packets to and from a physical or logical LAN medium. Each driver is unique to the adapter hardware and media, but the ODI eliminates the need to write separate drivers for each protocol stack. ODI allows LAN drivers to function with protocol stacks independent of the media frame type and protocol stack details.

MLIDs interface with a network board and handle the appending and stripping of media frame headers. They also help de-multiplex the incoming packets by determining their frame format.

### Link Support Layer (LSL)

The LSL is a software module that implements the interface between drivers and protocol stacks. It essentially acts like a switchboard, directing packets between the drivers and protocol stacks. Any ODI LAN driver can communicate with any ODI protocol stack through the LSL. The LSL handles the communication between protocol stacks and MLIDs.

### Media Support Module (MSM)

The MSM standardizes and manages primary details of interfacing ODI MLIDs to the LSL and operating system. The MSM handles generic initialization and run-time issues common to all drivers.

### Topology-Specific Module (TSM)

The TSM manages operations unique to a specific media type, such as Ethernet or Token-Ring. Multiple frame support is implemented in the TSM so that all frame types for a given media type are supported.

### Hardware-Specific Module (HSM)

The HSM is created for a specific network board. The HSM handles all hardware interactions. Its primary functions include adapter initialization, reset, shutdown, and removal. It also handles packet reception and transmission. Additional procedures may also provide support for timeout detection, multicast addressing, and promiscuous mode reception.

## OPTICAL DISK

A form of removable media used to store data. An optical disk can be one- or two-sided. Some optical disks are read-only; others can be written to as well.

## OSI MODEL

(Open System Interconnection) The ISO standard for communications that defines a framework for implementing protocols in seven layers. Control is passed from one layer to the next, starting at the application layer in one station, proceeding to the bottom layer, over the channel to the next station and back up the hierarchy.

Similar functionality exists in all communications networks, although layers may not correspond exactly. Most vendors have agreed to support OSI in one form or another. For a description of the OSI layers, see Chapter 3: The Physical Network.

### NetWare protocols

NetWare 4.0 has six layers of communication between an application and the hardware in the computer. These layers are based on the OSI model. The six communication layers are

- Application Layer
- Service Protocol Layer
- Communication Protocol Layer
- Link Support Layer
- Driver Layer
- Hardware Layer

In the server, communication protocols allow the Service Protocol Layer to communicate with the Link Support Layer (LSL). IPX, part of the operating system, is the default communication protocol.

You can use more than one protocol on the same cabling scheme because the LSL, part of the Open Data-Link Interface (ODI), allows the LAN driver for a network board to service more than one protocol.

# P

## PACKET

A unit of information used in network communication. Messages sent between network devices are formed into packets at the source device. The packets are reassembled, if necessary, into complete messages when they reach their destination.

## PACKET BURST PROTOCOL

A protocol built on top of IPX that speeds the transfer of multiple-packet NCP (NetWare Core Protocol) file reads and writes. The Packet Burst Protocol speeds the transfer of NCP data between a workstation and a NetWare server by eliminating the need to sequence and acknowledge each packet.

Packet Burst Protocol is more efficient than the one-request/one-response protocol in NetWare versions prior to 3.11/4.0. With Packet Burst Protocol, the server or workstation can send a whole set (burst) of packets before it requires an acknowledgment. By allowing multiple packets to be acknowledged, Packet Burst Protocol reduces network traffic.

## PACKET SWITCHING

Technique for handling high-volume traffic in a network by breaking apart messages into fixed length packets that are transmitted to their destination through the most expedient route. All packets in a single message may not travel the same route (dynamic routing). The destination computer reassembles the packets into their proper sequence.

This method is used to efficiently handle messages of different lengths and priorities in large networks, such as Telenet, Tymnet and AT&T's Accunet. X.25 is the international standard for such a network. Packet switching networks also provide value added services, such as protocol conversion and electronic mail.

### PAP

See *Printer Access Protocol* under the entry *AppleTalk protocols*.

### PARITY

A method of checking for errors in transmitted data.

### PASSIVE HUB

See *hub*.

### PASSIVE STAR

Network topology that joins wires from several nodes without providing any additional processing. See *active star*.

### PHONENET

Communications products from Farallon Computing, Inc. that extend LocalTalk distances to 3000 feet and use unshielded twisted phone lines instead of shielded twisted-pair. Configurations include daisy chain and passive star as well as active star topologies for both EtherTalk and LocalTalk.

## PORT

### Hardware port

A connecting component that allows a microprocessor to communicate with a compatible peripheral. On the PC, serial and parallel ports. The Macintosh includes a SCSI port.

### Software port

A memory address that identifies the physical circuit used to transfer information between a microprocessor and a peripheral. The DOS devices COM1-4 and LPT1-3 are software ports.

## POST

(Power On Self Test) Series of built-in diagnostics that are performed when the computer is first started. Proprietary codes are generated (POST codes) that indicate test results.

## PROTECTED MODE

The mode that 80286, 80386, and 80486 processors run in by default. When running in protected mode, these processors aren't subject to the same memory constraints as 8086 processors.

The 80286 processor uses a 24-bit address bus, and can address up to 16 MB of memory. The 80386 and 80486 processors use a 32-bit address bus, and can address up to 4 GB of memory.

Protected-mode operation provides the capability of multitasking (running more than one application or process at a time). Protected mode allocates memory to various processes running concurrently so that memory used by one process doesn't overlap memory used by another process.

By contrast, 8086 processors can address only 1 MB of memory, and can run only one application or process at a time. 80286, 80386, and 80486 processors can be set to run in *real mode*, in which case they emulate an 8086 processor (and are subject to its memory constraints).

## PU

(Physical Unit) In SNA, software responsible for managing the resources of a node, such as data links. A PU supports a connection to the host (SSCP) for gathering network management statistics.

# R

## RAID

(Redundant Arrays of Inexpensive Disks) Cluster of disks in which data is copied onto multiple drives. It provides faster throughput, fault tolerance (mirroring) and error correction. Level 3 is used for large block transfers (images, satellite feeds). Level 5 is most common. The levels are as follows:

| | |
|---|---|
| 0 | Disk striping only |
| 1 | Mirroring (100% duplication) |
| 2 | Complex error correction |
| 3 | Parallel transfer, parity drive |
| 4 | Independent transfer, parity drive |
| 5 | Independent transfer, no parity drive |

## REAL MODE

See *Protected Mode*.

## REDIRECTION

Diverting data from its normal destination to another; for example, to a print queue instead of the printer port, or to a server's disk instead of the local disk.

## REMOTE CONNECTION

A connection between a LAN on one end and a workstation or network on the other, often using telephone lines and modems. A remote connection allows data to be sent and received across greater distances than those allowed by normal cabling.

## REPEATER

A device that amplifies or regenerates the data signal in order to extend the distance of the transmission. Available for both analog and digital signals.

## RESOURCE FORK

See *Macintosh files*.

## RIP

See *Router Information Protocol*.

## ROUTER

A device that examines the destination address of a message and selects the most effective route. It is used in complex networks where there are many pathways between users. A NetWare router runs as part of a NetWare server. It connects separate network cabling topologies or separate networks with functions built into NetWare.

## ROUTER INFORMATION PROTOCOL (RIP)

A protocol that provides a way for routers to exchange routing information on a NetWare internetwork. RIP allows NetWare routers to create and maintain a database (or router table) of current internetwork routing information. Workstations can query the nearest router to find the fastest route to a distant network by broadcasting a RIP request packet.

Routers send periodic RIP broadcast packets containing current routing information to keep all routers on the internetwork synchronized. Routers also send RIP update broadcasts whenever they detect a change in the internetwork configuration.

### RS-232-C
EIA standard for a serial interface between computers and peripheral devices.

### RTS
(Request To Send) RS-232 signal sent from the transmitting station to the receiving station requesting permission to transmit.

### RTMP
See *Routing Table Maintenance Protocol* under the entry *AppleTalk protocols*.

# S

### SAA
(System Application Architecture) Introduced in 1987, a set of IBM standards that provide consistent interfaces among all IBM computers from micro to mainframe. It is made up of user interfaces, programming interfaces, and communications protocols, as follows:

1 · Common User Access (CUA)—Interfaces based on the graphics-based Presentation Manager of OS/2 and the character-oriented interfaces of 3270 terminals.

2 · Common Programming Interface (CPI)—A common set of application programming interfaces (APIs) that would, for example, allow a program developed on the PC to be easily moved to a mainframe. The standard database language is SQL.

**3 ·** Common Communications Support (CCS)—A common set of protocols, including LU 6.2 (APPC) and HLLAPI.

## SAP
See *Service Advertising Protocol.*

## SCSI
(Small Computer System Interface) An industry standard that sets guidelines for connecting peripheral devices and their controllers to a microprocessor. The SCSI interface defines both hardware and software standards for communication between a host computer and a peripheral.

## SDLC
(Synchronous Data Link Control) Primary data link protocol used in IBM's SNA networks. It is a bit-oriented synchronous protocol that is a subset of the HDLC protocol.

## SEQUENCED PACKET EXCHANGE (SPX)
A NetWare DOS Requester module that enhances the IPX protocol by supervising data sent out across the network. SPX verifies and acknowledges successful packet delivery to any network destination by requesting a verification from the destination that the data was received.

The SPX verification must include a value that matches the value calculated from the data before transmission. By comparing these values, SPX ensures not only that the data packet made it to the destination, but that it arrived intact.

SPX can track data transmissions consisting of a series of separate packets. If an acknowledgment request brings no response within a specified time, SPX retransmits it. After a reasonable number of retransmissions fail to return a positive acknowledgment, SPX assumes the connection has failed and warns the operator of the failure.

## SERIAL COMMUNICATION

The transmission of data between devices over a single line, one bit at a time.

## SERIALIZATION

Each NetWare operating system has a unique serial number. If two NetWare operating systems with the same serial number exist on the same internetwork, each NetWare server displays a copyright violation warning at the server console and at each logged-in workstation. Depending on the version, error messages may mention serialization.

## SERVICE ADVERTISING PROTOCOL (SAP)

NetWare servers advertise their services with SAP, allowing routers to create and maintain a database of current internetwork server information. Routers send periodic SAP broadcasts to keep all routers on the internetwork synchronized. Routers also send SAP update broadcasts whenever they detect a change in the internetwork configuration.

Workstations can query the network to find a server by broadcasting SAP request packets. When a workstation logs in to a network, it broadcasts a "Get Nearest Server" SAP request and attaches to the first server that replies.

## SFT

See *System Fault Tolerance.*

## SMB

(Server Message Block) Message format used in the Microsoft/3Com file sharing protocol for PC Network, MS-Net and LAN Manager. Used to transfer file requests between workstations and servers as well as within the server for internal operations. For network transfer, SMBs are carried within the NetBIOS network control block (NCB) packet.

## SMDS

(Switched Multimegabit Data Services) High-speed data services in the 45 Mbps range proposed by local telephone companies that will allow companies to build private MANs.

## SMTP

(Simple Mail Transfer Protocol) E-mail protocol used in TCP/IP networks.

## SNA

(Systems Network Architecture) IBM's primary networking strategy, introduced in 1974. SNA is made up of a variety of hardware and software products that all interact together.

## SNMP

(Simple Network Management Protocol) Format used for network management data. Data is passed between SNMP agents (processes that monitor activity in hubs, routers, bridges, etc.) and the workstation used to oversee the network. Originating in the UNIX community, it has spread to VMS, DOS, NetWare and other environments.

## SOCKET

The part of an IPX internetwork address, within a network node, that represents the destination of an IPX packet. Some sockets are reserved by NetWare for specific applications. For example, IPX delivers all NCP request packets to socket 451h. Third-party developers can also reserve socket numbers for specific purposes by registering those numbers with Novell.

## SONET

(Synchronous Optical NETwork) International standard for broadband transmission through fiber optic cables in the 50 megabit to 13 gigabit per second range. It is included in the Broadband ISDN (BISDN) specification.

## SOURCE ROUTING

IBM's method of routing data across source-routing bridges. NetWare source routing programs allow an IBM Token-Ring network bridge to forward NetWare packets (or frames). IBM bridges can be configured as either single-route broadcast or all-routes broadcast. The default is single-route broadcast.

- ▸ *Single-route broadcasting.* Only designated single-route bridges pass the packet and only one copy of the packet arrives on each ring in the network. Single-route bridges can transmit single-route, all-routes, and specifically routed packets.

- ▸ *All-routes broadcasting.* Sends the packet across every possible route in the network, resulting in as many copies of the frame at the destination as there are bridges in the network. All-routes bridges pass both all-routes broadcasts and specifically routed packets.

## SPS

(Standby Power System) see *Uninterruptible Power Supply*

## SPX

See *Sequenced Packet Exchange.*

## STAR NETWORK

Communications network in which all terminals are connected to a central computer or central hub. PBXs are prime examples, as well as IBM's Token-Ring, AT&T's Starlan LANs, and 10BaseT Ethernet.

## STOP BIT

A signal that indicates the end of a character.

### STP

(Shielded Twisted-Pair) Telephone wire wrapped in a metal sheath to eliminate external interference. See *twisted-pair*.

### SURGE PROTECTOR

Device that protects a computer from excessive voltage (spikes and surges) in the power line. See *Uninterruptible Power Supply*.

### SYNCHRONOUS TRANSMISSION

Transmission of data in which both stations are synchronized. Codes are sent from the transmitting station to the receiving station to establish the synchronization, and data is then transmitted in continuous streams. Modems that transmit at 1200bps and higher often convert the asynchronous signals from a computer's serial port into synchronous transmission over the transmission line. See *asynchronous transmission*.

### SYSTEM FAULT TOLERANCE (SFT)

A means of protecting data by providing data duplication on multiple storage devices; if one storage device fails, the data is available from another device. There are several levels of hardware and software system fault tolerance; each level of redundancy decreases the possibility of data loss.

# T

### T-CARRIER

Digital transmission service from a common carrier. T-carrier service requires multiplexors at both ends that merge the various signals together for transmission and split them at the destination. Multiplexors can analyze the traffic load and vary channel speeds for optimum transmission.

## T1

1.544 megabit T-carrier channel that can handle 24 voice or data channels at 64 Kbps. The standard T1 frame is 193 bits long, which holds 24 8-bit voice samples and one synchronization bit. 8000 frames are transmitted per second.

## T3

44.736 megabit T-carrier channel that can handle 672 voice or data channels at 64 Kbps. T3 requires fiber optic cable.

## TCP/IP

(Transmission Control Protocol/Internet Protocol) An industry-standard suite of networking protocols, enabling dissimilar nodes in a heterogeneous environment to communicate with one another.

The File Transfer Protocol (FTP) and Simple Mail Transfer Protocol (SMTP) provide file transfer and e-mail capability. The TELNET protocol provides a terminal-emulation capability that allows a user to interact with any other type of computer in the network. The TCP protocol controls the transfer of the data, and the IP protocol provides the routing mechanism.

## TDM

(Time Division Multiplexing) Technique that interleaves several low-speed signals into one high-speed transmission. For example, if A, B and C are three digital signals of 1000 Bps each, they can be mixed into one 3000 Bps as follows: AABBCCAABBCCAABBCC. The receiving end divides the single stream back into its original signals. See *baseband, FDM.*

## TERMINATION

Placing a terminating resistor at the end of a bus, line, chain, or cable to prevent signals from being reflected or echoed.

## TOKEN PASSING

Communications network access method that uses a continuously repeating frame (the token) that is transmitted onto the network by the controlling computer. When a terminal or computer wants to send a message, it waits for an empty token. When it finds one, it fills it with the address of the destination station and some or all of its message. Every computer and terminal on the network constantly monitors the passing tokens to determine whether it is a recipient of a message, in which case it "grabs" the message and resets the token status to empty.

## TOKEN RING NETWORK

IBM LAN that uses a special twisted wire cable and the token passing access method transmitting at four or 16 Mbps. It uses a star topology in which all computers connect to a central wiring hub, but passes tokens to each of up to 255 stations in a sequential, ring-like sequence. Token-Ring conforms to the IEEE 802.5 standard.

## TOKENTALK

Software for the Macintosh from Apple that accompanies its TokenTalk board and adapts the Mac to 4 Mbps Token-Ring networks.

## TROJAN HORSE

Program routine that invades a computer system by being secretly attached to a valid program that will be downloaded into the computer. It may be used to locate password information, or it may alter an existing program to make it easier to gain access to it.

## TWISTED-PAIR

Abbreviated "UTP" (Unshielded Twisted-Pair), a pair of thin-diameter (22 to 26 gauge) insulated wires commonly used in telephone wiring. The wires are twisted around each other to minimize interference from other twisted pairs in the cable. Twisted pairs have less bandwidth than coaxial cable or optical fiber.

# U

### UDP

(User Datagram Protocol) TCP/IP protocol that allows an application to send a message to one of several applications running in the destination machine. The application is responsible for reliable delivery.

### UNINTERRUPTIBLE POWER SUPPLY (UPS)

A backup power unit that supplies uninterrupted power if a commercial power outage occurs.

Types of UPS are online and off-line:

▶ *Online UPS.* Actively modifies the power as it moves through the unit. If a power outage occurs, the unit is already active and continues to provide power. An online UPS is usually more expensive than an off-line UPS, but provides a nearly constant source of energy during power outages.

▶ *Off-line UPS.* Monitors the power line. When power drops, the UPS is activated. The drawback to this method is the slight lag before the off-line UPS becomes active. However, most off-line UPS systems are fast enough to offset this lag. Also known as SPS (Standby Power Supply).

### UPS MONITORING

The process NetWare uses to ensure that an attached UPS (uninterruptible power supply) is functioning. When a power failure occurs, NetWare notifies users. After a timeout specified in SERVER.CFG, the server logs out remaining users, closes open files, and shuts itself down.

# V

## V.32

CCITT standard (1984) for asynchronous and synchronous 4800 and 9600 Bps full-duplex modems using TCM modulation over dial-up or two-wire leased lines. TCM encoding may be optionally added. V.32 uses echo cancellation to achieve full-duplex transmission.

## V.32BIS

CCITT standard (1991) for asynchronous and synchronous 4800, 7200, 9600, 12,000 and 14,400 Bps full-duplex modems using TCM and echo cancellation. Supports rate renegotiation, which allows modems to change speeds as required.

## V.42

CCITT standard (1989) for modem error correction that uses LAPM as the primary protocol and provides MNP Classes 2 through 4 as an alternative protocol for compatibility.

## V.42BIS

CCITT standard (1989) for modem error correction and data compression. It uses V.42 error correction with a compression technique (British Telecom Lempel Ziv) that increases transmission speed up to four times the Bps rating.

## VALUE-ADDED PROCESS (VAP)

A process that ties enhanced operating system features to a NetWare 2.*x* operating system without interfering with the network's normal operation. VAPs run on top of the operating system in much the same way a word processing or spreadsheet application runs on top of DOS.

NLMs provide this type of enhancement for NetWare 3.x and 4.0. (See *NetWare Loadable Module (NLM)*.

### VSAT

(Very Small Aperture satellite Terminal) Small earth station for satellite transmission that handles up to 56 Kbps of digital transmission. VSATs that handle the T1 data rate (up to 1.544 Mbps) are called TSATs.

### VTAM

(Virtual Telecommunications Access Method) Also called ACF/VTAM (Advanced Communications Function/VTAM), software that controls communications in an IBM SNA environment. It usually resides in the mainframe under MVS or VM, but may be off-loaded into a front-end processor that is tightly coupled to the mainframe. It supports a wide variety of network protocols, including SDLC and Token-Ring. VTAM can be thought of as the network operating system of SNA.

# W

### WAN

See *wide area network*.

### WATCHDOG

Packets used to make sure workstations are still connected to the NetWare server. If the server hasn't received a packet from a station in a certain time, a watchdog packet is sent to the station. If the station doesn't respond, another watchdog packet is sent. If the station still doesn't respond, the server assumes that the station is no longer connected and clears the station's connection.

## WIDE AREA NETWORK (WAN)

A network that communicates over a long distance, such as across a city or around the world. A LAN becomes a part of a WAN when a link is established (using modems, remote routers, phone lines, satellites, or a microwave connection) to a mainframe system, a public data network, or another LAN.

# X

### X.25

CCITT standard (1976) for the protocols and message formats that define the interface between a terminal and a packet switching network.

### X.400

CCITT standard mail and messaging protocol that is OSI compliant.

### X.500

CCITT standard mail and messaging protocol that includes the capability of maintaining directories of users. X.500 is OSI compliant.

### XON/XOFF

A handshake protocol that prevents a sending system from transmitting data faster than a receiving system can accept it.

# Z

### ZONES

See *AppleTalk Filing Protocols.*

# Index

## A

ABEND error messages, **25**, **28**, 32, 335
Access Control Lists, 260
accessing services and devices, **288–289**.
   *See also* security
  dial-in, **200–201**
  file, **289–290**
  printer, **290–292**
  trouble in, 5, 7–8
  from Windows, **292–294**
ACF/VTAM (Advanced Communications
   Function/VTAM), 432
active hubs, 113, 402
active star topology, 382
Address Resolution Protocol (ARP), 382
addresses, 393
  with IPX/SPX, 105
  with Macintoshes, 332
  with TCP/IP, 279
  with WANs, 20, 245–247, 404
Admin object, 338
Advanced Interactive Executive (AIX)
   system, 382
Advanced Research Projects Agency
   Network (ARPANET), 385
AFIX2.ZIP program, 331
AFP (AppleTalk Filing Protocol), 275,
   330, 383
AFP.NLM file, 276–277
AIF (Automatic Installation Files), 297
AIX (Advanced Interactive Executive)
   system, 382
aliases for directories, 261
all-routes broadcasting, 426
Alloc Short Term memory report, 192

American National Standards Institute
   (ANSI), 264
American Standard Code for Information
   Interchange (ASCII), 385
analog dial-up connections, 237
ANSI (American National Standards
   Institute), 264
anti-static precautions, **184**
Anti-Virus for NetWare program, 364
APPLDATA.AFP file, 276
AppleShare software, 383
AppleTalk Filing Protocol (AFP), 275,
   330, 383
AppleTalk Phase II, 275–276
AppleTalk Print Services (ATPS), 159,
   275, 332
AppleTalk protocols, 24, 106, **383–384**
  connecting, 74
  gateways for, 278
  printing with, **154–155**, **168–170**
  troubleshooting, **131–135**
  WANs with, **274–278**
application layer in OSI, 108, 416
applications, **288–289**
  e-mail, **298–299**
  as fault points, 13, 55–56
  file services for, **289–290**
  with networked modems, **299–301**
  NLMs for, 15, 31
  in printing, 148, **290–292**
  restoring, **216**
  on servers, **294–296**
  upgrading, **322**
  in Windows, **292–294**
arcing in power cords, 184
ARCnet (Attached Resource Computer
   Network) protocol, **113–114**, 384
  node numbers for, 413

in physical layer, 105
with TCP/IP, 279
with Windows, 293
ARCSERVE 5.0, 338
ARP (Address Resolution Protocol), 382
ARPANET (Advanced Research Projects
  Agency Network), 385
AS/400 minicomputers, 385
ASCII (American Standard Code for
  Information Interchange), 385
Asynchronous Transfer Mode (ATM),
  238–239, 264, 385
asynchronous transmissions, 385
ATCON.NLM, 276, 332
ATDISK.DSK driver, 336
ATM (Asynchronous Transfer Mode),
  238–239, 264, 385
ATPS (AppleTalk Print Services), 159,
  275, 332
ATPS.CFG file, 160
ATTACH utility
  for OS/2, 272
  from Windows, 293
Attached Resource Computer Network.
  See ARCnet (Attached Resource
  Computer Network) protocol
attaching to servers
  mail, 298–299
  multiple, 258
  with OS/2, 272
attributes, file, 282, 333
AUI (thick Ethernet) cable, 100, 109–110
AUTOEXEC.BAT files
  as fault points, 55
  login names in, 200
  for printing, 159, 164, 167
  problems in, 325–326
  saving, 63, 185
  for UDFs, 297
AUTOEXEC.NCF file, 15, 23
  ABENDs from, 25
  for RAM boards, 18
  skipping, 336
  for UNIX, 283
  for upgrades, 31
AUTOEXEC.SYS file, 14, 23, 30

Automatic Installation Files (AIF), 297
Available Cache Buffers report, 192

**B**

backbones, 386
backups, 175–176
  for binderies, 30
  capacity of tape drives in, 176
  costs in, 177
  for disasters, 206, 225
  documenting, 189
  with Macintoshes, 330–331
  reliability in, 178
  restoring from, 212–216
  of SERVER.EXE and NET$OS.EXE,
    27–28
  software for, 176–177
  speed of, 177
  strategy for, 178–179
  support for, 178
  before upgrading, 30, 308–309, 311
  for workstations, 179–180
bad blocks, hot fix redirection area for,
  22, 185
banner pages, 149, 291
base addresses, 386
baseband communications, 386
baselining, 246
  monitoring server in, 190–195, 223
  utilities for, 195–196
Basic Input/Output System. See BIOS
  (Basic Input/Output System)
batteries
  for CMOS RAM, 390
  for configuration, 62
  as fault points, 55
battery-powered power supplies, 180
baud rate, 264, 386–387
*Beyond Computing*, 347–348
BIND command, 24
binderies, 30
  documenting, 200
  duplicate names in, 308, 316
  FATs for, 211

*Italic* page numbers refer to figures

repairing, **28–29**, 210–212
restoring, 214
BINDFIX utility, **28–29**, 210–212
  problems with, 329
  tips for, **334–335**
  with upgrades, 313, 316–317
BIOS (Basic Input/Output System), 387
  as fault point, 12–13, 55
  for printers, 132
  for SCSI drives, 19
  shadow RAM for, **20**
  for Windows, 89
BISYNC protocols, 387
BIX (Byte Information Exchange)
        database, 359
BLOCK.NDS file, 30
BNC connectors, 387
books, **349–350**
boot records, 395
booting
  DOS, testing for, 4–5, 7
  emergency disks for, 209
  Macintoshes, 69, 330
  PC-compatibles, 59, **324–325**
  from SCSI drives, 18–19
  workstations, testing for, 47, 49
bridges, **117**, 387
  monitoring, 246
  troubleshooting, 241–242
  for WANs, **233–234**, 236, 241–242
broadband transmitting, 388
broadcasting, 426
brouters, 235, 388
buffers, 14, 191–194, 388
BUFFERS setting, 67
buildings, WANs between, **235–236**
bulletin boards, **356–359**
bus mastering mode, 21, 62
BVEquip program, 367
Byte Information Exchange (BIX)
        database, 359

**C**

cabling
  AppleTalk, **131–135**
  ARCnet, **113–114**
  changing, **127–131**
  coaxial, 390
  different types, connecting, 234
  documenting, **117–118**
  Ethernet, **109–110**
  fault points in, 54, **99–100**, *101*,
        120–121, 124, 126, 130–131,
        134–135
  and hardware standards, **108–114**
  installing, **92**, **118–121**
  length of, **110–115**, 236
  LocalTalk, **112–113**
  for printing, 146, 151–152, *152*, 164
  and protocols, **105–108**
  with repeaters, 236
  Token-Ring, **111–112**, **124–126**
  and topology, **100–104**, *102*
  troubleshooting, **93–96**, **115–117**,
        **121–135**
Cache Buffer Hits report, 194
cache buffers, 14, 191–194, 388
CapsLock indicator lights, 48
CAPTURE utility, 164
  problems with, 147
  setting up, **149–150**
  for special requirements, 153
  updating, 290–291
  on WANs, 258
  from Windows, 293
cards, 412
  for AppleTalk support, 277
  compatibility of, **60–61**
  conflicts with, 61, 327
  fault points in, 12–13, 55
  for Macintoshes, 70
  network interface, **412**
  for PC-compatibles, **59–61**
  for WANs, 223
  for Windows, 89

Carrier Sense Multiple Access/Collision Detection (CSMA/CD) access method, 392
case sensitivity in configuration files, 23–24
CCITT (Consultative Committee for International Telephony and Telegraphy), 264, 388–389
CCS (Common Communications Support), 423
CD-ROM, 349, 361, 389
CD-ROM extensions, 389
CD-ROM XA, 389
Certified NetWare Administrators, 362
Certified NetWare Engineer Professional Association (CNEPA), **361–362**
Certified NetWare Engineers, 362
change as source of problems, 57
channels, 389
Check-It LAN program, 367
checksums, 389–390
CHKDSK command with Windows, 328
clients, 390
CMIP (Common Management Information Protocol), 253, 390
CMIS (Common Management Information Services), 390
CMOS RAM, 55, 390
CNEPA (Certified NetWare Engineer Professional Association), **361–362**
Coax/Twinax card, 278
coaxial cable, 390
collisions, 109, 392
comments in configuration files, 23
Common Communications Support (CCS), 423
Common Management Information Protocol (CMIP), 253, 390
Common Management Information Services (CMIS), 390
Common Programming Interface (CPI), 422
Common User Access (CUA), 422
communication protocol layer, 416
comp.sys.novell forum, **359–360**

compatibility
  of cards, **60–61**
  of fax modems, 299
compression of files, 16, 243
COMPSURF, 19, 22
CompuServe, **351–356**
Computer Select, 349
COMSPEC setting, 67
concentrators. *See* hubs
CONFIG.SYS files
  as fault points, 55
  problems in, **325–326**
  saving, 63
  for UDFs, 297
  for Windows, 67
configuration and configuration files
  in applications, 295
  changing, 11
  documenting, 188
  for DOS, **63–64**
  as fault points, 55, 217
  forms for, *371–380*
  for Macintoshes, **72–73**
  for networks, *377*
  for NFS, 280
  for PC-compatibles, **62**, **325–326**
  for print queues, *380*
  for printers, 153, *379*
  for RAM boards, 18, 36
  for servers, **23–24**, *371–374*
  in upgrading, 306, 308, 320
  for users, *378*
  for WANs, 245, **247**
  for Windows, 90
  for workstations, *375–376*
conflicts
  with adapters, 20
  with fax modems, 299
  with interrupts. *See* interrupts
  in Macintoshes, **73–74**, 321
  in PC-compatibles, **61–62**, **326–327**
  in printing, 152, 159, 321
  from TSRs, 48, 63
  on WANs, 24, 37, 245–247
  in Windows, **66–67**, 328
  in zone numbers, 155

*Italic* page numbers refer to figures

connection numbers, 391
connection-oriented protocols, 391
connectionless protocols, 391
connections, 99
  bridges for, **233–234, 236**
  between buildings, **235–236**
  as fault points, 54
  for long distances, **236–239**
  maintaining, **184**
  to other systems. *See* WAN (Wide Area Networks)
  in PC-compatibles, **59–61**
  to printers, 146
  remote, 421
  repeaters for, **236**
  routers for, **234–235**
  on workstations, **56–57**
  world-wide, **239–240**
connectors, 115–116
  for AppleTalk, 74
  BNC, 387
consultants, 362
Consultative Committee for International Telephony and Telegraphy (CCITT), 264, **388–389**
contacts, corroded, 60
containers in NDS, 259–261
contaminants, **183–184**
contention, 391. *See also* conflicts
contexts in NDS, 263, 337
continuity testers, 94
Control Panel in Macintoshes, 72
controllers for duplexing, 32–33, *33*, 186, *186*
*Corporate Computing*, 346–347
corroded contacts, 60
corrupted files
  FATs, 335
  in Macintoshes, 74
  NET$OS.EXE, 7, **27–28**
  SERVER.EXE, **27–28**
  in WANs, 245
costs
  analysis tools for, 251
  in backups, **177**
  of installation, 108

CPI (Common Programming Interface), 422
CPU use, reports on, 192, 194
CRC (Cyclic Redundancy Checks), 391
CSMA/CD (Carrier Sense Multiple Access/Collision Detection) access method, 392
CUA (Common User Access), 422
Cyclic Redundancy Checks (CRC), 391

**D**

daemons, 155, 392
DAT (Digital Audio Tape), 392
Data Communications Equipment (DCE), 151, 393
data communications protocols, **105–107**
data files, restoring, 214
data forks, 407
data link protocol, 392
data loss. *See* disasters; preventing disasters
Data Service Unit/Channel Service Unit (DSU/CSU) devices, 396
Data Set Ready (DSR) signal, 396
Data-Tech Institute, 363
Data Terminal Equipment (DTE), 151, 396
Data Terminal Ready (DTR) signal, 396
databases for technical support, **360–361**
Datagram Delivery Protocol (DDP), 383
datagrams, 383, 393, 430
datalink layer in OSI, 107
DCE (Data Communications Equipment), 151, 393
DDAEMON.EXE file, 68
DDP (Datagram Delivery Protocol), 383
default login scripts, 25
dependability considerations, 108
DESKTOP.AFP file, 276
desktops for Macintoshes, 276–277, 330
DET (Directory Entry Tables), 398
Device-Independent Backup Interface (DIBI), 314

devices
  codes for, 393
  drivers for. *See* drivers
  inaccessible, 5, 7–8
  numbering, **393–394**
diagnostic programs, 365–366
  for servers, **29**
  for WANs, **251–256**
  for workstations, **59**
dial-in access, **200–201**
dial-in/dial-out servers, 243
dial-up connections, **236–237**
DIBI (Device-Independent Backup
    Interface), 314
Digital Audio Tape (DAT), 392
digital connections, **237–238**
Digital Signal (DS) speed, 395
DIR command, 329
Direct Memory Access (DMA), 395
directories
  aliases for, 261
  dots for, 293, 329, 334
  fake root, 296, 397
  levels of, 315
  for Macintoshes, 276
  managing, 366
  NetWare Directory Services, 15–16, **30**,
    **259–263**, *260*
  for OS/2, 272
  for queues, 148, 150
  in upgrading, 306, 315
Directory Entry Tables (DET), 398
directory maps, 261
directory tables, 394
disaster-recovery services, **202, 208**,
    **216–217**, 226
disasters, **206–207**
  attitude during, **207–208**
  emergency kits for, **209**
  LAN failures, **218**
  mechanical failures, **208–217**
  physical recovery in, **210–211**
  preventing. *See* preventing disasters
  reconstructing networks, **219**
  recovery software for, **211–217**
  from software problems, **217–218**

  viruses, **220–221**
disk drives. *See* drives
Disk Request Serviced From Cache
    report, 191
Distributed Queue Dual Bus (DQDB)
    standard, 264
DLLPATH for OS/2, 272–273
DMA (Direct Memory Access), 395
DNS (Domain Naming System), 395
documentation. *See also* resources,
    informational
  baselining for, **190–196**
  of binderies, 200
  of cabling, **117–118**
  for disasters, 206, 219, **225–227**
  of hard disk drive type, 62
  network plans and logs for, **188–189**
  on-line, 343
  in upgrading, **307–308**
Domain Naming System (DNS), 395
Don't Use Interrupts option, 339
DOS
  booting, testing, 4–5, 7
  configuration of, **63–64**
  as fault point, 55
  loading, 13, 47, 49
  for printing, 139–140, 142–143, 147
  with TCP/IP, 279
DOS boot record, 395
DOS partitions, 22
DOS versions
  problems with, 49, 55, 321–322
  for VREPAIR, 336
  for Windows, 90
dots (.) for directories, 293, 329, 334
downsizing, 257
DQDB (Distributed Queue Dual Bus)
    standard, 264
DRFORUM forum, **356**
Drive Light Status setting, 337
DRIVER.COM file, 65
driver layer, 416
DRIVER.SYS file, 68
drivers, 64, 393–394
  for cards, 65
  for disk drives, 14, 31, 394

*Italic* page numbers refer to figures

problems with, 49
for servers, **23**
for workstations, 47, 49, 313
drives
  documenting, 62
  duplexing, **32–33**, *33*, **186**, *186*, 394
  failures in, 191, **208–217**
  fault points with, **39**
  formatting, **19**, **22–23**, 70
  full, warnings for, 193
  mirroring, 18–19, **32–33**, *33*, **186**, *186*,
    *187*, 394
  partitions on. *See* partitions
  repairing, **27**, 42, 210–212, 335–336
  SCSI. *See* SCSI (Small Computer
    System Interface) devices
  and security, 198
  verifying writes to, 185
DS (Digital Signal) speed, 395
.DSK files, 14, 31
DSR (Data Set Ready) signal, 396
DSREPAIR program, 338
DSU/CSU (Data Service Unit/Channel
  Service Unit) devices, 396
DTE (Data Terminal Equipment),
  151, 396
DTR (Data Terminal Ready) signal, 396
DUPBIND.EXE utility, 308, 316
duplexing, **32–33**, *33*, **186**, *186*, 394
duplicate bindery names, 308, 316
duplicate network addresses, 20
dust, **183–184**
dynamic memory allocation, 14, 192
Dynamic Memory Pool Statistics Peak
  Usage report, 191
dynamic routing, 418

EMM386.EXE program, 328
EMMEXCLUDE command, 61, 66–67
EMSNETx.COM drivers, 64
encapsulation, 396
ENDCAP utility, 290
Enhanced mode in Windows, 327
Enterprise Certified NetWare
  Engineers, 362
ENTRY.NDS file, 30
equipment, quality of, **182–183**, 222
Error Message Log, 6
error messages, 6
  ABEND, **25**, **28**, 32, 335
  with SERVER.EXE, 7
ET (ElectroText) documentation, 343
Ethernet configuration, 100, 105,
  **109–110**, **396–397**, 413
EtherTalk protocol, 106, 275, 397
  connecting, 74
  printing with, **168–170**
  on workstations, 277
EVERYONE access
  in NDS, 263
  for printing, 257
  for UNIX, 283
exclusive locks, 289
expandability considerations, 109
expanded memory for drivers, 64
expanded memory managers, 365
EXPORTS file, 281
extended memory for drivers, 64
extensions
  CD-ROM, 389
  for Macintoshes, **73–74**
External Data Representation (XDR), 281

## E

e-mail applications, **298–299**
EISA bus, interrupts on, 21, 62
electromagnetic interference, 115, 126
electronic mail applications, **298–299**
ElectroText (ET) documentation, 343
emergency kits, **209**

## F

failures
  documenting, 189
  mechanical, **208–217**
fake root directories, 296, 397
fans, checking, 57
FAQ (Frequently Asked Questions), 360

FAT (File Allocation Tables), 211,
    335, 398
fault points
    in cabling, **99–100**, *101*, 120–121, 124,
        126, 130–131, 134–135
    in printing, **144–147**, *145*, 160–161,
        165, 168, 170
    in servers, **11–13**, *12*, 39–40, **43–44**
    in WANs, **240–247**
    in workstations, **52–56**, *53*, 79–80,
        82–85, 87–88
fault tolerance, 185, 398, 427
    as hardware consideration, 108
    mirroring and duplexing, 18–19,
        **32–33**, *33*, 186, *186*, 222–223
    SFT level III, **33–34**, *34*, 187, *187*,
        222–223
fax machines
    networked, **299–301**
    protection for, 182
FCONSOLE utility
    for documentation, 189–191
    information from, 26
    for routers, 246
    for servers, 6, 8
    for traffic flow, 255
FDDI (Fiber-optic Data Distribution
        Interface) standard, 105, 264, 398
    with TCP/IP, 279
    for WANs, 238–239
FDM (Frequency Division
        Multiplexing), 398
fiber channel standard, 398
fiber optic cable, 238, 425
Fiber-optic Data Distribution Interface
        (FDDI) standard, 105, 264, 398
    with TCP/IP, 279
    for WANs, 238–239
Fiber Optic Inter Repeater Links
        (FOIRL), 399
File Allocation Tables (FAT), 211,
        335, 398
file-creation masks, 282
FILE HANDLES setting, 67
file migration, 16, **311–312**, 316, 318
file rights, 199

file servers, 217, 289
file structure in upgrading, **307**
File Transfer Access and Management
        (FTAM), 399
File Transfer Protocol (FTP), 281, 399
files
    attributes for, 282, 333
    locking, 282, 289–290, 399
    Macintosh, 407
    services for, **289–290**
    sharing, 289
    translating, 235
    in UNIX, 282
FILES setting, 67
FILESERV file, 339
filtering packets, 254
floppy drives
    boot, 209
    and security, 198
FOIRL (Fiber Optic Inter Repeater
        Links), 399
fonts
    printer, 159–160, 292
    problems with, 86
    with Windows, 294
form feeds in printing, 149
formatting drives, **19**, **22–23**, 70
forms for configuration, 370
    of networks, *377*
    of print queues, *380*
    of printers, *379*
    of servers, *371–374*
    of users, *378*
    of workstations, *375–376*
FORWARD setting, 283
fractional services, 238, 399
frame relays, 399
frames, 399
freezing, 48, 245, 256
Frequency Division Multiplexing
        (FDM), 398
Frequently Asked Questions (FAQ), 360
FTAM (File Transfer Access and
        Management), 399
FTP (File Transfer Protocol), 281, 399

*Italic* page numbers refer to figures

## G

gateways, **117**, 400
  for AppleTalk, 278
  monitoring, 246
  troubleshooting, 242
  for WANs, **235**, 242, 268, *269*, 271
GET LOCAL TARGET STACKS
    setting, 67
GOSIP (Government Open Systems
    Interconnection Profile), 400
graphics, printing, 291–292
grounding precautions, 60, 184
groups
  login scripts for, 25
  in NDS, 16
  for printing, 164, 166
GROUPS file, 281
growth, planning, 190
.GRP files, 297
GUEST access
  in NDS, 263
  for printing, 257

## H

half-duplex transmissions, 400
handshaking, 400
hard disk drives. *See* drives
hardware
  cabling. *See* cabling
  for Macintoshes, **69–73**, *71*
  passwords for, 198
  patch panels, repeaters, and hubs,
    **116–117**
  in PC-compatibles, *58*, **59–62**
  routers, bridges, and gateways, 117
  for servers, **17–18**
  upgrading, 309, **319–321**
  for WAN troubleshooting, **251–254**
  for WANs, **240–244**
hardware layer, 416
hardware ports, 419
Hardware-Specific Modules (HSM),
    415–416

hardware standards, **108–109**
  ARCnet, **113–114**
  Ethernet, **109–110**
  LocalTalk, **112–113**
  Token-Ring, **111–112**
Hayes-compatible modems, 243
HBA (Host Bus Adapters), 389, 401
HDLC (High-level Data Link
    Control), 401
headers, 401
help. *See also* resources, informational
  for disasters, 208
  on-line, **249–250**
Help! utility, 364
HFS (Hierarchical File System), 401
hidden directories with upgrades, 315
High-level Data Link Control (HDLC),
    401
High Performance File System
    (HPFS), 272
histories, network. *See* documentation
hop counts, 401
Host Bus Adapters (HBA), 389, 401
host computers, 401
HOSTS file, 281
hot fix redirection area, 22, 185
HPFS (High Performance File
    System), 272
HSM (Hardware-Specific Modules),
    415–416
hubs, **116–117**, 391, 402
  with ARCnet, 113
  with Ethernet, 109
  and repeaters, 236
  troubleshooting, 100

## I

ICONDATA.AFP file, 276
ICONINDX.AFP file, 276
IDs for SCSI devices, 19, 71–72
IEC (International Electrotechnical
    Commission), 402
IEEE (Institute of Electrical and
    Electronic Engineers), 264, **402–403**

Boldface page numbers indicate primary references and explanations

IF MEMBER OF construction, 25, 164, 166, 296
IFCONFIG tool, 75
incremental backups, 176
independent long distance providers, 238
indicator lights on keyboards, 48
informational objects in NDS, 261–262
informational resources. *See* resources, informational
*Infoworld*, 346
infra-red lasers, 235
inherited rights masks, 25
.INI files, 297
INITpicker utility, 364
Inits, problems with, 86, 330
InocuLan 2.0 program, 364
in-place upgrades, 312
insects, 183
INSTALL programs, 19, 22, 31
installing
  cabling, **92, 118–121**
  NetWare, **22**
  NLMs, **31–32**
  servers, **17–31**, 35–40
  workstations, **76–80**
Institute of Electrical and Electronic Engineers (IEEE), 264, **402–403**
Integrated Services Digital Network (ISDN), 237–239, 265, 405
interfaces
  as fault points, 55
  for printing, **151–152**
  for UPS, 181
interference, 126
  from arcing, 184
  from cabling, 99, 111
  and connections, 54
  and performance, 115
intermittent problems
  with cabling, **95–96**
  with SCSI drives, 19, 72
  with servers, **8**
internal network numbers, 245
International Electrotechnical Commission (IEC), 402

International Standards Organization (ISO), 106, 265, 405
Internet, **359–360**, 403
  protocols for, 105–106
  and TCP/IP, 279
Internet Packet Exchange Open Data-Link Interface (IPXODI), 49, 404
Internetwork Packet Exchange. *See* IPX (Internetwork Packet Exchange) protocol
internetworks. *See* WAN (Wide Area Networks)
interrupts
  conflicts in, 20–21, 36, **61–62**
  in Macintoshes, 70
  in Micro Channel bus, 68
  nonmaskable, 413
  in PC-compatibles, **61–62**, 326–327
  in printing, 152, 159, 339
  for SCSI drives, 19
inventory systems, 9, 29, 250, 366–367
I/O Error Count report, 191
IP protocol, **105–106**
IPX (Internetwork Packet Exchange) protocol, 24, 105, 403
  addresses for, 247
  creating packets for, 64, 77
  drivers for, 49, 293
  for Macintoshes, **277–278**
  network numbers for, 245, 404
  with TCP/IP, 280
  with Windows, 66
IPX.COM program, 148, 158
IPX RETRY COUNT setting, 339
IPX.SYS file, 68
IPXODI (Internet Packet Exchange Open Data-Link Interface), 49, 404
IPXODI.COM file, loading, 65
IRQs. *See* interrupts
ISA cards, conflicts with, 21, 61
ISADISK.DSK driver, 336
ISDN (Integrated Services Digital Network), 237–239, 265, 405
ISO (International Standards Organization), 106, 265, 405

*Italic* page numbers refer to figures

## J

jabbering, 256
jumpers, 77, 413

## K

keyboards
  cleaning, 184
  as fault points, 54
  on workstations, testing, 48

## L

labeling backup tapes, 213
LAI (LAN Automatic Inventory)
    utility, 366
LAN (Local Area Networks), 406. *See
    also* networks
  failures in, **218**
  multiple, **20**, **233–239**
  NLMs for, 14, 31
LAN Automatic Inventory (LAI)
    utility, 366
*LAN Computing*, 345–346
.LAN files, 14, 31
*LAN Magazine*, 346, 348
LAN Server Watch utility, 366
LAN Tachometer utility, 366
*LAN Technology*, 346, 348
*LAN Times*, 345
LAN WorkGroup, **296**
LAN WorkPlace programs, 279–280
LANalyzer, 248
LANalyzer for Windows, 190, 246, 248,
    255–256, 283
LANDesk Manager program, 367
LANlord program, 367
LanProtect program, 363
LAP (Link Access Protocol), 383
Large Internet Packets (LIP), 406
large networks. *See* WAN (Wide Area
    Networks)
laser printers with UPSs, 181

LaserWriter printers, conflicts with, 321
LASTDRIVE settings, 66
LatticeNet, 113
.LCK files, 289
leaf objects in NDS, 259–261, *260*
leased connections, **237–238**
length of cabling, **110–115**, 236
light meters, 116
Line Printer Daemon (LPD),
    155–156, 281
linear bus topology, 100–102, *102*, **104**
Link Access Protocol (LAP), 383
Link Support Layer (LSL), 406, 415–417
LIP (Large Internet Packets), 406
LOAD AFP CDT option, 330
LOAD command, 24
loading
  DOS, 13, 47, 49
  drivers, 47, 49, 65
  NetWare, testing for, 5, 7
  NetWare 2.x, **13–14**
  NetWare 3.x, 15
Local Area Networks. *See* LAN (Local
    Area Networks); networks
local printers setting, 64, 149
LocalTalk protocol, **112–113**, 275, 406
  printing with, **168–170**
  speed of, 106
  on workstations, 277
Lock Daemon (LOCKD) utility, 282
locking files, 282, 289–290, 399
logging onto servers, testing, 47, 50
logical maps
  for cabling, 117–118
  for LAN structure, 189
logical numbers, 393
logical topology, 103
LOGIN.EXE file, 272
login names in AUTOEXEC.BAT, 200
LOGIN script, 335
logins and login scripts
  multiple, **258**
  in NDS, 261, 263
  security in, **200**
  standardizing, 63
  tips for, **335**

types of, **25**
with upgrades, 315, 319
logs, 6, 27, **188–189**. *See also*
  documentation
long distances, WANs for, **236–239**
LPD (Line Printer Daemon),
  155–156, 281
LPSCAN utility, 364
LPT port, 148–149, **291–292**, 294
LSL (Link Support Layer), 406, 415
LSL.COM file, 65
LSL.SYS file, 68

---

**M**

MAC.NAM file, 330
Macintoshes
  cards for, 70
  configuration of, 72–73
  conflicts in, 73–74, 321
  files for, 407
  hardware for, 69–73, *71*
  IPX for, **277–278**
  networking with, 74
  power-on sequences for, **69–70**
  printing with, **74–75**, **154–155**
  SCSI devices for, **71–72**, *71*
  and servers, 24
  software for, **73–75**
  with TCP/IP, 279
  tips for, **330–332**
  troubleshooting, **85–88**
  in upgrades, 317
  WANs with, **274–278**
MacIPX protocol, 277–278
*MacWeek*, 345
magazines, **344–349**
mail applications, **298–299**
maintenance, preventive, **183–185**, 222
MAKEUSER utility, 310
MAN (Metropolitan Area Networks),
  265, 407
management agents, 411
management utilities
  NLMs for, 15, 31

for WANs, **248–251**
manuals, 196, **342–343**
MAP utility
  for fake root directories, 296
  from Windows, 293
maps, 189
  of cabling, **117–118**
  of LAN structure, 189
  for multiple servers, 258
  in NDS, 261
  tools for, 250
  of UNIX permissions, 282
  for upgrading, 306
MAU (Media Access Units), 111, 407
Maximum Packet Receive Buffer Size
  setting, 280
Maximum Physical Receive Packet Size
  setting, 280
mechanical failures, **208**
  emergency kits for, **209**
  physical recovery in, **210–211**
  software for, **211–217**
Media Access Units (MAU), 111, 407
Media Support Modules (MSM), 415
memory
  for drivers, 64
  dynamic allocation of, 14, 192
  for Macintoshes, 275, 331–332
  for NetWare 2.x, 336
  for servers, **18**, 36, 38, 190–192
  with TCP/IP, 280
  testing, 59, 69
  in upgrading, 313, 316
  for Windows, 322
memory conflicts, 61
  with PC-compatible computers,
    **326–327**
  with VGA adapters, 20
  with Windows, **66–67**, 328
MESSAGES utility from Windows, 293
Metropolitan Area Networks (MAN),
  265, 407
MHS (Message Handling Services),
  **298–299**, 407
mice, 183
Micro Channel bus, **68**

*Italic* page numbers refer to figures

Micro-Scope utility, 365
microwave relays, 238
migration utility, 16, **311–312**, 316, 318
Minimum File Cache Buffer Report
    Threshold setting, 194
mirroring, **32–33**, *33*, 394
  partition size in, 19
  for preventing disasters, **186**, *186*, *187*
  SCSI adapters for, 18
miscellaneous objects in NDS, 262
mismatched equipment, 130
misspellings in configuration files, 23
MLID (Multiple Layer Interface Drivers),
    408, 415
MODE command for printing, 147
modems
  consolidating, 243
  dial-in access for, **200–201**
  interfaces for, 151
  networked, **299–301**
  protection for, 182
  standards for, **243–244**
Modify DOS Attributes setting, 282, 333
MONITOR utility
  for documentation, 190, 192, 194
  information from, 26
  for processes, 337
  for routers, 246
  for servers, 6, 8
  for traffic flows, 255
  for WANs, 256
monitors, 9
  as fault points, 54
  for servers, **190–195**, 223, 366–367
  for WANs, **248–251**
motherboards
  fault points in, 55
  POST for, 59
  problems with, 80–81
Mount Protocol services, 281
MPR (MultiProtocol Routers), 117, 242
MSAU (Multiple Station Access Units),
    111, 407
MSM (Media Support Modules), 415
multiple-byte characters, 408

multiple LANs, **20**. *See also* WAN (Wide
    Area Networks)
  between buildings, **235–236**
  at one site, **233–235**
Multiple Layer Interface Drivers (MLID),
    408, 415
multiple logins, **258**
Multiple Station Access Units (MSAU),
    111, 407
multiplexing, 265, 398, 408, 428
multiplexors (MUX), 408
multiport repeaters, 236, 241
MultiProtocol Routers (MPR), 117, 242
multi-server networks, 408
multitasking, 419
MUX (multiplexors), 408

## N

.NAM files, 14, 31
Name Binding Protocol (NBP), 383
name spaces, 409
  for backups, 177
  for Macintoshes, 275, 330–331
  for NeXTStep, 273
  for NFS, 279–280
  NLMs for, 14, 31
  repairing, 211
  for restoring, 214–215
  for UNIXWare, 274
  for upgrades, 30, 315–317, 319
National Institute of Standards &
    Technology (NIST), 413
NBACKUP program, 30
NBDAEMON.EXE file, 68
NBP (Name Binding Protocol), 383
NCN (Network Control Blocks), 409
NCOPY command, 295
NCP (NetWare Core Protocol), 410
NDS (NetWare Directory Services),
    15–16, **30**, **259–263**, *260*
NET.CFG files, 410
  for dots in directories, 293, 329
  as fault points, 49, 55
  for printing, 339–340

settings in, 64–65
for UNIX, 283
for Windows, 67
NETBEUI (NetBIOS Extended User
    Interface), 409
NET$BIND.SYS FILE, 30
NetBIOS (Network Basic Input/Output
    System), 24, 106
NETBIOS.COM file, 65
NETBIOS.EXE file, 410
NetBIOS Extended User Interface
    (NETBEUI), 409
NETBIOS.SYS file, 68
NET$BVAL.SYS FILE, 30
NetModem/E, 300
NET$OBJ.SYS FILE, 30
NET$OS.EXE program
    corrupted, 7, 27–28
    errors in loading, 22
    executing, 13–14
    with upgrades, 313
NET$PROP.SYS FILE, 30
NETremote+ utility, 366
NetShield program, 363
NETSTAT tool, 75
NET$VAL.SYS FILE, 30
NetView program, 410
NETW2X forum, 355
NETW3X forum, 355
NetWare
    diagnostic tools in, 255
    as fault point, 55
    installing, 22
    loading, testing for, 5, 7
    restoring, 214
    tips for, 334–338
    upgrading, 30–31
    utilities for, 366–367
    versions of, 13
    for WANs, 268, 270, 271
    Windows with, 66–68, 292–294
NetWare 2.x, 13–14, 15
    configuration changes with, 11
    server monitoring in, 191
    tips for, 336
    upgrading from, 310–315

NetWare 3.x, 14–15, 15
    server monitoring in, 192–193
    tips for, 336–337
    upgrading from, 311–312, 315–319
    upgrading to, 310–315
NetWare 4.x, 15–17, 15
    server monitoring in, 194–195
    tips for, 337–338
    upgrading to, 311–312, 315–319
NetWare Access Server, 300
NetWare Applications Notes, 343
NetWare Connection, 362
NetWare Core Protocol (NCP), 410
NetWare Directory Services (NDS),
    15–16, 259–263, 260
NetWare DOS/Windows Client Kit, 329
NETWARE.DRV file, 67
NetWare Express, 410
NetWare for Macintosh, 275–277
NetWare for UNIX, 279, 283–284
NetWare Loadable Modules. See NLM
    (NetWare Loadable Modules)
NetWare Management Agents, 411
NetWare NFS, 271, 279–283, 334, 413
    printing with, 155–156
    with TCP/IP, 279
NetWare Requester for OS/2, 411
NetWare Runtime, 411
NetWare Support Encyclopedia (NSE),
    360–361, 412
NetWare Tools for Windows, 293–294
NetWare UNIX Client (NUC), 273, 280
NetWare Users International (NUI),
    362, 414
NetWare Workstation Kits, 327
NetWire service, 351–352, 412
Network Advisor, 246, 248, 250
network analyzers, 29, 126, 132–133, 189
Network Basic Input/Output System
    (NetBIOS), 24, 106
Network Computing, 346–347
Network Control Blocks (NCN), 409
Network File System (NFS), 271,
    279–283, 334, 413
    printing with, 155–156
    with TCP/IP, 279

*Italic* page numbers refer to figures

Network Information Center, 245
network interface cards (NIC). *See* cards
network layer in OSI, 107
network monitors, 124
*Network News*, 346–347
Network Operating Systems (NOS), 13
networked modems, **299–301**
*Networking Management*, 347–348
networking software, **64–66**
networks
  adapter connections for, 59–60
  addresses for, **20**, 105, 279
  configuration of, *377*
  drivers for, 47, 49, 90
  inventory systems for, 9, 29, 250,
    366–367
  large. *See* WAN (Wide Area Networks)
  nodes for, 412
  numbers for, 24, 37, 233, 245, 404
  plans for, **188–189**
  reconstructing, **219**
  virus scanning software for, 197, 220
NETWORKS file, 281
NETx drivers, 64, 77
  in printing, 148, 158
  problems with, 49
  for Windows, 66, 293
NETX shell, 412
newsletters, 348
NeXTStep operating system, 273
NFS (Network File System), 271,
    **279–283**, 334, 413
  printing with, **155–156**
  with TCP/IP, 279
NFSADMIN utility, 333
NIC (network interface cards). *See* cards
NIST (National Institute of Standards &
    Technology), 413
NLM (NetWare Loadable Modules), 411
  as fault points, 13, 192
  installing, **31–32**
  types of, 14–15, 31
.NLM files, 15, 31
NMI (nonmaskable interrupts), 413
NMPIPE.SYS file, 68
nodes, 105–106, **412–413**

NodeVision program, 367
nonmaskable interrupts (NMI), 413
Norton Utilities, 365
NOS (Network Operating Systems), 13
NOTIFY file, 339
NOVA forum, **353**
NOVB forum, **353–354**
NOVC forum, **354–355**
Novell Authorized Education
    Centers, 362
Novell Press, books by, **349–350**
Novell publications, **343–344**
*Novell Research Reports*, 344
NOVLIB forum, **352**
NPRINT utility, 150, 290
NPRINTER utility, 148
  interrupts with, 339
  with Windows, 329
NPSERVER.SYS file, 68
NSE (NetWare Support Encyclopedia),
    **360–361**, 412
NUC (NetWare UNIX Client), 273
NUI (NetWare Users International),
    362, 414
number signs (#) for comments, 23
NumLock indicator lights, 48
NWADMIN utility, 262
NWDAEMON.EXE file, 68
NWIFS.IFS file, 68
NWREQ.SYS file, 68
NWTOOLS.EXE program, 293–294

## O

objects in NDS, 16, **259–262**, *260*
ODI (Open Data-Link Interface),
    **414–416**
ODI drivers
  loading, 65
  problems with, 49
  for Windows, 293
ODINSUP (Open Data-link
    Interface/Network driver interface
    specification support), 414
off-line UPSs, 430

off-site backup storage, 179, 209, 225
on-line help, **249–250**, 343, **351–360**
online UPSs, 430
Open Data-Link Interface (ODI),
    **414–416**
Open Data-link Interface/Network driver
    interface specification support
    (ODINSUP), 414
Open System Interconnection (OSI)
    model, 24, **106–108**, 265, **416–417**
operating systems
    as fault point, 55
    standardizing, 63
    upgrading, **321–322**
    on workstations, **272–274**
optical cabling, 116
optical disks, 416
Organization objects in NDS,
    259–261, *260*
Organizational Unit objects in NDS,
    259–261, *260*
OS/2 operating system, **272–273**
    NetWare Requester for, 411
    with TCP/IP, 279
    workstations with, **68**
OSI (Open System Interconnection)
    model, 24, **106–108**, 265, **416–417**
over-voltages, protection from, 180,
    221–222

**P**

Packet Burst Protocol, 417
packet decoders, 29, 218, **252–254**
Packet Receive Buffers report, 193
packet switching, 417–418
packets, 417
    filtering, 254
    headers in, 401
    protocol analyzers for, 29, 218, **252–254**
    with TCP/IP, 280
    tracking, 246–247, 249
    watchdog, 432
PAP (Printer Access Protocol), 384
parallel interfaces for printing, **151–152**

parallel ports for workstation
    backups, 180
parity, 418
PARTITIO.NDS file, 30
partitions, 395
    corruption of, 328, 338
    creating, **19**, **22–23**
    repairing, 211
    restoring, 214
    in upgrading, 313
passive hubs, 113, 402
passive stars, 418
passwords, **198–200**
patch panels, **116**
PAUSE command, 325
PC-compatible computers
    boot errors with, **324–325**
    boot sequence in, **59**
    cards and connections in, **59–61**
    configuration of, **62**, 325–326
    hardware in, *58*, **59–62**
    interrupt conflicts in, **61–62**, 326–327
    software in, *58*, **63–66**
    workstations with, **58–66**, *58*
PC Tools Deluxe utilities, 365
*PC Week*, 346
PCONSOLE, 150, 159
    checking, 139, 142
    connecting, 146
Percentage of Long Term Cache Hits
    report, 194
Percentage of Utilization report, 192
periods (.) for directories, 293, 329, 334
permissions
    for applications, 295–296
    for mail, 298–299
    problems from, 24–25, 217
    in UNIX, 75, **282–283**
    in Windows, 294
phone lines, protection for, 182
PhoneNet products, 418
physical addresses, 393
physical layer protocols, 105, 107
physical maps
    for cabling, 117
    for LAN structure, 189

*Italic* page numbers refer to figures

physical network. *See* cabling
physical security, **198**
physical topology, 103
Physical Units (PU), 420
PING command, 75, 283
PKWARE utilities, 365
planning
 baselining for, 190
 for networks, **188–189**
 for recovering data, **202–203**, **224–227**
 for upgrading, **304**, **306–310**, 312–313, 316–318
 for WANs, **245–247**
polarity checkers, 254
portability of protocol analyzers, 253
Portable NetWare, 271, **283–284**
portable tape drives, 180
ports, 419
 for modems, 243, 300
 for printers, 146, 158
POST (Power-On Self Tests), 419
 for PC-compatible computers, 325
 for workstations, 46, 48, **59**
PostScript printers, **154**, **157–161**, 291–292
pound signs (#) for comments, 23
power
 for printers, 146
 protecting, **180–182**, 221–222
power cords, arcing in, 184
power-on sequences for Macintoshes, **69–70**
power supplies as fault points, 12, 54
PowerBooks, SCSI devices with, 71
Preferred Server setting, 65
presentation layer in OSI, 108
preventing disasters, **174–175**
 backups for, **175–180**
 baselining for, **190–196**, 223
 equipment quality for, **182–183**, 222
 fault tolerance for, **185–187**, *186*, *187*, 222–223
 network plans and logs for, **188–189**
 power for, **180–182**, 221–222
 preventive maintenance for, **183–185**, 222

recovery planning for, **202–203**, 224–227
 security for, **198–201**, 223–224
 user training for, **196–197**, 223
 virus checking for, **197**
preventive maintenance, **183–185**, 222
PRINT file, 339
PRINT.DAT file, 335
Print Header setting, 65, 149
print servers, 146, 217
PRINT TAIL setting, 149
printcap file, 156
PRINTCON program, 150, 153, 159, 258
 for interrupts, 339
 for job definition files, 335
 with Windows, 293
Printer Access Protocol (PAP), 384
printer-related NDS objects, 261
printers, **153–154**
 checking, 141
 configuration of, 153, *379*
 forms for, *379*
 for Macintoshes, 276, 332
 ports for, 146, 158
 problems from, 132
 setting up, 138–139, 141, **157–161**
PRINTGRP.EXE utility, 308, 316
printing
 on AppleTalk, **154–155**, **168–170**
 from applications, 148, **290–292**
 CAPTURE for, **149–150**
 fault points in, **144–147**, *145*, 160–161, 165, 168, 170
 interfaces for, **151–152**
 to LPT1, **291–292**, 294
 with Macintoshes, 74–75, **154–155**
 with NFS, **155–156**
 process of, **147–149**
 PSERVER for, **151–153**
 queues for. *See* queues
 redirection in, **148–149**
 routers for, **161–165**, *163*
 tips for, **339–340**
 troubleshooting, **138–143**
 WAN reports, 255
 on WANs, **257–258**

from Windows, 290, **293–294**
from workstations, 146, **165–168**
PRINTUSR.EXE utility, 308, 316
processes in UNIX, 283–284
Processor Utilization report, 194
processors
  in upgrading, 313, 316
  for Windows, 89
properties of NDS objects, 259
protected mode operation, 16, 419
protocol analyzers, 29, 218, **252–254**
protocols, **105–107**
  for AppleTalk, **383–384**
  bridges for, 234
  connection-oriented and
    connectionless, 391
  gateways for, **235**
  routers for, 234–235
  for servers, **24–25**
PS/2 systems, **68**
PSERVER programs, **151–153**, 159
  checking, 139, 141–142
  connecting, 146
  drivers with, 340
  functions of, 147
  interrupts with, 339
  location of, 148
  with routers, 148, 162–164
  updating, 290
  with upgrades, 317
PU (Physical Units), 420
publications. *See* resources, informational
punch-down blocks, 116–117
PUPGRADE, 317

**Q**

QEMM-386 expanded memory
  manager, 365
quality of equipment, **182–183**, 222
QUEUE file, 339
queues, **150–151**
  accessing, **291–292**
  directories for, 148, 150

forms for, *380*
setting up, 146

**R**

radio transceivers, 235
RAID (Redundant Arrays of Inexpensive
  Disks), 420
railroads, fiber-optic cable services
  from, 238
RAM. *See* memory
read-after-write verification, 185
read-only files, 199
README files, **342–343**
real mode, 419
rebooting servers, 6
reconstructing networks, **219**
record keeping. *See* documentation
record locking in UNIX, 282
recovering data. *See* disasters; preventing
  disasters
recovery services, **202**, 208,
  **216–217**, 226
redirection, **148–149**, 420
Redirection Blocks, 22, 185
Redundant Arrays of Inexpensive Disks
  (RAID), 420
REGISTER MEMORY command, 18, 38
reliability in backups, **178**
remote connections, 421
remote control programs, 201
remote management software, 241
remote printers, 159
repairing
  binderies, **28–29**, 210–212, 313,
    316–317, **334–335**
  disk drives, **27**, 42, 210–212, 335–336
repeaters, **116**, 122, **123**, 421
  extending cabling with, 100, 236
  troubleshooting, 241
  for WANs, **236**, 241
replacing components, 81
Request To Send (RTS) signal, 422
resource forks, 407

*Italic* page numbers refer to figures

resources, informational
  books, 349–350
  bulletin boards, 356–359
  CNEPA, 361–362
  consultants, 362
  magazines, 344–349
  manuals, 342–343
  Novell publications, 343–344
  software, 363–367
  technical support, 351–361
  training, 362–363
RESTORE upgrade method, 307
restoring from backups, 212–216
rights, 25, 199, 282–283, 297
  in NDS, 259–263
  in upgrading, 313
rightsizing, 257
ring topology, 100–104, 102
RIP (Router Information Protocol),
    421–422
root directory for applications, 296, 397
Root objects in NDS, 259–260, 260
Router Information Protocol (RIP),
    421–422
routers, 117, 421
  monitoring, 246
  for printing, 161–165, 163
  problems from, 218
  PSERVER on, 148, 162–164
  troubleshooting, 242
  for WANs, 234–235, 242
routing
  dynamic, 418
  source, 426
Routing Table Maintenance Protocol
    (RTMP), 384
RPRINTER program, 146, 159
  function of, 148
  interrupts with, 339
  with Windows, 329
RS-232 interfaces, 151, 422
RTMP (Routing Table Maintenance
    Protocol), 384
RTS (Request To Send) signal, 422

**S**

SAA (System Application Architecture),
    422–423
SALVAGE utility, 175, 218
SAM antivirus program, 365
SAP (Service Advertising Protocol), 424
satellite communications, 238, 240,
    265, 432
saving files on server, 289–290
SBACKUP program, 30, 338
scanning software, 197, 220
screwing down connections, 56, 60
scripts. *See* logins and login scripts
SCSI (Small Computer System Interface)
    devices, 423
  compatibility of, 60–61
  in loading, 14
  for Macintoshes, 71–72, 71
  for servers, 18–19, 37
SDLC (Synchronous Data Link Control)
    protocol, 423
SECURE CONSOLE command, 198
security, 223–224
  dial-in access, 200–201
  for hardware, 116
  in logins, 200
  passwords for, 199
  physical, 198
  with print servers, 159
  rights for, 199
  for servers, 21
SEND utility from Windows, 293
Sequenced Packet Exchange (SPX)
    protocol, 24, 105, 423
serial communication, 243, 424
serial interfaces, 151–152
serial numbers in logs, 188
serial ports, 243
serial printer cables, 151–152, 152, 164
serialization, 424
SERVER.CFG file, 14, 23, 30
SERVER.EXE program, 7, 15, 22, 27–28
Server Message Blocks (SMB), 24, 424
server-related NDS objects, 261
server-to-server migration, 311–312, 316

servers
 ABEND error messages with, **25, 28**
 applications from, **294–296**
 binderies for, **30**
 boot diskettes for, 209
 configuration files for, **23–24**, *371–374*
 data recovery on, **210–212**
 diagnostic tools for, **29**
 documenting, 188
 drivers for, **23**
 fault points with, **11–13**, *12*, 39–40,
  **43–44**
 formatting and partitioning drives for,
  **19, 22–23**
 hardware for, **17–18**
 installing, **17–31**, 35–40
 installing NetWare on, **22**
 intermittent problems with, 8
 interrupts with, **20–21**, 36
 logging onto, testing, 47, 50
 login scripts for. *See* logins and login
  scripts
 management tools for, 250–251
 memory for, **18**, 36, 38
 monitoring, **190–195**, 223, 366–367
 multiple adapters with, **20**
 for NetWare for Macintosh, 275
 and NetWare versions, **13–17, 30–31**
 network addresses for, **20**
 NLMs with, **31–32**
 protocols for, **24–25**
 rebooting, 6
 repairing binderies for, **28–29**
 restoring backup files to, **214–215**
 SCSI adapters for, **18–19**, 37
 security for, **21**
 shadow RAM for, **20**
 software for, **22, 27–29**
 system error logs for, 27
 system fault tolerance for, **32–33**
 troubleshooting, **4–9**, 40–44
 VGA adapters for, **20**
 VREPAIR tool for, 27, 42
 for WANs, 271
 Windows from, **296–298**
 vs. workstations, 17

Service Advertising Protocol (SAP), 424
Service Processes report, 192–193
service programs, 182
service protocol layer, 416–417
SERVMAN program, 194
session layer in OSI, 108
SESSION utility from Windows, 293
SET command, 192
SETPASS utility from Windows, 293
setup, printer, 138–139, 141, *157–161*
SETUP program, 62, 297
SETVER.EXE command, 322
SFT (System Fault Tolerance), 185,
  398, 427
 as hardware consideration, 108
 mirroring and duplexing, **32–33**, *33*,
  186, *186*, 222–223
 SFT level III, 17, **33–34**, *34*, 187, *187*,
  222–223
shadow RAM for BIOS, **20**
shareable applications, 295
shareable locks, 289
shareware for server monitors, 195
sharing files, 289
SHELL.CFG files
 for dots in directories, 293, 329
 for printing, **148–149**, 158–159, 339
 settings in, **64–65**
 for Windows, 67
SHELLGEN, 55, 64
shielded twisted-pairs (STP), 427
SHOW DOTS setting, 293, 329, 334
Simple Mail Transfer Protocol
  (SMTP), 425
Simple Network Management Protocol
  (SNMP), 116–117, 218, 250, 253
sine wave power supplies, 181–182
single-port repeaters, 236
single-route broadcasting, 426
size of mirrored partitions, 19
Small Computer System Interface. *See*
  SCSI (Small Computer System
  Interface) devices
SMARTDRV.SYS program, 328
SMB (Server Message Blocks), 24, 424

*Italic* page numbers refer to figures

SMDS (Switched Multimegabit Data Services), 425
SMTP (Simple Mail Transfer Protocol), 425
SNA (Systems Network Architecture), 425
sniffers, 29, 218, **252–254**
SNMP (Simple Network Management Protocol), 116–117, 218, 250, 253
sockets, 425
software
  for backups, **176–177**
  for data recovery, **211–217**
  disasters from, **217–218**
  documenting, 188
  for Macintoshes, **73–75**
  for PC-compatibles, *58*, **63–66**
  for servers, 22, **27–29**
  upgrading, **321–322**
  for viruses, **363–365**
  for WANs, **245–247**, **254–255**
  for workstations, **365–367**
software ports, 419
SONET (Synchronous Optical Networks), 425
source routing, 426
spaces in zone names, 276, 332
SPDAEMON.EXE file, 68
speed
  of backups, **177**
  Digital Signal, 395
  shadow RAM for, 20
spikes, protection from, 180, 182, 221–222
SpinRite II program, 366
SPS (Standby Power Supplies), 180–181
SPX (Sequenced Packet Exchange) protocol, 24, 105, 423
SPX ABORT TIMEOUT setting, 339
SPX CONNECTIONS setting, 67, 149, 159, 340
SPX.SYS file, 68
SQE Test lights, 57
STACKS setting, 67
standards
  for hardware, **108–114**

for messages, 433
in telecommunications, **243–244**, 431
Standby Power Supplies (SPS), 180–181
star topology, 100–102, *102*, **104**, 382, 418, 426
STARTUP.NCF file, 15, 23
  ABENDs from, 25
  for buffers, 193–194
  for directory levels, 315
  for disk-full warning, 193–195
  skipping, 336
  with upgrades, 31
static electricity, 60, **184**, 222
status lights, 57, 60, 99–100
stop bits, 426
STP (shielded twisted-pairs), 427
strategy for backups, **178–179**
SUM II utilities, 365
superservers, 4
supervisor password, 200
support
  for backups, **178**
  technical, **351–361**
  for upgrading, **309–310**
surge protectors, 180, 182, 221–222, 427
Switched Multimegabit Data Services (SMDS), 425
Synchronous Data Link Control (SDLC) protocol, 423
Synchronous Optical Networks (SONET), 425
synchronous transmissions, 427
SYS volume in upgrades, 305, 307
SYS:ETC directory, 280
SYS:MAIL directory, 298, 335
SYS:_NETWARE directory, 30
SYS:PUBLIC directory, 199, 315
SYS:SYSTEM directory, 148, 150
  for bindery files, 30
  protecting, 199
  in upgrades, 315
SYSCON program
  for error logs, 6, 27
  for user numbers, 298, 335
System 7 in Macintoshes, 74, 330–331

System Application Architecture (SAA), 422–423

System Error Logs, 27

system extensions for Macintoshes, 73–74

System Fault Tolerance (SFT). *See* SFT (System Fault Tolerance)

SYSTEM.INI file, 61, 66–67

system login scripts, 25, 315

*System Messages* manual, 28

System ROMBreakPoint setting, 67

Systems Network Architecture (SNA), 425


## T

T-1 services, 238–240, 428

T-3 services, 238, 240, 428

T-carrier services, 427

t-connectors, 101, 103, 122–124, 130

tabs in printing, 149, 291

tape drives. *See* backups

TCP/IP (Transmission Control Protocol/Internet Protocol) standard, **105–106**, 428

  with AppleTalk, 278

  support for, 24

  with UNIX, 75

  WANs with, **278–284**

TCPCON utility, 246, 255, 283

TCPIP.COM file, loading, 65

TDM (Time Division Multiplexing), 428

TDR (Time Domain Reflectometry), 254

Technical Bulletins, 344

technical support

  databases for, **360–361**

  on-line, **351–360**

  serial numbers for, 188

telecommunications standards, 243–244, 431

telephone company services, **236–240**, 244–245

Telnet services, 281

10Base2 (thin Ethernet) cable, 100–101, **109–110**

10BaseT (twisted-pair Ethernet) cable, 100, **109–110**

Terminate and Stay Resident (TSR) programs, 48, 63

termination, 428

  checking, 116

  of SCSI drives, 19, 72

testing

  backups, 177–178, 213, 308, 311

  memory, 59, 69

  upgrades, 306

thick Ethernet (AUI) cable, 100, **109–110**

thin Ethernet (10Base2) cable, 100–101, **109–110**

throughput considerations, 108–109

Time Division Multiplexing (TDM), 428

Time Domain Reflectometry (TDR), 254

time synchronization, 317

token passing, 429

Token Ring networks, 103, 105, **111–112**, 429

  node numbers for, 413

  with TCP/IP, 279

  troubleshooting, **124–126**

tokens, 111

TokenTalk program, 106, 429

topology, **100–104**, *102*

Topology-Specific Modules (TSM), 415

traffic

  analyzing, 249, 255

  baselining for, 190

training

  sources of, **362–363**

  users, **196–197**, 223

transceivers

  connections for, 59–60

  status lights on, 57, 99–100

  for translating cabling, 99–100

translating files, 235

Transmission Control Protocol/Internet Protocol. *See* TCP/IP (Transmission Control Protocol/Internet Protocol) standard

transport layer in OSI, 108

trends

  analyzing, 249, 253, 255

*Italic* page numbers refer to figures

documenting, 189–190
Trojan horses, 429
true sine wave power supplies, 181–182
trustee rights, 25, 199, 282–283, 297
TRUSTEES file, 283
TSM (Topology-Specific Modules), 415
TSR (Terminate and Stay Resident)
    programs, 48, 63
tunneling, 280
twisted-pair wiring, 429–430
  connecting, 99, 115
  Ethernet (10BaseT), 100, **109–110**
  shielded, 427
Type 1, 2, and 3 cable, **111–112**

## U

UDF (User Definition Files), 297–298
UDP (User Datagram Protocol), 430
uninterruptible power supplies (UPS),
    180–181, 222, 430
UNIX systems, 75
  NetWare on, 279, **283–284**
  permissions on, **282–283**
  printing on, **155–156**
  protocols for, 105–106
  security on, 201
  and servers, 24
  tips for, **333–334**
  WANs with, **278–284**
UNIXWare operating system, **274**
unshielded twisted-pair (UTP) cable, 111
Untouchable Network program, 364
updating virus checkers, 220
upgradability, considerations for, 108
UPGRADE utility, 30, 307, 310, 314
upgrading
  backups for, 30, **308–309**, 311
  documentation in, **307–308**
  file structure in, **307**
  hardware, **319–321**
  hardware considerations in, 309
  NetWare, **30–31**
  Netware 2.x to 3.x, **310–315**
  Netware 3.x to 4.x, **311–312**, **315–319**
  planning, **304**, **306–310**, 312–313,
    316–318
  saving old hardware, 185
  software, **321–322**
  support files in, **309–310**
  work flow disruptions from, **305–306**
UPS (uninterruptible power supplies),
    180–181, 222, 430
Use Interrupts option, 159–160
USENET, 360
user contexts in NDS, 263
User Datagram Protocol (UDP), 430
User Definition Files (UDF), 297–298
USERLIST utility from Windows, 293
users
  binderies for, **30**
  configuration of, forms for, 378
  disasters from, **217–218**
  as fault points, 56
  login scripts for, 25
  in NDS, 16, **259–263**
  in printing, 147, 167
  training, **196–197**, 223
USERS file, 281
UTP (unshielded twisted-pair) cable, 111

## V

V.32 standard, 431
V.32bis standard, 431
V.42 standard, 431
V.42bis standard, 431
vacuuming, 183–184
Value Added Processes (VAP), 275,
    431–432
VALUE.NDS file, 30
ventilation, 183–184
VER command (DOS), 49
verification
  of backups, 177–178, 213, 308, 311
  of disk writes, 185
Very Small Aperture Terminals (VSAT),
    265, 432
VGA adapters, **20**
VIPX.IFS file, 68

Virtual Loadable Modules (VLM), 65–66
Virtual Telecommunications Access
    Method (VTAM), 432
VirtualHDIRQ setting, 67
viruses
  checking for, 64, 131, **197**, **220–221**
  software for, **363–365**
VLM (Virtual Loadable Modules), 65–66
VLM.EXE program, 65–66
VOLINFO utility from Windows, 293
voltage checkers, 254
Volume Low Warning Reset Threshold
    setting, 193–194
Volume Low Warning Threshold setting,
    193–194
volumes with multiple partitions, 22–23
VPICD.386 driver, 327
VREPAIR utility, **27**, 42, 210–212
  after ABENDs, 335
  problems with, 336
VSAT (Very Small Aperture Terminals),
    265, 432
VSHELL.SYS file, 68
VTAM (Virtual Telecommunications
    Access Method), 432

**W**

WAN (Wide Area Networks), 232, 265,
    **268–271**, *269*, *270*, 403, 433
  addresses on, **20**, 245–247, 404
  bridges for, **233–234**, **236**, 241–242
  between buildings, 235–236
  conflicts on, 24, 37, 245–247
  connecting, **232–240**
  diagnostic tools for, **251–256**
  dial-in/dial-out servers for, 243
  fault points in, **240–247**
  gateways for, 235, 242, 268, *269*, 271
  hardware for, **240–244**
  for long distances, 236–239
  with Macintoshes, **274–278**
  management tools for, **248–251**
  multiple logins on, 258
  NDS for, **259–263**, *260*
  at one site, **233–235**
  operating systems on, 272–274
  planning for, 245–247
  printing on, **257–258**
  repeaters for, **236**, 241
  routers for, **234–235**, 242
  services across, **257–258**
  software for, 245–247
  telephone company services for,
    244–245
  with UNIX, **278–284**
  for world-wide connections, **239–240**
WAN analyzers, 29
Wang, Kevin, 360
warnings
  for cache buffers, 194
  for disk-full, 193–195
warranties for power protection, 180–181
watchdogs, 432
Wide Area Networks. *See* WAN (Wide
    Area Networks)
WIN.COM file, 297–298
WINA20.SYS file, 327
Windows, **273**
  fonts in, 292
  with NetWare, **66–68**, 292–294
  printing in, 290, **293–294**
  requirements for, 322
  from server, **296–298**
  with TCP/IP, 279
  tips for, **327–329**
  troubleshooting, **88–90**
  versions of, 90
WinSleuth program, 366
WINSTART.BAT file, 327
wireless connections, 235
wiring. *See* cabling
workstations, 46
  AppleTalk support on, 277
  backups for, **179–180**
  boot diskettes for, 209
  booting, 47, 49
  cabling of, 100
  configuration of, forms for, *375–376*
  connections on, **56–57**
  data recovery on, **211–212**

*Italic* page numbers refer to figures

documenting, 188
drivers for, 47, 313
fault points in, **52–56**, *53*, 79–80,
    82–85, 87–88
installing, **76–80**
keyboards on, testing, 48
loading DOS on, 47, 49
logging onto servers with, testing,
    47, 50
with Macintoshes, **68–75**, *71*, **85–88**
modems on, 201
network drivers on, 47, 49
operating systems on, 272–274
with OS/2, **68**
with PC-compatibles, **58–66**, *58*
POST for, 46, 48, **59**
for printing, 146, **165–168**
with PS/2, **68**
restoring backup files to, **215–216**
security for, 198
vs. servers, 17
troubleshooting, **46–50**, **80–85**
UNIX, 75, **333–334**
upgrading, 304
utilities for, **364–366**

with Windows, **66–68**, **88–90**
world-wide connections, **239–240**
WSGEN program, 49, 77

## X

X.25 standard, **239**, 265, 433
X.400 standard, 433
X.500 standard, 433
XCONSOLE.NLM, 281
XDR (External Data Representation), 281
XMSNETx.COM drivers, 64
XON/XOFF protocol, 433
XTree program, 366

## Z

00006f00.000 file, 30
*Ziff Desktop Information*, 361
Zone Information Protocol (ZIP), 384
zones, 155, 275–276, 332, 384
ZTEST, 19, 22

Boldface page numbers indicate primary references and explanations

# Basic Principles of NetWare Problem-Solving

1 · Don't be afraid to experiment—just be sure you can return to the configuration you had when you started.

2 · Check the simplest things first—loose connections, incorrect configurations, and spelling errors cause more network problems than do hardware failures.

3 · Back up your server. Back up your server. Back up your server.

4 · Isolate the problem into small pieces, then check each piece methodically to see if it's causing the problem. Any big problem can be made into a bunch of little problems this way.

5 · Replace elements in a broken system one at a time. If the new piece doesn't help, put the old one back. This is the only way to isolate the piece that isn't working. The same principle applies to software.

6 · Look for common elements—do all users who are having a problem have the same type of workstation or use the same version of the shell? Are all the PCs that can't connect to the server on the same leg of the repeater?

7 · Understanding how things *should* look is essential for spotting problems—be sure you know what the normal traffic patterns on your network look like, the versions of software and their correct dates and sizes, what messages should display as the server boots, and so on...

8 · Don't underestimate the user's ability to make your life more difficult—verify that the PC is turned on (not just the monitor), or that they spelled their login name correctly before you assume the hardware's broken.